D0301310

Race and Practice in Archaeological Interpretation

Archaeology, Culture, and Society

Ian Hodder and Robert Preucel, Series Editors

A complete list of books in the series is available from the publisher.

Race and Practice in Archaeological Interpretation

Charles E. Orser, Jr.

PENN

University of Pennsylvania Press

Philadelphia

Copyright © 2004 University of Pennsylvania Press
All rights reserved
Printed in the United States of America on acid-free paper

10 9 8 7 6 5 4 3 2 1

Published by
University of Pennsylvania Press
Philadelphia, Pennsylvania 19104–4011

Library of Congress Cataloging-in-Publication Data

Orser, Charles E.
 Race and practice in archaeological interpretation / Charles E. Orser, Jr.
  p. cm. (Archaeology, culture, and society)
 ISBN 0-8122-3750-1 (cloth : alk. paper)
 Includes bibliographical references and index.
 1. Archaeology—Philosophy. 2. Race—History. 3. Ethnoarchaeology.
I. Title. II. Series
CC72 .O77 2004
930.1′028′5—dc21   2003053743

Contents

Illustrations

Preface

Scholars who investigate race—a label that asserts the identification of individuals based upon real or perceived physical differences—realize that they face a formidable task. History records that learned academicians, committed political activists, well-intentioned relief workers, empowered citizens, and disfranchised outcasts have variously contested and condoned, debated and denied race throughout modern history. That a complete and thoroughly accepted understanding of race has not emerged with the start of the twenty-first century merely demonstrates the tenacity of the concept, the perseverance of those who would seek to construct their world around racial notions, and the concomitant investigative hurdles that must be negotiated in the analysis of race.

Part of the difficulty of reaching a wholly satisfactory notion of race stems from the historical reality of racialization—the conscious labeling of individuals and groups as members of a "race" based upon specific criteria. Racialization is a process that seeks to define and compartmentalize the human community on the basis of outward characteristics. Individuals intent on racializing others have felt justified in using physical appearance, cultural practice, religious belief, and many other attributes as their defining variables. The process of racialization is never entirely harmless or disengaged from social ranking, because one implication of the process is the construction of social inequality. An added historicity of racialization is that the classifiers are completely free to change their classificatory attributes at any time. The mutability of the process mandates that the study of racialization is immensely laborious and fraught with pitfalls.

A contributing factor in the historical chimera of race is that racialized men and women may decide to accept an imposed label as a symbol of unity, group consciousness, and empowerment. Thus, while race does not exist as a biological reality, and racialization is a vastly mutable process, the assignment of race is a social fact with concrete reality in the daily lives of countless individuals.

Anthropologists, sociologists, and others who investigate race and racialization in present-day communities fully appreciate the obstacles that such study presents. The very mutability of the concepts, both across space and through time, dictates the complexity of race among living peoples. Knowing this, we can fully appreciate that the examination of race in the past is even more problematic. The addition of archaeological data to the universe of available information merely intensifies the problems because of the notorious difficulty of social interpretation in archaeology. To be sure, the many detailed ethnographic accounts of race and racialization serve as substantive cautionary tales for archaeologists.

This book is presented with the full understanding that race and racialization are profoundly complicated concepts that have had, and still have, clear social practices associated with them. The project to understand the archaeological dimensions of race and racialization in the modern world is only just beginning, and archaeologists will undoubtedly sustain the analytical effort for many years. This book is presented to offer one way to engage the examination of historic race.

In an important way, this book is a continuation and substantive refinement of A Historical Archaeology of the Modern World (1996). In that exploration, I outlined ideas about the importance of an archaeology of the modern world in light of the notion that because archaeology exists in the present, its practitioners have a responsibility to address research questions that have both historical and present-day significance. The onus of relevance is particularly strong on historical archaeologists because the history they study is still being enacted in various ways throughout the world.

The primary concern of the earlier book was to explore the major themes of the modern world and to consider how archaeologists might contribute to understanding their historical trajectories. These themes— colonialism, Eurocentrism, capitalism, and modernity—forever hover around the practice of historical archaeology. That these four topics can be controversial in today's scholarship amply demonstrates the continued force they exert on modern life.

Many readers misread the use of the term "haunts" to describe the major themes of the modern world as an attempt to promote a totalizing scheme for world history or to propose an Eurocentric view of modern history. Nothing could have been further from the objective because the goal was to demonstrate that capitalism, colonialism, Eurocentrism, and modernity have had, and continue to have, significant and locally variable impacts on the peoples of the world.

The initial attempt at framing a modern-world archaeology, however, was not without problems. In concentrating so deeply on the overarching, broad themes, many topics of seminal, social significance were glossed over or ignored. Race and racialization were a most glaring omission.

When thinking about an archaeology of race and the process of racialization, the works of two French scholars, Pierre Bourdieu and Henri Lefebvre, have been most helpful, even though neither of them engaged race in any substantive way. Neither was trained in archaeology, nor did either ever write about archaeological interpretation. Their lack of familiarity with archaeological practice, however, does not mean that their perspectives and insights have no utility in archaeology. On the contrary, their works are immensely important to helping frame a way of explicating an archaeology of race.

The application of race praxeology to early nineteenth-century rural Ireland may strike some readers as unusual. A strong case can be built for an explicit archaeology of race by reference to African American history. Not only have archaeologists provided a wealth of new information about the daily lives of slaves throughout North America, South America, and the Caribbean, but issues of race have tenaciously held a central place in American history. All residents of the United States have engaged race and racialization in one form or other. Even so, a case study focused on Ireland provides two important advantages. First, it presents materials from a region that has yet to receive sustained archaeological attention. Nine years of archaeological fieldwork in northern County Roscommon in the Republic of Ireland, at three pre-famine (1800–1850) evicted villages but concentrated at one, Ballykilcline, have demonstrated the wealth of information this research arena offers. The abundance of textual sources and the richness of the archaeological data combine to provide a well-developed sociohistorical context for the period. Second, a focus on early nineteenth-century Ireland offers an occasion to investigate race and racialization among a people who are today viewed as white, but who were not always so viewed in the past. Several authors from diverse disciplines have examined Irish racialization and whiteness, and many of them have provided explicit details about the historical strain of thought that linked rural Irish men and women with African Americans. A consideration of Irish racialization also has the power to link the sociohistorical situation in Ireland with similar situations in those places where Irish emigrants settled. The racial element of Irishness is thus clear, even though its full understanding is only now emerging.

During the course of the research and writing of this book, I have received the assistance of numerous individuals. Much of my earliest thinking about an archaeology of race was significantly developed by numerous discussions and interactions with David Babson, Stephen Brighton,

Nicholas Canny, James Delle, Terrence Epperson, Maria Franklin, Katherine Hull, Mark Leone, Christopher Matthews, Paul Mullins, Tadhg O'Keefe, Thomas Patterson, Robert Paynter, and Marion Willetts. I can neither presume to have captured their best ideas in this book, nor to think that they would necessarily agree with the way in which I have approached race and racialization. Nonetheless, I owe each of them a sincere debt of gratitude. I especially wish to thank Katherine Hull, Stephen Brighton, and David Ryder for graciously allowing me time away from the fieldwork in 2002 to finalize this manuscript

I would also like to acknowledge my debt of gratitude to Ian Hodder and Robert Preucel for their much appreciated assistance in preparing this book. I especially wish to thank Robert Paynter for his careful reading, insightful observations, and profoundly useful suggestions. The final version of this book is significantly better because of their input and engagement.

The archaeological fieldwork in Ireland was facilitated by grants from the following Irish agencies: the Famine Commemorative Commission, the National Committee for Archaeology, the Heritage Council, and the Roscommon County Council. The fieldwork occurred under the terms of an excavation license granted by Dúchas, The Heritage Service, Dublin. I would like to thank all the individuals in those institutions who made the field research possible. In particular, I wish to express my deep gratitude to Kevin Barton, Terry Berry, Tom Condit, Conleth Manning, Charles Mount, Nessa O'Connor, and John Waddell. Illinois State University also supported this research effort, and I wish to thank Nick Maroules and everyone else for their continued support.

Anyone who knows me realizes the profound debt I owe to Janice Orser. Many years of discussion with her have significantly increased my understanding of modern society, and my continued collaboration with her is the only way that any of this happens.

Chapter 1
Problematizing Race in Archaeology

During a journey through Ireland in 1835, French traveler Gustave de Beaumont, who had recently returned to Europe after an extended sojourn in the United States, experienced a startling revelation. Prior to visiting Ireland, he had believed that the living conditions he had observed among the dispossessed Native Americans and enslaved Africans in the United States represented the deepest deprivations human beings could suffer. But when visiting the Irish countryside, de Beaumont was so astonished by what he saw that he was forced to rethink his perceptions. He was compelled to conclude that the conditions faced by the lower orders of the Irish were the absolute worst that humanity could endure: "I have seen the Indian in his forests and the negro in his irons, and I believed, in pitying their plight, that I saw the lowest ebb of human misery; but I did not know the degree of poverty to be found in Ireland. Like the Indian, the Irishman is poor and naked; but he lives in the midst of a society which enjoys luxury, honours and wealth" (de Beaumont 1839, 1:204). After encountering rural Ireland, de Beaumont was obliged to conclude that the Irish had neither "the freedom of the savage nor the bread of servitude." In lacking both "freedom" and "bread" the Irish were the worst of the lot.

De Beaumont's bewildered observations initially appear to be uniquely discordant, and his comparisons between Native Americans, New World Africans, and rural Irish seem contrived and unbelievable. But these three disparate peoples—whom scholars and antiquarians for years had labeled the Red, Black, and White "races"—had had their histories and customs intertwined for decades, especially during the early nineteenth century, just when de Beaumont was writing. Visiting Ireland in 1842, the renowned English novelist William Makepeace Thackeray reported how an Irishman had expressed glee when he informed him that he had told de Beaumont "*such* a set of stories." As a proud member of the British Empire, Thackeray could perhaps easily accept that a gullible Frenchman had been fooled by a clever Irishman into believing that rural living conditions were wretchedly deplorable. Though Thackeray possessed the novelist's gift of insight into the vagaries of human nature, he could not help but observe that the "wretched hovels" of the rural Irish were very much like the "Hottentott" kraals of South Africa (Thackeray 1990: 101, 368). Five years later, in a year that would become widely known in Ireland as "Black '47" because of the devastation wrought by the starvation and disease that accompanied the potato blight, the American reformer Asenath Nicholson was moved to make a different, albeit equally impassioned, comparison: "For it is no more than justice to observe that there are some kind slaveholders in the United States, and there are some kind landlords in Ireland, but in too many cases both are synonymous terms, so far as power may be equal" (Nicholson 1998:43). Frederick Douglass strove to end the many comparisons between the rural Irish—as the "white slaves" of Ireland—and the New World's black slaves during his speaking engagements in Ireland (Blassingame 1979: 77–78), but the comparisons continued unabated. For instance, both Nicholson (1847: 260) and Quaker Jonathan Pim (1848: 116) compared the Irish rural cabin to "an African Kraal."

The comparisons between the rural Irish and the far distant Khoi of southern Africa were not simply harmless observations intended to promote cross-cultural comparison. Irish relief workers like Nicholson and Pim may have been seeking to stress, in the starkest terms possible, the desperate circumstances faced by both peoples, but their independent linkage of the rural Irish and the Khoi had a sinister, one hopes unintended, racial consequence. As far as most Western observers were concerned, the so-called "Hottentots" were some of the most reviled people on earth. As early as 1620, one European traveler observed that the "Hottentots" were "the most miserable savages which have been discovered up to now" (Fagan 1984: 28). Such pernicious ideas die hard, and the *Oxford English Dictionary* still includes, as one meaning for "Hottentot," "A person of inferior intellect or culture; one degraded in the scale of civilization, or ignorant of the usages of civilized society." The correlation of the rural Irish with the far-away Hottentots spoke to more than poverty and degradation; it stressed the linkage between social position and perceived race and in an unmistakable manner relegated those of the inferior race to the lowest social-structural positions. At the same time, Irish American novelists tenaciously struggled to appropriate whiteness, and through their literary pursuits they attempted to distance the oppression of the Irish from that being contemporaneously pressed upon enslaved Africans (Eagan 2001).

The comments of Nicholson, Pim, and Thackeray were not mere aberrations or literary devices used for dramatic effect. Many early nineteenth-century commentators drew transcultural comparisons, such

as those between the infamous "coffin ships" that transported Ireland's evicted tenant farmers and the death ships of the Middle Passage
(Woodham-Smith 1991: 228). In referring to the harbor at Cobh, the
port from which thousands of Irish immigrants left their homeland forever, one observer noted that it was popularly known as "the Harbor of
Tears" (Laxton 1996: 217), a term eerily reminiscent of the Cherokees'
Trail of Tears. Both terms denote deep sadness at the horror of forced
removal and the remembrance of life as it had once been lived.

Comparisons between rural Irish farmers, Native American villagers,
and African American slaves, however, were even commonly expressed
before the beginning of the nineteenth century. As early as the 1560s,
English adventurers and colonists drew such comparisons when they first
encountered the world's non-European cultures (see Allen 1994; Canny
1976: 160–63; Collins 1990: 42; Doan 1999; Quinn 1966: 22–26). After
having conjured up a temporally resilient image of the "wild Irish," it was
easy for English observers to create parallel images of the other "uncivilized" people they encountered during their many transoceanic voyages
(Gibbons 1991: 98–99).

The conceptual juxtaposition of Native American, African, and Irish
men and women is not merely a historic coincidence, a quaint expression
of misunderstanding with no deeper meaning. The referencing of these
three peoples in the same sentence incorporates a significance that
extends into a racialized understanding of the human condition. Comparing the homes of the rural Irish to those of the detested "Hottentots"
was designed to instill a sense of inferiority in both peoples, a dual de-
famation that would be immediately recognized and tacitly acknowledged by early nineteenth-century middle- and upper-class English men
and women.

In addition to sharing a perceived similar condition of debasement,
symbolized by material poverty, the entanglement between individuals of
Irish and African descent contained a physical element as well. For example, during a visit to Sligo in 1860, the virulently anti-Catholic Charles
Kingsley made the following observation: "I am haunted by the human
chimpanzees I saw along that hundred miles of horrible country. . . . But
to see white chimpanzees is dreadful; if they were black, one would not
feel it so much, but their skins, except where tanned by exposure, are as
white as ours" (quoted in Gibbons 1991: 96). During this period, it was
not uncommon for prominent English-language newspapers to publish
images that portrayed the Irish as having simian features at a time when
peoples of African descent were regularly equated with apes and mon-
keys (L. Curtis 1996; L. P. Curtis 1971). At the same time, practitioners
of an embryonic anthropology commonly referred to the Irish as "Afri-
canoid" (Young 1995: 72), and Thomas Moore composed a poem entitled

"Paddy's Metamorphosis," in which Irish men and women transplanted to the West Indies actually become black:

> About fifty years since, in the days of our daddies,
>   That plan was commenced which the wise now applaud,
> Of shipping off Ireland's most turbulent Paddies,
>   As good raw material for *settlers*, abroad.
>
> Some West-India island, whose name I forget,
>   Was the region then chosen for this scheme so romantic;
> And such the success the first colony met,
>   That a second, soon after, set sail o'er the Atlantic.
>
> Behold them now safe at the long-look'd for shore,
>   Sailing in between banks that the Shannon might greet,
> And thinking of friends whom, but two years before,
>   They had sorrow'd to lose, but would soon again meet.
>
> And, hark! from the shore a glad welcome there came —
>   "Arrah, Paddy from Cork, is it you, my sweet boy?"
> While Pat stood astounded to hear his own name
>   Thus hail'd by black devils, who caper'd for joy!
>
> Can it possibly be?—half amazement—half doubt.
>   Pat listens again—rubs his eyes and looks steady;
> Then heaves a deep sigh, and in horror yells out,
>   "Good Lord! only think—black and curly already!"
>
> Deceived by that well-mimick'd brogue in his ears,
>   Pat read his own doom in these wool-headed figures,
> And thought, what a climate, in less than two years,
>   To turn a whole cargo of Pats into niggers! (1857: 562)

The frequent connections drawn between Ireland and Africa are not merely nineteenth-century relics. In Roddy Doyle's novel *The Commitments*—immortalized in the 1991 film by the same name—three friends sit in a Dublin pub and discuss popular music, when one of them says: "Wha' class are yis? Workin' class. Are yis proud of it? Yeah, yis are. Say it once, say it loud, I'm black an' I'm proud. . . . The Irish are the niggers of Europe. . . . An' Dubliners are the niggers of Ireland. . . . An' the north-side Dubliners are the niggers o' Dublin" (Doyle 1995: 13). (This dialogue was sanitized in the film version by replacing "niggers" with "blacks.") In a similar vein, Bono, lead singer with U2, made a similar comment: "I was called a 'White Nigger' once by a black musician, and I took it as he meant it, as a compliment. The Irish, like the blacks, feel like outsiders" (Hewson 1988: 190). In the same vein, emotional and practical links were established between the civil rights movements in the United States and Northern Ireland (see Dooley 1998; Rolston and Shannon 2002).

The easy linkage between Ireland and Africa is an artifact of a historic process of racialization. Racialization is "a dialectical process of signification" that consists of assigning men and women to essentialist groups, based upon physical appearance or some other readily identifiable characteristics, that allow them to be perceived as biologically inferior or socially unequal (Miles 1989: 75). Racialization permits those classified as Other to be held in contempt by the collective members of the defining group (Fanon 1968: 212–13; Herzog 1998: 306–7; Omi and Winant 1983: 51). Men and women in dominant social positions and more powerful circumstances have thrust racialization on indigenous peoples around the globe, interconnecting them in one classification and then disuniting them in another. The assignment of people to a "race"—a discrete group of people who share "actual or imputed physical differences" (Cox 1970: 320)—is a historical and global phenomenon that serves to link disparate individuals in webs of interaction and interconnected awareness. It creates social groupings where they may not have otherwise existed and seeks to naturalize distinction as an objective feature of human existence.

Historians who have examined the beginnings of racialization argue that racism as it is currently expressed was not a social reality until the beginning of European global expansion (see, e.g., Hannaford 1996; Smedley 1993; Snowden 1991). The physical characteristics typically referenced as central factors in the act of racialization—skin pigmentation, eyelid and orbital structure, nose form, hair color and texture, and head shape (Blackburn 2000: 7–13)—were not employed until the early eighteenth century by European scientists. Thus, "Race is one of the central conceptual inventions of modernity" (Goldberg 1993: 3).

The association of racial constructs with the modern era, however, is not meant to imply that distinctions based on both physical appearance and cultural practices were unknown prior to the late fifteenth century. Christian scholars who lived during Europe's Middle Ages tended to classify people using the simple dichotomy of Christian and non-(or potential) Christian, or in other words, "those who believed like Us and Those who did not" (Muldoon 2000). Accordingly, when Isidore of Seville wrote *Etymologies* between 622 and 623, he divided the world's peoples into two categories: those who worshiped idols and those who were Christians (Hodgen 1971: 58). Members of the western Church typically identified themselves merely as "Latins," because many nationalistic names, such as "Franks," were amorphous and indistinct (Bartlett 1993: 19–20; Boas 1999: 7–8). Premodern men and women typically defined human variability in terms of differences in customs, language, and law. People who were like "Us" had our words and grammar, our system of justice, and our ways of doing things, whereas those who had different laws, customs, and language were decidedly "Not Us." Even so, bias against people with different skin colors was not unknown in the ancient world, and racist expressions occurred in India, China, and Egypt as early as the third century B.C. (Gossett 1963: 3–4). The Greeks classified the peoples in the known world as "Leucodermi: white-skinned; Xanthodermi: yellow-skinned; and Melanodermi: black skinned" (Benedict 1942: 23).

A perplexing characteristic of racialization is that it can create a historically mutable web of social meanings because it can be focused on physiognomy, skin pigmentation, and/or way of life (Brah 1996: 155). Perhaps the most significant feature of racialization that has archaeological relevance is the reality that race, though a social construct, creates real social distinctions that have sociohistorical meaning (Smaje 1997). Based on the long history of racialization in one form or another, archaeologists must be able to distinguish between the use of racial language (the creation of classificatory distinctions based upon identifiable, overt characteristics) and the creation of racial hierarchies, the institution of fairly rigid social positions apportioned at least in some respect based on perceived racial characteristics (Bonilla-Silva 1997). The conduct of a racially sensitive social archaeology relies on the identification of race-based social structural elements in past sociohistorical formations.

Situating Race in Archaeology

The socially contextual significance of race and racialization in past sociohistorical formations immediately and forcefully anticipates the development of an archaeology of race, especially within the archaeology of the recent past. If racialization truly became a defining social attribute within the world during the monumental transition from the medieval world to the modern world, then it is reasonable to suppose that archaeology should have a seminal role in investigating the materiality of racialization. Much of the earth's social world was forever transformed when Europeans took their conceptions of human variability beyond the limits of their traditional homelands and effectively turned "non-Christian" Native Americans, Africans, and others into scientific subspecies defined by physical appearance and cultural expression. If archaeology is to live up to its potential as a meaningful social science, then archaeologists should be able to investigate the historical nature of race and racialization in important and insightful ways.

Scholars from practically every discipline in the social sciences and the humanities have been or are in the process of investigating race from every conceivable angle. Investigators in such diverse fields as sports (e.g., Entine 2000; Hoberman 2000; Shropshire 1996), law (e.g., Bell 2000; Flagg 1998; Haney-López 1996), and art (e.g., Lucie-Smith 1994; Savage

1997) are seeking to graft their personal and disciplinary perspectives onto race, and these multidisciplinary research efforts will undoubtedly continue for some time. The sheer breadth of investigation demonstrates the supreme challenge that historical racialization presents to scholars, for race is subtle, historical, nuanced, and irrepressibly mutable. Its analysis is seldom straightforward or easy, and the difficulties are compounded when the subject is historical and much of the information is archaeological.

Archaeologists have typically chosen to focus on ethnicity rather than race, undoubtedly for many complex reasons. But not all archaeologists chose to avoid race and racialization, and even before 2000, several of them labored to demonstrate the importance of race to archaeological analysis as it pertained to a more complete understanding of the socio-historical realities of life on New World plantations, in colonial settlements, and at other kinds of habitations (see, e.g., Babson, 1990; Blakey 1988, 1990; Epperson 1990a, b, 1996, 1997, 1999; Mullins 1996; Orser 1988a; Otto 1980; Paynter 1990; Paynter et al. 1994). In particular, Epperson (1990a, 2001) has effectively shown, for example, that race, as a purely social construct, was not a naturally occurring characteristic of Western society, even within the inhuman plantation regime. While seventeenth-century Virginia planters did use the term "Negro" to identify their enslaved chattel, they juxtaposed this term with "Christian" and "English." The transition to "white" and "black" came later, and its reified special status within the established body of law soon made the distinction appear natural and timeless. Those men and women deemed white had legally protected rights, whereas those deemed non-white did not. Understandings such as these, when coupled with archaeological research have seminal importance for demonstrating the power of race and its significance to the modern world.

Most archaeologists, however, with the exceptions noted above, have been remarkably reticent in the face of the burgeoning transdisciplinary exegesis on race. A general reluctance to engage the historical and theoretical natures of race has permeated American historical archaeology, a field whose practitioners investigate places and times most definitely impacted by strategies of racialization.

Even though archaeologists have generally avoided race, race has been present within much past archaeological research. Racial issues prompted the first tortured steps of American archaeology, and they also helped to shape European archaeology. Early attempts to imbue the mysterious "mound builders" and the ancient Celts with racial characteristics were neither accidental nor entirely free of ulterior motive. Confronted with their own often impassioned, class-motivated ideas of race within their home societies, and typically wrapping themselves in the protective

cloak of "unimpassioned science," many early archaeologists perpetuated racial bigotry in the name of archaeology. For example, the earliest
Roman archaeologists from Great Britain used a plethora of images to
help support British imperialism (Hingley 2000). In the most egregious
of examples, Nazi fringe archaeologists used their "excavated findings"
to bolster their warped racial views and to justify their program of mass
human destruction—all in the name of race (see e.g., Arnold 1990;
McCann 1988, 1990). Even today, clever pseudo-archaeologists peddle
racial bigotry in the name of their self-proclaimed "courageous" archaeological interpretations. These aspects of the archaeological project—
some noble, some misguided, and some horrendous—bring the archaeological community to a point in its maturity in which its practitioners
can no longer glibly ignore race and racialization.

Within the archaeological world, no group bears more responsibility
for the study of racialization than historical archaeologists. Since racialization has been assigned socially prominent roles in modern history, it
is imperative for historical archaeologists to contribute their multidisciplinary approaches and interpretive insights to the growing body of
research on racialization. Historical archaeologists, at least in some respect, should commit themselves to understanding and interpreting the
material dimensions of historically conceived and implemented racialization. As individuals privileged enough to have the social assignment
of scholarly activity, they have a responsibility to confront the process of
modernity, whatever its temporal boundaries. In fact, as practitioners in
the modern world, historical archaeologists should be doubly compelled
to confront issues of race and racialization because racialization was a
social reality in the history they study, just as it is a social reality in their
own daily lives. Many of today's archaeologists, as they tack back and
forth between the present and the past, regularly face torturous ethical
dilemmas that involve racialization in some way (see, e.g., Zimmerman
1989; Custer 2001).

Historical archaeologists must confront issues of race, because the sites
they examine are often (and perhaps even always) associated with race
in some manner. Each archaeologist must approach this realization in a
personal manner. Some archaeologists may develop their awareness from
their formative experiences while coming of age (e.g., Ferguson 1992:
121–23). For others, racialization is always undeniably present (Franklin
2001), and for still others, race lurks as a silent element of their own lives,
an unacknowledged factor that guides success and failure. As a result of
such personal variability, accepting the importance of the study of racialization in archaeological research requires a concomitant profession of
reflexivity.

My own realization of the significance of race developed through an intensive examination of Millwood Plantation in the South Carolina Piedmont in the early 1980s (see Orser 1988b). As a twentieth-century American, I knew that race was inherent within the social structure within which I operated, but at Millwood race became for the first time utterly impossible to ignore in my archaeological practice. During antebellum times (1834–1861), the plantation had been the home of a white planter and hundreds of black slaves; after the Civil War (1865–1925), most of the ex-slaves had become tenant farmers on the estate lands and, as such, lived and labored within an oppressive Jim Crow environment. This site-specific racial history was not merely a historical feature, however, because racialization touched almost everything that occurred during the archaeological research itself. The Millwood research unequivocally demonstrated that the true power of race lies in its ability to allocate power, privilege, and wealth (Smedley 1998). Even when I accepted this realization, archaeological convention caused me to be reluctant to acknowledge the significance of race to archaeological analysis and, while I argued for the necessity of recognizing race, I subordinated it to economics (Orser 1988a).

Unquestionably, part of my personal failure to conceptualize the full impact of racialization on past sociohistorical formations was guided by contemporary archaeological practice. As noted above, few archaeologists working in the late 1980s considered race to be a viable subject amenable to archaeological analysis. With the value of today's hindsight, it is now obvious that historical archaeology focused on the modern world is undoubtedly the intellectual site from which an archaeological conceptualization of race and racialization must come. The transdisciplinary data are too rich and the subject too important to think otherwise. In order to make the necessary commitment to an archaeology fully sensitive to matters of race and racialization, historical archaeology must be at least partially rethought and reconfigured.

Before we can reformulate the study of race in relevant archaeological terms, we are encouraged to consider why it has taken historical archaeology so long to "discover" race as a topic. What is it about the field that tends to make race epiphenomenal or even irrelevant? Much of the problem may lie within the history of the discipline, and so one place within which to locate a possible answer may concern the way in which historical archaeology has been traditionally designed. Additional, related problems may derive from three central deficiencies in the practice of historical archaeology: (1) its most prominent practitioners' use of the concept of culture, (2) the failure of historical archaeologists to take poverty seriously, and (3) the reluctance to employ multi-leveled models of social engagement. These three issues are inexorably entangled with race and racialization, and further exploration is necessary.

A Short Critique of Historical Archaeology

An important issue that must be briefly broached when considering the reluctance of historical archaeology, as a discipline, to confront the analysis of race is that historical archaeologists have traditionally had significant difficulty precisely defining their field. Uncertainty about the goals and aspirations of historical archaeology helped to retard the theoretical maturation of the field and served to distance the field's practitioners from substantive sociohistorical issues such as race and racialization. This early confusion has already been documented by many historical archaeologists and only cursory comments are required here, specifically as they pertain to the analysis of historical racialization.

Historical archaeology began to attain academic attention in departments of anthropology in the United States beginning in the late 1960s, but the field had an earlier function principally as a restorationist's tool (see Harrington 1952; South 1994). The project assigned to many of the earliest historical archaeologists was to provide exact architectural details that could help historic-site restorers and reconstructers to (re)construct historic buildings in ways that could be considered accurate. Within the parameters of this mindset, racialization was not conceptualized to play any role in building design or placement, and the subject was not broached.

The struggle for historical archaeology to distance itself from such particularistic research involved a forced and oftentimes tenuous engagement with anthropological thought (see e.g., Cleland and Fitting 1968 and the papers that accompany it; Noël Hume 1969). The many exercises in self-identification pursued by historical archaeologists are perhaps understandable in the sociohistorical context of the 1960s, because many prominent archaeologists were then striving to redesign their discipline's parameters and goals in terms of what Paul Martin (1971) described as a "revolution." Though several historical archaeologists stood behind Martin's intellectual barricade, agreement in the field was not immediate, and historical archaeologists continued their debates throughout the 1970s and 1980s (Deagan 1988; Deetz 1977, 1983; Leone et al. 1987; McKay 1975).

The definitional debate continued into the 1990s, although by this time it had grown more sophisticated, as it moved away from facile arguments over the disciplinary home of historical archaeology and toward more theoretically charged discussions. Gone were the early, superficial exchanges over whether historical archaeology was properly "historical" or "archaeological," or whether historical archaeologists should consider themselves anthropologists or historians. By the 1990s, a number of topics of historical and theoretical interest displaced the question of disciplinary identity as historical archaeologists generally turned to more substantive sociocultural issues (see Paynter 2000a: 2–5). Among these, two of the most prominent were (1) whether capitalism was the "proper" study of historical archaeology (Becker 1995; Hackbarth 1995; Leone 1995a, b; Leone and Potter 1994, 1999; Moore 1995a, b; Wesler 1996), and (2) whether the interpretive power of historical archaeology rested upon its ability to link prehistoric and historical archaeology in the study of cultural contact and change (Lightfoot 1995).

The historical archaeologists' first topic had been implicitly suggested in the 1960s by those archaeologists who mentioned colonialism and European expansion in their definitions of the field, even though they did not explicitly mention capitalism (e.g., Fontana 1965; Jelks 1968). The second topic has had an especially protracted history, because most of the pioneers of American historical archaeology had educational and practical backgrounds in the prehistoric archaeology of Native America. These scholars were generally comforted by the short intellectual leap from late prehistory to the early contact period, and they excelled in the analysis of cultural contact in diverse North American settings (see, e.g., Quimby 1966; White 1975; Wittry 1963; Woodward 1978). As anthropologically trained archaeologists, these historical archaeologists were able to retain their explicit focus on Native Americans, but with the addition of colonialist Europeans and their material culture.

It may appear at first consideration that the two topics debated by historical archaeologists in the 1990s were actually quite compatible. The proponents of both issues usually envision a historical milieu in which colonizing Europeans in North America brought with them either capitalism or the germ of its mercantilist idea as they established settlements in areas traditionally controlled by indigenous peoples. Surprisingly, however, the positions are actually almost mutually exclusive, because those archaeologists who give primacy to capitalism tend to agree that the introduction of that system into an indigenously controlled region represents a "qualitatively new phenomenon" (Wolf 1982: 85) and a "decisive break in world history" (Amin 1989: 1). Archaeologists of capitalism generally envision the so-called "historic period" to have begun with the invasion of Europeans, an intervention that effectively worked to create many new worlds among the indigenous populations. Within this viewpoint, the world became, quite simply, a different place after capitalist interpersonal relations were established. The precise nature of one's understanding and perception of this new world would largely depend upon where one was situated—socially and geographically—within it (Orser 1996a: 76–77; also see Blaut 1993).

The capitalism-as-engine-of-change position is controversial, because those archaeologists who perceive an unbroken temporal bridge between prehistory (without capitalist relations) and post-contact history (with capitalist relations of some sort) tend to put their faith in the powers of cultural maintenance. They tend to believe that, as indigenous men and women are faced with capitalism's new sociospatial relations, their culture will help them to create and maintain an acceptable place within that new social order using traditional social and ideational means (Wolf 1999: 15). However one may wish to envision the role of capitalism in historical archaeology, adherence to these theoretically disparate positions indicates that historical archaeology is not unified even in terms of something as basic to modern world history as the introduction, spread, and maintenance of capitalist relations and the many indigenous responses to them.

The internal controversy in historical archaeology did not cease with the beginning of the twenty-first century. Charles Cleland (2001)—who had been one of the first archaeologists to press for the development of an explicitly anthropological perspective for the field, and who, with James Fitting in the late 1960s, coined the concept that historical archaeology had a "crisis of identity" (Cleland and Fitting 1968)—asked whether historical archaeology was theoretically "adrift." In other words, Cleland was once again posing the question as to whether historical archaeology was still searching for its identity. (For more complete overviews of the intellectual history of American historical archaeology, see Deagan 1982; Little 1994; Orser 1996a: 1–28, 2001a; Paynter 2000a, b.)

Cleland's question shows that historical archaeology is not a coherent field of study. Today's archaeologists, accordingly, continue to use three meanings for "historical archaeology." Some define it as any archaeological practice in which an archaeologist bases his or her interpretations on the combination of excavated data and textual or even oral information. Others relate the term to the archaeology of a "historical" segment of time demarcated by literacy. For others, the focus of historical archaeology begins with modernization, a process that is generally associated with the global spread of Europeans and Europeanization, beginning in earnest in the fifteenth century, but undoubtedly with much earlier roots. The perspective adopted in this book is unabashedly committed to the last understanding of historical archaeology. Not only does this perspective promise to provide the most robust contribution to cultural and historical knowledge, it also has the potential to present unique, materially based information about the process of becoming modern. So important is the challenge to understand modernization that this special interest within broader historical archaeology (defined under the first usage) is best termed "modern-world archaeology."

The impetus for "modern-world archaeology" (Orser 1996a: 26–28) derives with some modification from the work of many noted historical archaeologists (Deagan 1988, 1991; Deetz 1977, 1991; Leone 1995a; Leone et al. 1987; Schuyler 1970; South 1988b), but with the important caveat that the study of racialization must form one of its integral and inseparable elements. During their prolonged debate over whether historical archaeology was "history" or "anthropology," the participants never explored the field's relationship to race, even during the inception of plantation archaeology in the United States and the Caribbean.

Any sort of modern-world archaeology, however, is not without its critics, among whom are archaeologists who appear satisfied with the status quo. In a particularly provocative analysis, John Moreland (2001: 106–7) argues that all archaeologies investigate the central elements of the "modern world," such as colonialism and the living conditions of the dispossessed and downtrodden. In his attempt to stretch the meaning and focus of historical archaeology, however, Moreland seriously misreads the intent of modern-world archaeology. His misunderstanding is adequately typified by his startling claim—in an avowed reverence for the written word (which he capitalizes as "Word")—that historians frequently make detailed examinations of history's "voiceless" men and women (Moreland 2001: 105). While correctly arguing that systems of writing can be used as a tool of oppression (a position few could deny), Moreland creates a model that not only is a tautology but is, or at least should be, untenable for archaeology: his all-consuming faith in the Word—a medium that more often than not creates stereotypic images of the lower orders—further relegates non-elites to the anonymity presented by the Word itself. In making such an assertion, he deftly chooses to ignore the significant contributions of the entirety of African American archaeology and precludes any serious archaeological examination of race.

Moreland's is an attempt to turn back the intellectual clock of historical archaeology, to reduce the field once again to a mere methodology, a way of linking "archaeological" and "historical" sources of information into a unified interpretive whole. Such efforts present the possibility of diluting the interpretive force of historical archaeology by turning it away from a critical analysis of the modern world. Modern-world archaeologists thus openly reject this approach because it (re)-condemns the discipline to the role of a particularistic and decidedly non-anthropological pastime.

The general trend within historical archaeology to ignore the effects of racialization coincides with the rejection of "modern-world archaeology," however it may be conceived.

A brief exposition of three shortcomings in contemporary historical archaeology will demonstrate reasons for historical archaeology's failure to confront the historical dimensions of race and racialization.

Historical Archaeology and the Concept of Culture

It was no accident that the intellectual profile of historical archaeology was raised from the "handmaiden to history" (Noël Hume 1964) and a kind of "restoration archaeology"—suited only to providing architectural details for historic reconstructions (Harrington 1952: 341–42)— to a fully anthropological endeavor during the ascent of processual archaeology. As American archaeology struggled to find its place within anthropology (Binford 1962; Longacre 1970), historical archaeologists faced the double challenge of first making a place for themselves within archaeology and then establishing their relevance within anthropology. At the time that processual archaeology was finding its intellectual voice, most prehistorians still considered historical archaeology to be the "unrespectable" wing of the field (Fontana 1968).

The challenge to raise the intellectual respectability of historical archaeology was most explicitly and successfully taken up by Stanley South (1977). He argued that the field could obtain disciplinary standing by fully accepting the nomothetic goals of the New Archaeology. South believed that, by adopting this scientific line of argument, historical archaeology, along with the rest of archaeology, could work its way into anthropology. South's commitment to processual archaeology closely coincided with Binford's, even to the point of having the same interest in White's neo-evolutionary paradigm (see South 1955; Orser 1989). Binford (1972, 1977) was also an early and strong supporter of South's endeavors on behalf of historical archaeology.

South's primary goal was to transform historical archaeology into an explicitly processual practice, an archaeology that would be openly "concerned with understanding past lifeways, culture history, and culture process by examining the material remains of culture reflecting these processes" (1977: xiii). His primary pathway to this significant contribution was through the conscious adoption of a "pattern concept." South's conceptualization of the "pattern" figured prominently in many historical archaeologists' understanding of culture.

The basic importance of the pattern concept was as an analytical tool that could permit historical archaeologists—investigating what South (1978: 223) termed "high energy cultural systems"—to use the recognition of patterned regularity in artifact assemblages to help understand the "dynamics of past cultural systems" (South 1977: 84). The foundational idea is that men and women enculturated within a particular cultural system should tend to behave in similar enough ways to permit the identification of a pattern within the remains they deposited in the archaeological record. To recognize the pattern in an archaeological collection, the analyst must group the excavated artifacts into categories and then examine the relative proportions of the categories. The resultant categorical profiles can then be compared against the profiles obtained for other artifact collections. If the collections are roughly the same, then they may represent one pattern; if they are significantly different, then two patterns may exist. In order for the pattern concept to sustain intellectual validity, however, the analyst has to understand culture, because it is culture that ultimately provides the patterned regularity in the artifact assemblages.

The concept of patterned regularity has been a mainstay of archaeological and anthropological research for many years. Though the word "pattern" has acquired many disparate meanings over time (Lesser 1961: 43), South (1977: 84) explicitly states that the patterns he searches for are analogous to Kroeber's (1919: 259) "great pulsations" and Steward's (1955: 88) "regularities." Kroeber was generally more explicit than Steward in linking culture with pattern, and it is with him that we must begin.

Kroeber is well remembered for his interest in broad cultural patterns. His interest in patterned regularity was first expressed in nascent form (1936), but it later blossomed into an exhaustive study (1944). Kroeber (1948: 311) explained patterns as "those arrangements or systems of internal relationship which give to any culture its coherence or plan, and keep it from being a mere accumulation of random bits. They are therefore of primary importance." As providers of cultural order, patterns theoretically could assume an infinite number of expressions, but Kroeber provisionally identified four types of patterns: the universal, the systemic, the societal or whole-cultural (also called "total-cultural"), and the style type.

The concept of the universal pattern, as an organizational scheme that could be applied to all ethnographic cultures, was known before Kroeber's formulation (Wissler 1923). Patterns of speech, material possessions, art, knowledge, religion, property, and politics were all part of the universal pattern, with each category having numerous subdivisions. For instance, the patterns of material culture included food, shelter, dress, weapons, and industries.

A systemic pattern consists of a complex of cultural material that persists by constantly demonstrating utility. The cultural complex thus exhibits a "functional consistency" (Radcliffe-Brown 1952: 43) that represents its significance generally "on a historical view" (Kroeber 1948: 313). The systemic building blocks of culture have a temporal consistency that describe "a common pattern persistent enough to be recognizable for a long time" (Kroeber 1948: 321).

Whole-cultural patterns represent national cultures, and Kroeber (1948: 316) mentions "an Italian, a French, [and] a British pattern." According to Kroeber, disparate peoples create whole-cultures by their distinctive customs and traditions. In order to perceive these patterns, the analyst can employ an analogy with art history and strive to recognize the patterns as different great styles (Benedict 1934: 48; Kroeber 1948: 318). These great patterns appear through time as the rise and fall of "civilizations" (Kroeber 1966: 18–27).

Kroeber argues that style patterns are used to represent a particular method of accomplishing a task, "a way of achieving definiteness and effectiveness in human relations" (Kroeber 1948: 329). Kroeber's (1919; Kroeber and Richardson 1940) famous studies of dress design indicate that diverse styles are created, temporarily used for an unspecified time, and then fall out of favor. Style patterns thus resemble art styles and so can be related to whole-cultural patterns.

Of these four cultural patterns, South (1977: 32) was most impressed with the whole-cultural and the style patterns, and stated that Kroeber's analysis of women's fashion was particularly applicable to "those archaeologists excavating sites of the historic period." According to South, Kroeber's research provides "an excellent model demonstrating the value of the nomothetic approach" to historical archaeology. Using Kroeber's conception of the whole-cultural pattern as a foundation, the historical archaeologist could "select a group of known domestic house ruins from varying areas and known cultures, such as those from British-American communities, German-American communities, French-American communities, and Spanish-American communities" and conduct a pattern analysis (South 1977: 84). The investigator could then link the resultant whole-cultural patterns to style patterns so that the invention, introduction, use, and abandonment of individual kinds of artifacts—such as tea cups—could be conceptualized as analogous to the great pulsations of the world's major civilizations.

The view of culture that South developed for historical archaeology—and which most historical archaeologists readily accepted—was certainly influenced by Kroeber's understandings. But as a cultural evolutionist, South also found it important to include Steward's (1955) notion of "regularity." Regularities are similarities of cultural form and content that occur "cross-culturally in historically separate areas" (Steward 1955: 88). In Steward's framework, regularities are causally related, and when compared across regions not historically related, can be used diachronically to chart multilinear evolution. Basing his formulation on the idea that "certain basic types of culture may develop in similar ways under similar conditions," Steward viewed multilinear evolution as a means of "searching for parallels of limited occurrence" (Steward 1955: 4, 14–15). As such, his methodology calls for a focus on discrete cultural entities whose regularities can be verified through empirical research.

South's adoption of Kroeber's ideas, and to a lesser extent those of

Steward, is central to understanding the historical archaeologists' use of culture because South has consistently been a respected and central figure in the creation of an explicitly anthropological historical archaeology. By linking a nomothetic approach and an overtly neoevolutionist perspective that included the search for empirical whole-cultural patterns, he situated historical archaeology firmly within mainstream processual archaeology (see Gibbon 1989: 69–73). In doing so, South developed a whole-culturological historical archaeology that quickly found many advocates throughout the discipline.

James Deetz was another prominent proponent of the use of a whole-culture model in historical archaeology. His views on this matter are most clearly presented in his exposition of the mental template, an idea that "the proper form of an object exists in the mind of the maker" (Deetz 1967: 46). The ideational basis for the development of the template, and indeed its historical consistency, derives from the overarching culture. Producers of artifacts know, because of their culture's rules, what attributes to assemble to make a particular object. The similarity of the mental template among members of a particular cultural unit produces an artifactual consistency within the unit's general material culture. Deetz would eventually drop the term "mental template" from his vocabulary, but the idea of the whole-culture is very much in evidence in his later works, as he sought to understand the subtle nuances of "European Colonial culture in North America" (Deetz 1968: 121) and "national European culture" (Deetz 1991: 3). Unlike the cultural evolutionist South, however, Deetz rooted his search for whole-cultural patterns within a commitment to a structuralist paradigm (Deetz 1983), based on an earlier program pursued by folklorist Henry Glassie (1975).

Antebellum slave plantations in the American South provide an excellent arena in which to demonstrate the disciplinary significance of the whole-culture approach to pattern recognition, because the antebellum plantation throws into stark visibility the issue of racialization. This exploration is all the more important because the archaeology of slave plantations has developed into one of the most important realms of study within New World historical archaeology (Singleton 1999), and it is from this intellectual site that the most far-reaching theoretical advances have been made in the discipline (see Orser 1990, 1998a).

When Charles Fairbanks began the overtly anthropological archaeology of antebellum slave plantations in the late 1960s, he did so within a culturalist framework that was entirely consistent with mainstream archaeology, even though his approach was not as developed or as explicit as South's or Deetz's perspectives. Fairbanks's central concern was to discover the material elements of African culture in the New World, as exemplified by the presence of "Africanisms" (Fairbanks 1983: 23), or "retentions" and "survivals" (Mintz and Price 1976: 27). Fairbanks's culturalist interest situated him directly within the anthropologically relevant debate between Frazier (1964) and Herskovits (1958) over the persistence of African cultural traits in the New World. The search for Africanisms—which for Fairbanks (1984: 11) existed as part of an endeavor that would eventually constitute "a systematic study of the whole fabric of Black culture"—had obvious whole-cultural elements because relict Africanisms would unambiguously signal the existence of African culture in the New World. They would offer tangible proof that the men and women who had survived the horrendous Middle Passage had carried with them elements of their traditional cultures.

Fairbanks soon discovered, and others have since reaffirmed, that irrefutable examples of Africanisms are decidedly difficult to identify, even though archaeologists have presented credible cases for the existence of such materials using both artifacts (see, e.g., Emerson 1994, 1999; Ferguson 1992, 1999; Handler 1997; Samford 1996; Young 1996) and biocultural remains (see, e.g., Handler et al. 1982). Having discovered the difficulty of locating single artifacts that could be classified as unambiguous Africanisms, most historical archaeologists abandoned the search and turned to providing an understanding of the material basis of slave life. These researches have documented several features of the slaves' daily lives, with the most important arguably concentrated in the areas of material possessions, housing conditions, diet, and religious beliefs (Orser 1990: 124–29, 1994a).

Most archaeologists concentrating on the archaeology of slavery during the earliest years of this disciplinary focus used Kroeber's whole-cultural concept, largely via South and Deetz, as a methodological framework. The link between the search for survivals of African culture in the New World and the culture-defining underpinning of South's views is amply demonstrated by the numerous archaeologists who in the 1980s either used South's specific pattern designations or else created new patterns explicitly rooted in his methodology (see, e.g., Drucker 1981; Moore 1981, 1985; Singleton 1980; Wheaton and Garrow 1985; Wheaton et al. 1983).

The reification of culture that existed as an integral element of the whole-culture paradigm began to shift in the 1990s, as archaeologists of New World slavery began to reflect upon the more complex and accordingly more realistic process of creolization. Scholars outside archaeology had developed creolization studies during the 1960s and 1970s (Gundaker 2000: 124), and the lag in interest among historical archaeologists probably reflects their overwhelming concern at that time with identifying whole-culture patterns. Since discovering the interpretive potentialities of creolization, several historical archaeologists have recognized it as a powerful conceptual tool that may offer a more nuanced view of ethnogenesis than the whole-culture model. Most historical archaeologists engaged in slave research now understand that in the face of the forced cultural fragmentation that accompanied bondage-for-life, slaves of African descent had to unite to create coherent communities to distinguish themselves—visibly and undeniably—from their owners (see, e.g., Higman 1998; Joyner 1984). An acceptance of creolization concomitantly raises the specter of racialization in historical archaeology because this paradigm incorporates the idea that slave communities were created within a racially based, oppressive environment that was intended to extend throughout the entire lives of the enslaved bondsmen and women.

Research by social historians reveals, however, that creolization is far from simplistic or universally designed and implemented. Studies in south Louisiana, for example—widely regarded as the locus of North American creolization—show that various definitions of "creole" exist, with the promoters of the purest form steadfastly maintaining that the term should be applied only to "a native Louisianian of pure white blood descended from those French and Spanish pioneers who came directly from Europe to colonize the New World" (Tregle 1992: 132). Acadians (Cajuns) are excluded under this definition, but the term would encompass American-born Germans if their ancestors traveled directly from Germany to Louisiana (Kniffen and Hilliard 1988: 128). At the same time, scholars have argued that Africans in south Louisiana created an "Afro-Creole culture" organized around the linguistic uniqueness of blended African and Caribbean languages (Hall 1992: 87).

The identification of specific individuals who can be considered "creoles" thus remains problematic. At least two meanings of "creole" exist in today's Louisiana, with one group being "socially and legally white" and the other "socially and legally colored" (Domínguez 1986: 149). The perceptions of each group accordingly vary. So-called "white creoles" tend to envision Louisiana's population as divided into two gross categories of people: "white" and "'colored" or "non-white," and they divide the whites into "Americans," Creoles, Cajuns, Italians, Irish, and Jews, and the non-whites into "mulattos" and "Negroes." Non-whites, however, perceive the creole social category quite differently. Some see whites as homogeneous and "coloreds" as divided into "creoles" and "blacks," whereas other non-whites perceive both "creoles" and non-creoles as being composed of whites and "coloreds" (Domínguez 1986: 149–53). Within this complex framework of perceived human variation, people can imagine "creoles" as a category that includes both whites and non-whites. Domínguez (1986) shows that, in addition to the social confusion caused by the use of the term "creole," the Louisiana judicial system has often been called upon to render legal decisions about what constitutes

Parsons, Boas, Kroeber, and Lowie, all of whom are justifiably remembered for their investigations into Native American life (Riley 1967). Much of their research was culturally and regionally based, focusing on the "tribes" or "contiguous tribes" within a particular "culture area" (Wissler 1927).

The idea that discrete polities inhabited Native North America, and indeed the rest of the pre-colonial world, is an undeniable reality. Diverse peoples throughout North America expressed their thoughts and attitudes in unique ways and maintained specific customs and traditions that were uniquely their own. To deny this reality would be to argue against Native American self-determination and to deny the significance of the early anthropological research.

The conceptual entropy that swirls around the notion of Native American whole-culture becomes perhaps most apparent when we consider termination. Faced with the cessation of federal recognition, which guaranteed them a special status both the United States and Canada, Native American peoples were forced to prove that they represented "organized" societies. The act of offering such legal proof is frequently advanced through substantiating a long-term territorial occupation and intricate kin associations (see, e.g., Elias 1993). The presentation of substantive evidence indicating long-term cultural cohesion makes it relatively easy to agree that Native American polities can be modeled as whole-cultures. But even so, many scholars of Native America have begun to substitute the word "nation"—a term that encompasses sovereignty—for culture (see, e.g., Bonvillain 2001; Josephy 1994; LaDuke 1992).

The use of "nation," however, is only a bit less problematic than "culture," because the word "culture" has the power to be used as a counterpoint against the Europeans who insisted that native peoples could not possibly have the sophistication to develop and maintain complex sociohistorical polities (see M. K. Green 1995). At the same time, it is also true that John Marshall, the first Chief Justice of the United States—and a person who has been described as someone who "did more to destroy American Indian cultures than even his contemporary, the noted Indian-hater Andrew Jackson" (Osborne 1995: 64)—used "nation" in the ponderous and consequential phrase "domestic dependent nation" in *Cherokee Nation v. Georgia* (1831) (Getches et al. 1979: 163) It is also noteworthy that two Supreme Court justices argued in the same case that Native Americans had no sovereignty at all. The easy reification of Native American peoples into whole-cultures—organized on a progressive evolutionary scale—helped to promote an "Us versus Them" mentality among early European American scholars and social engineers who could employ racist attitudes (both subtle and overt) to justify their Social

Darwinist beliefs (see Patterson 1995: 59; Trigger 1989: 111–12). Within this conceptual framework, Native Americans were the true "Vanishing Race," because they were perceived as culturally and biologically inferior to Europeans (Dixon 1972).

Archaeologists who have investigated Native American life have generally found it relatively easy to accept Native Americans as whole-cultures. Archaeologists working during the culture-historical phase often interchanged "culture" with "civilization," and many of them became preoccupied with the "labelling of geographically and temporally restricted assemblages of prehistoric archaeological material as cultures or civilizations" (Trigger 1989: 162). Using ideas formulated by researchers such as Gustaf Kossinna, who in the early twentieth century fanatically investigated German origins, it became commonplace for archaeologists to accept that "the relationship between people and material things is a direct and causal one" (Thomas 1996: 22).

The concept of culture has always presented problems to archaeologists engaged in Native American research. Even Willey and Phillips (1958: 12, 46–48), in their classic work on "culture-historical integration," recognized the difficulties with the identification of such a "maximum unit" as culture. As may be expected, archaeologists have selected various ways of resolving the problem identified by Willey and Phillips. Whereas some have proposed a Darwinian-style cultural evolution to examine broad cultural trends (Leonard 1993), others have opted to look inside "culture" and to focus on human agency (Dobres and Robb 2000a), a view of growing popularity at the start of the twenty-first century. Still others retain whole-cultural terms, but fully understand their limitations (see, e.g., Pettula 1993).

Archaeology and Poverty

Anthropologists, sociologists, social historians, and other social scientists have engaged poverty as an investigational topic for many years. With the rise of Western industrialization, social reformers began to pay greater attention to the plight of men, women, and children who did not seem to be benefiting from the production of wealth by a select few. Journalists and a few committed reformers began to produce photo-documented investigations of the conditions faced by the poor in the late nineteenth century (e.g., Riis 1971), and twentieth-century social historians have provided their own detailed examinations of poverty (e.g., Davin 1996). In anthropology, the most prominent and controversial explicit studies of poverty were Oscar Lewis's (1959, 1966) explorations into the "culture of poverty" (see also Leacock 1971; Winter 1971), though several rural sociologists and anthropologists did directly confront issues of poverty and race in diverse locations, particularly in the American South, during the 1920s, 1930s, and 1940s (see, e.g., Cox 1945; Davis et al. 1941; Dollard 1937; Hagood 1939; Park 1928; Raper 1936; Vance 1929, 1935, 1936; Warner 1936; Woofter et al. 1936). Immediately after the Second World War, as the chilly atmosphere of the Cold War settled upon the academic world, anthropologists began to perceive their discipline as focused almost exclusively on the "exotic," and their research became "divorced from the pressing issues of the day," including poverty and race (Patterson 2001: 133).

Archaeologists have had difficulties with culture, but we may well suppose that they have had more success investigating poverty. After all, archaeologists recover and examine pieces of material culture, and the abundance or paucity of material objects is commonly used to signal wealth or want. Scholars typically use the relative abundance or scarcity of personal possessions as a simplistic measure of well-being (particularly in the capitalist societies within which most archaeologists live), but even historical archaeologists have been reluctant to engage poverty as a legitimate topic of investigation. The failure to confront poverty undoubtedly is one reason why race has not been approached as a major concern of the field's practitioners. Even though the general disciplinary avoidance of poverty as a topic is a reality, it is also true that some historical archaeologists have been cognizant of its importance in social life.

In a seminal article published in the early 1970s, Robert Ascher (1974) provided a usually unacknowledged plea for what would later be termed "interpretive archaeology" (Hodder 1986), when he included "the poor" among "the inarticulate." By "inarticulate," Ascher (1974: 11) meant the socially "powerless": men and women "who did not write or who were not written about" in the chronicles of the past. Deagan (1982: 171) later reinforced Ascher's perspective by voicing a belief that was rapidly becoming commonplace among her colleagues: that they were often presented with special opportunities to study groups who have been "excluded from historical sources because of race, religion, isolation, or poverty." This "bottom-rung" perspective became more widely voiced in the 1990s. For example, Deetz (1991: 6) obliquely mentioned the poor when he stated that historical archaeology focuses on more than just "a small minority of deviant, wealthy, white males." The tacit implication, of course, was that historical archaeology studies Others: men and women who were neither "deviant," "wealthy," nor "white." And another historical archaeologist opined that "Giving voice to the voiceless of history—the poor, the oppressed, the disenfranchised—is among historical archaeology's most important contributions to anthropology" (Feder 1994: 16; for an opposing view, see Moreland 2001).

By the early 1970s, some historical archaeologists had at least recognized the role their field could potentially play in examining the myriad historical dimensions of poverty. Strangely enough, however, most historical archaeologists have neatly sidestepped the study of poverty just as they have done with race. This avoidance has been accomplished in two principal ways: (1) by examining impoverished peoples first and foremost as members of cultures—as a variant of whole-cultural analysis—or (2) by ignoring poverty entirely or concealing it within "socioeconomic status." The way in which archaeologists have used these two approaches can be illustrated by reference again to the archaeology of African Americans, the people that Ascher (1974: 11) identified as "the largest group of inarticulate Americans."

As noted above, when Fairbanks first decided to conduct archaeological research at African American slave sites in coastal Georgia and Florida, his interest was essentially to augment knowledge about the cultural lives of slaves, with the archaeology contributing "to defining the total picture of black lifeways in America" (Fairbanks 1983: 22). Fairbanks did not reference poverty in any way, and since then, many archaeologists have seemed to presume an intuitive notion of poverty in their African American studies, even though they seldom explicitly broach the subject. Most archaeologists prefer instead to adopt the view that the people under investigation were culturally rich—because they were able to survive and to build vibrant, living cultures from the wreckage of inhuman, personal bondage. Poverty is usually only tacitly included as one characteristic of enslavement within an otherwise optimistic picture of past cultural life. Deetz clearly expressed the culturally rich perspective in his examination of the Parting Ways settlement in New England, when he portrayed its African American residents as the "bearers of a life-style, distinctively their own" rather than as "simple folk living in abject poverty" (Deetz 1977: 154, 1996: 211). Deetz's culturological and undoubtedly well-intentioned treatment seeks to elevate the men and women of Parting Ways from the realm of downtrodden, disadvantaged members of an inherently unequal hierarchical system to individuals who struggled to retain their cultural traditions in the face of poverty, cruelty, and perpetual enslavement. Poverty is thus epiphenomenal to culture; it gets in the way, but does not inhibit it. The spirit of Deetz's intent concentrates on the dignity of the human spirit and the tenacity of traditions in the worse possible social conditions. Nevertheless, his elimination of poverty from the sociohistorical situation significantly reduces the impact of his analysis.

The more overtly sociological position has come closest to confronting poverty within historic African America. In an early study, for example, Drucker (1981) attempted to discern the "socioeconomic status" of the former residents of a historically undocumented homesite. She foregrounded questions of wealth and poverty, but, as was popular at the time—particularly in cultural resource management studies, from which her information derived—she employed South's (1977) pattern concept in her analysis, ensuring that the theory behind the research would be whole-cultural, and thus utterly unable to discern poverty.

Consumer-choice models would seem to provide a ready avenue to the archaeological investigation of poverty, but historical archaeologists have generally not used them to study poverty. Authors of studies written in the 1980s typically mentioned "socioeconomic status"and "social class" without giving much overt attention to the lower echelons of the social order (see, e.g., Henry 1991; Reitz 1987). Even so, the specter of poverty did occasionally appear in some of the studies, if only briefly and obliquely (see, e.g., Leone and Crosby 1987; Shephard 1987).

One of the most relevant attempts to explore an archaeology of poverty appears in the oft-cited research of John Solomon Otto (1977, 1980, 1984). Otto devised three social "statuses" as a baseline from which to examine the material culture of the antebellum Cannon's Point Plantation in coastal Georgia. A "racial/legal status" separated plantation inhabitants on the basis of skin color. Planters and overseers were situated in a free white caste, while African American slaves were relegated to an unfree black caste. A "social status" separated people on the basis of occupation: planters were managers, overseers were supervisors, and slaves were workers. Finally, an "elite/subordinate status" divided people based upon their power within the plantation regime. Planters, as members of society's elite, were at the apex of the hierarchy, followed by overseers and then slaves (Otto 1980: 8).

The theoretical foundation for much of Otto's analysis was rooted in the historical reality that on any large slave plantation one could reasonably expect to find wealthy planters, working managers, and enslaved laborers all living side by side. In light of the historical sustainability of this understanding and given the spatial proximities of early nineteenth-century plantation life, it was only logical for archaeologists to conclude that they should be able to discern the material culture distinctions among the three plantation groups. But poverty did not figure in even this nuanced portrayal in any significant way, even though race (as caste) did have a place. The prime issue for Otto was simple social inequality: white versus black, managers versus supervisors, managers versus workers, and elites versus subordinates. His interest rested upon "socioeconomic status" as a social measure that could account for the material inequalities excavated from the homesites of plantation owners, overseers, and slaves.

Otto's conceptual framework appears to combine scientific rigor with historical scholarship, and its apparent logic undoubtedly accounts for its wide acceptance among historical archaeologists (but see Orser 1988a). The weaknesses in Otto's approach, however, only become evident when the focal point of the analysis is moved beyond the spatial confines of the antebellum plantation South to a locale where the linkages between race and poverty can be examined without the overlay of bondage.

In 1943, Adelaide and Ripley Bullen (1945) excavated a homesite in Andover, Massachusetts, that had been inhabited by a woman named Lucy Foster. Foster died in 1845 at the age of 88 as an impoverished freedwomen who had been listed on the poor rolls since 1812, the date of her mistress' death. Several decades after the Bullens' pioneering excavation, Vernon Baker (1978, 1980) analyzed the ceramics the Bullens had recovered from the Foster site. In addition to describing the pieces owned and used by a freed African American slave, Baker (1980: 29) hoped that his analysis would illuminate "patterns of material culture distinctive of Afro-American behavior." In other words, he hoped to identify those characteristics of the ceramic collection that were indicative of African American ethnicity, but only in keeping with the general strictures of the culturalogical approach being pursued at the time. Baker compared the ceramics from Foster's home with those excavated from Otto's slave cabin in Georgia and from Deetz's Parting Ways site in Massachusetts. Upon completing his analysis, however, Baker (1980: 35) was confronted with a problem he had not foreseen: he could not determine whether the artifacts reflected poverty or "ethnicity." Thus stymied, he stated that a suitable resolution to his dilemma could only be found once archaeologists had excavated a number of sites inhabited by "poor whites." Upon comparison, if the collections were similar, then poverty would constitute the key variable, but if they were dissimilar, ethnicity would be of primary importance in affecting material possession. In drawing this conclusion, Baker anticipated the view that "whiteness" would provide "the key site of racial domination" and would accordingly develop into an important line of future inquiry (Harrison 1995: 63).

Baker had begun his analysis hoping to discover the material aspects of African American life as they were reflected in ceramics, but concluded by wondering whether poverty was more important than whole-cultural attributes. Ripley Bullen (1970: 128) had earlier framed much the same argument when he wrote that Foster, "although she was a person of low status, possessed a large collection of ceramic materials, much larger than might be expected." Calculating that a person of inconsequential personal wealth would not be able to purchase an abundance of ceramic objects, Bullen reasoned that Foster had probably obtained outdated vessels as handouts from her employers. He concluded that "the assessment of a person's social or economic status by the items found in their cellar hole or well must be done discreetly" (Bullen 1970: 128). His assessment thus leads directly to issues involving consumer choice.

The concepts underlying consumer-choice research seem reasonable to archaeologists because they ultimately rest upon the common sense of the capitalist marketplace, an environment with which most practicing archaeologists have first-hand experience. It is reasonable to conclude that men and women purchase objects that both appeal to them and are affordable. Even though the efforts of the consumer-choice archaeologists began with great promise, they have been less than successful in their overall research program, and most of them have not been able to go further than Baker or Bullen (see Chapter 5). Part of the analytical difficulty stems from the simple reality that "the poor are often not poor in their own eyes, and may also be despised in the eyes of the rich. They are often also an ethnic group, that is, they are not only different, they are sometimes thought of as profoundly other. And the otherness can be an escape as well as a source of integrity amidst exploitation" (Leone and Crosby 1987: 405).

As of this writing, most historical archaeologists have been willing to accept, albeit perhaps only tacitly, the widely held belief that race equals ethnicity. This facile understanding of race may have made it possible for politically conservative historical archaeologists to downplay or even ignore racialization, racial oppression, and racism as a means of creating and upholding the social inequalities of capitalist societies. If this assessment is true, it is perhaps likely that this avoidance was unconscious. A number of conservative scholars have attempted to demonstrate that racism is dead and that many nations are effectively becoming race blind as they create and present opportunities to all peoples (see, e.g., D'Souza 1995; Sowell 1994, 1998). The effects of racism are downplayed in such idealized circumstances, and the potentialities of the economic marketplace assume primary significance. In any case, and however it is construed, the conscious linkage of racialization and economic opportunity has been largely excluded from historical archaeological research (Orser and Fagan 1995: 213–19).

Even though the relationship between racialization and economic opportunity has not constituted a primary topic of analysis in historical archaeology, race and poverty are inexorably linked within the kinds of sociohistorical contexts typically studied by historical archaeologists. As a result, the connection between the two social variables can no longer be ignored. The structural importance of the link between race and economic potential was succinctly stated by heavyweight boxing champion Larry Holmes: "It's hard being black. You ever been black? I was black once—when I was poor" (Oates 1987: 62). For some, the linkage between poverty and race can easily become a foundational feature of the capitalist project because of the association of physical appearance and perceived social value: "Market theory starts from the principle that the efficiency of an individual, his capacity to produce goods and services, depends first of all on his innate qualities, such as intelligence, his physical strength, etc." (Redor 1992: 13). Comments such as these quickly and unambiguously establish the linkage.

But what exactly is poverty? It should come as no surprise that this concept, which at first seems so readily understood almost intuitively, is in fact infinitely complex in both historic and contemporary societies (see, e.g., Geremek 1997; MacPherson and Silburn 1998). In many ways, of course, poverty is a purely subjective measure, but as an appellation it often embodies ethnocentric and even racist characteristics. To cite one famous example, Adam Smith (1993: 8) wrote in 1776 that "savage nations of hunters and fishers" lived in a state of abject poverty. As an ardent supporter of the free market system, Smith found it easily palatable to identify hunting and fishing peoples as "poor" because of their lack of material possessions. Conversely, the educated Englishmen who traveled within Smith's social circle were decidedly "not poor." Most of today's anthropologists would vehemently disagree with Smith's ethnocentric assessment, and some may even suggest that hunters and gatherers maintained a quality of life that many industrialized peoples alive today would envy. But Smith's comment was not merely economically oriented, because the subtext of his observation was that hunting and fishing peoples, who would also not be considered white, were less educated and less adaptable to the advanced, modern age than were his white, English cohorts.

Smith's comment, however, is not insignificant, because for state-level societies organized with a capitalist superstructure, poverty is at its root an economic measure, defined as economic deprivation (Tabone 1998: 118). And, to ensure that poverty is quantifiable and thus readily recognizable, social scientists and policy makers in the United States, led by the federal Social Security Administration, established a baseline measure of poverty in the 1960s that incorporated a "poverty threshold" (Citro and Michael 1995: 17). The United States is one of the few nations to assume a purely quantified determination of poverty; most nations use a more relative measure (MacPherson and Silburn 1998: 9).

Using the quantitative threshold, the United States government annually calculates a poverty line to identify precisely who should be classified as "poor." The threshold is free to slide up or down, and the government's enumerators establish each year's threshold using a correlation between family income and family size. Thus, for 1989, the government ruled that "The average poverty threshold for a family of four persons was $12,674" (U.S. Department of Commerce 1993: B-27). The threshold is designed as a sliding scale that creeps upward as the number of individuals in the family increases, so that the threshold was $16,921 for a family of six, and $19,162 for a family of seven. In 1989, a family of nine or more could earn $25,000 and still be considered poor. As far as the U.S. government was concerned in 1989, a family of four lived in poverty if their income was below $12,674; a family of four with an income of $12,800 did not live in poverty. Apparently the reasoning behind this draconian measure is that a family of four needed $12,674 to maintain "a minimally adequate standard of living" that is "defined appropriately for the United States today" (Citro and Michael 1995: 19).

Viewed by the United States government, then, the poverty threshold is an absolute measure that effectively establishes American poverty. To fall under the line means that a family cannot command enough goods and services to live in a "comfortable" manner. But again, "comfortable" is a contextually relative term that can have ethnocentric and even racist roots, and as such is a term that bears an epistemological resemblance to the "color line" (see Chapter 4). In other nations, social analysts can assess the amount of poverty by using a $1/day measure, with households falling below that amount being considered poor. Statistics reveal that the highest percentage of poverty measured in this manner appears in Sub-Saharan Africa (where 48.5% of the population were considered poor in 1996) and in South Asia (42.3% of the population were considered poor in 1996) (Dietz 2001: 20). By some accounts, over one-fifth of the world's people earn less than $1/day (Hertz 2002: 55). For other social analysts, poverty is "defined as all persons belonging to families with a net equivalent income below half the median for all families" (Hedstrom and Ringen 1990: 93).

Capitalist states thus see poverty as ultimately an economic measure rooted in material deprivation (Citro and Michael 1995: 19; Sen 1982: 22). Though many kinds of deprivation may be imagined—including the lack of personal kindness, social mobility, and psychological well-being— most people usually perceive poverty in purely economic terms. Poverty is therefore widely perceived as a way of expressing "a people's lack of economic resources (e.g., money or near-money income) for consumption of economic goods and services (e.g., food, housing, clothing, transportation)" (Citro and Michael 1995: 19).

The idea that poverty relates to the consumption of economic goods and services has obvious relevance to archaeology, particularly as it pertains to the examination of the past five hundred years, a period that has witnessed an unprecedented explosion of global mass consumption (see Chapter 5). Most of the artifacts archaeologists excavate from post-Columbian sites were once commodities produced as part of a capitalist labor and exchange system. The relative frequency of artifacts that were pure commodities increases with time. Tangible, consumable commodities are the goods a family must acquire and command to stay above the poverty line. Large-scale commodity manufacturing systems existed among many ancient empire-states (see, e.g., Kardulias 1999), but only after the fifteenth century did huge numbers of non-elite men and women have the opportunity to purchase objects manufactured in far-away places. Only after the expansion of the European superpowers could non-elites become part of a global network of commerce that linked together Europe, Africa, Asia, and the New World (Wallerstein 1974, 1979, 1980). Commodities that were once out of reach quickly became attainable "objects of desire" for the masses (Forty 1986: 6–10). Even before this commodity revolution could gain a foothold in the Western imagination, a considerable multi-locale trade occurred in Asia and Africa (see Frank 1998; Levathes 1996). Even the earliest colonialist activities in North America created a consumer revolution, as Native Americans acquired hundreds of thousands of commodities from the mercantilist fur traders who regularly moved among them (Axtell 1992). The same commodity revolution occurred in most places that indigenous and colonialist peoples interacted and engaged in exchange.

Social scholars fully realize, however, that "poverty" references more than simply a lack of personal possessions, because social labeling usually accompanies the assignment of the word "poor" to actual individuals. The link between poverty and the capitalist project is indisputable, because poverty "was not merely its by-product, its social price, but one of its integral elements" (Geremek 1997: 109). Pejorative labels like "the underclass" and "the undeserving poor" are often attached to individuals who are assigned to poverty. In the United States, racial labels are "usually reserved for low-income people" because Americans do not generally use class labels (Gans 1995: 13). As a result, racialization often accompanies an identification with poverty, regardless of the perceived skin color of the person or persons being labeled.

The realization that poverty ultimately refers to economic deprivation perhaps helps explain why many archaeologists may hesitate to examine the poor: after all, archaeology is at least on some level about things and, given the high cost of excavation, archaeologists generally avoid excavating where they suspect they will find little or nothing in the way of past human activity. In the United States, for instance, legislators designed laws of cultural patrimony to mandate excavation and data recovery only in places where one can expect to find something that either already has "significance" or has the potential to be deemed "significant" along carefully crafted criteria (Hardesty and Little 2000; King 2000).

The argument against the archaeology of poverty in the United States is appealing when the legislation is viewed in conjunction with the notion that archaeologists would usually prefer to recover artifacts and other cultural remains. Since the poor in all capitalist societies by definition suffer economic deprivation—and are usually so labeled—is there any reason to assume that the poorest members of a society could have obtained significant numbers of commodities that are amenable to archaeological discovery? The apparent commonsensical link between poverty and the paucity of material possessions may lead to the conclusion that an archaeology of the poor would provide little in the way of material culture evidence. Phrased in this manner, the excavation of sites known to have been inhabited by economically disadvantaged men and women seems professionally risky. What can an archaeologist expect to learn except that the people had little in the way of personal possessions, and do we not already know this from our pedestrian understanding of poverty and from the accounts so painstakingly provided by historians? Some archaeologists would respond in the affirmative: "What seems at first sight to be the material trace of the ordinary person all too often turns out to be the debris of those with power and influence. Slaves were owned. They owned little of their own and by and large left as faint a trace in the material record as they did in the written documentation" (Hall 2000: 19).

On one level, such logic appears unassailable. But archaeology has progressed far beyond the simple search for artifacts, no matter how important the objects from the past continue to be for helping to frame archaeological interpretations. More to the point, perhaps, archaeology conducted at sites associated with historically documented, economically deprived inhabitants has produced artifacts, and often in large numbers. For example, the Bullens recovered fragments of 113 individual ceramic vessels of many forms and decorations from Lucy Foster's homesite (Baker 1978: 109), and Otto (1977: 115) found the remains of 80 tableware vessels in a slave cabin at Cannon's Point Plantation. By comparison, he recovered only 78 vessels at the overseer's cabin. These two examples alone serve to deny any easy correlation between artifact occurrence and poverty.

Multiscalar Network Theory and Modern-World Archaeology

At first consideration, poverty may appear to constitute a purely autochthonous and internal social-structural phenomenon in which some individuals are classified as controlling little in the way of personal wealth when compared to others within the social organization. Such an assertion can easily be promoted when analysts turn their intellectual gaze inward and envision poverty as society-specific and historically constrained. Within the parameters of this framework, it would be equally possible to imagine racial identification (when linked to material possessions) in the same light, so that each culture is seen to identify its human variations in distinct, culturally meaningful ways. The application of the internalized perspective would be correct in one sense, because cultural members do design social structures that are consistent with their world views, beliefs, and understandings. And, though each sociohistorical situation is unique, internalizing the linkage between race and poverty in the post-Columbian world would be shortsighted and misleading.

Numerous historians and social scientists have fully documented the global spread of mercantilist and capitalist sociohistorical formations after about A.D. 1500 (e.g., Wolf 1982). To take just one example, the Atlantic slave trade dramatically altered the social realities and wealth-holding structures both in parts of Africa and throughout the New World (e.g., Curtin 1990; Gilroy 1993; Miller 1988; Thornton 1992). Structurally similar sociohistorical changes accompanied the expansion of the marketing system, of which racialized slavery was but one element.

Any intensive understanding of the modern world, however one wishes to define it and to establish its parameters, must rely to some degree on the notion of social interaction. Rather than envisioning individuals like marbles that occasionally and temporarily crash into one another in the course of their existence, a critical understanding of life must incorporate the idea that humans produce relationships as an integral facet of their existence (Godelier 1986: 1). The relational-determinative perspective has been termed "mutualism," a view that rests on the foundational concept that social actors "do things with, to, and in respect of each other" (Carrithers 1992: 34). In other words, people are self-aware and other-aware.

The mutualist connections between individuals and groups are understandably intertwined, historically situated, and multifaceted because human life is complicated. Archaeologists investigating the history of state-level organizations, especially those that incorporated a complex web of mercantilist and capitalist relations, must acknowledge that multidimensional and multihistorical interlinkages may have operated in the past sociohistorical formation. They must also recognize that these many connections were temporally mutable. As a result, modern-world archaeologists must incorporate network theory—social and geographic—as they seek to interpret the past. The investigation of race especially demands a sociospatial network perspective because racial assignment was imposed from the outside, by individuals who were in contact—either directly or figuratively—with men, women, and children whom they labeled The Other.

The most geographically expansive expression of network theory is world-systems theory. Though far from perfect, world-systems theory offers applicable concepts that can be employed within the archaeological search for racialization in past social systems. But world-systems theory is not a unified way of perceiving the world. On the contrary, it is best perceived as an overarching theoretical perspective that incorporates three important understandings: a hesitancy to accept the independent validity of reified cultural and social units, such as nations, tribes, and races, an emphasis on a concept of multiscalar relations to account for the interconnectedness between cultural and social units, and a concept of systemic (geographically expansive) processes to help explain the nature of these relationships (Peregrine 1996: 1; Reno 1996: 6). World-systems theory developed as part of the intellectual exercise directed toward comprehending modernity, and as such, it has explicit relevance for modern-world archaeology (Orser 1996a).

As currently formulated, world(-)systems theory has two varieties, each one associated with a particular proponent. World-systems theory (with hyphen) was initially identified with sociologist Immanuel Wallerstein, and world systems theory (without hyphen) with Andre Gunder Frank. Archaeologists have used both varieties of the theory (e.g., Algaze 1993; Blanton and Feinman 1984; Blanton et al. 1992; Champion 1989; Chase-Dunn and Hall 1991; Crowell 1997; Edens 1992; Hall and Chase-Dunn 1993, 1996; Kardulias 1999; King and Freer 1995; Kohl 1987; McGuire 1986; Pailes and Whitecotton 1979; Peregrine 1995; Peregrine and Feinman 1996; Rowlands at al. 1987; Sanderson 1995; Schortman and Urban 1987, 1992, 1994; Upham 1982, 1986).

As explained by Wallerstein and his colleagues, the basis of world-systems theory is that since the sixteenth century, a single, capitalist world economy has been the driving force behind the creation of the modern world (Wallerstein 1974, 1980). This "modern world-system," though exceedingly complex in its specific, local details, incorporates three central features: a single expanding economy, referred to as the "capitalist world-economy," expanding multiple states, and the capital-labor relation (Hopkins 1982: 11).

The capitalist world-economy is distinguished by a mode of production organized on the basis of profitable exchange within a market environment (Wallerstein 1979: 159). As a world-economy, capitalism incorporates a single division of labor—divided most simplistically into owners and workers—located within numerous sociohistorical settings. But even with all the influence its agents can wield, capitalism is an economic rather than a purely political system. The integration of the system is maintained by the economic interdependence between the political units, not necessarily by political alliances (Chase-Dunn 1992: 11). The politicization of the system, however, is quite possible (Stearns 2001: 126–27), as the various interconnected nodes vie for control, seek independence, or struggle for self-sufficiency.

Spatiality, in addition to structured social inequality, is a central facet of world-systems theory. As the world-economy spreads outward from its core, its agents and local collaborators create spatial polities that maintain various historically relevant links with the center. The precise characteristics and components of cores, semi-peripheries, and peripheries have been the subject of considerable debate within the archaeological community (see the citations above). For present purposes it is acceptable to simplify the various historically mutable formations by noting that the cores in the capitalist world-economy are central places from which production and capital emanate. Conversely, the peripheries are locales that are dependent on the cores (Wallerstein 1979).

As originally outlined by Wallerstein, world-systems theory is a post-Columbian phenomenon. Many scholars, including many archaeologists, have rejected Wallerstein's idea that large-scale, global systems must necessarily be capitalist in form and post-Columbian in date. These dissenting scholars see nothing particularly unique about the post-Columbian expansion of mercantilism and capitalism and argue instead that world systems have existed for centuries. The major proponent of the so-called "continuationist" school is Andre Gunder Frank (Chase-Dunn 1993: 407).

Frank in fact anticipated Wallerstein's work by a number of years. In an influential article (Frank 1966), he proposed that the global spread of capitalism tended to institutionalize societal underdevelopment. As the agents of capital moved outward from metropolitan centers (cores), they created numerous dependent satellites (peripheries). As the centers exploited the satellites for their own benefit, their agents created and enforced social inequality. Frank coined the now-famous term "the development of underdevelopment" to characterize the unequal relations forged by the agents of the powerful core.

During his widely ranging study of unequal global relations, Frank concluded that world systems existed long before the Age of European Expansion. Employing the research of anthropologists as a springboard (Ekholm and Friedman 1982; see also Freidman 1994; Wilkinson 1987), Frank argued (1993a, b, 1998; Frank and Gills 1993; Gills and Frank 1992) that the features of the world-system that appeared with the commencement of post-Columbian history were in truth an element of a larger Afroeurasian cycle that had operated for thousands of years before the birth of Columbus (Chase-Dunn 1996: 247). For Frank, the rise of Europe in the sixteenth century was only one expression of a cycle that witnessed the rise and fall of core states, a process that extended back in time at least to the Bronze Age and possibly into the Neolithic period (Abu-Lughod 1989; Hall 1999: 7).

No way currently exists to determine precisely when it is proper to speak about the development of worldwide systems of interaction. The application of world(-)systems theory in archaeology has consequently been controversial (see e.g., Frank 1999). Archaeologists investigating pre-Columbian history and wishing to reject world(-)systems theory out of hand can simply argue that capitalism did not operate in any significant way before either the sixteenth (Wallerstein 1974) or the eighteenth century (Wolf 1982: 298). Pre-Columbian archaeologists interested in the concept of interactive, global networks can employ Frank's temporally broader perspective. To extend the applicability of world systems theory into the pre-Columbian world, archaeologists can merely refer to world systems as "core/periphery structures" (Hall and Chase-Dunn 1996: 16). This useful term suggests the longevity of the basic sociospatial structure without the necessity of including capitalism. As another option, archaeologists can reject the theory outright on the grounds that it is too intellectually confining and totalizing (see, e.g., Feinman 1996; McGuire 1996; Kohl 1987).

The complete rejection of world-systems theory is impossible for modern-world archaeologists, and a number of historical archaeologists have successfully adopted the tenets of the theory in their research, albeit with various degrees of rigor (see, e.g., Crowell 1997; Deetz 1991; Gaughwin 1992; Jeans 1988; Orser 1996a; Paynter 1982; Reno 1996; South 1988a, b). But even in historical archaeology, the use of world-systems theory is not without its severe critics. Perhaps the most facile rejection of world-systems theory is practical, incorporating the simple argument that archaeologists only investigate individual sites one at a time. This line of reasoning maintains that because archaeologists "do not excavate on a global level" (Schuyler 1988: 41), they must forever be restricted to studying individual sites. The logic of this perspective is unassailably obvious but shortsighted, because it seeks to establish artificial boundaries around a site, effectively segregating its inhabitants and creating a bounded community. By turning the perspective inward, the analyst loses the opportunity to understand the broader networks within which the site's inhabitants found themselves enmeshed.

In a more thoughtful critique, Leone and Potter (1988: 4–5) envision the eventual value of world-systems theory, but only after its proponents overcome three significant shortcomings. First, proposing that world-systems theory is an evolutionary model, Leone and Potter argue that the theory accordingly cannot account for failure, irrationality, or emotion. Because it ultimately rests on a "goal-directed" motivation, world-systems theory discounts sociohistorical phenomena that do not serve the functioning of the system. In their unrelenting march toward understanding capitalist human-human and human-land relations, world-system theorists tend not to notice the often tiny, though sometimes quite significant, sidesteps where "progress" is hampered by individuals who wish to remain outside the system. Second, Leone and Potter state that world-systems theory cannot provide an understanding of native cultures. World-systems theorists may be expert at identifying and interpreting the frontiers the center's representatives erected between the cores and the peripheries, but they are less skilled at interpreting the realities faced on the indigenous side of the equation. According to Leone and Potter, the interpretive gaze of the world-systems theorists is uniquely directed toward the powerful and away from the weak. And finally, Leone and Potter argue that world-systems theory is a universalizing perspective. World-systems theory is in essence merely a functionalist project, and one that embodies "the basic functionalist assumption that the elements of a society can be fitted together to achieve a view of how that society works or worked, and the corollary assumption that societies achieve some functional end" (Leone and Potter 1988: 3).

The deficiencies in world-systems theory noted by Leone and Potter are indeed difficult to deny. World-systems theorists, for example, have overwhelmingly focused on the actions of the superpowers' agents to press their economic dominance throughout the world. And, when examined in its entirety with the insights of today's hindsight, world-systems theory does appear totalizing and goal oriented.

To have utility, however, world-systems theory need not be perceived as intellectually confining. It is undeniable that an archaeologist can assume a priori that world-systems theory has merit as an overarching, structuralizing feature of history. Once this determination is finalized, the archaeologist can simply strive to mold the findings to fit the model. Rather than demonstrating the inherent deficiency of the model, however, such usage merely demonstrates that any complex formulation can be misunderstood and misapplied. Elements of world-systems theory can be adopted in modern-world archaeology, not so much as an explanatory device, but as an interpretive tool to help disentangle the largest scale sociospatial interactions that operated in a past sociohistorical situation. At a minimum, the structural framework provided by world-systems theory offers an intellectual grid upon which issues of race and racialization can be understood.

Any archaeological understanding of culture, poverty, and multiscalar social dynamics is necessarily complex and historically situated, especially when race is conceptualized as a social assignment that interlinks many social entities. The interpretive difficulty is perhaps even more formidable for archaeologists than for sociologists, because of the archaeologists' need to understand the material culture dimensions of racialization within a sociohistorical context that is multidimensional by definition. The mutable, historical relationships between race and material culture represent a major interpretive challenge to today's historical archaeology. I offer one avenue of inquiry that has the potential to advance historical archaeological research to a full appreciation for the study of race and racialization. As a necessary starting point, however, it is instructive to examine briefly archaeology's history of investigating race. This disciplinary history, because it includes a widespread reification of race, has led to a theoretical dead end in the archaeological investigation of racialization. This checkered history may constitute one contributing factor to explain the paucity of racial analysis in today's archaeology, as modern-day practitioners have sought to distance themselves from the mistakes of the past.

Chapter 2
The Prehistory of Race and Archaeological Interpretation, Part I
Inventing Race for Archaeology

When considering an archaeological interpretation of race, it is instructive to retreat from the present and delve into archaeology's past. A withdrawal into archaeological history accomplishes two important tasks. First, it provides a perspective on the development of archaeological thought as it pertains to race and racialization, and second, it helps to bring into sharper focus the need for a new program of research.

The use of the word "prehistory" in the title of this and the next chapter deserves some comment. As applied here, the term is not meant to indicate a "time before history" or "history before writing." The term is instead intended to signify approaches to the archaeology of race that have been used prior to this writing. The three examples cited in this chapter refer to "properly prehistoric" peoples, whereas the examples in the next chapter mostly refer to men and women who lived during the past five hundred years, within the period commonly though arbitrarily demarcated as "history." The term "prehistory" is employed in the next chapter as well, because it still represents the early history of the archaeological analysis of race and racialization. The specialized and idiosyncratic use of "prehistory" here is meant only to suggest the distinction between more facile analytical approaches to an archaeology of race and those that are capable of being pursued in the twenty-first century.

Each of the three examples presented in this chapter has significant archaeological dimensions. Two of the examples derive from real archaeological subjects—the North American Mound Builders and the European Celts—but the third example involves the mythical lost continent of Atlantis. These case studies span the history of archaeological research, from the earliest investigations in Europe and the United States to the present day, and they range from serious archaeological exploration and thought to the utter fantasy of pseudo-science.

The inclusion of Atlantis is not presented flippantly. On the contrary, the racial interpretation of Atlantis has a substantial, if fringe, relevance to the way race and archaeology have been linked in history. Archaeologists are, of course, well acquainted with the story of the Mound Builders, but the creation of a fully racialized Atlantis may be less understood, because professional archaeologists frequently dismiss as irrelevant the often outlandish claims of pseudo-archaeologists. The racialization of the mythical Atlantis, however, presents "archaeological interpretation" at its worst.

The Mound Builders

It is no exaggeration to state that the image of the Mound Builders created the impetus for serious archaeological research in the Americas. Scientifically minded and historically curious Americans would undoubtedly have "discovered" archaeology without the Mound Builders, but the controversy that surrounded this "mysterious race" provided an early, immediate, and long-term acceleration of archaeological research in the New World.

Mound Builder archaeology encompassed the entirety of the nineteenth century (Willey and Sabloff 1993: 39), and its history has been recounted many times (for excellent overviews, see Silverberg 1986; Kennedy 1994). For present purposes, the search for the Mound Builders is instructive for two principal reasons. First, the conscious creation of this "race" represents the invention of a racialized whole-culture in a manner that is generally representative of the entire history of racial analysis in archaeology. Second, the invention of the Mound Builders was predicated on the assignment of significant racialist elements to a past population, such that it would have been virtually impossible to invent the Mound Builders without the accompanying racialist philosophy.

It was not accidental that the scientific interest in the Mound Builders developed alongside the expansion of the United States. Men and women of both European and American descent who migrated westward into the continent's hinterland—often in collusion with the government to dispossess the Native Americans in their path (Hinsley 1989: 83)—encountered many magnificent earthen monuments. Most of these settlers and the scientists who accompanied them found it difficult to explain the presence of the mounds within the confines of their understanding of humanity. The intellectual curiosity the mounds engendered coincided with the rise of American sovereignty, as citizens of the new nation came into direct conflict with Native Americans who had lived in their traditional homelands for generations and who, by their very presence, represented an obstacle to nationalism (Patterson 1995: 27–28).

Because the monuments the migrants encountered in the Ohio and Mississippi valleys were especially impressive, they generally found it impossible to equate their construction with the Native Americans who either still survived in the region or who had recently been removed.

Soon after the existence of the earthen monuments was made public, scholars chose sides based upon their perception of who was responsible for the monuments' construction. Some argued that ancestors of Native Americans had built the mounds, while others attributed them to more "civilized" peoples. Assuming that large monuments implied an advanced civilization, the scholars who discounted Native American involvement in the mounds usually argued that non-indigenous people must have built them. Their principal candidates were the Lost Tribes of Israel, the Welsh, the Vikings, and even a Mysterious Lost Race.

Tales of the advanced, albeit unknown "race" began to circulate throughout the embryonic United States. For example, in *The History of the American Indians,* published in 1775, James Adair (1968: 11–12) observed that contemporary scholars believed that Native Americans represented one of three cultures: "Pre-Adamites," "a separate race of men," or descendants of the Chinese. Adair was not persuaded by any of these arguments and instead issued twenty-three reasons why Native Americans were "descended from the Jews." He focused on many of the cognitive elements of life—from the worship of Jehovah to traditions of marriage and divorce—but he also considered the nature of Native American ornamentation. Just as the "Israelites were fond of wearing beads and other ornaments" so too were "The Indian nations . . . agreed in the custom of thus adorning themselves with beads of various sizes and colours" (Adair 1968: 169–70). The physical evidence was unassailable because these North American people of Israel had worn shell beads long before European traders had given them glass beads.

Adair was impressed by the skin color of Native Americans and used this characteristic in his attempt to prove their Semitic origin. In fact, the first sentence in his history reads: "The Indians are of a copper or red-clay colour." Accepting their Middle Eastern origin on faith, Adair was compelled to explain the physical appearance of Native Americans by proposing "That the Indian colour is merely accidental, or artificial." As support for this position, he said that in 1747 he observed a Pennsylvanian, "a white man by birth, and in profession a Christian" who, after long exposure to the sun "was tarnished with as deep an Indian hue" (2–4). For him, the skin color of Native American men, women, and children was explainable merely by long exposure to the sun. This neat climatic explanation allowed Adair to retain his view of Native American origins and at the same time to account for their physical appearance.

Adair is most remembered by historians and anthropologists for his observations on southeastern Native American polities, but it is clear that he generally recognized "the Indians" as a kind of whole-culture that had come from the Holy Land by way of Beringia sometime in the far distant past (1968: 219). These intercontinental immigrants had later subdivided themselves: "As the Israelites were divided into Tribes, and had chiefs over them, so the Indians divide themselves" (15).

Adair's belief that Native Americans were descended from the "Lost Israelites" meant that he was not particularly interested in the mounds of Eastern North America. As an advance man for the British Empire, however, one of his primary interests was to ensure that the empire thrived. In the appendix to the *History*, he provides "Advice to Statesmen," in which he offers expert testimony for the course of action to follow to dispossess the native residents of the American Southeast. He says of the Muskogees, for instance, that "This haughty nation is directly in the way of our valuable southern colonies" and that if "they renew their acts of hostility against us" that they should be given a "severe correction" or be driven "over the Mississippi" (457).

Adair's comments, though not specifically focused on the Mound Builders, indicate that he employed both his positions regarding their ethnogenesis—either as the ancestors of eighteenth-century Native Americans or as a distinctly separate "race"—tacitly and overtly to denigrate the Native Americans' rights to their ancestral lands (Patterson 1995: 28). Even individuals who believed that Native American ancestors were responsible for the mounds could still promote the pernicious notion of cultural degeneration, and argue that the Native Americans who "stood in the way" of American national expansion were inferior to their ancestors, the builders of the majestic mounds. The case was easy to formulate and to press forward. After all, the mounds in the Ohio valley and in the vicinity of what would eventually become St. Louis were magnificent constructions that exemplified complex geometry. In juxtaposition to these masterworks of architecture and engineering, many American scholars perceived the nearby natives to be lazy, ignorant, and intellectually incapable of creating technological marvels that required long-term commitments of labor and significant organizational skills (Williams 1991: 72).

The racialist argument was even more straightforward for those who ascribed the mounds to an "advanced race" from outside Native North America. These writers simply compared the condition of the indigenous peoples around them with the mythicized image they had created of the outsiders. Individual creators of the Mound Builders were free to envision them any way they wished. In fact, they could invent them specifically as a counterpoint to the visible, contemporary Native Americans around them.

In either case, we must recall that the native peoples in the Ohio Valley—in alliance with other groups facing the same assimilationist and even genocidal pressures within the American South—had engaged in a protracted "spirited resistance" to American encroachment and dispossession, with many groups openly rejecting the invaders' alcohol, artifacts, worldview, and religion (Dowd 1992). The American settlers' memories of these often-intensive struggles for territory made it relatively easy for them to support either one of the Mound Builder arguments with gusto. Either the present-day Native Americans had degenerated from a glorious past, or they were merely peoples who had earlier been dispossessed by an advanced, immigrant race. The dispossession of resistant Native Americans could be intellectually legitimated with either argument.

The natives' struggle for respect and sovereignty certainly did not endear them to the American colonizers who were poised along the continent's east coast. The earliest speculations about the Mound Builders of the Ohio Valley had coincided with the period of armed native resistance beginning around 1745, during the French and British imperialist contest for a North American empire, and ending around 1815, at the close of the War of 1812. Caleb Atwater is today credited with creating the first systematic account of the eastern mounds. Completely discounting Native American involvement, he argued that Tartars from southern Asia or possibly even "Hindoos" had constructed the monuments. It is not coincidental that Atwater moved to Ohio from Massachusetts in 1815, directly after the cessation of open hostilities. He conducted his famous survey shortly thereafter (Bieder 1986: 110; Williams 1991: 40–41). The invention of the Mound Builders as a whole-culture allowed American settlers, such as Atwater, to separate the mysterious and magnificent "race" of earthmovers from the many "degenerate" peoples who were allied against them west of the Appalachians, as well as all those other "primitive" peoples Lewis and Clark had only recently reported on further west.

The first serious work in Mound Builder archaeology, *Ancient Monuments of the Mississippi Valley* by Ephraim Squier and Edwin Davis, published in 1848, was only possible with American sovereignty. The goal of Squier and Davis in this well-known archaeological classic was to explore the antiquity, origin, and identity of the mysterious Mound Builders, and ultimately to put a scientific slant on the speculations that were then rife throughout America (Meltzer 1998: 1). In keeping with the goals of early nineteenth-century science, scholars generally believed that careful observation of the mounds and measured contemplation about their history would chart a way to understand them. A few individuals had produced written accounts of the mounds, but their observations were neither systematic nor scientific. Based on the quality and scope of previous thinking about the mounds in the eastern United States, "It was concluded that if these monuments were capable of reflecting any certain light upon the grand archaeological questions connected with the primitive history of the American Continent, the origin, migrations, and early state of *the American race,* that then they should be more carefully and minutely, and above all, more systematically investigated" (Squier and Davis 1998: xxxiii-xxxiv; emphasis added). In providing this scientific service, Squier and Davis modeled the Mound Builders as a whole-culture, and their characterization obtained for many years.

Squier and Davis (1998: 301) outlined the cultural characteristics of the Mound Builders as they were able to discern them from their field investigations. The distribution of the monuments indicated that, while the Mound Builders were a "numerous and widely spread" people, they were still "essentially homogeneous, in customs, habits, religion, and government." The authors were also convinced that the Mound Builder whole-culture represented an essentialized "ancient race." In a perfect description of a whole-culture, Squier and Davis argued that

the mound-builders were an agricultural people, considerably advanced in the arts, possessing a great uniformity throughout the whole territory which they occupied, in manners, habits, and religion—a uniformity sufficiently well marked to identify them as a single people, having a common origin, common modes of life, and, as an almost necessary consequence, common sympathies, if not a common and consolidated government. (1998: 45)

That the Mound Builders were distinguishable from America's many diverse groups of "Indians" was duly represented by subsistence alone: the Mound Builders were "stationary and agricultural," whereas Native Americans were "hunters averse to labor" (Squier and Davis 1998: 45).

Squier and Davis's survey foregrounds the notion that early anthropology is largely a story of various authors attempting to explain the physical (nature) and the cultural (nurture) differences between the world's peoples, with "race" figuring either totally or prominently in the mix. Beginning with Johann Friedrich Blumenbach's "De generis humani varietate nativa," published in 1775, scholars and scientists have sought to describe human diversity through categorization. Though Blumenbach used samples of hair and eyewitness portraits of human variation to frame his conclusions, his primary emphasis centered upon the comparison of eighty-two skulls from different "races" (Voget 1975: 105–6). Blumenbach believed in five races: Caucasian (white), Mongolian (yellow), Ethiopian (black), American (red), and Malayan (brown). He also understood, however, that these categories were somewhat arbitrary, because gradations of skin color could occur (Malefijt 1974: 259).

Treatises like those written by Blumenbach helped to fuel the debate between the monogenists and the polygenists, with the polygenists generally including an apology for the enslavement of African peoples as an offshoot of their argument (Harris 1968: 89–90). Using this logic, the separate creation of Africans must have occurred for a divine reason, perhaps one known only to the Creator. But the reification of essentialist races was so prevalent that even scholars who opposed slavery, but who were still polygenists, could also promote racist beliefs that reinforced the "scientific" basis of human bondage. For example, *An Account of the Regular Gradation in Man*, published in 1799 by Charles White, an opponent of slavery, stressed that men and women of African descent had small brains, large sex organs, and an apelike odor; they were, in fact, more like apes than Caucasians (Harris 1968: 89). But as Malefijt (1974: 260) explains, studies like Blumenbach's created controversies simply through their existence, because they helped to legitimate an early period of scientific racism. The "scientific" part of the equation was guaranteed by the quantification of cranial measurements, a process that appeared clinical, scientific, and unbiased.

The myth of the Mound Builders was intimately connected with the examination of ancient crania. The creation of scientific-sounding indices rooted in the ratios of various skull measurements appeared to provide tangible evidence of racial identification and, by extension, intelligence and ultimately long-term physical survival. Many of the earliest American researchers who employed skulls as data for racial studies obtained their specimens from prehistoric earthworks. For example, a Philadelphia physician named Montroville Wilson Dickeson excavated some 200 mounds and obtained "about 60 tolerably perfect skulls" (Meltzer 1998: 17). Squier and Davis knew about Dickeson's study, and while they condemned his methods, they had no intellectual argument with this intent. In a letter to Squier, Davis excoriated Dickeson because his techniques in "moundology" lacked scientific rigor. Davis called Dickeson a "journalist" because he only sketched the mound while slaves did the actual labor (Bieder 1986: 116). The charge of being merely a "journalist" could also be made against Thomas Jefferson, the oft-venerated doyen of scientific archaeology (Wheeler 1956: 58), who also employed slave labor in his mound excavations.

The seminal work in the study of human crania was Samuel G. Morton's *Crania Americana*, published in 1839, with the provocative subtitle: *Or, a Comparative View of the Skulls of Various Aboriginal Nations of North and South America to Which is Prefixed an Essay on the Varieties of the Human Species*. Morton, who has been identified as the creator of American physical anthropology (Brace 1982: 17), examined 256 crania (147 of them from native peoples in North and South America) and concluded that the Native American skulls were morphologically different from those of Caucasians, Africans, Mongolians, and Malays (Bieder 1986: 69). Scholars know today that Morton's methods were biased (see, for example, Gould 1981: 54–60), but nineteenth-century scholars, including Squier and Davis, tended to accept his detailed, scientific, and seemingly well-documented study. Acknowledging that Morton had used skulls taken from mounds—including two that "may be regarded as genuine remains of the mound-builders"—Squier and Davis dutifully reported cranial measurements in their survey (Squier and Davis 1998: 290–92). The skulls they found within the mounds were usually either crushed by the weight of the earth above them or almost completely decomposed. As a result, they were able to present the measurements for only one skull. They recognized that "no general conclusion as to the cranial characteristics of the ancient people can be based upon a single skull," but they nonetheless observed that their measurements placed the skull within the parameters of the "American race" (Squier and Davis 1998: 289).

Mound Builder scholarship continued apace after the pioneering efforts of Squier and Davis, and most of the completed research contained a racial element usually designed around the idea that nineteenth-century Native Americans could not possibly be the descendants of the Mound Builders. Until the final years of the nineteenth century, authors commonly designated the Mound Builders as "a race" who were not amenable to satisfactory, final identification. Most scholars identified their favorite candidates for the Mound Builders, with many of them pointing to Central America and Peru, a linkage also favored by Squier and Davis (1998: 301). The explanatory interest in Central and South America was undoubtedly not coincidental, because shortly before Squier and Davis's *Ancient Monuments* had appeared, John Lloyd Stephens had published *Incidents of Travel in Central America, Chiapas, and Yucatán* (in 1841) and *Incidents of Travel in Yucatán* (in 1843), complete with Frederick Catherwood's stunning illustrations (Coe 1993: 92). These books, and the magnificent ancient civilizations they revealed to an eager public, ignited and fueled the perception that the Mound Builders either had migrated from Central America *to* Ohio or had gone to Central America *from* the Ohio and Mississippi valleys. As American Midwesterners, Squier and Davis were most comfortable with the second idea, thus putting the cradle of Mound Builder civilization squarely within the United States.

One of the best-known studies of the Mound Builders was John Wells Foster's *Pre-historic Races of the United States of America*, published in 1873. Foster, then president of the Chicago Academy of Science, was positively aghast at the idea that Native Americans could stand in the way of American Manifest Destiny, even after the Cherokees had traveled the Trail

eft behind. He felt confident
n intelligible opinion" about
nse, proficiency in art, habits
utes of migration (311). Cit-
er of conclusions: that the
"the ancient inhabitants of
tchez Indians" as well as the
Mound Builders buried "the
ith their dead as did the Chi-
arly Christians; and that the
fice, like the Scythians, the
les living in Mexico and Cen-
d that the Mound Builders,
curative powers of salt, built
national religion" (350–51).
ially telling, because it hark-
as exhibiting the character-

examine the origin, history,
s had Squier and Davis. He
color. He writes, for exam-
any to be the primitive type
his day; while the Caucasian
f society, and of more favor-
Darwin, von Humboldt, and
zzle of the Mound Builders'
nied and could not propose
today, however, we can pos-
e believed that the Mound
of his skin-color scale than

ast for professional archae-
4) at the end of the nine-
vestigation of the mounds
rs, and conclusively proved
tive Americans. His study
ve Americans and Mound
lish that any effort to prove
summary at the beginning
ertly attacked the idea that
ulture, separate from the
d-builders of the area des-
eoples bearing about the

ry
at
th
"A
to

to
ess
mo-
that
as
rton
are
und
rms
ess,
alley
51).
here
ified
itled
–60)
rt to
ojec-
stles,
pper
mon-

ke the
ark of
of veg-
n with
a mere
bed in

s were
erland
ast in
ll. His
ilized,"

nic Re-
s it was

revealed in the earthen monuments they
that he could develop from the remains "
Mound Builder architecture, systems of def
and pursuits, religious observances, and r
ing copious authorities, he drew a num
Mound Builders were sun worshipers lik
Central America, Mexico, [and]. . . the N
Scythians and the Babylonians; that the
most useful or most highly-prized" objects
nese, the "Aryans of the Vedas," and the e
Mound Builders engaged in human sacr
inhabitants of Stone Age England, and peop
tral America (310–17). He also conclude
unlike Native Americans, understood the
long lines of defense, and maintained "a
Foster's use of the term "national" is espe
ens back to the essence of the whole-cultur
istics of a nation-state.

But for Foster, it was not enough simply t
and characteristics of the Mound Builders
was also interested in considering their ski
ple, that "The Negroid type is believed by r
of mankind, and has remained constant to
type is the result of a more improved state
able external influences" (336). Foster cited
other scientists to tease a solution to the pu
"race," but in the end he was completely sty
any firm conclusion. From our vantage poin
tulate—based on the rest of his text—that
Builders were closer to the "Caucasian" end
to the "Negroid" end.

The Mound Builder whole-culture was, at
ologists, demolished by Cyrus Thomas (18
teenth century. Thomas made a careful i
studied by Squier and Davis, Foster, and oth
that they were the product of ancient N
demonstrated that the links between Nati
Builders were so numerous and easy to estab
otherwise was absurd. As the first entry of a
of his lengthy analysis, Thomas (1894: 17) o
the Mound Builders were a distinct whole-
Native Americans, concluding that: "the mou
ignated consisted of a number of tribes of

same relations to one another and occupying about the same culture-status as did the Indian tribes inhabiting this country when first visited by Europeans."

At the beginning of the twenty-first century, the Mound Builders, as a distinct, non-Native American whole-culture, exist only in the minds of pseudo-archaeologists. For example, Barry Fell (1976: 163) intimates that the Mound Builders had an Old World origin, and David Hatcher Childress (1992: 349–53) seems to think that they were people of giant stature who may have been associated with the ancient Egyptians or the early Nestorian Christians. What is most interesting about these outrageous ideas is that their inventors model the Mound Builders as a whole-culture in the same manner as scholars a century earlier. Though professional archaeologists have long since abandoned the concept of the Mound Builders as a distinct people, the Mound Builders are not truly gone from modern-day, albeit outlandish, associations with archaeology. Regrettably, the "prehistory" of the Mound Builders, as a racialized people, has not entirely disappeared, because pseudo-archaeologists regularly promote it with the collusion of a gullible media.

The Celts

By the end of the twentieth century, the word "Celtic" had assumed almost mythic proportions. The live show *Riverdance* had brought global acclaim to Celtic history and artistic expression, optimistic economists widely referred to the tiny Republic of Ireland as the "Celtic Tiger," and the award-winning movie *Braveheart* had glorified the fearless exploits of the ancient Celts as they struggled for freedom in the face of seemingly overwhelming odds. Professional writers have also produced a stunning array of books about the Celts and their mysterious ways (e.g., Dames 1992; Matthews 1996; Pennick 1996), and the Celts quickly became the inspiration for a New Age growth industry as men and women around the world attempted to learn the secrets of Celtic religion and naturalistic mysticism. The excitement generated about the Celts has been predicated on the idea that they were a deeply spiritual and intensely knowledgeable people who had lived through a venerable history begun long before the rampant materialism of our modern age.

The history of the actual Celts, though wrapped in the mysteries of time and confused by their popular image, appears to be relatively straightforward. They were a largely animistic people who held reverence for the earth and its creatures, but who, when called upon to do so, could defend themselves vigorously. They had a rich oral tradition and a profound worldview that rested on an ancient foundation. Reality, however, seldom matches the invented image, and the archaeological evidence for the Celts is infinitely more complex than the popular picture would imply. In fact, the term "Celt" is so problematic that one prominent archaeologist has suggested that scholars should abandon the term altogether (Renfrew 1996: 132–33). "Celt" is today so equivocal that its usage tends to cause more problems than it solves. Even so, the idea of a "Celtic World" in the past is still very much alive, appearing in many standard archaeological texts (e.g., Clark and Piggott 1966: 314–32; M. J. Green 1995; Piggott 1965: 215–66).

Unlike the Mound Builders, the Celts were an actually identifiable people with a discrete material culture, at least according to some observers. They were certainly not a "lost race," a people like the Mound Builders who had disappeared before the presence of literate individuals who could record impressions of their lifeways, attitudes, and belief systems. But like the Mound Builders, the Celts have often been mythicized as a discrete "race," an inward-looking population with distinctly identifiable physical features. The racial characteristics attributed to the Celts are perhaps even more relevant to our discussion than those ascribed to the Mound Builders, because while most scientists gave up on the existence of the Mound Builders in the late nineteenth century—with Thomas's (1894) definitive examination—the image of the Celtic race continues into the present.

Part of the difficulty with the word "Celt" is that it is a "much-abused term" that has a minimum of three distinct meanings. "Celtic" can refer to a language family, an art style, and a whole-culture with identifiable "racial" characteristics, concretely based on contemporary written accounts (Fitzpatrick 1996: 242; Flanagan 1992: 54). The variance among these three meanings and the possible confusion that can be perpetuated by their usage have meant that the most discerning and meticulous scholars recommend that "Celtic" be strictly reserved for reference to the language (Evans 1995: 9). The linguistic sense of the term is probably the intellectually safest—other than Renfrew's total abstinence—because it refers to a group of Indo-European languages that are classified as "Celtic." These languages include Irish, Scots Gaelic, Manx, Welsh, Cornish, and Breton.

For present purposes, the second and third senses of "Celtic" are most relevant. When European archaeologists conceptualize "Celtic," they typically envision a Late Iron Age archaeological manifestation called La Tène. La Tène, a town on Lake Neuchâtel in Switzerland, was identified as the locus of the type-site for the La Tène cultural expression (Phillips 1980: 252; Schutz 1983: 191). Artifact-rich burials constitute perhaps the greatest source of information about the people who created La Tène, with burials exhibiting wooden chambers covered by substantial earthen mounds containing two-wheeled chariots and carts, bronze cauldrons, ornamental brooches and belt clasps, and gold jewelery (Champion 1996: 379; Phillips 1980: 252–53; Wells 2001: 57). Most scholars recognize the La Tène expression by the intricate swirls and interlinked designs that characterize its artistic style. Given the unique character of La Tène artistic expression, some scholars argue that "'Celtic art' is synonymous with 'La Tène' art of the period c. 500 B.C. to A.D. 100" (Megaw and Megaw 1995: 346; see also Herity and Eogan 1977: 224). Other scholars, more circumspect about making this correlation, maintain that the geographical expansion of the La Tène style does not necessarily reflect a concomitant "spread of the Celts," even though the use of the style could indeed refer to some notion of shared identity (Wells 2001: 68). Others, however, do not even use the term "Celtic" when referring to ancient European art and prefer instead to use the more restrictive, descriptive terms "Hallstatt" and "La Tène," the two archaeological whole-cultures that refer, respectively, to the Early and Late Iron Age (Champion 1995: 411; Milisauskas 1978: 254). Regardless how one designates it, an important feature of La Tène art is its obvious borrowing from Mediterranean peoples, most notably the Greeks (Megaw and Megaw 1995: 361; Wells 1980: 104, 2001: 60–63, 69).

The association of a people called "Celts" with La Tène art is significant because it goes to the heart of how archaeologists identify past peoples who strove to express self-identity with portable material culture. But what is most immediately pertinent here is that the first literate people who wrote about the Celts—Greeks and Romans—originally identified them as members of a distinct "race." It was through their writings that Greek and Roman authors, beginning with Herodotus in the fifth century B.C., essentially created the Celts as a whole-culture (Wells 2001: 104). Classical authors applied names inconsistently to various peoples, and in many cases their works promote a picture of cultural stasis where in fact great fluidity existed. Wells (2001: 114–18) makes a convincing case that Caesar, for one, consciously invented the Celts (as a people who lived west of the Rhine) and the Germans (as a people who lived east of the river) as part of an effort to advance the impression that he had encountered unified peoples who were exceedingly formidable warriors.

Caesar noted that Gaul was divided among three distinct peoples, as a fair number of people can still recite: "The whole of Gaul is divided into three parts, one of which the Belgae inhabit, the Aquitani another, and the third a people who in their own language are called 'Celts,' but in ours 'Gauls.' They all differ among themselves in respect of language, way of life and laws" (see, e.g., Hammond 1996: 3). Caesar's account is presented as fact, but he was not an ethnographer and "It was not his business to ask himself or to inform his readers whether the Belgae, the Celtae and the Aquitani were homogeneous groups, or whether each group was an aggregate or a mixture of different races" (Holmes 1899: 245). In the late nineteenth century, Paul Broca concluded, after examining a collection of crania (in the manner of Morton and others) in addition to official census returns that included information on personal stature, that "The true Celts, the Celts of history. . . were the mixed race whom Caesar called Celtae" (Holmes 1899: 287).

Recent research suggests that it is likely that the names Greek and Roman writers used to identify the "Celts" were not in fact the names the people themselves used. It remains possible, however, that the people may have accepted the appellation on some level, just as many Native Americans came to accept the term "Indian"or to think of themselves as being "red" in color (Hubert 1966: 24; Shoemaker 1997: 641–42; Wells 2001: 104–5). Most scholars today accept that the "Celts were not a race, but a group of peoples, or, to speak more accurately, a group of societies" (Hubert 1966: 33). It is extremely likely that the peoples referred to as "Celtic" did not think of themselves as a single cultural entity (James 1993: 9; Norton-Taylor 1974: 11; Renfrew 1996; Ross 1974: 33).

The idea that the Celts were a static "race" with a distinct artistic tradition is nonetheless an idea that quickly took root, in essence transforming the La Tène style into the marker for a racialized whole-culture. The Celts accordingly have been described as "the first great nation north of the Alps" (Powell 1958: 13). Based on the writings of Mediterranean observers, many people have come to equate this "great nation" with certain physical characteristics.

The physicality of the "Celts" was originally based on the works of ancient writers who provided descriptions of the Celts' appearance, with Posidonius—a Stoic philosopher of the first century B.C.—offering one of the most thorough early descriptions (Freeman 2001: 33–34; Rankin 1987: 132). Most outside observers were initially struck by the stature of the "Celts." For example, the Greek historian and geographer Strabo (c. 64 B.C.-after A.D. 21) said that he had seen Celts in Rome who towered over the tallest people in the city, even though the Celts were neither as tall nor as fierce as the "Germans" (Hamilton 1887: 1: 297, 443; Lloyd-Morgan 1995: 103). For his part, Caesar attributed the size of the Celts to their being permitted to live as they saw fit when young (Rankin 1987: 134), even though it remains entirely possible that he exaggerated their physical appearance to increase his status as their conqueror (Wells 2001: 115–16).

The Celts, however, had more readily identifiable characteristics than merely their height. One writer notes, "The Celts were remarkable to Mediterranean eyes for their height, their fair skin, muscularity, blue eyes and blond hair" (Powell 1958: 66). Ancient writers, beginning with

Polybius (c. 200–118 B.C.), also promoted the distinctly "Nordic" image of the Celts (Holmes 1899: 283).

Scholars who have carefully evaluated the classical writers' physical descriptions of the Celts have noted the inconsistency of their accounts. Some specialists have concluded, for example, that Posidonius and Caesar actually described different people: "a large proportion of the people whom Caesar called Celtae were short, dark and brachycephalic or sub-brachycephalic; that is to say that they differed essentially in physical characters from the Gauls or Celts whom the ancient writers [including Posidonius] with one voice describe as tall, and whom nearly all of them describe as fair" (Holmes 1899: 293). What is most relevant here is that some scholars find the distinction relatively easy to explain. Using material culture as their guide, they argue that Posidonius's account suggests that he was observing La Tène II people, whereas Caesar's description relates to La Tène III people (Nash 1976: 122–23). The dates of La Tène II (or B) are roughly 375–250 B.C. and of La Tène III (or C) 250–150 B.C.(Schutz 1983: 246; for the various dates of the La Tène periods, see Crumley 1974: 33–34).

In any case, the idealized image of the Celts as tall and fair-haired has led to the formulation of perhaps the most egregious racial ideas about them. In fact, the idea that the Celts were a distinct "race" entered legitimate physical anthropology as an extension of the monogenist-polygenist debate that also swirled around the Mound Builders (Harris 1968: 93). While scholars had some difficulty deciding the skin color of the Mound Builders—because several options existed—those seeking to assign skin color to the Celts could simply look at the parts of Europe they deemed most "advanced" or noble and conclude that the Celts were the ancestors of those modern-day Europeans. As a result, the Celts became white.

The idea that the Celts constituted part of a distinctly "white race" appears as an element of what is widely known as the Teutonic Origins Theory (Gossett 1963: 84–122). Scholars throughout Europe and the United States initially used the works of Roman historian Tacitus to promote the notion of virtue and greatness among the "white race," and the noble Celts were perfect candidates to be assigned to that color.

Daniel G. Brinton did much to promote the Teutonic Origins Theory in his influential book *Races and Peoples: Lectures on the Science of Ethnography* (1890). As was true of many scholarly works written in the late nineteenth century, Brinton's book promotes scientific racism, including such comments as "it is a common statement that to our eyes all Chinamen look alike, or that one cannot distinguish an Indian 'buck' from a 'squaw.' Yet you recognize very well the one as a Chinaman, the other as an Indian" (Brinton 1890: 18).

Brinton believed in the empirical reality of racial types and also argued that the term "European race" was synonymous with "white race." He also believed in the fixed hierarchy of the races, and proposed that the hierarchy could be scientifically demonstrated through the measurement of various body features. He argued, for instance, that quantifiable testing had proven that peoples of African descent have longer arms than "whites," and concluded from this that "The long arms are characteristic of the higher apes and the unripe fetus, and belong, therefore, to a lower phase of development than that reached by the white race" (28).

In addition to using the racialized studies of nascent physical anthropologists, Brinton also recognized the importance of "the science of 'prehistoric archaeology'" (83). Brinton was intrigued by archaeology because he believed it provided the best means for producing information that could be used to unravel the mystery of the creation of the races.

Using mostly archaeological evidence, therefore, Brinton offered the opinion that the "white race" is synonymous with the "Eurafrican race," because Africa was the locus of the original whites. But the physiological complexity of humanity, including the Eurafricans, meant that several types of whites existed, including two Celtic types. The first Celtic type was tall, red-haired and freckled, with a square jaw, a broad face, and prominent cheek bones. For Brinton (1890: 106–7): "This is the type we see preserved in some of the Highland Scotch clans, and in the 'Tuatha de Danann' of Ireland, recalling the large-limbed and red-haired 'Caledonians' of Tacitus, and those ancient Britons who, under Queen Boadicea, withstood so valiantly the Roman legions." The second Celtic type was smaller in stature with darker hair and eyes. These Celts appear as "the dark clans of the Highlanders, the Irish west of the river Shannon, the Manx, the Welsh, the Bretons of France, the Auvergnats, and Walloons of Belgium and the Ladins of eastern Switzerland" (107).

Brinton also believed that the racial traits he observed in the world's peoples were related to mental characteristics. Using language reminiscent of observations that were contemporaneously being made about Native Americans, Brinton said that the Celts were a "decaying group" destined to disappear. His description of the Celts indicates why he perceived them to be headed for complete extinction:

turbulent, boastful, alert, courageous, but deficient in caution, persistence and self-control, they never have succeeded in forming an independent state, and are a dangerous element in the body politic of a free country. In religion they are fanatic and bigoted, ready to swear in the words of their master, rather than to exercise independent judgment. France is three-fifths of Celtic descent, and this explains much of its history and the character of its inhabitants. (155)

Brinton's opinion transmits as much about his personal view of the French as about the ancient Celts.

Following on the work of Brinton, another book of considerable importance in promoting the scientific image of the Celts as a distinctly European race was William Z. Ripley's *The Races of Europe*, published in 1899. Ripley was a sociologist who was interested in the diverse "forces" that acted upon and influenced human society. In accordance with much of the environmental-determinist scholarship of the time, he perceived the physical environment and race as the two most important forces that affected the human condition. His book represents his intellectual effort to "disentangle" these two "forces."

To begin the task of disentanglement, Ripley first had to understand the meaning of language, nationality, and race. He understood that "It is impossible to measure race by the geographical distribution of arts or customs" because they, like language, "migrate in complete independence of physical traits" (1899: 28). In his mind, men and women tenaciously cling to their "fireside" customs and folklore, even though their "racial" characteristics can be lost in the "mingling" of blood. In other words, even though "racial" intermarriage could easily occur, the individuals involved did not necessarily surrender all their customs and traditions simply through the act of marriage and procreation. Language, as a cultural trait, was not lost through marriage. As far as the "Kelts" were concerned, the spread of their language—taken in conjunction with the cultural features archaeologists were discovering at their past habitation and burial sites—did not "imply a new race of men" (28). Rather, the "Keltic language and culture" belonged only to a tiny, dominant aristocracy. For reasons that are not entirely clear, Ripley believed that this ancient aristocracy probably had not introduced "new arts"— unfamiliar customs and traditions—to the masses along with their language. As far as nationality was concerned, Ripley understood that "race" cross-cut artificial national boundaries and existed independently of political considerations: "Race denotes what man *is*; all these other details of social life [customs and folklore] represent what man *does*" (32, emphasis in original).

Based on the principal characteristics of head form (cephalic index), hair and eye color, and stature, Ripley posited that three European races existed. His exploration of hair and eye color is especially pertinent because he based his analysis on a refutation of the power of skin color to represent "race" (58–77). Even though distinct skin colors exist throughout the "several varieties of the human species," Ripley said that there appears to be no direct correlation between skin color and "anatomical structure." After having made this claim, however, he nonetheless noted that the world's peoples can be divided into four groups based on skin color. A "jet or coal black" group appears in sub-Saharan Africa and in the islands southeast of New Guinea; a "brownish" group has skin that "shades off from deep chocolate through coffee-colour down to olive and light or reddish brown and includes "negroes," Australians, "the aborigines of India," "American Indians," and Polynesians; and a third group "in which the skin is of a yellow shade," includes most of Asia, the northern third of Africa, Brazil, the "Hottentots," the "Eskimos," and the people of Malaysia. The skin color of the third group "varies from a dull leather colour, through a golden or buff to a muddy white" (60). The "white race" is Ripley's fourth group, so-called even though "many of its members are almost brown and often yellow in skin colour" (60–61). The "white race" appears in Europe, "part of modern Africa north of the Sahara, which geologically belongs to the northern continent," and parts of Asia. What is especially interesting is that after this long discussion of skin color groups, Ripley posited that skin colors really do not have much intellectual weight because of simple human variation. The "real determinant characteristic" of race is "not the skin at all but the pigmentation of the hair and eyes" (61).

Ripley's specific analyses communicate much about his attitudes toward race. In his analysis of stature, for instance, Ripley understood the significance of environment but nonetheless established a dichotomy between "savages" and "civilized peoples," with "savages" being more prone to environmental influence. Thus the savage "Hottentots" tend to be taller than the "Bushmen," even though both are "physically of the same race" (80). The situation is, as we might expect, more complex for "civilization," because one must take into account a number of diverse factors, including the amount of local industrialization, the availability and sustainability of natural resources, and "economic prosperity." The last variable is particularly important for explaining the "degenerate physique of the peasantry, especially marked in its stature" (85). "Economic prosperity" undoubtedly referred to the market-based economy within which Ripley lived, and the material well-being of the "peasantry" undeniably related to income poverty.

Ripley asserted "that there is no single European or white race of men" (103) and employed his primary characteristics of human variation to argue for the existence of three European races: the Teutonic, the Alpine (or Celtic), and the Mediterranean (Table 2.1). Ripley's second "race," the Celtic, is of greatest pertinence here. He stated that to understand the correlation between the Celtic "race" and the amassed knowledge about the history of Celtic peoples—including the information derived from archaeology—it is first necessary to come to terms with the "Celtic question" (124).

The initial part of the "Celtic question" involves the uncritical acceptance by "the leading ethnologists prior to 1860" of the comments of classical writers, who easily linked the "Celts" with the "tall, blond peoples of northern Europe" (Ripley 1899: 124). The problem with this characterization, said Ripley, is that scientists have learned that not all "Celtic" individuals were in fact blond, blue-eyed, and tall. On the contrary, some so-called Celts could be short and brunette. Falling back on the unmistakable fact that linguists had identified a family of Indo-European languages which they have labeled "Celtic," Ripley argued that linguists are the only scholars who can legitimately use the term (128). They cannot, however, use the term "race." Then, referencing the known archaeological information of the time, Ripley noted that the distribution of the "first stage of iron culture," Hallstatt, seems to correlate with what is known about the geographical extent of the Celtic language. In the final analysis, however, he concluded that the designation "Alpine" is probably the best racial term for the "Celtic" people. This term would avoid the inevitable confusion caused by references to the Celtic languages. Speaking specifically of Ireland, a place often referred to as the most Celtic of places—largely because the Romans never conquered it (Dames 1992: 13)—Ripley stated that Americans are familiar with "two types" of Irishmen and women: a freckled, red-haired variety, and a variety with "black or dark brown hair and steel-blue iris" (321). The latter variety is "known to the older anthropologists as the 'light Celtic eye.'"

Ripley's study is complicated and thorough for its time, but for all his apparent rigor, he clearly wished to create a reified Celtic "race." Having concluded a priori that a Celtic physical type existed, Ripley's task was to isolate its characteristics in terms of his primary "racial" features: Height, head shape, and hair and eye color. His numerous frontal and profile black and white pictures of examples of the various European races

TABLE 2.1. The Physical Characteristics of Ripley's Three European Races

Race	Head	Face	Hair	Eyes	Stature	Nose
Teutonic	long	long	very light	blue	tall	narrow, aquiline
Alpine (Celtic)	round	broad	light chestnut	hazel-gray	medium, stocky	variable, rather broad, heavy
Mediterranean	long	long	dark brown or black	dark	medium, slender	rather broad

Source: Ripley (1899: 121).

strike us today as a bizarre reflection of racist science, even though he may in fact have had the best of intentions. His discussion of the attempts of others to classify Europe's "races" demonstrates that he was aware of the difficulties inherent in the process (597–606). But his major debate with the earlier research was with the specific "races" the investigators had identified, not with the actual process of identification itself. In considering the findings of a Dr. J. Deniker of the Natural History Museum in Paris, for example, Ripley noted that Deniker's identification of six European races and four secondary races was merely an exercise in the classification of "existing varieties" (598). For Ripley, the anthropologists' use of the word "race" is analogous to the way zoologists use the word "type."

It is an interesting intellectual point to note that Ripley's research to extend the concept of European races occurred at just about the same time as Thomas was demolishing the existence of the Mound Builder race. Beginning with the date of Thomas's publication (1894), the myth of the Mound Builders had begun to be relegated exclusively to pseudo-archaeology. At the same time, however, the myth of the Celtic race was still garnering serious scientific attention. The themes pursued by Ripley were not simply a manifestation of late nineteenth-century science. Other scholars—some overtly racist, others more reservedly so—promoted ideas that were either analogous to Ripley's or directly adapted from his work.

A German author named Hans Günther advanced a particularly racist account of the "European races" in his *The Racial Elements of European History*, first published in 1927. Günther (1970: 3) defined "race" as a characteristic that "shows itself" in a human group through its unique "bodily and mental characteristics" (3). In a departure from Ripley, Günther proposed the existence of five European races, which he defined in the following terms:

The Nordic race: tall, long-headed, narrow-faced, with prominent chin; narrow nose with high bridge; soft, smooth or wavy light (golden-fair) hair; deep-sunk light (blue or grey) eyes; rosy-white skin;

The Mediterranean race: short, long-headed, narrow-faced, with less prominent chin; narrow nose with high bridge; soft, smooth or curly brown or black hair; deep-sunk brown eyes; brownish skin;

The Dinaric race: tall, short-headed, narrow-faced, with a steep back to the head, looking as though it were cut away; very prominent nose, which stands right out with a high bridge, and at the cartilage sinks downward at its lower part, becoming rather fleshy; curly brown or black hair; deep-sunk brown eyes; brownish skin;

The Alpine race: short, short-headed, broad-faced with chin not prominent; flat, short nose with low bridge; stiff, brown or black hair; brown eyes, standing out; yellowish-brownish skin;

The East Baltic race: short, short-headed, broad-faced, with heavy, massive under jaw, chin not prominent; flat, rather broad, short nose with low bridge; stiff, light (ash-blond) hair; light (grey or whitish blue) eyes, standing out; light skin with a grey undertone. (1970: 3–4)

Having established these "races," Günther (51–63) easily assigned each with "mental characteristics" (Table 2.2). This exercise represents both the worst conflation of physical attributes and mental abilities.

Günther did not dwell on the Celts, as had many other writers, but he did provide enlightening comments about his perception of them. In his discussion of the mental characteristics of the "Mediterranean Race," he said that "Sinn Fein in Ireland" represented the kind of secret plotting that Mediterranean peoples often undertake (57). In terms of ancient history, Günther argued that some "Kelts" were members of the Nordic "race," and concluded that "In the prehistory of Europe two races only have shown themselves to be truly creative, and these must be looked on as the true European races: the Nordic and the Mediterranean, the Nordic first and foremost as the true history-making race of prehistoric and historic times" (116–17). During Hallstatt times, said Günther, Dinaric peoples transmigrated into the Alpine region and began to intermarry with Kelts, creating "Nordic-Dinaric-Alpine tribes." The Nordics, being more creative and dedicated than either the Alpine or the Dinaric races, dominated within the region and gave the historic homeland of the Kelts a Nordic flavor. Ireland, for example, represented a combination of the Nordic and Mediterranean races (86).

Günther's views are clearly unacceptable by modern standards, and only racist individuals would today give them any consideration or merit. But views similar to Günther's were also present in mainstream anthropology, including in the work of physical anthropologist Carleton Coon. Coon's perspective, though not as despicable as Günther's, strongly relied on Ripley's research. In fact, Coon made a conscious decision to reuse Ripley's title, and he even dedicated his *Races of Europe* thus: "To Professor William Z. Ripley, author of the earlier and classic *RACES OF EUROPE*, at whose suggestion the present work was begun and in whose honor it is named" (Coon 1939: v).

The plan behind Coon's book was to pursue Ripley's research in light of the advances in physical anthropology that been achieved in the early decades of the twentieth century. Like Ripley, Coon fully recognized the confusion caused by the use of the word "race," but he nonetheless presented his *The Races of Europe* as a detailed examination of the "white race," beginning with Chapter II, "Pleistocene White Men." Accordingly, Coon used archaeological, osteological, historical, and linguistic information "to trace the development of racial entities in the territory occupied by the white race, from the earliest human times to the Middle

Ages, the threshold of the modern period" (241). As part of his historical investigation, he presented the "Kelts" as members of the white race
(186–93).

Coon wisely noted that the identification of the Celts had been extremely controversial, and he insightfully observed that many scholars
had seen Celts wherever they wished to search for them. Some of the
Celts had been brachycephalic brunets, while others had been dolichocephalic blonds. Even though most scholars had been somewhat loose
with their identification of the Celts, Coon (186) categorically stated that
"there *was* a Keltic physical type" that began with the La Tène "civilization" around 500 B.C. To sort out the origin of the Celts before La
Tène times—in other words, during the Hallstatt phase—Coon relied
upon the few skulls that until then had been excavated from Iron Age
gravesites. He found little homogeneity in the remains, however, as some
La Tène skulls are dolichocephalic and some are brachycephalic. Skulls
from Austria and the Alpine are mostly mesocephalic, with some being
brachycephalic; skulls from Great Britain are typically mesocephalic with

TABLE 2.2. The "Mental Characteristics" of the Five European Races According
to Günther

Race	Characteristics
Nordic	men: truthful, energetic, highly developed sense of reality, prudent, reserved, steadfast, calm in judgement, trustworthy, creative, can be extravagant; women: maidenly, tender, proud
Mediterranean	men: passionate, excitable, loves strong colors, takes a deep, often childish interest in others, eloquent, talkative, not hard-working, lazy, swayed by sexual life, disposition to cruelty and animal torture, exhibits a tendency toward lawlessness and anarchy
Dinaric	rough strength, trustworthy, brave, warm feelings toward nature, love of home, inclined to sudden outbursts, quick anger, lives for the moment, strong business sense, exhibits language skills
Alpine	men: reflective, hard-working, narrow-minded, reserved, sullen, mistrusting, slow, patient, sober, practical, lacks boldness of thought, careless, suspicious, no sense of humor, inclined toward Catholicism; women: plodding, soulless
East Baltic	slow, confused, moody, irresolute, no creative power, cannot distinguish between good and evil, lively sense of patriotism but requires leadership, cunning, revengeful, brutal in sexual relations, inability to handle money, exhibits little personal or household cleanliness

Source: Günther 1927 (1970: 3).

almost no brachycephalic examples. Based on such evidence, Coon was compelled to conclude that "the Kelts were a mixed group in race as in culture" and that "out of this combination, the Kelts developed an easily identified *national* type, of considerable constancy" (193; emphasis added). Once again, the use of the word "national" recalls Kroeber's whole-culture.

Regarding the Irish, those easily recognized Celts of the modern age, Coon offered the following description:

The composite Irishman, representing the mean of ten thousand of his countrymen, is 35 years old, 172 cm. tall, and weighs 157 pounds. He is well built, muscular, and large boned, with shoulders 39 cm. broad, and a trunk length which is 53.3 per cent of his total height. His arms are long, and his span is 105.3 per cent of his stature. . . . His head is large, for Ireland has consistently the largest head size of any equal land area in Europe. (377)

His description bears a strong similarity to the idealized version of the Celt created by classic authors (Rankin 1987: 134–35). In a rather bizarre departure from physical anthropology, Coon also argued that Irish Catholics were the genetic descendants of Cro-Magnons, whereas the Anglican Protestants were more "Nordic"(378–79).

Based on the assignment of the Irish to a physical type that Coon would refer to as "national," it is important to consider the archaeology of Iron Age Ireland. As shown in Chapter 1, Ireland provides an excellent site to examine the hierarchical elements of race construction. Given the oft-cited association of the "Celts" with La Tène art, coupled with the notion that Ireland is a Celtic nation, Ireland should be a place where the archaeology of the Iron Age Celts is relatively straightforward. After all, "In Ireland the La Tène Iron Age continued unbroken by Roman interference, though modified by Christianity and its carrier-waves of Greco-Roman classicism" (Rankin 1987: 13). When archaeologists discovered objects having stylistic features resembling La Tène forms—such as the Turoe Stone in County Galway—the easiest conclusion was that Celtic peoples had emigrated to Ireland and brought La Tène art with them. The problem is that no archaeological evidence exists for any large-scale immigration into Ireland (Waddell 1998: 288). Irish archaeologists accordingly find it difficult to speak of a "Celtic Iron Age" on the island. As Waddell (1998: 289) notes, if by "Celtic Ireland" individuals mean "Celtic-speaking Ireland" then no problem exists. Ireland is, officially and in some places actually, a nation that speaks a language classified as Celtic. The difficulty arises when scholars attempt to designate the "Irish Celts" as a whole-culture. They often present the whole-culture notion in terms of ethnicity (Collis 1996: 173; Crumley 1974: v), a topic further explored in Chapter 3. Because artifacts with

La Tène influence appear most often in the northern part of Ireland (Cooney and Grogan 1994: 202–3; Raftery 1996: 155–56), most Irish archaeologists refer to the La Tène expression as a "horizon" (e.g., Raftery 1996: 155) or "phase" (e.g., Cooney and Grogan 1994: 185). This culture-historical designation is applicable because continuity exists between the Late Bronze Age and the Early Iron Age. Thus, the presence of objects such as scabbards and torcs decorated with La Tène stylistic motifs may represent an increased demand for prestige items rather than any sort of mass migration (Cooney and Grogan 1994: 186).

One of the historical features of the Irish Iron Age that supplements the notion of a "Celtic" Iron Age is the association of some of the island's most impressive monuments with legendary Celtic personages and events. Navan Fort in County Armagh, for instance, is associated with Emhain Macha, the seat of the kings of Ulster (Harbison 1988: 157), and Rathcroghan in County Roscommon is linked to Queen Maeve and her consort Ailill, King of Connacht, Ireland's westernmost province (Waddell 1998: 347). Both sites are associated with the famous Cattle Raid of Cooley, the *Táin Bó Cúailgne*, sometimes referred to as "the most famous epic in mythology" (Ellis 1991: 216). Such associations add to the creation of a "Celtic Iron Age" in Ireland, at least in the minds of many non-archaeologists, and to the creation of the Celts as a distinct, often nationally based "race."

White Atlantis

It seems to be an odd departure to discuss Atlantis in a serious investigation of race and archaeological interpretation. Archaeologists, historians, and avocationists are divided in opinion as to whether this mysterious, sunken continent ever even existed. Most scholars would argue that Atlantis never existed (see, e.g., Jordan 2001), but other serious investigators believe in the essence of the Atlantis story and have situated it at Troy (Zangger 1992), on the island of Thera (Santorini) (Pellegrino 1991), and on Minoan Crete (Castleden 2001). The lost continent of Atlantis has also spawned a huge pseudo-scientific literature in which various authors, of diverse talents and imagination, have situated the mysterious island everywhere on the globe from Antarctica to the center of the earth.

The tenacious pseudo-scientific interest in Atlantis has understandably repelled many professional archaeologists from considering the place worthy of mention, and many professors strongly dissuade their first-year students from broaching the subject. Some archaeologists even see Atlantis as dangerous because its proponents, through their misapplied zeal, usually project a false image of archaeological research (Cole 1980: 15–17;

Feder 1984: 534). Careful reflection suggests, however, that—through Indiana Jones movies and a constant stream of pseudo-archaeological "expeditions" documented on television—many non-archaeologists may already have a woefully inaccurate understanding of archaeology precisely because the Atlantis myth simply will not quietly recede into history. But it is exactly the dangerous element of Atlantis that is most important here, because the myth hides within it a substantial racial character. Simply put, the modern-day conceptualization of Atlantis is steeped in racialization, and today's popular conception of the island is irrepressibly racial in intent and design.

The goal of this brief exploration into Atlantis is neither to explore the story of the continent in depth nor to evaluate the truth of the account. Others have previously accomplished this task with great success, and no need exists to repeat their work (see, e.g., de Camp 1970; Ellis 1999; Feder 2002: 177–203; Stiebing 1984: 29–56; Wauchope 1962: 28–49; Williams 1991: 130–55). The only intent here is to explore the often overlooked racial elements of the Atlantis tale.

The story of Atlantis begins with Plato's original account presented in the *Critias* and *Timaeus*, written around 355 B.C. The basis of the story is an account that Solon (c. 640–560 B.C.) reportedly learned from Egyptian priests, in which a powerful, highly advanced civilization called Atlantis attempted to conquer and enslave ancient Athens. The goal of the story was really intended to create an image of the ancient greatness of Athens, because the greater Atlantis could be made to appear, the more remarkable was Athens's victory over it. True to this ideal, Plato described Atlantis as a place of rich palaces, high walls covered with luxurious gold, great buildings with ivory roofs, active race tracks, lush gardens, busy docks, and magnificent bridges.

But for all its apparent majesty, ancient scholars began to debate the veracity of the Atlantis tale almost as soon as Plato died, around 347 B.C. (de Camp 1970: 16–18). The philosophers who immediately followed him did not know exactly what point Plato had attempted to make with the Atlantis story, and many thought he was simply offering a morality tale, using the fictitious paradise for emphasis. Strabo, in his *Geography* (published in 7 B.C.), believed that the sunken continent was once a real place, but added that "Poseidonius [the scholar who also wrote about the Celts] thinks that it is better to put the matter in that way than to say of Atlantis: 'He who brought it into existence can also cause it to disappear'" (Hamilton 1887: 154).

The history of Atlantis as recounted by Plato in the two dialogues is easily summarized (Lee 1977). "Once upon a time," the gods divided the earth among themselves, giving Poseidon Atlantis, an island situated opposite the strait called "the Pillars of Heracles" (for most scholars the

Strait of Gibraltar). Already resident on the island were the earth-born Evenor and his wife Leucippe, who had a daughter named Cleito. When Evenor and Leucippe died, Poseidon fortified the island and took Cleito as his consort. Before long, Cleito gave birth to five pairs of male twins, and when they reached maturity, Poseidon gave one-tenth of the island to each of his sons. The sons of Poseidon and Cleito were the patriarchs of several generations of Atlanteans, and the island became a utopia in every way, supplying all that its residents could ever want. With time, however, the people of Atlantis began to take their richness for granted, and once they lost their self-control and their morality, Zeus was forced to destroy the island "in a single dreadful day and night" (Lee 1977: 38).

Plato provided no information about the physical appearance of the common men and women of Atlantis, and he did not say what happened to them after the destruction of their island. All we really know is that they were by ancestry part-human and part-deity. Since we know little else about them, and since there is no source not derived from Plato for Atlantis, how did the lost continent become racialized?

The idea that Atlantis was an actual place receded from consciousness soon after Plato's death, and the place became just another mythical island somewhere outside Europe, like Hy-Brasil (Westropp 1912). With the global expansion of the European superpowers in the sixteenth century, however, Atlantis once again rose to importance, because it provided an easy explanation to account for the peopling of the Western Hemisphere. In 1535, Gonzalo Fernández de Oviedo y Valdés first promoted the idea that Atlanteans fleeing their doomed island had settled in the New World (Wauchope 1962: 30). His idea quickly gained support among European colonialists, because it provided an ready answer for the wealth of some native peoples, particularly in Mexico. The sixteenth-century interpretation of Atlanteans in the New World still attracts numerous pseudo-scientific proponents (e.g., Allen 1998).

As soon as scholars made the connection between the peoples of the New World and Plato's ancient island, many found it only a short intellectual leap from the termination of the original story—ending in cultural degeneration and dissolution—to racist notions about all those peoples around the globe who were not of European ancestry. In the framework of such racialist thinking, it was possible to make the following "scientific" argument: (1) Atlantis was inhabited by an advanced people, (2) who through their own fault had degenerated, (3) causing a divine power to destroy their island; (4) some Atlanteans must have escaped from the island and settled somewhere else; (5) the peoples of the New World were clearly "less civilized" than the men and women of the colonial European superpowers; (6) therefore the peoples of the

New World must be the descendants of Atlantis; if so (7) then as cultural degenerates—forsaken by god—they are eligible for assimilation or genocide.

Of all the writers who made this argument, the Irish American Ignatius Donnelly was by far the most successful. Donnelly's invented conception of Atlantis is largely today's commonly held view. So important is his work on Atlantis that he is rightly considered to be the "father" of today's pseudo-archaeology. His *Atlantis: The Antediluvian World*, first published in 1882, was a phenomenal bestseller, and the methods he presented in this text have been faithfully repeated by almost all the pseudo-archaeologists who have followed him (Orser 2000a). Donnelly was largely responsible for mainstreaming the idea that refugee Atlanteans developed the world's greatest "civilizations," and he saw the influential hand of the Atlanteans wherever great cultures flourished: Egypt, Peru, Central America, and Bronze Age Europe. He neatly linked the Mound Builders and the Celts to Atlantis, making these peoples nothing less than descendants of the island's semi-deities. Regarding the Mound Builders, for instance, he imagined them and their Atlantean ancestors as sun worshippers and even included the ancient Peruvians in the equation, undoubtedly to link them with the Mound Builders (Donnelly 1976: 2).

As the son of first-generation Irish immigrants in Know-Nothing America, Donnelly was intent on understanding the physical makeup of the Atlanteans, and he was eager to prove that "Atlantis was the original seat of the Aryan or Indo-European family of nations." His Chapter V, dedicated to "The Question of Complexion," is particularly pertinent to our exploration (183–97).

One of the strengths of Donnelly's methodology is that he made frequent use of anthropological knowledge as it had advanced by the late nineteenth century. His use of the physical anthropological understanding of race, for example, included the observation that learned scientists were then defining race in terms of head shape, height, and hair, eye, and skin color. Citing Tylor, Donnelly stated:

There is a general misconception as to the color of the European and American races. Europe is supposed to be peopled exclusively by white men; but in reality every shade of color is represented on that continent, from the fair complexion of the fairest of the Swedes to the dark-skinned inhabitants of the Mediterranean coast, only a shade lighter than the Berbers, or Moors, on the opposite side of that sea. (183)

Donnelly offered an impressive series of quotes to reinforce the scientific proposition that the "complexion" of the world's various peoples was widely variable. His goal, however, was not to demolish the notion of essentialist racial identification, but only to promote the idea that human variation can be accounted for by the interbreeding of the Atlanteans with the world's indigenous peoples. In his mind, scholars should forget "the Mortonian theory that the aborigines of America are all red men, and all belong to one race" (197). Native Americans, like people living throughout the world, represent commingled "dark and light races."

Speaking specifically of the Aryans, Donnelly proposed that the center of "the Aryan migrations" was Armenia: "If we admit, then, that it was from Armenia the Aryans stocked Europe and India, there is no reason why the original population of Armenia should not have been themselves colonists from Atlantis" (457). From this realization, it is only a short step to proposing that the "Kelts were originally part of the population and Empire of Atlantis."

Where did the world's "dark and light races" originate? For Donnelly, the answer was, of course, Atlantis, and his clever reasoning explained human variation:

The people [of Atlantis] represented at least two different races: a dark brown reddish race, akin to the Central Americans, the Berbers, and the Egyptians; and a white race, like the Greeks, Goths, Celts, and Scandinavians. Various battles and struggles followed between the different peoples for supremacy. The darker race seems to have been physically, a smaller race, with small hands; the lighter-colored race was much larger—hence the legends of the Titans and Giants. (473)

Surprisingly, Donnelly decided that the small-handed, darker race was the "more civilized" because its people worked in metal and made ships. As he imagined it, the European Bronze Age was peopled by small-handed men and women.

Donnelly's book firmly established the racialized foundation of the lost continent of Atlantis, and his formulation was readily adopted by numerous Atlantologists who followed him.

One of the most prominent early twentieth-century writers about Atlantis was Lewis Spence, the one-time editor of the *Atlantis Quarterly* (de Camp 1970: 91). Spence believed Plato's story in its entirety and spent years attempting to prove its veracity. He offered his views about the "races of Atlantis" in his *History of Atlantis*, first published in 1926.

As a true believer in Plato's account, Spence felt confident that the Greek scholar had been accurate when he said that the destruction of Atlantis had occurred about 9,640 years before the birth of Christ (Spence 1995: 75). Given this early date for such a technologically advanced civilization, Spence was compelled to devise a way to account for the long history of the Atlanteans. He found his creative solution with the Cro-Magnons, "the first of those immigrant waves which surged over Europe at a period when the continent of Atlantis was experiencing cataclysm after cataclysm" (85). He glowingly described the Cro-Magnons as a "remarkable," "highly-developed race," "animated with a compelling sense of truth." To improve the image of these advanced Cro-Magnon Atlanteans even more, Spence described them in the following terms: "The average height of Cro-Magnon man was 6 feet 1 ¼ inches, he had relatively short arms, *a sign of high racial development*, the brain-case being extra-ordinarily large in capacity" (80; emphasis added). Spence believed that the Cro-Magnons had peopled the world, including North America, after leaving Atlantis. His association of the Cro-Magnons with the Atlanteans justifiably has the appearance today of the worst kind of pseudo-science, but it is worth remembering that Coon (1939) regarded the Cro-Magnons as members of the "Pleistocene White Race."

The hyperdiffusionist, racial interpretation of Atlantis—bizarre as it may appear—became an integral part of the story of the lost continent through the writings of Spence and others. For example, in *The Shadow of Atlantis*, first published in 1940, Alexander Braghine focused intently on the "racial" composition of the Atlanteans. Most so-called Atlantologists, including those of today, use degeneration as a prime explanatory device to explain what became of the one-time greatness of the Atlantean culture. Atlantologists like Braghine begin with the assumption that Atlantis represented the pinnacle of cultural development. All the cultures that were originally derived from Atlantis, but were "primitive" or "barbaric" in modern-day or historic times, had obviously degenerated. The use of cultural degeneration in this manner is a variation of G. Eliot Smith's heliocentric theory (Harris 1968: 380–81), in which Atlantis simply replaces Egypt as the cradle of advanced civilization.

Braghine was intent on demonstrating the worldwide migration of Atlanteans through his understanding of "races." He envisioned "ethnic waves" moving from Asia to North America and from there to Europe. Asians settled in South America, then moved to Europe, becoming the "forefathers of the so-called Celts" among others (Braghine 1997: 122). His perception of race as reified in physical appearance extends throughout his conceptualization: the "new-comers in Europe had to sustain a cruel struggle with the European aboriginal tribes, the descendants of the Neanderthal race"; "white-skinned" Indians still live in Venezuela; an ancient race arrived in Europe "during the Neolithic Period and was of the dolichocephalic type" (39, 122, 148). Braghine also noted that "Almost all mysterious nations of the Mediterranean basin were remarkable for the reddish colour of their skin and the scantiness of the beard save the Jews and Arabs. . . .The Aryan peoples, on the contrary, are rich in facial hair and are white-skinned and brachicephalic" (148). In making this argument, Braghine essentially transferred to Atlantis the then-current state of physical anthropological research on race.

Donnelly began the technique of coopting legitimate research for his own fantastic claims about the lost continent, and all pseudo-archaeologists have since adopted it with varying degrees of success. The use of race in this manner has woven together the peoples of the world—including the Mound Builders and the Celts—into descendants of Atlantis. Today's conceptualization of Atlantis would not be possible without the addition of essentialized race.

Skin color still figures prominently in the identification of Atlanteans. For example, for those pseudo-scientists who argue that Egypt was the doomed continent's first colony, the Atlanteans were "red" because that was how Egyptian artists portrayed their people (e.g., Wilson 1999). Their common "redness" was an irrefutable "racial" marker. The designation of the Atlanteans as red also helped explain how Native Americans—who were equally "red"—could also be the descendants of Atlantis (Flem-Ath and Flem-Ath 1995: 79).

Psychics have significantly added to the modern conception of a racialized Atlantis, so much so that many non-archaeologists probably accept their ruminations as a matter of fact. Edgar Cayce, the so-called "Sleeping Prophet" (Beyerstein 1996; Bro 1989; Stearn 1967), was by far the most famous American clairvoyant to mention Atlantis. Cayce gave thousands of "readings," compiled during trance-like sessions, and many of them included the entire course of human history. As part of this body of work, Cayce identified the existence of five human "races"—black, white, red, brown, and yellow. Like many mystics and pseudo-scientists, Cayce believed outdated ideas, including polygenism, and said that each of the five races had been simultaneously created on earth but in different places. According to him, "the red race developed in Atlantis and its development was rapid" (Cayce 1968: 57). Cayce further said that two factions or "races" had developed on Atlantis: the Sons of Belial and the Sons of the Law of One. The Sons of Belial were the descendants of the "monstrosities," or "soul-entities" who had assumed many different "strange and grotesque bodies in order to experience material existence in the earth" (Robinson 1976: 52). The mixture of the monstrosities with the animals on Atlantis caused some of them to be as much as twelve feet tall. The Sons of Belial were self-centered and materialistic, while the Sons of the Law of One were spiritual and creative. Cayce departed from Plato's original statement that Atlantis had suffered from one major catastrophe, saying instead that three distinct periods of destruction had rocked the continent, with the last one coming as a result of severe antagonism between the two factions. Following Donnelly, Cayce said that members of each faction had emigrated to new homes throughout the world. He implied that the Sons of the Law of One—the good race—had established the library at Alexandria, Egypt, and that they had sent leaders to various places including the Pyrenees. The Sons of Belial, on the other hand, traveled to the land of the Maya and to North America—including the land of the Mound Builders—though some of them also may have gone to Spain (Cayce 1968: 109–10, 126).

Most writers in this tradition have perceived great wisdom in Cayce's pronouncements and most have generally agreed with them. In contrast to Cayce's five races, however, British psychic Murry Hope (1991: 161–62) proposed that only three "races" existed on Atlantis:

1. Tall, white, gentle, bearded strangers with fair or auburn hair, who were the bringers of knowledge, law, science, and medicine.
2. A red or copper-skinned people, akin to the American Indians, who possessed features not dissimilar to those depicted in Aztec art.
3. Shorter, dark-haired people with fair skin and hazel or brown eyes.

Hope is not particularly forthcoming as to how she devised these races—Plato certainly did not mention them—except to cite Donnelly, "ancient Aryan writings," and the *Popul Vuh*. Nonetheless, a clear similarity exists between her "tall, white, gentle" strangers and Cayce's Sons of the Law of One.

Pseudo-archaeologists continue to perpetuate the idea that Atlantis was a racialized place. David Hatcher Childress, one of the most flagrant violators of basic archaeological reasoning, has provided perhaps the most outrageous racialized vision of Atlantis. In discussing Tiahuanaco in Bolivia—as a palace built long before any Native South Americans were present—Childress proposes that the majestic site could only have been constructed by the "Atlantean League." The league was composed of mythic seafarers who "sailed the world spreading a megalithic culture, and wore red turbans *over their blond hair*" (Childress 1986: 139, emphasis added). Nowhere did Plato, the only actual source on Atlantis, mention the blond hair of the Atlanteans. Plato did mention that the men and women of Atlantis, being semi-divine, were inherently good:

For many generations, so long as the divine element in their nature survived, they obeyed the laws and loved the divine to which they were akin. They retained a certain greatness of mind, and treated the vagaries of fortune and one another with wisdom and forbearance, as they reckoned that qualities of character were far more important than their present prosperity, so they bore the burden of their wealth and possessions lightly, and did not let their high standard of living intoxicate them or make them lose their self-control. (Lee 1977: 145)

The correlation between goodness and whiteness is thus obvious in Childress's formulation and in much else that has been written about Atlantis. Childress's point of view, and that of other pseudo-scientists, may have developed from the racialization of Atlantis that began with Donnelly's best-selling book, or it may have derived simply from the racialized attitudes that are commonly expressed in Western society at large.

Because pseudo-scientists have situated Atlantis everywhere on the globe, it is not surprising that some authors believe it was located in northern Europe and that it gave birth to the "Aryan Race." The idea of a northern Atlantis was the brainchild of Jean-Sylvain Bailly, a late eighteenth-century French scientist and revolutionary. Bailly believed that Plato's Atlantis had been located on the far northern islands of Greenland, Spitsbergen, and Novaya Zemlya (Godwyn 1996: 47). Other writers situated Atlantis further south, in southern England, Denmark, or southern Sweden. Gerhard Herm (1976: 93), for example, proposes that a cursus monument near Stonehenge was possibly the race track mentioned by Plato at Atlantis (Lee 1977: 140–41). The idea that cursuses were race tracks for the chariots of ancient Britons began with William Stukeley in the mid-eighteenth century, but this interpretation has now been completely discarded by serious archaeologists (Harding and Barclay 1999: 3). Still others argued that the homeland of the Indo-Europeans ranged between latitudes 45 and 60 and included much of northern Europe (Schrader 1890: 89). In any case, the notion that Atlantis was located in northern Europe, and that it was a technologically super-advanced civilization, correlated well with the idea that the Aryans had originated in the Arctic and had migrated south from there (Goodrick-Clarke 1998: 37–38).

The mention of an Aryan race in northern Europe understandably conjures images of the Nazi reign of terror throughout Europe in the 1930s and early 1940s. It is unlikely that Hitler himself had much interest in such an esoteric subject as Atlantis (see Anderson 1995), but it is known that Nazi archaeologists, under the leadership of Heinrich Himmler, were directed to examine archaeological and pseudo-archaeological matters. Himmler believed that the Aryans, as Nordics, were ancient Germans who had developed advanced scientific knowledge. He accordingly ordered his archaeologists to conduct research on Atlantis to determine whether the lost continent was the source of Aryan greatness (McCann 1990: 79). When the idea that Atlantis was located in northern Europe is united with Cayce's pronouncements that the Atlanteans had electric and even atomic power (Cayce 1968: 74–77), the supposition can follow that the Aryans were indeed Atlanteans. The argument may be structured as: (1) the Atlanteans were highly advanced people; (2) the Atlanteans knew about electricity and other modern sources of power long before anyone else; (3) Atlantis was located in northern Europe; (4) twentieth-century Germans had substantial historical roots in northern Europe; and so (5) the Germans must be the descendants, either figuratively or literally, of the Atlanteans.

Any connection between Atlantis and the ancient Germans is pure fabrication, but the basic idea—that proto-Germans were an extremely ancient people in northern Germany—had to be taken seriously by archaeologists (McCann 1988: 52). The most persuasive spokesperson for the ancient greatness of Germany was Gustaf Kossinna, a fanatically patriotic German national. As Bruce Trigger (1989: 164) explains, Kossinna's 1911 book, *The Origin of the Germans*, "was a mixture of important theoretical innovation and a fanciful glorification of German prehistory as that of a biologically pure master race." Kossinna accepted that Germans were the descendants of long-headed, blond Aryans and proposed that racial characteristics determined human behavior. Kossinna's work was serious enough to garner Childe's interest, and, though Childe rejected Kossinna's jingoism, he did agree with other elements of his formulation (Trigger 1980: 37–55). In *The Aryans*, Childe advanced the following nuanced perspective of the Nordic people:

it must be remembered that the Nordic cultures in Germany are very far from homogeneous. Some people buried their dead collectively in megalithic tombs, others in regular cemeteries of separate graves; the variety of the pottery is bewildering; both long and short-headed skulls are met. We get the impression of a tumultuous flood of rudimentary clans or tribal groups in continuous interrelation. Often they were at war, for the multitude of stone weapons is innumerable. But regular trade relations subsisted between the various groups illustrated by the diffusion of amber and other commodities. (1926: 173)

Childe was willing to imbue ancient Europeans with native creativity and, though he did envision diffusion and migration in European prehistory, he was not such a hyperdiffusionist that he had to reinvent Atlantis as an explanatory whole-culture (Trigger 1980: 47–48).

Race and Archaeological History

The above three examples recount the creation of three disparate albeit oddly interlinked "races" in archaeological thought—the Mound Builders, the Celts, and Atlantis. The goal of this chapter is to demonstrate that an initial phase of the archaeology of race was characterized by a commitment to correlating the differences in archaeological expressions to human physical variation. Archaeologists like Childe were intent on understanding the history of Europe's many peoples and, employing the language of the day, even he was drawn to the study of "race" as a reified representation of discrete human populations. Childe certainly understood the challenge that he and other archaeologists faced when they attempted to unravel the "racial" differences of ancient peoples: "The path of the prehistorian who wishes to draw ethnographical conclusions from archaeological data is often beset with pitfalls. The correlation of cultural with racial groups is generally hazardous and speculative" (Childe 1926: 200). The problem that Childe and other serious scholars faced was of course that race at this point in history was considered an essential and unshakable fact of life, something that men, women, and children carried around with them. What is more, scientists seriously believed that they could measure human variation in the simplest ways, using the presence and absence of readily visible traits. Accepting that race was an actual physical attribute, the central issue these scientists faced was how to measure it. Was the primary attribute head shape, skin color, language, or some complicated combination of these? And, if physical anthropologists could indeed identify the most important physical traits, how could archaeologists contribute to the study of the origin of races? How were material manifestations of past life related to racial differences?

We must remember that the racial science of the nineteenth century, being practiced just when archaeology was being established as a legitimate field of study, was not unbiased or wholly objective. Quite the contrary, the preeminent scientific perspective was that racial dominance— white over non-white—was a permanent and irreducible fact of life (Wade 2000: 39). The perspective of dominance was undeniably interjected into archaeology by the field's many early, European-descended practitioners who unquestionably accepted racial superiority as their birthright. In anthropology, Boas and Ruth Benedict worked simultaneously to problematize race, but much of the research of early women ethnographers on race was marginalized or ignored (Bauer 2000). As Patterson (1995: 41) points out, the tenets of scientific racism were readily accepted in those societies, like the United States, that were experiencing a substantive increase in immigration of "non-white peoples." Books such as Ripley's (1899) provided a legitimate, scientific rationale for the belief in inherent racial superiority. Archaeologists—upper middle- and upper-class, educated elites with no fear of having to work in the industrial factories and sweatshops that would consume thousands of immigrants—generally embraced scientific racism because it helped to legitimate their own positions of authority and inherited privilege. Racism in legitimate archaeology was both overt and subtle, running the gamut from the Mound Builders to the Celts. In one of its more subtle expressions, late nineteenth- and some early twentieth-century archaeologists proposed the existence of cultural stasis among ancient, non-European peoples. Even Thomas—who destroyed the myth of the Mound Builders as a mysterious, lost race—argued for the static nature of aboriginal culture (Trigger 1989: 124).

Atlantologists have unquestionably provided the most overtly racist readings of the past, and professional archaeologists interested in the invention of race cannot afford to ignore their many arguments about past race. In a departure from many archaeologists who would argue that it is pointless to consider Atlantis and other pseudo-archaeological subjects at all, the brief outline above should demonstrate that archaeologists must engage the widely broadcast, racial pronouncements of pseudo-archaeologists. Pseudo-archaeologists merely demonstrate their profound lack of knowledge when they refer to themselves as "courageous" intellectuals (Von Däniken 1970), when they denigrate professional archaeologists for having "no understanding of science" (West 1993: 234), when they promote catastrophist geology (Childress 1986: 132–33), and when they claim that archaeologists are engaged in a conspiracy of silence about the "truth" of human history (Cremo and Thompson 1993: 25–26; Hancock and Bauval 1996: 116; West 1993: 240). Much about pseudo-archaeology can easily be disregarded as patently ridiculous, but pseudo-archaeologists are far more dangerous when they promote the existence of a lost "race of mankind" that was far smarter than the indigenous Greeks, Egyptians, Native Americans, or any other human population (Hancock 1995, 2002; Hancock and Faiia 1998; Wilson and Flem-Ath 2001). Ancient Atlanteans and alien space travelers have largely been excised from today's most successful pseudo-archaeology, but they have been replaced with a far more mysterious, albeit equally advanced, people. Along with their tenacious attachment to nineteenth-century science, many pseudo-archaeologists maintain their belief in nineteenth-century racialist ideas.

In his study of student beliefs about pseudo-science, Kenneth Feder (1984: 529) discovered that considerable numbers of undergraduate students either believe in the existence of Atlantis or are willing to keep an open mind about it. Other surveys (see, e.g., Gallup and Newport 1991; Harrold and Eve 1995) indicate that adults have regularly been exposed to pseudo-science on television and in college classrooms, and at the beginning of the twenty-first century, about one-third of high school biology teachers provide classroom instruction in scientific creationism (Moore 2001). Prominent Native American commentator Vine Deloria Jr., (1995) promotes the ideas that dinosaurs and humans cohabited the earth and that the Bering land bridge never existed. The early history of race and archaeology, beginning with the Mound Builder controversy, continues into the twenty-first century in the guise of pseudo-archaeology. Though this continuation represents a "prehistory" of thought, it is a prehistory that is still very much with us.

Pseudo-science carries the label because its practitioners make claims that appear scientific but which lack any sort of supporting evidence or, in the case of pseudo-archaeology, even plausibility (Shermer 1997: 33). Pseudo-archaeologists have constantly perpetuated the perspectives of nineteenth-century archaeology, replete with old-fashioned explanations and even racist thinking. Professional archaeologists have long since abandoned such notions. The search for the Mound Builders, the identification of modern Germans with the Celts, and the racialized presentations of Atlantis provide one element of the prehistory of race and archaeological interpretation. Serious archaeologists, however, have pursued research into another topic that many individuals often equate with race: ethnicity.

Chapter 3
The Prehistory of Race and Archaeological Interpretation, Part II
Ethnicity over Race

Archaeologists have been interested in documenting the relationship between human variability and the material expressions of daily life ever since they realized that artifacts from the past could be visualized as more than historical documents. As an anthropological-historical approach gained acceptance in archaeology, greater numbers of the field's practitioners were compelled to attempt "to draw ethnographical conclusions from archaeological data" (Childe 1926: 200). As shown in the previous chapter, the convention of the late nineteenth and early twentieth centuries usually dictated that "race" was the frame of reference of most pioneering social archaeologists. By the 1960s, however, professional archaeologists had largely abandoned the concept of race as a reified, subjective entity, and had substituted for it the more anthropologically supportable concept of ethnicity. As a result, if Childe had published *The Aryans* in 1986 instead of 1926, he probably would have chosen the term "ethnic" over "racial" in his assessment that "The correlation of cultural with racial groups is generally hazardous and speculative" (1926: 200).

Processual archaeologists, because of their overt interest in social and cultural systems, quickly recognized the importance of ethnicity. David Clarke (1968), for example, wrote about the archaeology of "ethnic subcultures." Employing the systems theory jargon of the New Archaeology, Clarke (1968: 236) perceived an ethnic subculture as a type of "cultural assemblage system" composed of "genetically related and discrete minorities existing within an 'alien' culture, either as engulfed authochthons or as intrusive immigrants." His use of the term "genetically related" suggests perhaps that a subtle racial strain still existed within archaeological thought at this time. Clarke proposed that archaeologists can recognize ethnic subcultures by their "traditional attributes and artefacts," but said that these subcultures would lose their identity over time. He thus proposed that archaeology offered a unique avenue for identifying the cultural traits of relict ethnic subcultures before they had suffered the effects of culturally modifying assimilation. The anthropological relevance of the archaeological task outlined by Clarke was immediately clear to archaeologists who desired to transform archaeology into a more socially oriented discipline.

As some archaeologists began to think specifically about cultural complexity and social variation, many began to debate the effects of divergent group variation as opposed to evolutionary change. In a famous example, François Bordes (1973; Bordes and De Sonneville-Bordes 1970) equated different styles of paleolithic tool kits with "different cultural variants" that could be shown to be contemporaneous. Binford challenged Bordes's view that the "cultural variants" could be constructed with ethnic meaning, and cited Bordes's failure to document unambiguous ethnic distinctions within the various archaeological assemblages (Binford 1973; Binford and Binford 1966). The Binford/Bordes debate is still somewhat unresolved (Renfrew and Bahn 1991: 343), but Bordes's interpretation is significant—independent of its veracity—because it aptly demonstrates the difficulty identified by Childe as early as 1926.

The archaeological consideration of ethnicity became more sophisticated as archaeologists familiarized themselves with more ethnographically grounded understandings of ethnicity (see Horvath 1983). Perhaps the greatest advance in archaeologists' understanding of ethnicity came with Fredrik Barth's (1969) conception of an "ethnic group" as a discrete aggregate of people who seek to maintain their sense of self through the maintenance of ethnic boundaries. Barth's ideas represented a significant turning point in ethnic group research (McGuire 1982: 160–61; Jones 1997: 60), because, for example, archaeologists, especially those trained in documenting large-scale cultural histories, understood the many problems posed by cultural boundaries.

The concept of ethnic boundary maintenance transformed the attempt to identify past ethnic groups through the accompanying perception that a people united in lifeways and traditions will strive to maintain this unity. Conceivably, their material culture should also reflect their cultural unity and concomitantly, their base-level differences from other peoples. In a purely archaeological sense, then, ethnic differences should appear as distinct assemblages of objects. Thus the associated archaeological identification of past ethnicity initially appears relatively straightforward. Nonetheless, it remains the case that the determination of ethnicity from archaeological collections "is as difficult today as it has ever been" (Dongoske et al. 1997: 600). Even among living peoples

"Ethnicity has a will-o'-the-wisp quality that makes it extremely hard to analyze" (Maybury-Lewis 1997: 59).

Through the examples they have presented in their detailed ethnographic accounts of living peoples, ethnoarchaeologists have demonstrated the complexity of associating ethnic identity with material culture. The assignment of ethnicity through material remains is neither straightforward nor easy. For instance, in the American Southwest, Michael Stanislawski (1978) discovered that Native American artisans working within one specific pottery tradition, Hopi-Tewa Whiteware, were free to choose among a number of decorative techniques. He learned that the style variations they employed could relate to a potter's guild membership, age, sex, or social standing. Potters from twelve different Hopi and Hopi-Tewa clans (who resided in five villages and composed two distinct linguistic and ethnic groups) shared the Whiteware style. In a similar study conducted in a Tarascan community in Mexico, Margaret Hardin (1979) realized that a particular potter's use of decorative techniques rested upon the individual's competence and degree of social interaction with other potters. In a study in Sierra Leone, West Africa, Christopher DeCorse (1989) discovered that 200 years of material culture related to three distinct ethnic groups—Limba, Yalunka, and Kuranko—revealed no appreciable differences. The only clear distinctions among the groups appeared in certain aspects of ritual behavior that were not transferred to material culture.

In a more detailed ethnoarchaeological study also conducted in Africa, Ian Hodder (1982) concentrated specifically upon the correspondence between the archaeological concept of "culture" and the living ethnic groups who lived in the Baringo district of north-central Kenya (also see Hodder 1979). Hodder's interest was rooted in the growing dissatisfaction among Anglo-American archaeologists with the use of the culture concept. Even processual archaeology, with its unabashed interest in sociocultural lifeways, usually only offered functional explanations, scientifically legitimated with principles of ecological adaptation. In keeping with the then-developing tenets of ethnoarchaeology, Hodder believed that the observation of living cultures within the Baringo region—the Tugen, Njemps, and Pokot—would permit a more nuanced understanding of the use of material culture by ethnic groups and provide information on material boundary maintenance that would have archaeological relevance.

Hodder's research indicated that the Tugen, Njemps, and Pokot visibly and unambiguously transmitted their group affiliation along with their ornamentation. So concrete was the correlation of identity with group membership that an individual who chose to change residence from one group to another would also modify his or her personal ornaments to conform to the new group's fashions. Even though the three cultures experienced a great deal of interaction and cooperation, they each nonetheless maintained the unique character of their material culture. The social situation was actually much more complex, however, because it actively involved material culture in disparate ways. Whereas pottery may have been used to mark ethnic differences, spears and calabash decorations cross-cut ethnic boundaries. This finding indicated that "there is a continual tension between boundary maintenance and boundary disruption; the one exists in relation to the other. And it is the material symbols which actively constitute the different emphases and which have to be continually brought in to justify and support the differing strategies of the subgroups within societies" (Hodder 1982: 73). As a result, the people in the Baringo region differentially used material symbols to emphasize the various social relations they enacted between and within the ethnic groups (as well as between and within age, sex, prestige, and kin aggregates). It may very well be true, for instance, that material divisions seemingly apparent in archaeological collections may not be indicative of social distance and the lack of personal interaction at all. On the contrary, distinctions within and between material culture assemblages may have constituted a point of association, a coming together that fostered between-group social interaction.

Hodder's intensive ethnoarchaeological research, focused as it was on the theoretical underpinnings of the concept of the archaeological culture, allowed him to stress that archaeologists who wish to construct associations between excavated material culture and past ethnic groups must be knowledgeable about the group's internal system of social relations as well as the way the group tends to symbolize social variables. Acquiring this sociocultural knowledge is of course exceedingly difficult for archaeologists investigating extinct cultural expressions, and Hodder (1982: 229) acknowledges that historical archaeologists, given the nature of their data, have greater interpretive potentiality in this realm, even though the presence of textual sources does not ensure straightforward ethnic identification in the past (see Shennan 1989: 12, 14). As a result, the archaeologists' continuing difficulty with ethnicity deserves exploration.

Ethnicity

Social archaeologists have been interested in ethnicity for many years. Their long-term desire to link an archaeologically discovered material culture with individuals who in history self-identified as a discrete group has meant that ethnicity has remained a staple of archaeological research (see, e.g., Olsen and Kobylínski 1991; Shennan 1991). The publication of books and journals dedicated solely to the subject amply demonstrates both the complexity of ethnicity and the importance social scientists attach to it. As Hodder (1982: 3) makes clear, most archaeologists in the early twentieth century who strove diligently to link material culture with ethnic affiliation generally glossed material differences as racially based, adopting the terms and concepts employed by the physical anthropologists of the period. Throughout the twentieth century, as archaeology matured as a sociocultural pursuit, the analysis of past ethnicity became increasing sophisticated (McGuire 1982; Shennan 1989), even though some archaeologists continued to argue that the search for prehistoric ethnicity was fruitless (see, e.g., Atherton 1983: 93). Archaeological perspectives on ethnicity have generally become more nuanced and mutable over time, with many archaeologists obtaining an understanding—based on both ethnographic and ethnoarchaeological research—of the subtle, often situationally sensitive characteristics of ethnicity.

What is ethnicity? In the simplest terms, ethnicity refers to a complex set of interrelating characteristics that collaborate to provide a sense of "peoplehood" to an interacting group of individuals (Gordon 1964: 24–29). The invention of peoplehood for archaeologists must constitute more than a simple spatial similarity of material culture when compared with other places, because ethnicity incorporates self-conscious identification (Shennan 1989: 14). Ethnic groups are social constructs that serve the dual purpose of providing ascriptive and exclusive membership into "us" and "them" categories, while also permitting members to confine their primary personal and intimate interactions and frames of reference to the "us" group (McGuire 1983: 193). The composition of ethnic groups can assume many forms, including artificially created "nationalities," a process termed "ethnonationalism" (GAP 1987: 24–25), and groups of individuals who share traditions but who may have originated in widely diverse geopolitical units, such as Gypsies (Rose 1974: 13) and Irish Travelers (Gmelch 1976; O'Connell 2002).

The precise identification of an ethnic group is difficult because, being self-defined, its membership is free to vary as individuals decide whether they wish to belong to the group. Many analysts have aptly demonstrated the inherently malleable nature of ethnic group identity, but a study presented by Pyong Gap Min and Rose Kim (2000) is especially informative. In their investigation of Asian American professionals, Min and Kim learned that the ethnic awareness of the individuals they interviewed tended to increase as they grew older. Young children and adolescents tended to eschew traditional Asian values as they attempt to conform to the ideals of American society. Upon growing older, however, these same individuals may acquire greater degrees of passion for the traditions and customs of their ancestors. Thus, while individuals may always have a strong, personal identification with their ethnic group, they need not always communicate this attachment in the same way, if at all. From a purely archaeological standpoint, we may well imagine that the material remains left by the individuals in Min and Kim's study would present different messages about their ethnic identity. Based on what period of history is represented, the archaeological remains may variously suggest an American and an Asian identity. Even this facile conclusion is unsatisfactory because of the term "American identity." Such a term is easily politicized to become a weapon against those people who do not conform to what are perceived to constitute the basic elements of this overtly nationalistic identity. For instance, ardent anti-immigrationists might argue that "American identity" is a largely anglicized phenomenon and that to conform one must surrender all ancestral traditions: religion, foodways, dress, language, and so forth. Other commentators might counter that the "American identity" is now and always has been multicultural in composition.

The research reported by Min and Kim (2000) and many similar studies illustrates the difficulties of defining ethnicity in living populations, but it also starkly illustrates the problems that archaeologists confront when they attempt ethnic identification among past populations. Cross-cultural research among living peoples demonstrates that even the names employed to refer to specific ethnic groups may have diverse meanings. Group names can be "traditional" (referring to ancient self-identifiers, such as "the people"), pejorative (names assigned by conquerors or neighbors and then adopted by the people themselves, such as "Yoruba"), rooted in lifestyle (terms such as "Bedouin," which refers to dwelling in the desert), administrative (referring to a group's ruler, such as being considered Swedish in the Middle Ages without actually being able to speak Swedish or having Swedish traditions), economic-functional (such as referring to members of the Hanseatic League as "Hanseatics"), geographical (indicating a group's homeland, such as "Viking," a term originally used to refer to people who lived around Oslo fjörd), or religious (Wallerström 1997: 309–11).

The problem with delineating ethnic groups and their boundaries in the past is indeed a difficult one. But an equally significant problem occurs when archaeologists attempt to link ancient ethnicity with living peoples, or in other words when they strive to link past and present ethnically. Paul Barford, Zbigniew Kobylínski, and Dariusz Krasnodębski (1991) discovered the problem in their examination of ethnicity in the northeast corner of Poland, a region with a long history of cultural admixture. Their analysis began with the Neolithic era and extended to the sixteenth century and beyond. Their findings assumed an especially sharp edge when they were forced to confront issues of ethnicity in recent times: "When the ethnic interpretation of an archaeological culture remains an academic hypothesis divorced from reality, it causes few problems; many modern cultures however have their roots in the past, which cannot be separated from the present" (Barford et al. 1991: 152). It is thus clear that ancient ethnicity may exist in the minds of many of today's archaeologists in a manner similar to the way in which Carl Becker (1955) wrote about historical facts: in order for these to exist, archaeologists have to create and selectively use them in their analyses. Barford, Kobylínski, and Krasnodębski indicated that some ethnic groups, such as the so-called Przeworsk Culture, could not be studied for thirty years because Nazi archaeologists had examined their history in order to identify them as Germanic. As a result, their serious examination constituted a prolonged archaeological taboo.

Modern-world archaeologists are unavoidably called upon to confront the difficulties of ethnic affiliation, and even though many historical groups are perhaps easier to identify nominally, they are no easier to define archaeologically (Orser 1991a: 109). The analytical problems are compounded when archaeologists, perhaps unconsciously, set ethnicity against race. If we define ethnicity in its simplest terms as a self-imposed, anthropocentric category and race as an imposed category, we may well imagine the interaction between race and ethnicity. Using the findings of Min and Kim (2000) as a guide, we may well suppose, for example, that an individual's degree of ethnic expression has the potential to be racially motivated. Individuals may openly express their "degree of ethnicity" based upon perceptions and expectations pressed upon them from the outside. Individuals can have varying degrees of ethnic and racial identity:

Whereas their ethnic identity is related closely to the ethnic subculture practiced in their parents' home and in their parents' home country, their racial identity stems from the consciousness of their non-white status in a white dominated society. To state it alternatively, their racial identity is related closely to the perception that as non-whites they are not fully accepted in American society. Their non-white racial identity is expressed as either pan-Asian or Third World (people of color). (Min and Kim 2000: 751)

This insightful observation indicates that in the modern world ethnicity and race can exist in tandem, two aspects of the same characteristics given voice in different ways.

As noted above, archaeologists have been interested in ethnicity for many years, but an avowed and serious concern with the investigation of race dates only to the 1990s. This same trend in research also characterized much of the anthropological project (Sanjek 1994: 8–10). Based on

this disciplinary history, it is instructive to survey the historical archaeologists' analysis of ethnic groups in the United States, a nation that has
had a long association with multiculturalism. For the sake of brevity, the
concern here is only with three distinct ethnic groups: Asian, Hispanic,
and Irish immigrants.

Archaeology and Overseas Chinese Ethnicity

Historical archaeology in the United States began largely as an East
Coast pursuit, as its earliest practitioners turned their initial attention
to those places first visited by European explorers or later settled by their
countrymen and women (Harrington 1952). Only sporadic archaeological work appeared further west, where most Asian immigrants lived.
Even in the western United States, much of the earliest research was
situated at Spanish colonial outposts or urban centers, but even in cities
the programs of inquiry were usually not specifically directed toward
or particularly mindful of the Asians who lived in the area (see, e.g.,
Landberg 1967). When archaeologists did mention Asians, they typically
did so only obliquely, in order to discuss the material culture the archaeologist associated with them. The earliest studies involving Chinese topics were thus neither planned nor operationalized as examples of social
archaeology with the expressed goal of explicating Asian American cultural history. For example, historical archaeologists have long been
interested in Chinese export porcelain (Noël Hume 1969: 257–65; von
der Porten 1972), Chinese coins (Beals 1980; Farris 1979; Olsen 1983),
and Chinese opium pipes (Etter 1980), but their interest in Asian peoples themselves developed only later.

The failure of American archaeologists to investigate Asian culture
and history undoubtedly arose from several causes, the eastern focus
of most research perhaps primary among them. The internment of
Japanese-Americans during the Second World War and the rise of the
Communist state in the People's Republic of China may have contributed in some fashion to the archaeologists' inattention, even though
both events occurred prior to the formal creation of academically based
historical archaeology. It may have been impossible, or at least extremely
unpopular, to conduct archaeological research on Asian-occupied sites
during the 1950s, when considerable research was already underway at
numerous colonial-period sites associated with European settlers along
the eastern seaboard. It is also possible that racism played some role in
the archaeologists' general failure to investigate sites associated with
Asians. In this vein, it must be noted that the excavation of sites associated with peoples of African descent was also not regularly performed

during the 1950s, making the Bullens' excavation of Lucy Foster's home even more remarkable.

Interest among archaeologists in sites inhabited by Asians, most notably those associated with Overseas Chinese, grew in tandem with the burgeoning interest in African American archaeology in the late 1960s (Schuyler 1980a, b). The initial goals of the earliest research on Overseas Chinese sites were modest in scope and design, often concerned only with "consciousness-raising" and with the further attempt to make American historical archaeology overtly anthropological (Kelly and Kelly 1980: 137). As may be expected, perhaps, the earliest attempts to examine the material remains of Asian Americans from a social (ethnic) perspective were simple in design and facile in findings. Roberta Greenwood's (1980) examination of the Chinese community in nineteenth-century Ventura, California, provides an excellent example.

In a further comment on the state of historical archaeological research, it is especially revealing that Greenwood's research began as a study of the eighteenth-century San Buenaventura Mission. Mission sites, being both old and related to European settlement, were legitimate foci for study in the 1970s. Upon excavating at the mission site, however, Greenwood discovered "The first evidence of the Chinese presence on Main Street" composed of "utilitarian ceramics, small glass medicinal vials, and opium pipe bowls found within the mix of aboriginal, Mission, and 19th century materials on a very disturbed site" (Greenwood 1980: 114–15). Her further excavation of a well and a trash pit allowed her to isolate certain "Chinese" objects—rice bowls, tea cups, ginger jars, and soy bottles—within the larger collection. More importantly, her discovery of these objects allowed her (1980: 118) to present a summary of material traits associated with Chinese and non-Chinese features (Table 3.1).

Though in hindsight it is tempting to denigrate Greenwood's formulation, we must keep the times firmly in mind and recognize that even this now facile view was somewhat revolutionary when presented. One important point to note is that she presented the assemblage as a unified set of material culture rather than as individual goods. While this manner of presentation has the potential to represent itself as a whole-culture, her assemblage perspective significantly encouraged historical archaeologists to abandon the individual-artifact-as-ethnic-marker model that was initially part of Fairbanks's search for African survivals in the American Southeast. Greenwood thus provided an informed and much needed point of view, especially if we remember that her study represented "one of the first contextual assemblages of Chinese goods to be reported" (Greenwood 1980: 120).

Another centrally significant feature appears in Greenwood's early analysis, though it was perhaps not as prominent a feature as was the artifact assemblage information. Greenwood fully understood that she needed to contextualize the Asians in California historically to understand the nature of their life in the United States. Within the parameters of the time, and given that her research was so pioneering, it would have been easy for her simply to present the material culture from the site, to provide a brief statement about the nature of the archaeological deposits, and then to conclude that more research was required before archaeologists could provide much new information about Asian American life. Importantly, however, Greenwood explicitly mentioned the forces of anti-Asian racism that were arrayed against Chinese men and women in Ventura. She noted the "exclusion" of Chinese people from non-Chinese life in the town, and observed that the Chinese settlement enclave continued to exist even in the face of "openly expressed hostility" (Greenwood 1980: 117). Faced with forced segregation and overt aggression, the Chinese in Ventura were compelled to create their own

TABLE 3.1. Greenwood's Material Traits for Chinese and Non-Chinese Features

| Function | Object | |
	Chinese	Non-Chinese
Tableware	porcelain spoons porcelain cups predominantly bowls	metallic cutlery glass tumblers predominantly plates

Cooking	iron pots
	stoneware shipping jars
	brass utensils
	predominantly pork
	  and seafoods
		enamelware utensils
		glass canning jars
		metallic cutlery
		predominantly beef
		  and sheep

Recreation	opium smoking accessories marbles, dolls, other toys go counters, die, coins	clay pipes marbles, dolls, other toys arms and ammunition
Medicinal	glass vials and brass cans herbal remedies	glass bottles patent and prescription remedies
Other	shirt buttons only	wide variety of buttons and clothing fasteners
	wringer, sad irons, ink bottles	occupational tools
		chamber pots, cuspidors

Source: Greenwood (1980).

community. Unlike the local Native Americans, who experienced the paternalism of the nearby mission, the Chinese were shunned and forced to engage the "cultural and racial solidarity among the whites" (121). In a conflation of racist attitudes of nearby Los Angeles, the area within which the Chinese lived was widely known as "Negro" and even "Nigger Alley" (Greenwood 1996: 9–11).

The hostility shown toward Chinese immigrants in the mid- to late nineteenth century was a problem rooted mostly in labor, as Chinese immigrants were courted as workers who could replace the emancipated African Americans in the agricultural fields of the postbellum American South. Immediately after the American Civil War, one observer noted that many Chinese immigrants came to the United States eager to work: "Instead of coming to us in a state of mental depression from cruel treatment [presumably as former slaves would have done], the Chinaman comes buoyant with hope and zeal" (Merrill 1869: 588). Even commentators who supported the introduction of Chinese hands in the fields of the American South often based their commitment on their racialist preconceptions. Opinion among southern landlords was largely divided as to whether the Chinese would be psychologically malleable enough for southern agricultural labor or whether they would prove as intractable and bothersome as many of the former bondsmen and women. Writing in a journal dedicated to staunch southern boosterism, one observer noted that the Chinese were "a race as incongruous to the whites as the negroes, and far less docile and respectable than the negroes. They will come, but like mules, they must be perpetually renewed" (Anonymous 1869a: 709–10).

The idea that the Chinese communities in the western United States were beleaguered by the racist attitudes of their more politically powerful, non-Chinese neighbors is broached by John Olsen (1983) in his analysis of East Asian coins found in Tucson, Arizona. Seeking to understand the ways in which physical things can be used to promote social cohesion and the construction of shared identity, Olsen (1983: 53) argues that the continued use of Chinese coins after the demonetization of foreign coins in the 1850s "attests to their continued importance as intracommunity tokens of exchange which served to strengthen the traditional cultural bonds which were apparently an important feature in these frontier ethnic enclaves." In other words, the late nineteenth-century circulation of Chinese coins, after they were useless as currency, was a social (and probably also political) act intended to project ethnic unity. Olsen comes dangerously close to promoting the single-artifact-as-ethnic-marker model, but even so, we must acknowledge that racism and overt hostility worked in tandem with ethnic pride to reinvent the coins as potential ethnic markers, even if they were not used as currency (Akin

1992). The coins thus serve as a surrogate indicator of an East Asian presence, even though archaeologists have found many Asian coins in Native American contexts (e.g., Beals 1980).

The historical reality that Chinese immigrant communities operated within a social environment that was generally unfriendly and unwelcoming has given rise to an interest in assimilation among historical archaeologists. This interest is understandable because historians have provided significant evidence to document that immigrant Chinese did not readily assimilate to mainstream nineteenth-century American life (Staski 1993: 129). Chinese immigrants tended to create and maintain their ethnic boundaries, only manipulating their limits when they chose to do so. Acculturation and assimilation have been common topics of archaeological research for many years, having been used initially to investigate the cultural changes experienced by Native American peoples as they adapted to or rejected European-American patterns of life and material objects (Orser 1996a: 60–65).

Many reasons may account for the maintenance of ethnic boundaries by Chinese immigrants, but one of the primary reasons must be that most men and women did not plan to remain in the United States for long (Greenwood 1996: 10). Most immigrants hoped to establish a business concern or to obtain a job, to save their money, and then to return to Asia. The idea of the "returning immigrant" was not unique to men and women from Asia; the tug-of-war between assimilation and cultural preservation caused many immigrants to return to their ancestral homelands after only a few years (see Wyman 1993: 63–66).

In agreement with the earliest historical archaeological research on Native American peoples (see, e.g., Quimby 1939, 1966; Quimby and Spoehr 1951), most archaeologists investigating Overseas Chinese sites have wondered about the degree of assimilation (a set of processes that eventually eliminate an ethnic group) and acculturation (unique behavioral patterns that serve to identify ethnic membership and nonmembership) experienced by the people who once lived at the sites under investigation (Staski 1993: 128). Assimilation and acculturation models thus have been the engine of much archaeologically based Chinese ethnic study in the United States. One particularly promising avenue of inquiry has involved the analysis of faunal collections for evidence of discrete Chinese dietary patterns.

In their examination of the diet of a household of Chinese gardeners in Tucson, Arizona—inhabited between 1892 and 1905—Michael Diehl, Jennifer Waters, and Homer Thiel (1998) conclude that foodways can constitute an important aspect of ethnic identity. Their underlying assumption is that because cultures tend to be conservative in their eating habits, food usage can help to preserve group identity (Glassie 1968:

216, 237). An obvious and important corollary of this understanding is the related assumption that the people using the food remains will have deposited them at their habitation sites. Using ethnographic information collected in 1974 in Tucson, Diehl et al. argue that Chinese residents in the city, even the second and third generations, maintain a diet that is regulated by a complex set of food-belief associations. Some foods are eaten during and after specific ceremonies, but even across the entire diet, the Chinese strive to seek a balance between starchy foods and meat and vegetables. Examining the macrobotanical evidence, faunal remains, and food-related containers from the gardeners' house, Diehl et al. suggest that the individuals who lived there attempted to maintain their traditional diet by careful substitution and innovation. They tended gardens that contained "Irish" potatoes, sweet corn, and other locally viable species, but they also imported spices, dried meats, and other foods that were not readily available in the local area. The gardeners used Chinese vessels for food preparation and service, but often supplemented these with European, Hispanic, and Native American (Tohono O'odham) vessels. Even though it appeared that the gardeners tended to adopt certain non-Chinese behaviors, Diehl et al. propose that they still maintained some sense of their ethnic heritage through their food, if not with other objects: "Although household members may have dressed in western clothing, used western tools, and become enmeshed in the economy of Tucson, archaeological evidence suggests that the gardeners maintained their cultural identity by recreating the dietary practices that they enjoyed in the faraway homeland" (31).

In a similar study of faunal remains associated with Overseas Chinese immigrants, Sherri Gust (1993) attempted to obtain a pan-Chinese perspective by using a sample from several sites: Sacramento, California (dating to 1850–60), Woodland, California (1870–80), Tucson, Arizona (1880–1910), Ventura, California (1890–1910), and Lovelock, Nevada (1920–30). Her explicit goal was to determine whether she could isolate "shared and distinctive features" across the assemblages. Her approach appears to hold great promise because the presence of similarities at different sites could be interpreted to have had important social meaning. The problem, of course, is in deciding whether the perceived meaning can plausibly be related to ethnic or to racial factors. Gust's analysis suggested that two groups could be isolated in the remains (Gust 1993: 208). The first group, composed of the Sacramento, Woodland, and Lovelock sites, contained "large amounts of pork, a large percentage of chicken, higher status cuts of meat, and less intense butchering of pork." Group two, containing Tucson and Ventura, presented just the opposite profile in every regard. For example, whereas the Sacramento, Woodland, and Lovelock sites contained 16 percent, 19 percent, and 16 percent pork loin respectively, the Tucson and Ventura sites contained only 8 percent and 6 percent respectively. In terms of butchering, Gust (1993: 193) found that between 20 percent and 40 percent of the pig bones in her samples had been severed with a cleaver, whereas only 10 percent of the cow bones were butchered with this tool. Regarding the presence of obvious ethnic markers among the faunal remains, Gust (1993: 208) concluded: "There appear to be few valid indicators of Chinese ethnicity for bone deposits, excepting butchering marks on cat and dog bones."

In a similar study, Edward Staski (1993: 140–41) discovered that the faunal remains from Chinese-related sites in El Paso, Texas, indicated that pork was the most common food among the Chinese men and women there, with beef being second in importance. In addition, 57 percent of Staski's pig remains had been cut in a nontraditional manner, using a saw. The remaining pieces had been cut with a cleaver.

The studies of cut marks on domestic animal bones are not trivial because they can provide unique information about Chinese ethnic boundary maintenance. It could be argued that Chinese men and women, living in a foreign and largely hostile environment, struggled to maintain their traditional foodways as one measure of their ethnic unity. Given the historical context, however, it is not surprising that many Chinese individuals were compelled by circumstances to adopt certain non-Chinese characteristics. This basically assimilationist interpretation initially appears logically sound, but at some point in the analysis we must ask ourselves whether it really mattered to Chinese ethnic identity whether their pork was cut with a cleaver or with a hand saw. In other words, did cut marks on bones really have ethnic relevance?

This question is of course exceedingly difficult to resolve, but one of the shortcomings of even posing the question can be illustrated by reference to another study of the Chinese in California. Focusing on their research in Sacramento, Adrian Praetzellis, Mary Praetzellis, and Marley Brown (1987) present a considerably nuanced perspective on acculturation and ethnic identity by openly rejecting the proposition that "the Chinese" were ever a homogeneous group amenable to archaeological analysis as a unified ethnic group. They argue that archaeologists, in their efforts to investigate acculturation through the relative frequencies of Chinese versus non-Chinese artifacts, have usually negated the social variability that operated within every Chinese community. To correct the often facile archaeological understanding of culture change, therefore, Praetzellis et al. propose that archaeologists must obtain a deeper understanding of the contextual dynamics of the specific community under investigation. One avenue toward pursuing this kind of analysis is with a conscious concentration on individual households. The existence of ample historical documentation allowed Praetzellis et al. to pursue this approach and to establish the social and economic characteristics of the various households in the sample.

Focusing on a section of I Street occupied by Chinese residents in the mid-nineteenth century, Praetzellis et al. use excavated archaeological remains in conjunction with historical records to investigate the social identity of the Chinese community's merchants. Merchants formed an important segment of the community because by maintaining connections with members of the non-Chinese community they could influence the way the Chinese community's individuals were perceived beyond the limits of Chinatown. The excavations in Sacramento revealed that many of the artifacts discovered within the merchant contexts were European American in origin. Within the linear assimilation model, the presence of non-Chinese objects could be construed as indicating that the merchants had experienced acculturation, or in other words, that they were becoming Americanized. Once we appreciate, however, that the artifacts were associated with merchants, we can retreat from any simple acculturationist model and develop a more contextually nuanced interpretation. The presence of non-Chinese objects in the merchant assemblage may simply represent the merchants' access to nontraditional goods. The objects may also signal that Chinese merchants used European American goods to communicate their distinctive place within the Chinese community as merchants and as inter-ethnic intermediaries (see also McIlroy and Praetzellis 1997: 167). The possible use of non-Chinese ethnic boundary markers by Chinese merchants reinforces the notion that archaeologists interested in ethnicity must understand the sociohistorical contexts of the peoples they investigate, especially when they seek to understand such a complex and mutual social attribute as ethnicity. The approach adopted by Praetzellis and his colleagues dissolves any reliance on any sort of totalizing framework within which the ethnicity of a site's occupants can be construed as natural.

In another study of the Chinese merchants of Sacramento, Mary Praetzellis and Adrian Praetzellis (1997: 289–95) further explore the complex relation between material culture and ethnic boundary maintenance. Again arguing for the heterogeneity of the Chinese community, Praetzellis and Praetzellis situate the individual members of the community within a social structure that had a dual social dynamic. A class-based, internal dynamic operated to distinguish between Chinese individuals based upon relative wealth and influence, and an external dynamic—ethnically and racially based—operated to connect the community's Chinese merchants with the world outside Chinatown. Concentrating on a boardinghouse site, Praetzellis and Praetzellis argue that three groups interacted in the first dynamic: merchants and agents of the Chinese District Association (an organization dedicated to the maintenance of the community), the staff members of the Association (servants, cooks, and nurses), and temporary lodgers. Class-based relations played an important role in the internal social dynamic because the lodgers would have had significantly lower life chances (and hence relative social value) than the other residents. The Association's agents also had the power to affect the diet of the lodgers. The external dynamic was characterized by a system of personal relationships called *guanxi* which created entangled networks of reciprocity and trust that stretched across and beyond the Chinese community, connecting its members with non-Chinese merchants, business leaders, and politicians. The operation of the *guanxi* relations could promote good will with the non-Chinese world, but they were effective only as long as the good will outpaced the racist attitudes of the non-Chinese. In other words, the successful employment of the *guanxi* relationships could be hampered and even precluded during periods of intense hatred against the Overseas Chinese community.

Praetzellis and Praetzellis (1997; also see Praetzellis 1999) also recognize that the proportions of Chinese to non-Chinese artifacts constitutes more than merely a facile marker of acculturation. They discovered that specific objects, even the chinoiserie ceramic vessels from the English ceramics industrial machine, could be used to help create and maintain the ethnic boundaries of the Chinese community. At the same time, however, the same artifacts could also project an overt if possibly misleading Chinese acceptance of Victorian values of hard work and frugality (for further comments on Victorian expression in Sacramento, see Praetzellis 1991).

Archaeology and Hispanic Ethnicity

Historical archaeologists have made tremendous strides since the 1960s in examining the local expressions of Spanish colonialism in the United States, the Caribbean, and Latin America. Archaeologists in these regions have been so prolific that the literature is too vast to cite in detail (but see, e.g., Deagan 1985; Gasco et al. 1997; Fournier-García and Miranda-Flores 1992; McEwan 1993; Thomas 1989, 1990, 1991). As is true of research at Overseas Chinese sites, archaeologists have made prodigious efforts to understand the material nature of Hispanic ethnicity.

In keeping with the general trend in historical archaeology, the earliest research on Spanish colonialism focused on artifact identification and analysis and, like much archaeological research of all periods, commenced with the study of ceramics (Goggin 1960, 1968). More recent studies have supplemented this early research (e.g., Deagan 1978, 1987, 2002; James 1988; Lister and Lister 1976, 1978).

As might also be expected, archaeologists interested in the social aspects of Spanish colonialism directed their earliest research toward the examination of the interactions between indigenous peoples and the newcomers. This body of research led directly to acculturation studies, focusing both on the Native American residents of the American Southeast and on the Spanish who traveled among them. Much of the archaeological research, beginning with sporadic work in the late 1940s, concentrated on mission sites. From a purely intellectual standpoint, missions were places where Spanish colonists, religious functionaries, and government agents could regularly interact with indigenous peoples, often on a daily basis (Weisman 1993: 165). From a purely practical viewpoint—as is clearly demonstrated by Greenwood's (1980) research on the Ventura Chinatown—mission sites are often focal points of modern-day reconstruction and renovation projects.

Kathleen Deagan (1983), whose pioneering research centered on St. Augustine, Florida, was perhaps the first archaeologist to provide rigorous analyses of colonial Spanish-indigenous acculturation in the New World. After a decade of excavation in "America's oldest city," Deagan (1983: 99, 271) concluded that the Spanish settlers there were actively engaged in the process of inventing a unique Hispanic-American cultural tradition, facilitated largely by the practice of *mestizaje*, or Spanish-Indian intermarriage and descent. But the new tradition was not a straightforward recreation of Iberian culture with a New World twist. Rather, it was specifically designed to incorporate a simple dualism: the elements of the culture that were male-focused and public tended to retain their Spanish appearance, whereas those cultural elements that were female-centered and focused on the household tended to be more amenable to acculturation. Objects of display retained their Spanish character, but objects that were less open to public consumption were more Native American in nature than strictly Spanish. This dualistic character allowed Deagan (1995: 452) to propose that Spanish-Native American acculturation was "sex-linked" in such a way that Spanish sexism mitigated Spanish racism (Deagan 1995: 452). In other words, colonial Spaniards—living far from their traditional homeland—were willing to overlook the Native American heritage of local women in order to attain marriage and procreation partners. For Deagan, a creolized identity constitutes the central characteristic of the emerging Hispanic-American cultural tradition in the New World (also see McEwan 1992: 104, 1995: 223).

Deagan's ideas about acculturation and creolization were later tested by Charles Ewen (1991) at the sixteenth-century site of Puerto Real, Haiti. Focusing on an area designated Locus 19, Ewen investigated the nature of Spanish colonial identity formation and concluded that Deagan's hypothesis was essentially correct: the ceramic collection (which was ostensibly more or less private) was composed of types of both Spanish and Native American manufacture, whereas the more visible objects—tablewares and items of clothing and personal adornment—were almost exclusively European in origin (1991: 116). Similarly, architecture and internal home furnishings, perhaps the most publicly visible of all material culture, were also consistent with Spanish conventions. Ewen's findings, taken in conjunction with further research, tend to reinforce the general pattern of Spanish visibility and aboriginal invisibility (that is, as purely public/private expressions) throughout the eastern Spanish colonies. In general, aboriginal ceramics in colonial Spanish contexts tend always to outweigh European ceramics in Spanish households (Deagan 1987: 104). This research finding is not trivial because it speaks directly to identity formation in colonialist settings.

Archaeologists have also developed ideas about two-way acculturation in Spanish-aboriginal contexts—which created syncretic cultural expressions—through their analyses of graveyards. For example, excavating at the cemetery of the sixteenth- and seventeenth-century Mission Santa Catalina de Guale in present-day Georgia, David Hurst Thomas (1988, 1993) discovered that the 431 interments he investigated contained a wide variety of both Native American and Spanish objects, including chipped stone projectile points, a rattlesnake shell gorget, brass hawk's bells, a rosary, glass beads, majolica plates, and Roman Catholic religious medallions. The inclusion of these objects in mortuary contexts tends to argue for a strong element of acculturation among the natives, at least in terms of their traditional belief system. In addition to making a case for the acculturation of the native peoples who lived near the mission, the skeletal population also documents the negative impact of colonization on the biological health of the natives, including the disruption of normal growth curves, the introduction of smallpox and measles, and the increased incidence of osteoarthritis indicative of escalating labor demands (Larsen 1993). In this context, then, Native Americans—as at many other locations throughout North American later in time—faced a double-edged cultural and physical stress: their physical bodies were being attacked by infectious, fatal diseases, while their cultural expressions were also being devastated.

Using information from six early nineteenth-century Spanish mission contexts in California, Paul Farnsworth (1992) completed one of the most explicit investigations of Native American acculturation during the era of Spanish colonialism. Farnsworth began by assessing earlier classifications designed to quantify acculturation by the relative occurrence of specific kinds of material culture, starting with Quimby and Spoehr's (1951) schematic outline. In accordance with these earlier ideas, Farnsworth argued that it should be possible to invent indices of cultural continuity and change that would reflect native acculturation. In other words, once the archaeologist can understand the relationship between the process of acculturation (when viewed as a continuum stretching from no acculturation to total assimilation) and precise examples of material culture, it should be relatively easy to chart the course of the acculturative process using excavated artifacts.

Farnsworth (1992: 26–27) sought to accomplish this analysis by devising a six-point, step-wise model that extended from "Imported artifacts to the area with no traditional counterparts" (e.g., brass buttons) to "Traditional artifacts which do not fit into the new culture in the area" (e.g., stone tools). Having devised these categories, his next task was to create six indices, expressed as percentages, that were calculated by adding and dividing the various categories: "Continuity of Traditional Culture," "Continuity of New Culture," "Intensity of Cultural Exchange," "Availability of Imported Goods," and "Degree to Which New Culture is Supplying Unchanged Traditional Culture." After calculating the indices for the mission site contexts—all of which date to the early nineteenth century, Farnsworth concluded that the indices suggest that the Native Americans at the missions were generally able to maintain "a high level of traditional culture"(33). The Native Americans in contact with Spanish missions in California thus appeared to retain their traditional identities with little modification. The indices termed "Intensity of Cultural Exchange" and "Continuity of Traditional Cultural Elements" are the specific sites which Farnsworth believes are most relevant to the study of identity formation, because it is in the process of exchange and cultural maintenance that we should expect to observe the effects of acculturation and creolization.

In his examination of the remains he excavated from the Mission of Nuestra Senora de la Soledad, established in 1791, Farnsworth obtained the indices for two contexts, the Neophytes' Barracks remains and the Missionaries' garbage pit (Table 3.2). The garbage pit is important because the implication is that the low percentages of both measures indicate European presence. Part of Farnsworth's interpretation is based

TABLE 3.2. Indices for the Mission Soledad Contexts

Context	Number of artifacts	Continuity of traditional cultural elements (%)	Intensity of cultural exchange (%)
Neophytes' barracks	161	67.1	9.3
Missionaries' garbage pit	69	14.5	4.3

Source: Farnsworth (1992: 29).

on his findings from the excavation of the La Purisima Concepción Mission located south of the Soledad Mission. At La Purisima, a Continuity of Traditional Cultural Elements index of 32.0 percent and an Intensity of Cultural Exchange index of 4.0 percent, "most likely represent the presence of a *mestizo* with a dual cultural heritage, rather than a European" (Farnsworth 1992: 31). In further disassembling the contexts at Mission Soledad, Farnsworth discovered greater, rather than less, cultural continuity among the native peoples through time. He attributes some of the retention of native cultural elements, and by extension native identity, to the increased population of Native Americans at the mission from 1795 to 1805, during which the indigenous population increased by over 200 percent.

Charles Cheek (1997) provided another contribution to acculturation studies in the world of Spanish colonial influence, but in his study the Spanish appear only on the periphery as individuals unable to force complete cultural dominance. Cheek analyzed three sites associated with the Garifuna, a unique people usually known by anthropologists as Black Caribs, who live in present-day Honduras. History records that the Black Caribs were originally shipwrecked Dutch slaves who had intermarried with Caribs on the island of St. Vincent. After losing a war with the English in the 1790s, the Black Caribs—who by then had established themselves as a discrete cultural group—were deported by the English from St. Vincent to the island of Roatan off the coast of Honduras, directly opposite the Spanish town of Trujillo (Cheek 1997: 101–2). Ethnographic and ethnohistoric research indicates that the Garifuna worked diligently to build a distinct cultural expression in an environment that included intense conflict between English and Spanish forces actively seeking to control the coast of Honduras (Gonzales 1988). Garifuna sites appear to present a rare opportunity to investigate identity formation and cultural retention in a colonial setting, because the Garifuna struggled so diligently to create their own completely new identity during this period.

Cheek studied three separate archaeological sites associated with the Garifuna: Campamento, located west of Spanish Trujillo, and inhabited by the Garifuna by 1799; Site 8, southeast of Trujillo, probably occupied from about 1800 to 1830; and Site 1, in Cristales, on the western edge of Trujillo, inhabited from the 1830s to the 1880s. Focusing on the ceramic collections, Cheek discovered that the assemblages contained three cultural traditions: Hispanic (represented by majolicas and wheel-thrown redwares), English (represented by decorated Staffordshire wares), and indigenous (represented by handmade, red-painted water jars).

In an intriguing analysis, Cheek devised an innovative way to examine the Garifuna acceptance of foreign cultural traits by analyzing changes in their foodways behavior as represented by the presence of nontraditional, European ceramic vessel forms at the three sites. His interest focused on the presence of cups, under the assumption that these vessels should signal the adoption of decidedly nontraditional consumption patterns. Cups played an important role in the creation and continued performance of the English tea ceremony (Roth 1961), and archaeologists in the eastern United States have examined this ceremony using different perspectives (e.g., South 1977: 40–41; Wall 1994b; but cf. Monks 1999: 209). The underlying assumption of tea-ceremony research is based on the historical reality that it was initially a practice strictly reserved for the English upper class, but that, as tea and tea wares became more widespread throughout the English-dominated world, greater numbers of individuals in the middle and working classes also adopted the practice of drinking tea. Cheek's idea was that an increase in vessels associated with tea drinking among the Garifuna would signal "an attempt to emulate the English food and drinking habits, whether or not tea or coffee were drunk regularly" (Cheek 1997: 107). The analysis of the three sites revealed that the occurrence of cups did indeed increase through time. Because Campamento, the earliest site, contained only Spanish ceramics and no tea wares, the suggestion is that the Garifuna initially had no interest in English foodways. Site 8 had 4.9 plates per cup, whereas Site 1, the most recent of the three, had 3.8 plates per cup. Though these ratios of plates to cups do not mirror those calculated for European-occupied sites along the eastern seaboard of the United States, they nonetheless appear significant within the Garifuna context (Cheek 1997: 109).

One significant sociocultural characteristic of Garifuna life is that they have constantly worked to retain their unique identity as a distinct people, frequently incorporating new elements in their traditions and daily patterns of life (Gonzalez 1988). When it came to adopting foreign cultural traits (or perhaps only habits), however, they chose through time to gravitate toward the English rather than toward the Spanish. The reasons for this decision are not entirely clear, but it does appear that the Garifuna adopted nontraditional, European ceramics as part of their identity formation process.

As is true for sites associated with the Overseas Chinese, some historical archaeologists have concentrated on examining faunal collections as possible avenues toward understanding ethnicity at sites related to Spanish colonial occupation. The assumptions made in such studies, where they concern identity construction and the maintenance of identity boundaries, are typically the same as for the Chinese: greater reliance on non-traditional species may indicate culture change and a concomitant transformation of identity.

In an effort to reconstruct the subsistence patterns of sixteenth-century Spanish colonists in Florida, Elizabeth Reitz and Margaret Scarry (1985) specifically explored how ethnicity and acculturation might be represented in archaeologically collected faunal and floral remains. Their analysis generally revealed that "In Spanish Florida, acculturation can be seen in the rapidity with which Native American subsistence items and techniques were incorporated into the settlers' subsistence system" (Reitz and Scarry 1985: 95). Spanish colonists, entering a natural environment unlike anything they had known in the Iberian peninsula, quickly decided to exploit the local flora and fauna as a practical means of survival. The perception of their rapid acceptance of what they found readily available is appealing and logical; after all, people must eat to survive. But Reitz and Scarry urged caution when attempting to relegate this process of acceptance to acculturation. Spanish colonists need not have necessarily acculturated to ensure their physical survival; they may simply have developed their New World subsistence strategies as an example of adaptation. Spanish colonists in the southeastern corner of North America would simply have experienced an initial period of trial and error as they experimented with the local species and as they adjusted to their colonial lives.

In their careful analysis of several archaeological sites once inhabited by Spanish colonists in Florida, Reitz and Scarry fully document the colonists' use of wild plant and animal species and their retention of traditional patterns of consumption. An indication that this process of acceptance and resistance was not universal appears in Reitz and Scarry's documentation that the exploitation of wild and domestic species was not consistent across the Spanish Southeast. Part of the variation was undoubtedly biological, because some natural species occurred only in certain ecozones. For example, the exploitation of gopher tortoises was much greater at St. Augustine (35 individuals accounting for 7.96 kg of biomass) than at the more northern outpost of Santa Elena, in present-day South Carolina (3 individuals constituting only 0.11 kg of biomass).

Regarding culture change, Reitz and Scarry (1985: 99) conclude that the Spanish inhabitants of colonial Florida both adapted and acculturated. Iberian men and women retained what they could of their traditional foodways, they adapted to their new environment by exploiting plants and animals strange to them, and they learned from Native Americans with whom they came in contact. Their conclusion adds further weight to Deagan's (1983) original interpretation about the creation of a creolized Hispanic-American culture in the Spanish New World beginning with the earliest days of their presence there (also see Reitz 1992, 1993; Scarry 1993).

The amount of research conducted at Spanish colonial-period sites throughout the southeastern and southwestern United States, in the Caribbean, and in Latin America is indeed impressive, and it continues to expand and to be reported (see, e.g., Deagan and Cruxent 2002a, b). Archaeologists, however, have shown considerably less interest in examining more recent sites inhabited by Hispanic peoples. A few illustrative studies nonetheless have been completed.

Employing Barth's notion of boundary maintenance, Randall McGuire (1983) examined the relationship between ethnicity and material culture in his study of the late nineteenth-century Rancho Punta de Agua in southern Arizona. McGuire's central idea was that archaeology could provide important information about ethnicity when the excavated artifacts are perceived as material symbols of ethnic identity. McGuire eschewed the idea that unambiguous symbols of ethnic identity would appear in archaeological deposits, but argued that the material correlates of specific ethnic ideologies and behaviors should be present. In keeping with the thinking of the time, McGuire suggested that consumption patterns, as demonstrated by the remains of trash deposits, as well as the floor plans of dwellings, should provide information about ethnic identity and the maintenance of ethnic boundaries. In other words, the way ethnicity was expressed should be imprinted on the material remains in some fashion. The history of the rancho appeared to provide a perfect arena in which to examine ethnicity. Pioneers of German ancestry originally built and inhabited the rancho (1855–1866/67), and individuals of Hispanic heritage lived there later (1868/71–c. 1877). The various deposits created by each sociohistorically distinct household provided an opportunity to formulate inferences about the symbolic markers of ethnic identity.

Late nineteenth-century historical records indicate that Mexican Americans in southern Arizona were usually assigned to lower economic positions than nearby Anglo families. Though both Mexican Americans and Anglos were economically stratified according to labor position and hence wage, the Hispanics of each level were consistently paid less than their Anglo counterparts. McGuire used the historical information in conjunction with contemporary wage and price lists for selected commodities and empirically demonstrated the historical gap between the two groups. When he investigated ethnicity specifically, however, he was forced to conclude that "very little at the Rancho appears to reflect the social dimensions of ethnicity" (McGuire 1983: 200). The paucity of distinctive ethnic symbolism ran directly counter to the situation that obtains today, where significant ethnic markers are found in Tucson, located only about four miles north of the rancho site. Since the archaeological evidence provided no clear differences that could be attributed to nineteenth-century ethnicity, McGuire (201–2) concluded that the social distance between the two groups is greater today than in the past.

Edward Staski (1987) conducted a similar investigation into Hispanic ethnicity in El Paso, Texas, a city located directly across the Rio Grande from the Republic of Mexico. The materials he excavated dated to the 1850–1920 period, and because they were collected from domestic contexts that Staski differentially identified as Mexican and Euroamerican, he believed that they offered an excellent opportunity to examine a number of anthropologically relevant topics, not the least of which was ethnic group dynamics. Staski focused his attention on twelve trash pits discovered during his excavation, four of which dated to the 1850–1881 period, with the other eight dating to 1881–1920. The temporal variance is significant because the earliest deposits derive from the period before the railroad had reached the city. Historical documents indicate that during the pre-railroad era, "ethnic separation" in the city was practically nonexistent. Historians have tended to envision a general homogeneity of the city's population in the pre-railroad era, when the residents were unable to differentiate themselves by their selective purchase of consumer goods. Staski faced a significant problem, however, in that it was impossible for him to correlate any of the trash pits to particular individuals or households. His ability to separate the "Mexican" and the "Euroamerican" deposits was thus severely limited. He felt confident in circumventing this problem by proposing that "certain behaviors of both Mexicans and Euroamericans were affected by the transition of El Paso from a small isolated community to a major center within the American national economic system" (Staski 1987: 52). In other words, the two ethnic groups could be combined into a third group, "El Pasoans." The most important variable in the trash pits, then, was not ethnic identity but date of creation.

Staski's analysis of the ceramics from the trash pits indicated that wares manufactured in traditional Mexican ways and in the United States and Europe were present in all contexts. That he discovered little variation among the trash pits in terms of quantity or variety of Mexican ceramics implies a certain homogeneity of ceramic usage during the pre-railroad period of close ethnic interaction. Even though greater amounts of European and American ceramics would have been available during the post-railroad era, Staski discovered that the Mexican types actually increased in variety. As far as ceramic vessels were concerned, it did not appear that the men and women of Hispanic heritage in early El Paso experienced assimilation. The faunal remains, however, provided other information. When he examined the remains to determine what species of meat the early El Pasoans consumed, Staski discovered both a growing homogeneity of diet and an increased reliance on the national American market. Staski (1987: 55) interpreted this increased similarity as evidence of assimilation.

Staski's findings in El Paso reinforce the development of a syncretic culture similar to that modeled by Deagan for the earliest colonial Spaniards, in addition to a later assimilation into the "American melting pot." Staski's interpretation is significant because it calls into question the concept of the "Border Culture," the sociohistorical formation along the Mexico/southwest United States border. This culture is characterized by a retention among Mexicans of much of their traditional culture but a concomitant surrender to American material culture. Though some geographers have termed the border region a culture area, designated as the "Hispanic-American Borderland" (e.g., Nostrand 1970), it is perhaps more correctly termed a "bi-cultural" zone (see Glidersleeve 1978: 42–48).

In another study published the same year as Staski's investigation of El Paso, Susan Henry (1987) compared "Mexican-American" and "Euro-American" contexts in Phoenix, Arizona. Her archaeological deposits were all urban in context and were collected from twelve privies and three trash pits used from about 1880 to 1940. Henry could link the individual archaeological contexts with specific individuals, because of the late dates of the sites and the availability of contemporary city directories. The directories also provided information about the professional occupations of most of the area's heads of household. Henry's primary goal in the analysis was to investigate consumer behavior in Phoenix by examining the variation between the contexts. The underlying idea was that different percentages of objects would yield socially relevant information about the men and women who produced the deposits, with Henry's main dimension of distinction being occupational ranking. In the fully capitalist setting Henry was investigating, occupation served to indicate a household's "socioeconomic status," a shorthand appellation for purchasing power within the marketplace (for contrary views on the use of this measure, see Monks 1999; Orser 1988a).

Focusing part of her analysis on the faunal remains—and adopting the assumption that humans tend to be conservative in their foodways habits—Henry believed that "ethnic group membership" may account for some of the variability she found in the distribution of remains. Differential occurrence of beef, mutton, and pork remains existed between the Mexican and the non-Mexican deposits, but no statistically valid difference was present in the distribution of chicken and wild game (Henry 1987: 374).

Archaeology and Irish Ethnicity

Archaeological studies of Irish ethnicity in the United States are extremely limited in number. Historical archaeology conducted in Ireland is usually defined as post-medieval archaeology. The archaeology of post-medieval history is a relatively new pursuit in the Republic of Ireland, though a longer tradition exists in Northern Ireland (see, e.g., Donnelly and Brannon 1998; Donnelly and Horning 2002; Horning 2001; Orser 1996b, 1997a, b, 2000b, 2001b). Some archaeological studies of Irish sites in the United States have not specifically mentioned ethnicity, instead choosing to focus on other issues (see, e.g., Orser 1992b; Praetzellis and Praetzellis 1990; Sopko 2000; J. E. Thomas 1993). Nonetheless, a few archaeologists have conducted examinations of Irish ethnicity using excavated information.

One of the first explicit investigations of the archaeological nature of Irish ethnicity in the United States was Sherene Baugher's (1982) study of Hoboken Hollow, a working-class neighborhood in Troy, New York, inhabited by Irish, English, and German immigrants from 1853 to 1929. Baugher was cognizant of the relevant archaeological literature about ethnicity then available, and properly judged the significance of ethnic study in historical archaeology. With an understanding of the nuances presented by ethnicity and the possible effects of other social variables on artifact ownership, she was interested in investigating whether archaeological remains could be used to infer ethnic identity among European immigrants. As a result, she explicitly designed her study around the question of ethnic visibility in archaeological deposits.

Baugher excavated a row house composed of six two-story units, each of which had housed one family. Though extant historical documents provided useful information about ethnic immigration to Troy, they offered no comparable evidence for the names or ethnic affiliations of the families who had lived in the excavated house units. And, because the records indicated that tenants tended to stay in the area for only three to five years, it was possible that each of the three ethnic groups had lived in the same housing unit at some time in the past. An analysis of the excavated artifacts was of no use in indicated the residents' ethnic affiliations, because the assemblages from each house unit contained the same kinds of objects. The ceramics from each unit were similar and included transfer-printed and undecorated whiteware, porcelain, and stoneware. The discovery of material culture homogeneity compelled Baugher (1982: 36) to conclude that all the immigrant families purchased the same kinds of dishes regardless of their perceived ethnicity. While the groups may have socially segregated themselves in member-restricted clubs and taverns, their ethnic distinctiveness apparently did not transfer to their material culture. This understanding led Baugher (1982: 36) to conclude that historical archaeologists should be cautious in their eagerness to assign ethnic affiliation to artifacts alone. When it came to material possessions, the families' economic positions (actually, their purchasing power)—which were all similar—seemed to outweigh their ability (or perhaps even their willingness) to display their ethnicity.

In a similar study of Irish ethnicity and its material correlates published a year later, Lu Ann De Cunzo (1983) investigated ten archaeological deposits found in six privies in Dublin, a working-class community in Paterson, New Jersey (also see Cotz 1975). People in various households in Dublin used the privies from about 1830 to the late 1890s and, with the assistance of historical documentation, De Cunzo was able to determine the ethnic affiliation of seven of the households. Her analysis was multidimensional in terms of understanding the social variables that may have affected the deposition of objects in the privies, with ethnicity being one of her principal foci.

Historical records indicated that almost all the individuals involved in the use of the privies either were born in England or Ireland, or were born in the United States of English or Irish parents. De Cunzo thus hypothesized that of the two groups, "the Irish are expected to maintain the strongest sense of ethnic consciousness, a consequence of their ascription to the lowest social and economic positions in Paterson (and American) society on their arrival in this country"(1983: 384). She conversely proposed that the English maintained less ethnic awareness, partly because of their better socioeconomic standing. De Cunzo judged that the behavioral implications of the divergent attitudes of the Irish and the English might appear in the realms of foodways and health care. She specifically hoped to discover patterned variability in the ceramic vessel forms, the relative occurrence of glass food and beverage containers, the differential presence of medicine bottles, and the presence of items derived from Ireland and England.

Any analysis of the kind envisioned by De Cunzo is exceedingly complex. A substantial amount of the interpretive difficulty was introduced by the historical reality that numerous individuals had access to the privies during their use. For example, privy deposit 1, associated with Numbers 1–4 Van Houten Street, was used by Peter Ryle, born in England, and his wife and two daughters, born in New Jersey; John and Sarah Manson, born in Ireland, their daughter, and two boarders born in the United States; and one boarder born in England. De Cunzo (1983: 403) readily acknowledged the difficulty of separating the deposits "along ethnic lines," but mostly because the "archaeological record should show considerable acculturation to have occurred." The underlying assumption is that both Irish and English individuals should have experienced the impact of United States acculturative pressures and that both groups should have independently become more homogeneous, at least in terms of their material culture usage.

De Cunzo discovered no obvious individual symbols of Irish identity, such as white clay pipes embossed with Irish harps or shamrocks, or any other objects that would signal membership in Irish-associated organizations. Her analysis of the ceramic vessel forms similarly yielded no obvious indication of ethnic affiliation. Two of the deposits contained more teawares than tablewares, but one of the deposits was associated with individuals of English, Scottish, and American birth, while the other was linked to persons of Irish, American, and English birth. All the deposits contained food storage vessels in different amounts, but no unambiguous, ethnically relevant variation was identifiable. The jumble of indefinite findings forced De Cunzo (1983: 405) to conclude that "Ethnic differences in foodways may be masked by the integrated residence pattern. Judging from the discarded ceramics, however, differences which did exist in diet, tea and coffee consumption, and food reparation and storage were not related to ethnic background." The distribution of beverage bottles similarly appeared to be a function of both ethnicity and date. The earliest deposits contained only wine bottles and stoneware jugs, whereas the later deposits included these vessels, but also beer, soda water, mineral water, and liquor bottles. The archaeological remains thus suggested that the people of Irish heritage in the area preferred soda water and beer to the wine and liquor consumed by the nearby non-Irish residents. Even with these ambiguous findings, however, De Cunzo was confident enough to use them to estimate the ethnicity of three households in her sample whose ethnicity was not mentioned in the historical records. She concluded that these household were "almost certainly of native or English background" (De Cunzo 1983: 411).

De Cunzo (1983: 439) was careful to propose that the acceptance of American-made objects did not necessarily imply acculturation because the Irish may simply have adopted the goods of United States factories as a "symbolic" effort "to update the group's image in the eyes of the host society by adopting its strategy in the marketplace." As shown above, archaeological research at Chinese-affiliated sites in the western United States suggests that the immigrant Chinese also sought to manipulate the image they presented to the non-Chinese, highly racialized, dominant world.

By far the most ambitious effort to examine the nature of Irish settlement in the United States has occurred in relation to research conducted at the old Five Points district in lower Manhattan, New York City (see Yamin 2001). Identified by the intersection of Park, Worth, and Baxter streets, the area of the Five Points was widely regarded in the nineteenth century as a focal point for ramshackle tenements, dark alleyways, and disreputable people. Even Charles Dickens, long-time vocal opponent of the evils of urban social inequality, refused to visit the area without a police escort (Yamin 1997: 46). The scope of the archaeological work conducted at the Five Points is massive, with over one million artifacts recovered from 22 stone- or brick-lined privies and cess pools on 14 different city lots. The sheer magnitude of the research suggests that archaeologists will present significant findings from this site for many years (see Yamin 2000). One feature that makes the Five Points research so consequential is that the residents of the area derived from many different national communities, including a substantial number of immigrants from Ireland.

Given the national diversity represented by the residents of the Five Points, as indicated by abundant historical records, it was inevitable that the project's archaeologists would be influenced to investigate the material representations of ethnicity. One might minimally expect that the Five Points deposits would permit archaeologists to address important anthropologically relevant topics like acculturation and the maintenance of identity within the confines of an active, multicultural environment. The authors of the Five Points analyses have had the benefit of the earlier, often facile archaeological examinations of ethnicity, and so their studies tend to be considerably more nuanced and sophisticated than many of the earlier works cited here.

Heather Griggs (1999) specifically explores Irish ethnicity at the Five Points but links it closely with class. She considers the analytical problems earlier archaeologists encountered when they sought to engage ethnicity, and states that archaeologists have generally pursued two conceptually invalid approaches (1999: 88): either they have attempted to identify discrete "ethnic markers" in their archaeological collections—those one or two objects that unambiguously signal ethnic identity and are analogous to African "survivals" in the New World—or they have sought to identify the material boundaries between two distinct ethnic groups. The last approach is considerably more sophisticated than the first, because it rests on the archaeologists' acceptance of Barth's (1969) notion of ethnic boundary maintenance. Griggs argues against both approaches on the grounds that each is too facile to interpret the intricate real world of social interaction. Any sociohistorical variable as complex as ethnic identity conceivably must be symbolized with more than one or two personal possessions (like soy sauce bottles or white clay smoking pipes embossed with shamrocks). More important, the archaeologists' efforts to identify ethnic boundary markers tend to reinforce reified, artificial "us" and "them" categories—some of which are historically charged and hotly contested. The use of such categorizations effectively

distracts archaeologists from the class distinctions that were operationalized within the various immigrant communities.

Regarding the Irish specifically, Griggs argues that the urge to create
a "them" category called "The Irish" simply masks the inequalities that
existed in Ireland and were undoubtedly transferred to the United States.
This is a significant point, because Griggs is arguing that when "the"
Irish are perceived as a homogeneous group within North America, they
are essentially being tagged with a racial label. It makes no difference, on
a purely intellectual level, whether the label is imposed by nineteenth-
century Know-Nothing racists or by present-day, otherwise well-meaning
archaeologists.

Griggs specifically focuses her analysis on the artifacts recovered from
a cesspool that contained over 100,000 artifacts associated with the residents of a five-story tenement house located at 472 Pearl Street. Among
the large array of artifacts, ceramic analysts were able to identify a
minimum of 355 vessels, including 207 tea and table wares. Two decorated glass objects are of particular interest because Griggs (1999: 94)
terms them "high quality items": an elaborate cruet with diamond cuts
and basal fluting and a castor. She identifies these objects as being of
"Anglo-Irish manufacture" and concludes that they "may have been
brought from Ireland as family heirlooms" (94). She also notes that the
objects in the cesspool do not contain "a full complement of serving vessels," in contradistinction to the general rules of genteel Victorian etiquette. Griggs believes that the meaning of the incomplete set of serving
vessels may relate to "ethnically oriented" dining habits, as does the
"presence of unusually high quantities of pork, including large numbers
of pig's feet which were commonly consumed in rural Ireland" (94).

In another study using the Five Points material, Claudia Milne and
Pamela Crabtree (2000) present an analysis of the faunal remains that
is methodologically similar to other investigations cited above. Their explicit goal is to examine approximately 65,000 animal bones to determine "whether differences in food choices can be seen as expressions of
ethnicity in what was a diverse, multiethnic immigrant neighborhood"
and also to consider the extent that "socio-economic status" affected
dietary habits (Milne and Crabtree 2000: 130). Regarding the Irish specifically, Milne and Crabtree examined 18,900 bone fragments extracted
from the deposits of the cesspool at 472 Pearl Street, the same deposit
Griggs used in her study. Their analysis revealed a few simple differences
between the Irish and the other ethnic groups in the area. For example,
the Irish residents of the tenement regularly consumed ham hocks
and pigs' feet, while the members of the nearby Polish-German households seldom ate these portions. Like their non-Irish neighbors, however, the Irish ate little poultry. Overall, the Irish appeared to consume

a substantial amount of meat, with pork dominating. The abundance of pork initially appears to provide visible evidence of ethnic variation, but an associated difficulty that makes this conclusion impossible to accept with assurance is that pork was also the least expensive meat available in New York at the time. The Irish may simply have purchased pork because they could afford it. The low incidence of poultry also appears to constitute a somewhat widespread feature of lower-class dining habits, with no obvious ethnic associations (185). One obvious "ethnic marker" of Irish Catholic food consumption patterns would conceivably be a relatively high amount of fish bones. The relatively low percentage of fish remains, however, compelled Milne and Crabtree to conclude that the Irish in the area ate less fish than any other New Yorkers who have been archeologically investigated.

In another Five Points study, Michael Bonasera and Leslie Raymer (2001) examined medicine bottles and other health care items for evidence of ethnicity. Their analysis revealed that most of the proprietary medicines at the site derived from Irish-related deposits. This finding suggested that the Irish "apparently chose, and were able, to spend a large portion of their wages on their health" (2001: 59). At the same time, and as discovered earlier by De Cunzo (1983) in Paterson, New Jersey, the Irish in the Five Points had a "pronounced preference" for soda water, as well as for mineral water. But again, the linkage with ethnicity here is not clear cut, because the consumption of soda and mineral water may have had both class and ethnic associations (Bonasera and Raymer 2001: 61). Not only were soda and mineral water less expensive than medicines and other palliatives, these liquids "may have been used in an attempt to alleviate psychological distress and even the effects of alcohol" (see also Reckner and Brighton 1999).

Archaeologists from Sonoma State University conducted an equally extensive project in Oakland, California, that promises to offer significant new insights about the interaction of race, class, and ethnicity in the United States (Meyer and Stewart 2000; Praetzellis 2001a, b, c; Praetzellis and Stewart 2001; Stewart and Praetzellis 2001; Ziesing and Praetzellis 2001). Using historical records, the archaeologists were able to relate the excavated artifacts—deposited in hundreds of features excavated in 23 city blocks (and dating to the last half of the nineteenth century)—to many of the area's resident families, including several deposits created by Irish immigrants. The late date of the deposits meant that the archaeologists could correlate individual archaeological features with specific residents. Their investigation is pertinent here because one of the six explicit research themes was "ethnicity/urban subcultures."

The complexity inherent in the archaeological analysis of past social life can be adequately demonstrated by reference to the faunal materials.

In an effort to comprehend the relative economic positions of the residents, the faunal analysts used contemporary meat prices to divide the animal bones into three price groups: high, moderate, and low (Gust 2001) The profiles of meat prices for only eight of the Irish-associated contexts indicates the complicated relationship between race, class, and ethnicity and the price of cuts of meat (Table 3.3) because no obvious patterned variability emerges in the samples.

Wrestling with Ethnicity, Coming to Terms with Race

The above overview provides a descriptive indication of the ways in which historical archaeologists have investigated the material dimensions of past ethnic difference. The authors of each study made a serious and sincere effort to understand a social variable that was complex, mutable, and entangled with several other social attributes. Each study represents a well-intentioned effort to identify the material dimensions of social variability. The archaeologists cited above overtly recognized the difficulties they faced in attempting social analysis, and most acknowledged the tentative nature of their interpretations. Their self-conscious understanding of the explanatory obstacles before them illustrates that each was well prepared to undertake the search for ethnicity in archaeological deposits. That they could seldom present firm, unshakable conclusions merely reflects the depth of the interpretive difficulty.

Archaeologists who have conducted rigorous inquiries into group

TABLE 3.3. Prices of Meat for Eight Irish Contexts in Oakland, California, Late Nineteenth Century

Resident family	Location	Occupation	Meat price range (%)		
			High	Moderate	Low
Donavan	666 Fifth	sewer contractor	19.2	48.1	32.7
Breen	802 Brush	laborer	58.0	29.0	13.0
Tighe	762 Fifth	railroad car cleaner	43.0	53.0	4.0
Murray	822 Murtle	laborer/ gardener	35.5	40.2	24.3
Broderick	813 Filbert	laborer	31.1	28.3	40.6
Corrigan	824 Linden	boilermaker	58.6	32.4	9.0
O'Brien	1817 Goss	carpenter, lawyer	61.0	28.0	12.0
McNamara	1865 Goss	railroad laborer/ foreman	20.0	40.0	40.0

Sources: Meyer and Stewart (2000: 55); Praetzellis (2001a: 111); Praetzellis and Stewart (2001: 105, 307, 380); Stewart and Praetzellis (2001: 136, 278); Ziesing and Praetzellis (2001: 109).

identity during the past 500 years—during the second phase of the "pre-history of racial analysis"—were generally not much more successful than was Childe or any of the other early archaeologists who investigated ancient social variability. The general failure of historical archaeologists in the same arena of research raises identical, troubling questions about the efficacy of archaeological research to untangle the most complicated facets of human social interaction. The deficiencies may even be more glaring in historical archaeology because of the addition of often-abundant and informative historical documents. The presence of textual sources often means that archaeologists examining the past 500 years are on a firmer informational footing than their colleagues engaged in the analysis of ancient group identities. The above overview demonstrates, however, that the archaeological analysis of ethnicity remains problematic even with the existence of copious amounts of supportive information. It is not surprising, perhaps, that some of the most sophisticated, socially oriented studies in historical archaeology are situated within late nineteenth-century contexts, when the historical documentation is generally more complete and more profoundly expository than for earlier periods of history.

At the beginning of their search for social variability, archaeologists sought to view ethnicity in the simplest possible terms, seeking to discover one or two discrete "ethnic markers" that would unambiguously signal group identity. If it was true, for instance, that only Overseas Chinese individuals used opium pipes, then it was easy to assume that the discovery of an opium pipe in an archaeological context could be used to signal Chinese ethnicity. When archaeologists learned, however, that many non-Chinese also smoked opium—and that the promotion of the practice was a particularly despicable element of anti-Chinese racism (Wylie and Fike 1993)—they quickly realized that any sort of facile interpretation of opium pipes would not be possible. The same conclusion applied to other examples of "ethnic" artifacts, like smoking pipes, buttons, and anything else that could be printed or embossed with a meaningful symbol. Social archaeologists soon transformed the search for easily identifiable artifacts into an understanding that any material markers of a group's identity were more likely to have consisted of assemblages of objects rather than just one or two individual, highly charged "ethnic" pieces. To make matters more complex, as archaeologists increasingly acknowledged the role of symbolism in artifact usage, they began to accept that ethnic markers could go unrecognized. Even when archaeologists transferred their attention from single-artifact associations to assemblage-focused examinations, they were still merely conducting uniscalar investigations, with the sole focus being on the single sociocultural vector of ethnicity.

The appreciation that the analysis of only one dimension of social variability was not adequate to account for the complexities inherent in the sociocultural formations that were created and maintained in the modern world developed as soon as historical archaeologists began to adopt an explicit consumer-choice perspective. As explained by Suzanne Spencer-Wood (1987a: 1), consumer choice studies in historical archaeology seek "systematic connections between patterns in the archaeological data and patterns of participation in consumer behaviors of cultural [ethnic] subgroups." When situated in a modern-world setting, the identity of the various cultural subgroups is often (and perhaps always) influenced by their patterns of consumption. Men and women of the historic past used a diverse number of objects in discrete and different ways to create, reinforce, and signal their individual and group identities. The consumer-choice model immediately made considerable archaeological sense, because, as capitalist consumers themselves, all archaeologists operate in ways that are at least structurally similar to those of earlier consumers. The linkage between group membership and habits of consumption was an important staple of consumer choice studies by the 1990s, and ethnic affiliation was widely appreciated as an important feature of personal and group identity. Some archaeologists came to consider consumer choice as the window through which they could begin to understand the material dimensions of ethnicity (see, e.g., Henry 1991; Holt 1991; Huelsbeck 1991).

The conceptual addition of individual, family, and household wealth (usually expressed as purchasing power within the dominant economy) allowed historical archaeologists to begin more sophisticated, biscalar analyses in which they consciously connected class membership with ethnic affiliation. These studies usually included the concept of cross-cutting social vectors (McGuire 1983). Analyses conducted with this more sophisticated understanding became increasingly more nuanced, as individual archaeologists attempted to model the real-world complexities of historic men and women who were enmeshed in both class and ethnic membership structures. The growing analytical rigor of social analysis in historical archaeology was directly attributable to the archaeologists' understanding that consumption can serve as one important way for individuals and groups to create unique identities.

The adoption of biscalar analyses, even though a significant advance in the realm of socially oriented scholarship in historical archaeology, did not completely capture the complexities faced by men and women engaged in the process of becoming modern. Studies of ethnicity, even though the most rigorous were interlinked with social class membership, were still unable to investigate racialization in any substantive way. Many historical archaeologists, in their often uncritical (and perhaps even unconscious) use of a whole-culture paradigm, fail to engage poverty as a social reality, and their misunderstanding or complete avoidance of an extra-site, network perspective, shortchanged their social analyses. Even the most sophisticated biscalar investigations generally provide an incomplete contextualization that precludes any analysis of race and racialization. Most of the authors cited in the preceding overviews generally accepted the whole-culture perspective by promoting various ethnic groups as taken-for-granted sociocultural entities. Relying on both primary historical documents and secondary historical accounts, they knew, for example, that thousands of immigrants entered the United States from east and west during the nineteenth century. Employing such terms as "the" Chinese, "the" Hispanics, and "the" Irish, they unwittingly reified the social order and made racial analysis all but impossible. In all fairness, however, much of their usage was occasioned by the practical circumstances of the archaeology itself. The excavation of an urban privy used by 300 people of various ethnic affiliations living in a single five-story tenement is bound to cause an interpretive nightmare for archaeologists interested in social variability and ethnic boundary maintenance. The difficulty here is understandable, but more surprising, perhaps, is that many of the archaeologists who conducted otherwise significant consumer-choice studies generally avoided poverty by focusing on groups that were considered "middle class." Again, however, much of this bias may be related to the realities of the archaeological research because many of the most informed studies were completed within a sponsored-research environment. Archaeologists who work in this realm are not often free to select what portions of a site they wish to investigate. But, as noted in Chapter 1, even in many cases where archaeologists have complete freedom of site selection, they often fail to addresses poverty, preferring instead a whole-culture perspective that is less sociological and more overtly cultural. And, while most consumer-choice archaeologists readily admit that a marketplace of global extent operated at the time of their sites' habitation—after all, the non-local artifacts originated somewhere—even the most rigorous studies tend to employ a mechanistic approach that only permits the formulation of purely functionalist interpretations that incorporate measures of commodity flow practically devoid of social interference (see, e.g., Adams et al. 2001).

By bypassing poverty, ignoring the capitalist world economy, and adopting a whole-culture perspective, archaeologists investigating the modern era, have for the most part been able to overlook race and racialization. This neglect has meant that historical archaeologists have generally found it impossible to progress beyond biscalar analyses. Even within this intellectual environment, however, some archaeologists have provided analyses that could well have included in-depth considerations of racialization. For example, in her seminal studies of the Overseas Chinese, Greenwood (1980, 1996) repeatedly observed that the Chinese men and women of the American West lived in a hostile and unfriendly social environment. So central was this social reality to her understanding of Chinese life that she mentioned it in the first sentence of her 1980 article:

If acquired through the traditional avenues of historical research, knowledge of the early Chinese community in Ventura, California, would be limited to the facts that it existed, and that *its presence aroused hostility on the part of other settlers in this town* which grew from and around the Mission San Buenaventura. (Greenwood 1980: 113; emphasis added)

The creation of an Anti-Chinese League in Ventura, California, the actions of the Chinese Exclusion Societies in Los Angeles and San Francisco, and the passage of the federal Chinese Exclusion Act of 1882 (Greenwood 1980: 113, 1996: 11; also see 1993)—as well as several other, less well organized, local discriminatory actions—indicate that the Chinese individuals who inhabited the sites she investigated in both Ventura and Los Angeles lived under a state of racial siege. Undoubtedly influenced by Greenwood's early mention of racially designed bias against Chinese immigrants, as well as by the historical accounts they consulted, some archaeologists have mentioned racially motivated hatred toward Chinese men and women (Stapp 1993: 16; Fee 1993: 73). In a similar vein, Griggs (1999: 98), citing Noel Ignatiev's (1995) understanding of the racial oppression directed toward the Irish, also noted the significance of past racial bias in her analysis.

In a different but equally important take on racial bias, D. H. Thomas (1988: 74–75) explains the way in which Anglo historians have traditionally evaluated the "Black Legend" of the colonial Spanish. Thomas says that as historians express the legend, it incorporates four principal beliefs about the Spanish: (1) that they were never true colonists committed to long-term settlement, but were rather interested only in extracting wealth and bringing souls to God; (2) that they contributed little or nothing to New World civilization; (3) that they were universally cruel and unmerciful; and (4) perhaps most pertinent for our purposes, that "Something 'peculiar' in the national Spanish character fostered bigotry, pride, and hypocrisy" (Thomas 1988: 75). In Thomas's view, unwarranted Hispanophobic bias has significantly retarded serious research into the true character of Spanish colonialism in the New World. The significance of the historians' bias can be evaluated by considering that they were undoubtedly judging the Spanish against the colonial English. Colonial English were not only long-term settlers in the New World, they were also the progenitors of "American civilization," as well as the intellectual ancestors of the historians, if only by language. The equally pernicious myth of the English colonists' friendship and kindness toward their Native American neighbors constitutes a stalwart element of early formal education in the United States, as best exemplified by Thanksgiving portrayals. It is undoubtedly not an accident that the English are members of the Teutonic group, whereas the Spanish are placed in the Italic group in Brinton's (1890) racialist scheme.

Historical archaeologists actually conceptualize race when they present ethnicity as an element of social domination. For example, the statement "Ethnicity has little meaning until complex structures arose based on political domination" (Schuyler 1980b: vii) is actually more about race than it is about ethnicity. As the above overview indicates, however, many historical archaeologists have collapsed race into ethnicity, and in the process have diluted or erased the power of racial assignment and identification (see Perry and Paynter 1999: 307). Ethnicity has the appearance of intellectual safety and acceptability, whereas race as a topic may seem dangerous and political (Sanjek 1994). The propensity to consider race and ethnicity as synonymous is of course not confined to archaeology, and scholars in cultural anthropology, history, and other disciplines have also been forced to delineate the important distinction between race and ethnicity (see, e.g. Smedley 1993: 29–34; Wolf 1994). Archaeologists, like scholars in other fields of study, must recognize that race and ethnicity are not synonymous. Though race does not exist biologically, it does have an "essence" that relates to categorization from outside, the institution of racial hierarchy, and an ideology of othering (Bonilla-Silva 1999: 903). What is now necessary is for historical archaeologists to turn their attention to race and racialization.

Chapter 4
Archaeological Interpretation and the Practice of Race

The previous chapters demonstrate that archaeologists have long experience handling the concept of race, even though their understandings of this important social variable have changed over time. Many late nineteenth- and early twentieth-century archaeologists were inspired by the period's neophyte physical anthropologists, and so they tended to envision race as a biological objectivity with concrete, readily identifiable characteristics. Archaeologists, following the progressive intellectual leads of later anthropologists and sociologists, soon discovered that their conceptions of race were required to become increasingly sophisticated to have credibility and interpretive power within general social science. With the increased anthropologization of archaeology in the 1960s, however, many archaeologists interested in human variability turned away from race and began systematic examinations of past ethnicity. Historical archaeologists concomitantly developed their own interest in ethnicity and generally avoided race until the late 1980s and 1990s (see Orser 1998b, 2001d). Race is today developing as a topic of serious investigation by historical archaeologists (see, e.g., Franklin 2001; Orser 2001c), but it is still not a central focus of most long-term analysis.

The unambiguous interpretation of past ethnicity using archaeological materials has remained frustratingly elusive. Even with the aid of supplemental textual sources of information, most historical archaeologists' examinations of the relationships between ethnic affiliation and material culture have generally been less than entirely satisfactory. Many archaeologists at the beginning of the twenty-first century are diligently continuing their efforts to interpret ethnicity, and some are beginning to confront racialization as well. Today's social archaeologists acknowledge the copious data collected by physical anthropologists and readily recognize the fallacy of race as a biological reality. At the same time, they must admit that racialization has had in history—and continues to have in the present—a profound affect on human interaction.

Social archaeologists cannot afford to sustain the illusion that a universally supported method of interpreting racialization in archaeology can be devised immediately. At the same time, archaeologists interested in social theory must grant that the task is worth attempting, and thus must allow that the first step in the process of understanding is to concede that archaeologists, and especially archaeologists with recourse to text-based, supportive sources of information, at least have the potential to unravel the material and social dimensions of historical racialization. The pivotal question, of course, is precisely how this act of disentanglement is to be accomplished.

This chapter outlines a framework in which archaeologists may begin to make contributions to the investigation of modern-period racialization. To complete this task, we must explore a series of propositions and concepts that bear relation to the weaknesses proffered by the use of whole-cultural models, the avoidance of poverty as a topic of study, and the failure to employ a perspective that incorporates extra-site, network connections, which archaeologists often implement as a core-periphery model (see, e.g., Champion 1989; Chase-Dunn and Hall 1991). The development of an archaeology that can present useful interpretations about the historical nature of racialization must reach beyond these realms of investigation, because archaeologists must have an operative theoretical framework within which to conduct their analyses. Practice theory, an approach rapidly gaining adherents in the archaeological community, provides an elegant and powerful perspective for an archaeological effort to engage racialization.

Race, Power, Culture, and Hierarchy

The complex theoretical nature of racialization, coupled with its many historical faces, amply evinces the obstacles inherent in constructing an analytical framework that has archaeological relevance. One approach to confronting an archaeologically relevant notion of racialization is to begin by considering racism. This intellectual route, though it may initially appear slightly unusual, offers a conceptual base for an archaeological interpretation of race because of its overt concentration on the role of racialization in creating and maintaining systems of social stratification.

In an important essay, sociologist Eduardo Bonilla-Silva (1997) presents a structural theory of racism that is rooted in the concept of the racialized social system. According to Bonilla-Silva, the most prominent theories of race and racism incorporate the idea that racism exists as part of a personal, internalized belief system. This cognitive feature incorporates a doctrine of superiority as a matter of definitional necessity.

When racism is construed simply as a belief, it appears as an aberrant and irrational ideological construct. Individuals who express racist points of view appear to be somehow removed from society's mainstream, because they occupy a social space that is distinctly distant from the majority (at least nominally). History demonstrates that the internalization of a racist belief system can generate overt acts of racial oppression that truly do appear deviant. Such actions, which can run the gamut from subtle discrimination to the unspeakable horror of lynching, are judged by the majority to be abhorrent and criminal. Regardless of the infinite range of actions that can be employed to express racism, the racism-as-thought perspective maintains at its core the belief that racism is purely ideological. As race has no basis in human biology, racism can be nothing more than cognitive. Almost every perspective that incorporates racism-as-ideology adopts some social-psychological element at its base (Bonilla-Silva 1997: 466).

Two limitations of the ideological perspective have profound significance for social archaeological research. First, the adoption of the ideological construct effectively excludes racism from a social organization's structure. As a baseless, irrational belief, racism is utterly dependent upon other facets of the social order. In one reading, racism is epiphenomenal because it emerges from the psychology of class oppression. Being derivative, racism is thus not perceived as a central characteristic of the social order. Second, when racism is viewed as psychological, its perpetuation (and very existence) rests with individuals. Racism is thus attitudinal rather than structural. Individuals, not social institutions, are "racist" or "prejudiced." Racism is not constructed as an integral feature of the social organization's superstructure and once again appears as merely aberrant.

The understanding that racism is psychological leads to the application of a simple research methodology. To judge the amount of racism within any population, the researcher must simply conduct interviews with individuals within that social organization and then, using the amassed data, merely compute the percentage of racists within that population (i.e., as a function of those people who expressed racist sentiments). Thus, the members of population X can be judged to be more racist than the individuals in population Y if a greater percentage of X individuals make comments and express actions that equate intelligence, motivation, and attitudes with physical appearance or cultural background. Archaeologists can immediately judge the severe limitation of the ideological definition of racism when they consider the methodology required to capture it. As scholars who investigate defunct and relict sociohistorical formations, archaeologists have no ability to compile statements about personal attitudes on race. Even historical archaeologists attempting to employ a social-psychological methodology would quickly discover that the information they could obtain from written records would be extremely selective and sketchy.

Bonilla-Silva makes it abundantly clear that racism is much more than simply ideological. Racism creates action and affects practice. To circumvent the weaknesses inherent in the ideological notion of racism—and by extension, the construction of discrete human races—Bonilla-Silva (1997: 469–74) presents an alternative framework that is contingent on the perspective of racialized social systems (also see Bonilla-Silva 1999; Loveman 1999). Employing a structuralist framework, Bonilla-Silva models racist behavior as a set of practices that maintain institutional reality in the social system itself.

In Bonilla-Silva's view, the theoretical foundation of the process of racialization rests on the belief that the group in control of naming the various "races" is hierarchically dominant. Those individuals who are the subject of the dominant group's labels are subordinate. The creation of the social hierarchy—which is thus racially based—invents and defines social relations between the designated races (1997: 469). The individuals performing the naming tend to believe in (or at least tend to promote) the racial essence of their categories (typically with all the means within their control), usually employing physical and even cultural characteristics as racial markers (Smedley 1993: 32). Individuals deemed to belong to the nominally dominant race, but who are sympathetic to those who are dominated or who dispute the objective underpinnings of the racial designations, are often labeled "race traitors" (Ignatiev and Garvey 1996).

The historically constructed racial hierarchy carries with it serious implications, because the superordinate race has greater life chances than those judged to be racially inferior. The racialized social system—with its phenotypically or culturally based hierarchy—reproduces and reifies the established racial order, and all individuals, during their lifetimes, are assigned a racial identity whether or not they accept the designation (Omi and Winant 1983: 53). The structure of the hierarchy is not negated because some men and women can "pass" from one racial designation to another (Cox 1970: 430–31) or because some individuals may attempt to manipulate the racial order by having themselves legally declared to be a member of the socially identified superordinate race (Domínguez 1986: 1–5). In the final analysis, the theoretical basis of the racial hierarchy is relational, because each race stands in relation to the others in a truly dialectical fashion: to have meaning there must be "white" to stand in opposition to "black." The racial designations lose all social meaning in the absence of such dialectics.

The construction of racial hierarchies, like many elements of social organization, is fraught with considerations of power. The interests and aspirations of each designated race are shaped by the collective practices of the individuals as they struggle for power within the racialized social system. Significantly, the operation of race-based oppression does not imply that all other forms of oppression are negated or erased (Bonilla-Silva 1997: 470). Quite the contrary, other forms of oppression—class-based, gender-based—work alongside racism to reproduce a complex structure of oppression (see Franklin 2001: 110–11; Sacks 1989). In addition, the use of racial concepts, however constructed, produces reification as a social process (Brubaker and Cooper 2000: 5) that is inherently historically situated (Bonilla-Silva 1997: 470–71, 1999: 903). Frameworks of power thus constitute one avenue through which social analysts can begin to understand the historical performance of racialization, because the decisions about who is to be designed "white," "black," "red," "yellow," or whatever, reflect and affect the diverse elements of the struggle between the constituent "races" (Bonilla-Silva 1997: 472; Wolf 1999: 66).

Social scientists from diverse academic backgrounds have examined social power from many different perspectives, both theoretically and empirically, and have generated a huge literature on the subject (see, e.g., Adams 1975; Blau 1964; Boulding 1989; Lasswell and Kaplan 1950; Lenski 1966; Lukes 1974; Russell 1938; Wesolowski 1979; Wrong 1980). Classic theoretical sociologists (e.g., Mills 1959: 40–41; Weber 1963: 117–18) tend to view power as simply the ability of one person or group to obtain a certain outcome enacted by another person or group. Sociologists also tend to subdivide power into authority (legitimized power readily accepted by the obedient), manipulation (the subtle exercise of power unrecognized by the powerless), and domination (the ability to have a command obeyed without question). Given the breadth of research and subsequent interpretation, it is not surprising that power is "one of the most loaded and polymorphous words in our repertoire" (Wolf 1990: 586) and that "The concept of power is sociologically amorphous" (Weber 1968: 53). Even though scholars use the term in myriad ways, most of them agree that "power—seeking it, using it, abusing it, decrying it, coveting it, contesting and overthrowing it—is central to the human condition" (Lipman-Blumen 1994: 108). Human power relations also provide the basis for a racialized social structure, as men, women, and children are allocated to racial slots.

Archaeologists have been interested in power for several years, and many of them have investigated it from diverse angles using data sets too numerous to cite (but for recent works, see D'Altroy and Hastorf 2001; McAnany 2001; Sweely 1999). Power exists as a continuum that exhibits both historical specificity and broadly general properties (see Nowak 1983), but archaeologists have often conceptualized power as a simple distinction between "power to" (as in "to get something accomplished," that is, instruction, manipulation) as positive, and "power over" (as in "over others") as generally a negative force involving coercive domination (see Miller and Tilley 1984: 6; Orser 1996a: 175; Paynter and McGuire 1991: 11). "Power over" can be a coercive political tool that does not require the consent or acquiescence of those being dominated (Marquardt 1992: 106), but the idea that the dominated group will obey a command from above constitutes a classic sociological principle of power (Weber 1968: 53). "Power over" can also be hegemonic, achieved through consent rather that coercion (Bonilla-Silva 1997: 470). State-level organizations, with their codified laws, standing armies, police forces, and institutionalized bureaucracies, can even use their administrative power to assign categorical identities, including many that are properly considered racial (Brubaker and Cooper 2000: 15). The United States Census of 2000 presents a perfect example of how the state sought to assign racial identity along criteria they consciously created (Allen 2001; also see Kertzer and Arel 2002). Such efforts to objectify race—and thereby to fractionalize humanity—is a characteristic of a truly dominant political polity.

Dominated social groups can resist coercion, categorical assignment, or any other form of domination, but, as Marx and Engels (1970: 64–65) pointed out, the state can also create social distinctions that, when reified in practice, result in working-class divisions. Such often artificial classifications operate in contradistinction to ethnogenesis, a process that typically serves to unite individuals into self-identifying groups (Boswell and Dixon 1993: 685; Kurien 1994: 385). People labeled "subordinate" can of course renounce their classification, but when the superordinate group meets resistance from below, their "forces of coercion" struggle against the opposing "forces of resistance" and the outcome is always far from certain (Nowak 1983: 141–52; for archaeological examples of this process, see Frazer 1999). (For an important examination of the binary "master metaphor" of physical coercion and ideological persuasion—"power over"/"power to"—see Mitchell 1990.)

As Nowak (1983: 189–210) made abundantly clear, the degree of resistance that the subordinates express is directly proportionate to the extent of the domination. And as Bourdieu observed, the dominated within any sociohistorical formation can exert "a certain force," but in contradistinction to popular theories of resistance (e.g., Scott 1990), he argues that "the dominated seldom escape the antinomy of domination" (Bourdieu and Wacquant 1992: 80, 82). (For an uncritical acceptance of Scott's perspective in archaeology, see Hall 2000). Numerous sociologists have stressed that domination is distinct from power, and the most useful view of domination is that it occurs when rulers have the ability to interfere with the social relations among the ruled (Nowak 1983: 150–51). This is indeed a subtle distinction, but as can be surmised, the struggles that accompany a racialized social structure, or what Bonilla-Silva (1997: 473) terms "racial contestation," can take many forms. Race-based social action generally has as its final goal the institution of fundamental changes in the racialized social structure. In other words, the races judged to be subordinate seek to change their racial position in social space *relative to the other assigned races.* As Bourdieu (1998b: 56) notes, the dominant vision of the social order "has more often than not been imposed through struggles against competing visions." The struggle for the dominance of individuals deemed "white" occurred in many settings, over a number of years, and involved the interjection of frequently disreputable science.

The inherent interlinkage between the dominant and the dominated, the superior race and the inferior race(s), properly illustrates the significance of the network aspect of the racialized social order. To conceptualize the way in which power and domination relate to racialization and the invention of historically relevant social hierarchies, it helps to recognize that "the individual is born into an established network of people" and that the individual's "very person is a social phenomenon" (Wolf 2001: 2). The acceptance of a network structure of relations serves to track investigators away from the facile whole-culture perspective and toward a more nuanced, contextually embedded, network-based understanding of society. At a minimum, the acceptance of a network model—in which racialized peoples are relationally connected—allows archaeologists to conceptualize racialization in a way that has considerable interpretive potential.

The view that individuals arrange themselves in complex networks of interaction has a venerable history in formalized social science, extending at least to Durkheim's (1915: 426) view that "There is no people and no state which is not part of another society, more or less unlimited, which embraces all the peoples and all the states with which it first comes in contact, either directly or indirectly." Archaeologists have shown little interest in formal network theory (but see Orser 1996a; Trombold 1991), even though it has a long intellectual tradition with strong anthropological ties (see, e.g., Barnes 1972; Johnson 1994; Mitchell 1974; Schweizer 1997) . The reasons for this avoidance are unclear, but it may derive in part from the early association of formal network theory with the generally ahistorically inclined structural-functionalist cultural anthropologists (Scott 1991: 27–33). At variance with the essential synchronicity of much structural-functionalism, a network perspective permits archaeologists to conceptualize complex social realities like racialization because the assignment of groups to "races" is at its core a relational property of human involvement. A critical element of the network perspective is that it successfully and wholly negates the whole-culture because "neither societies nor cultures should be seen as givens, integrated by some inner essence, organizational mainspring, or master plan. Rather, cultural sets, and sets of sets, are continuously in construction, deconstruction, and reconstruction, under the impact of multiple processes operative over wide fields of social and cultural connections" (Wolf 1984: 396).

The use of a network perspective is only one element that will assist social archaeologists in their analyses of the racialized social systems of the past. Practice theory, as it originally emerged and is now being expanded and refined, provides another powerful avenue for an archaeological inquiry of race when linked with the relational vision of network theory.

Networks

Social scientists typically employ the term "social network" in one of two ways: in a metaphorical sense—in saying, for example, that a group of people interact in a complex manner that resembles a network—and in a more analytical sense to refer to interpersonal connections that can be measured and assessed (Barnes 1972: 1). Thus, when Georg Simmel (1955) referred to the "web of group-affiliations," he was actually using the network concept in a loose, metaphorical sense to model individual and group interconnection. On the other hand, when sociologists employ experimental methods to measure relational cohesion and power (Lawler and Yoon 1996), they are using "social network" in the second, more analytically rigorous sense. Both perspectives, however, incorporate the same characteristics when they model the idealized social network:

1. an overarching use of relational concepts and processes as a fundamental component of analysis;
2. an understanding that actors and their actions are interdependent rather than autonomous;
3. a view that the linkages between actors are channels for the flow of material and nonmaterial resources; and
4. an acknowledgment that network models conceptualize structure as the lasting patterns of relations between the actors (Wasserman and Faust 1994: 4).

Network analysts focus their attention on the interactions between individuals and social groups, and typically refer to the associations as the "relations that connect the social positions within a system" (Knoke and

Kuklinski 1982: 10). Network theorists have devised several sophisticated tools for measuring the dimensions of specific networks (see, e.g., Scott 1991; Wasserman and Faust 1994).

Much network analysis is conducted within sociological and social-psychological disciplinary environments and traditions, and involves the study of individuals whose actions and interactions can be directly observed and evaluated. Accordingly, most of the major assessment instruments used in social network analysis—questionnaires, interviews, behavioral experiments, and observations—have no archaeological relevance. Even archaeologists who employ oral interviewing as part of their research methodology would have little or no direct access to the actual operation of past social network relations through the comments of modern-day informants.

The inability of archaeologists to observe social networks in action does not mean that social network analysis in archaeology is impossible. In fact, many archaeologists can conduct social network analysis because of the availability of historical records. Many network theorists have successfully used archival sources to obtain information about human interaction in the past (Wasserman and Faust 1994: 50–51). Past social links can be discerned from a careful assessment of newspaper accounts, court records, journal articles, official documents, and many other kinds of historical records (Burt and Lin 1977). Network analysts can use historical records to construct time series that extend into periods for which individuals are not available for interviewing and direct observation. Historical records can also increase the sample size of the individuals who interact within a social network and expand the temporal parameters of investigation.

Textually based sources can also provide indispensable structural information about extinct social networks. Three brief examples, though not indicative of practice theory, can be used solely to demonstrate the importance of historical materials for the analysis of defunct social networks and to reinforce the idea that the use and evaluation of historical records is a staple of research in modern-world and other text-rich archaeologies.

In their analysis of early fifteenth-century Florence, John Padgett and Christopher Ansell (1993) investigate the way in which Cosimo de' Medici was able to seize control of the Florentine Renaissance state in 1434. They refer to their investigation as "an archaeological dig" designed to reveal the inner workings of the elite Florentine social network (Padgett and Ansell 1993: 1265).

History indicates that the Florentine state was in political and cultural turmoil during the late fourteenth century as an unsuccessful class revolt helped to consolidate power in the hands of a marriage-allied oligarchy.

Cosimo de' Medici—a shrewd manipulator who employed multiple personas in his daily activities and associations—was quickly able to rise to power within the elite group. Network relations were the foundation that supported the Medici empire, and the dynasty he created remained powerful for three hundred years.

Using the available historical evidence, Padgett and Ansell (1993: 1265–66) were able to reconstruct nine types of relationships that operated among the elite families of Florence: (1) a marriage link; (2) four economic ties (trading/business, joint ownership/partnership, bank employment, and real estate connections); (3) two political/economic links (patronage and personal loans); and (4) two personal friendship relationships (personal friendship and surety—a bond used to guarantee the good behavior of an exile). The actions pursued by members of the elite families were framed within the web of networks created by these complex personal partnerships.

Padgett and Ansell used information about 92 Florentine families, and assessed the way the Medicis manipulated the social environment in their rise to prominence. They learned that the network strategies employed by the Medicis were more diversified than were those of other elite families. In terms of friendship and marriage, for instance, they discovered that the Medicis were more introspective and careful in their selection of friends and marriage partners than were other elite families. In terms of economics, the Medicis were more willing than their upper class associates to interact with the "new men"—individuals who, like the Medicis, had risen from the middle class. Put another way, "old money" elites were less willing to associate with nouveau riche individuals than were the Medicis. The Medicis also established additional links with their economic and marriage partners that involved personal loans and patronage. Thus, while the old elite failed even to acknowledge the new men, the Medicis' attention to them—through a multiplex, overlapping network—created "an awesomely centralized patrimonial machine, capable of great discipline and 'top down' control because the Medici themselves were the only bridge holding this contradictory agglomeration together" (Padgett and Ansell 1993: 1285).

In a second study, Roger Gould (1996) investigated the role of patron-client connections in the Whiskey Rebellion of 1794. Localized in Pennsylvania's westernmost counties, the Whiskey Rebellion was organized to resist the imposition of a federal excise tax on the production of spirits. The government of Pennsylvania had implemented its own tax years earlier, but both passive and active resistance from the citizenry had effectively eliminated it. When rebellious western Pennsylvanians attempted a brief armed resistance against paying the new federally mandated tax, President Washington ordered federal troops to march against them. The rebels were cowed by the show of governmental force and the Whiskey Rebellion came to an inglorious end.

Gould noticed an intriguing paradox in his reading of the historical chronicle that detailed the events of the rebellion. The increased financial burden of the federal tax effectively meant that individuals who were once small producers of whiskey had to purchase spirits when they could no longer afford to manufacture them. The increased demand put more economic capital in the pockets of the largest producers—who were also the wealthiest landowners—because they were the individuals who could afford to remit the increased tax. The large landowners were thus largely unaffected by the burden of the tax. Still, many of them were also the individuals who were prominently engaged in organizing the resistance. Historians who initially attempted to understand the rebellion could not solve the paradox of the large landowners' complicity, so most interpreters simply retreated to an understanding that rested on an unsupported socio-psychological/ethnic interpretation. The roots of the Whiskey Rebellion were thus seen to lie in the democratic frontier spirit expressed by Scots-Irish immigrants who maintained a cultural tradition of animosity toward tax collectors (Gould 1996: 407). Not willing to accept this ideological non-explanation, Gould decided to conduct a network analysis using the official records compiled during the rebellion itself.

Consulting records that spanned the 1781–94 period, Gould compiled a sample of 45 members of the local elite, men who were defined by having held public offices on the local, state, and federal levels. In order to run for political office in early Pennsylvania, a candidate had to find someone (and often more than one person) who was willing to post a surety bond on his behalf. These bonds allowed for the reimbursement of any funds lost by the officeholder during his tenure in office and served as a hedge against liability. Since the bonds could reach as high as £1,000, the posting of a surety in someone's else's name was a serious matter. At a minimum, the surety created a strong social bond between the political candidate and the surety provider.

Gould's analysis of the historical records indicate that many of the members of the elite were connected—in a patron-client network— through the payment of sureties. Three distinct cohorts existed within the network, each of which occupied a different structural position in the patronage hierarchy: ten men who only posted bonds for others, six who posted bonds and had bonds posted for them, and eleven who posted no bonds but rather only had them posted on their behalf (Gould 1996: 419). The men in the first cohort can be considered true patrons because they accepted no surety bonds from anyone; everyone else in the network is a client. Significantly, however, seventeen men composed a fourth group of individuals who did not post surety for anyone else and who held public offices for which no surety was posted. The men who were not linked into the patron-client network—notably the seventeen isolates—were in the most danger of political exclusion when the federal government exerted its pressure during the rebellion. This group existed outside the patronage network and provided most of the rebel leaders. Gould's (1993: 423–24) analysis thus suggests that an individual's participation in the patronage network—rather than his or her economic position—appears to provide the best predictor for whether a wealthy landowner would have been involved in the Whiskey Rebellion. This interpretation was impossible without the insights offered by network analysis.

In a third study, Karen Barkey and Ronan Van Rossem (1997) examined another rebellion, this one a more subtle uprising that occurred in seventeenth-century Anatolia. Their investigation focused on peasant contention, but rather than concentrating on the collective dispute between distinct groups—the typical focus of most studies of mass protest—Barkey and Van Rossem concentrated on locally based village networks, community organization, and the location of villages within the vicinity of Manisa, a large administrative center. Barkey and Van Rossem learned that the small farmers in their Anatolian study area did not employ strategies that included collective, violent protest, as did many small farmers in Western Europe at the same time. The farmers of the Ottoman Empire instead usually chose individual forms of action, and frequently took their concerns to the courts rather than to the streets. The highly formalized judicial route to conflict resolution provided documentation for the peasants' claims.

Barkey and Van Rossem compiled a data set composed of 190 court cases heard in the 1650–1654 period. They discovered that the court records contained a rich reservoir of relational (intra- and inter-village) information about each case's claimants and defendants. Their data set was accordingly gleaned from the records along two relational vectors: content and identity. Barkey and Van Rossem were also able to describe three relational contents that embodied, in turn, conflict, cooperation, and neutrality. Conflict relations obtained where individuals were placed in adversarial positions. These relations typically involved plaintiffs and defendants, but other individuals could be drawn into the relation as well. Cooperative relations appeared when two or more people collaborated against a third party. In this instance, the adversarial dyad of the conflictual relation merely added a cooperative relation to the network matrix. Neutral relations were enacted in cases where neither conflict nor cooperation obtained, and in cases where individuals mentioned in the records were simply observers of the other two relations. The range of specific identities that operated within the relations—as represented in the court records— was enormous, but the most significant relations were based on kinship, friendship, acquaintanceship, trade, and patron-client links. The relations Barkey and Van Rossem identified also linked villages together using two content networks and three identity networks.

Barkey and Van Rossem analyzed the multirelational networks presented in the court records using a well-known approach in formal network theory called the blockmodel technique (see Wasserman and Faust 1994: 394–97). One element of blockmodel analysis is that it partitions actors in the network into subsets called "positions." Using this technique, Barkey and Van Rossem (1997: 1364–69) identified four blocks or positions of villages that were structurally similar. Their analysis revealed that villages located near the center of the region (as defined by the location of Manisa) and those that were isolated were not prone to contention. Individuals living in villages situated in the intermediate zone, however, were more apt to engage in contention. Strife in these villages was usually expressed through weak social ties where the identity relation hinged on mere acquaintanceship. Stronger kinship and friendship links characterized the noncontentious cases. Barkey and Van Rossem (1997: 1371–76) posited that their findings indicate that the peasants who lived in the intermediate villages experienced the greatest impact from the many sociohistorical changes that were being wrought in the seventeenth century. The people's regional position meant that they were more exposed to increased national and international competition at the same time that the state was seeking to increase their tax burden. In response to such pressures, the peasants were forced to begin growing new crops—rice, cotton, and sesame—for national and international markets. Instead of choosing to riot, the Ottoman peasants selected forms of contention that were sanctioned by the state. Everyday interaction, through cross-cutting intra- and inter-village networks, nurtured both conflict and cooperation.

These three examples illustrate the use of formal network theory and are presented here for two reasons. First, each study demonstrates the seminal role historical documents can play in investigating the nature and content of relations in social situations where it is no longer possible to interview participants or to observe them in action within social networks. Not all historical record sets contain relational information, to be sure, but many collections do include such information if the analyst is willing to extract it. The possibility that such information exists means that archaeologists intent on any kind of network analysis cannot discount textual information without first evaluating it for meaningful sociological information. Second, the three studies summarized above portray the profound significance social networks have in the operation of society.

Overtly accepting a network perspective allows investigators to acknowledge that human beings produce relations in order to live, that interconnections between individual men, women, and children do not simply happen by accident (Godelier 1988: 1). The "warp and weft of humans' interactive nets are constantly being changed as if by an overly fussy weaver" (Orser 1996a: 33). Network analysis thus appears to provide a rich body of theory and method for the further refinement of a social archaeology that truly combines sociological perspectives and techniques with data that are usually considered archaeological.

With the exception of ethnoarchaeologists, archaeologists do not have the ability to see interactions actually happening. As a result, perhaps the most important question for archaeologists rests on how they can use the overarching, foundational ideas of social network analysis in their investigations of past social situations. For present purposes, another central question is: where does racialization enter in? The three historic network studies outlined above suggest that the perception of race can easily constitute an identity relation, when two actors develop a conflictual or cooperative dyadic connection and when they interact as if they are members of different races. Racial consciousness can obviously help to structure the resultant relational matrix. But simply making this claim does not help archaeologists move toward conceptualizing race in the past. Fortunately, sociological practice theory can significantly advance the archaeological interpretation of historical race.

Practice Theory

The concept of practice theory for understanding human social interaction has had a long germination period, being noted by Marx (1983: 155) in 1845 in his "Theses on Feuerbach":

The chief defect of all previous materialism (including Feuerbach's) is that the object, reality, what we apprehend through our senses, is understood only in the form of *object* or *contemplation*; but not as *sensuous human activity*, as *practice*; not subjectively. Hence in opposition to materialism the *active* side was developed abstractly by idealism, which of course does not know real sensuous activity as such. (emphasis in original; also see Marx and Engels 1970: 58)

In keeping with a major scholarly trend in political economy at the time, Marx became overwhelmed with focusing on production, and he never truly designed a practice theory as such. The task of developing such an explicit and usable theory of practice, however, was completed in the late twentieth century by French sociologist Pierre Bourdieu.

Practice theory has increasingly begun to find its way into contemporary archaeological thought. The route for recognizing the potential utility of practice theory has often been through "agency theory," even though practice theory is not agency theory (Pauketat 2000: 114). Arguably the greatest conceptual problem with agency theory, as social analysts currently construct and pursue it, is that few individuals agree on a precise meaning of "agency." This theoretical deficiency is particularly acute in archaeology, as different practitioners employ an often weakly designed concept of agency in their analyses of the past (see Dobres and Robb 2000b).

The conceptual variation that has accompanied the term "agency" in archaeology has had the practical implication that "agency" has come to mean "anything that a person consciously or unconsciously does." Viewed in this light, agency is everything archaeologists find interesting, and so being transformed into everything, it becomes nothing. When agency is viewed as dynamic human action, the philosophical roots of agency can justifiably be understood to constitute a substantial element of the pedigree of Western philosophical thought. Agency studies thus can be perceived as having a significant archaeological heritage because, under the loosest of definitions, archaeologists have been studying agency for many years. In being broadly conceptualized, agency becomes "universalized and decontextualized" (Gero 2000: 37–38), and in some cases, even archaeologists claiming to use agency theory are not actually doing so (see Pauketat 2001: 79).

Agency theory thus appears to lack a clear body of thought and a unique perspective that archaeologists can use to provide new insights about past sociohistorical formations. Of course, it is possible to perceive the variance in the conceptualization of agency to be advantageous to postmodern analysis, but because it is so diverse in meaning, it becomes much too easy to apply to every possible human action. The urge merely to reconstruct a new image of the past, but simply with a new jargon, is always present in archaeology. Within the vast milieu of theoretical constructs that currently exist, however, practice theory appears to offer an enlightening avenue for examining race and racialization in past sociohistorical formations. But it must be made clear that diverse readings of practice theory are possible (see, e.g., Le Hir 2000; Lovell 2000).

Timothy Pauketat (2000, 2001) has emerged as one of the most erudite proponents of the application of practice theory in archaeology. So strong is his belief in the interpretative power it offers that he argues that its application is inventing a new paradigm in archaeological theory called "historical processualism." As a counterpoint to the interpretive power of practice theory, he offers a concise assessment of the three most prominent approaches used by archaeologists at the beginning of the twenty-first century—neo-Darwinism, cognitive processualism, and agency theory. Pauketat argues that archaeologists in each intellectual camp have all engaged the notion of human agency, but that none of them have fully embraced actual agency. He argues, for example, that "selectionist" neo-Darwinists have engaged agency by choosing largely to ignore it, while "individualist" neo-Darwinians have acknowledged its importance, but have only imbued a few socially prominent individuals with the ability to sway others to follow their lead. "Transmissionist" neo-Darwinists employ agency theory the most successfully, but in a mostly reductionist fashion, ultimately proposing that human agents are constrained by their cultural rules. People's practices simply give expression to their traditions.

Pauketat (2001: 79–80) convincingly argues that any archaeology that employs some notion of behavior is, in effect, distancing itself from a view that the creation of history is situationally constructed. Human action without practice becomes a scientific project composed of goal-directed performances reduced to a series of discrete "behaviors." The behaviors, thus reified, can be linked with ease to nationalized whole-cultures, in effect becoming synonymous with them (e.g., South 1977). Pauketat proposes to install practice theory in the place of such essentializing perspectives. Drawing on the work of practice theorists, including Bourdieu, he argues that human action—that is, practice—is the product of certain dispositions that are neither goal-directed nor a priori givens. Archaeologists adopting this perspective of practice can envision history as "the process of cultural construction through practice" (Pauketat 2001: 87). History is thus neither a series of cultural stages to be progressed through nor the expression of a preordained sequence. History is, quite simply, a web of human actions. The practice view of history creation allows Pauketat (2000: 115) to define practice theory as "the continuous and historically contingent enactments or embodiments of people's ethos, attitudes, agendas, and dispositions."

Pauketat (2000, 2001) uses his research at the Mississippian center of Cahokia to illustrate the power of practice theory. He argues against any understanding of the polity's development and persistence that installs as part of the interpretation the population's demographic profile, the incipient power of the elites, the richness of the natural environment before the polity's creation, or any other agent that was external to the practice of actual humans going about the business of constructing history on a daily basis. Some archaeologists have employed political power as a key attribute to posit that Cahokia's largest mound—Monks Mound—was constructed on the orders of the powerful to legitimate their exalted social positions. A temple atop a high mound would signal, both architecturally and symbolically, the power of the elites as literally "standing above" everyone else. But as Pauketat (2000: 118–20) asserts, Monks Mound was not built as an example of monumental architecture. Archaeological excavation reveals that the people of Cahokia raised the mound through a series of discrete practices that involved the concomitant establishment of new buildings with each act of construction. A practice perspective thus implores archaeologists to envision earthen-mound construction not as a *consequence* of a cultural process, but *as* a cultural process. The locus of change rests within the practice of tradition in such a way that different actions produce different history.

Pauketat further argues that the enactment of tradition is a collective element of life rather than a truly individual pursuit. A focus on group positions in place of individual placement is indeed a prominent feature of practice theory. Pauketat's view, however, must be conceptualized as a practical consideration for those archaeologists working without the benefit of textual sources of information, because of the improbability of clearly identifying individual action except in the rarest of circumstances. (This practical difficulty is a corollary of the problem of attempting to adopt full-scale social network analysis in archaeology.) The presence of textual sources of information makes possible, in the archaeology of the modern era, a further elaboration of the practices of individuals within past social networks of action. The presence of textual sources for much modern-world archaeology means, I believe, that these archaeologists often have the option of asking different questions from those of their colleagues who investigate ancient, non-textual history, simply because of the presence of an often diverse and frequently abundant body of supplemental evidence. It may be true that any segmentation of archaeology into neatly defined subsets is intellectually untenable, and that all archaeologists engaged in practice analysis examine the way in which traditions were employed to create history (Pauketat 2001: 87). These points are well taken when conceptualizing practice theory, and the linkages between text-aided and non-text-aided archaeologies deserve further contemplation. At this point, however, it appears that archaeologists of the modern era *at least have the potential* to create somewhat richer expositions of practice theory, if for no other reason than that they often have access to the observations of actors directly engaged in the historical processes being examined with archaeological data.

Many archaeologists who have explored the use of agency theory in their research, including Pauketat, probably discovered practice theory through two—possibly connected—routes: the assessment of the theory by cultural anthropologists (see, e.g., Friedman 1994: 148–49; Miller 1987: 147–57; Ortner 1984: 144–57), or the pertinent works of mostly European sociologists. As part of this process of exploration, it was inevitable that archaeologists would encounter the writings of Pierre Bourdieu, the most influential of the practice theorists. Though some archaeologists have referenced Bourdieu's early ethnographic research in Algeria among the Kabyle (for recent citations see, e.g., Allison 1999:

9; Earle 2001: 109; Goldberg 1999: 157; Thomas 1999: 45), the archaeological engagement with Bourdieu's theoretical pronouncements usually led archaeologists directly to his concept of "habitus."

Habitus

Many archaeologists were originally drawn to Bourdieu's notion of habitus because it appeared to provide more interpretive freedom than any teleological notion of behavior (Pauketat 2001: 79–80). But even though some archaeologists did offer early and generally sympathetic readings of Bourdieu (see Hodder 1986: 70–75; for general comments, also see Shanks and Tilley 1987: 128, 1988: 108, 113), it remains true that "The sociology of Pierre Bourdieu has never been fully applied to archaeology" (Glørstad 2000: 185). Archaeologists, like scholars in other disciplines (Wacquant 1992: 4–5), have tended to focus only on one or two of Bourdieu's works, ignoring those that do not appear immediately pertinent, even when they contain abundant restatement and reformulation of Bourdieu's essential points. The process of selective exclusion has generally characterized the archaeological use of Bourdieu's notion of habitus, as archaeologists have either merely referenced habitus in passing or have simply accepted it as a synonym for "activity" (see, e.g., Arnold 2000; Blanton 1994: 9–10; Cowgill 2000; Joyce 2000; Lawrence 1999: 137; Schiffer 1999: 22; Thomas 1996: 48; Wilkie 2000).

Many archaeologists who have used Bourdieu's concept of habitus in passing have effectively transformed it into the "theoretical deus ex machina" that Bourdieu himself has been accused of providing with the concept itself (DiMaggio 1979: 1464). In misreading habitus, some archaeologists have reformed it as a kind of socialization with a new name (Jones 1997: 88; Wilkie 2000) and in so robbing it of its theoretical substance have recreated habitus as a caricature of itself. Such loose users of habitus have in essence transformed the concept into an updated whole-culture, imbuing it with the same powers of mystification. Even with the obvious shortcoming, inculcated in the misuse of habitus, the word is familiar in archaeology but, as is true of many disciplines including sociology, it is "far from well understood" (Swartz 1997: 96). The key is to understand the essence of habitus as a route toward theory building in archaeology rather than as a reified essence that can be applied verbatim to every sociohistorical situation (Pauketat 2001: 79). The goal is to use the habitus concept, not merely to apply it.

It would be disingenuous to argue that habitus is an easy concept to grasp. Part of the problem with deciphering the exact meaning of the term undoubtedly resides in the problems inherent in the transnational adoption of a text originally written for a French academic tradition.

Bourdieu (1993a; Bourdieu and Wacquant 1992: 169) himself readily acknowledged this problem (also see Brubaker 1993; Simeoni 2000). Archaeologists and other scholars who have explicitly used habitus in their research (e.g., Jones 1997: 88) have typically reproduced Bourdieu's definition from *Outline of a Theory of Practice*:

The structures constitutive of a particular type of environment (e.g., the material conditions of existence characteristic of a class condition) produce *habitus*, systems of durable, transposable *dispositions*, structured structures predisposed to function as structuring structures, that is, as principles of the generation and structuring of practices and representations which can be objectively 'regulated' and "regular" without in any way being the product of obedience to rules, objectively adapted to their goals without presupposing a conscious aiming at ends or an express mastery of the operations necessary to attain them and, being all this, collectively orchestrated without being the product of the orchestrating action of a conductor. (1977b: 72)

Bourdieu later restated this definition in slightly clearer language in *The Logic of Practice*:

The conditionings associated with a particular class of conditions of existence produce *habitus*, systems of durable, transposable dispositions, structured structures predisposed to function as structuring structures, that is, as principles which generate and organize practices and representations that can be objectively adapted to their outcomes without presupposing a conscious aiming at ends or an express mastery of the operations necessary in order to attain them. Objectively "regulated" and "regular" without being in any way the product of obedience to rules, they can be collectively orchestrated without being the product of the organizing action of a conductor. (1990b: 53)

One must adopt classic hermeneutics to obtain a clear understanding of these definitions because their complexity far outweighs their length (105 words in the first version, 96 in the second). Disassembly can illustrate the significance the habitus concept holds for social archaeology in general and for the archaeological interpretation of race specifically. It is necessary to note at the outset—and his various definitions substantiate this—that Bourdieu slowly transformed the cognitive and normative demeanor of habitus into a practical and contextualized understanding of action (Swartz 1997: 102).

The conditions associated with a particular class of conditions of existence. This opening phrase in Bourdieu's definition promotes the historicity of a habitus. Though Bourdieu maintained an uneasy relationship with Marx—variously accepting and rejecting his ideas (Calhoun 1993: 67–68, 1995: 138–42; Lane 2000: 23; Swartz 1997: 39–40, 153)—we may interpret the initial phrase of his definition as reminiscent of Marx's (1970: 20) "material conditions of life" and Engels' (1974: 175) argument that people "must first of all eat, drink, have shelter and clothing" before they can make history. Additionally, Engels' (1974: 175) comment that historical materialism placed history "on its real basis" could just as easily be said about habitus. As Bourdieu (1990b: 54) phrased it: "The habitus, a product of history, produces individual and collective practices—more history—in accordance with the schemes generated by history." Practice theory weaves together individual moments of practice, precisely contextualized in time and space, and in the process "makes perfect history" (Pauketat 2001: 87). Bourdieu allows that interpersonal human action is "pregnant with the whole history" of the individuals themselves and of their relationships (Bourdieu and Wacquant 1992: 124), but openly rejects the application of any sort of meta-periodicity in historical analysis. His anti-teleologic understanding also makes it impossible to accept that late twentieth-century neoliberalism was as inevitable as its proponents have claimed (Bourdieu 1998a: 30). For Bourdieu (1990a: 41–42), as for archaeologists, social reality is inherently historical to the point that it is absurd to attempt to deny the significance of time. A habitus without history is impossible.

Durable, transposable dispositions. Bourdieu's concept of "dispositions" provides a key element of the habitus. The word "disposition" is meant to convey the idea that "choices do not derive directly from the objective situations in which they occur or from transcending rules, norms, patterns, and constraints that govern social life" (Swartz 1997: 100). Rather, actions develop from "practical dispositions" that incorporate the many inconsistencies and uncertainties encountered when acting within temporal and spatial contexts. The dispositions are indeed historical (in a sense of being accretionally created over time), but they are not necessarily operationalized in response to rules and norms. In an earlier definition of habitus, Bourdieu (1971: 83) noted that dispositions integrate past experience as "a matrix of perceptions, appreciations, and actions." In this sense, the habitus shares many characteristics with Robert Park's (1950) concept of "rote learning," and with Gramsci's (1971: 419) notion of "common sense" (for applications of common sense, see, e.g., Silverman 2001; Thompson 1993: 10–11).

Bourdieu's use of "disposition" allows that two components are central to the habitus: structure and propensity (Swartz 1997: 102–3). Habitus initially results from the early socialization process in which a person learns to internalize the external structures of life. These invented frameworks are analogous to the "epochal structures" of reformed historical materialism (Donham 1999) and the "vertical classifications" of sociology (Williams 1990). The parameters of the possible and impossible are durable—they last through time—and they are transposable—they can be analogically transferred from situation to situation. But because Bourdieu tends to foreground class position in his analyses of contemporary French society, the boundaries of the dispositions are related to the stratified position of the socialized. The internalized dispositions are formed in such a way that they correlate to aspirations, and in this manner, the dispositions both structure and are structured.

The idea that all individuals in a social position inculcate the habitus is a controversial element of Bourdieu's framework. How many of the dispositions are interchangeable as a person moves through history? Ethnographic observation suggests, for example, that individuals—particularly those facing intense intercultural contact—can adopt elements of more than one habitus (Miller 1994: 298). Based on such empirical evidence, it must be allowed that the habitus represents an array of dispositions, some of which may even appear to be contradictory. Accordingly, therefore, the habitus—rather than representing a cognitive whole—may be structured as a set of bits and pieces, partial connections between people and things (Strathern 1991).

Part of the ambiguity in the habitus concept derives from Bourdieu's hints that it does not govern all human behavior. The habitus may recede into the background in specific sociohistorical situations in which codified rules govern practice (Bourdieu 1977b: 20). Highly ritualized contexts may limit, though not totally eliminate, opportunities for active innovation as individuals correlate their actions with societal norms (Swartz 1997: 113). Bourdieu cites as an example of the lessened importance of the habitus the long-distance marriage alliances enacted among the Kabyle. He states that the intention of such marriage is purely political, with the participating woman serving merely as an operative tool. Being political rather than purely kin-oriented, the ritualized marriage ceremony is carefully regulated and profoundly significant. In fact, "The stakes are so high and the chances of a rift so great that the agents dare not rely entirely on the regulated improvisation of orchestrated habitus" (Bourdieu 1990b: 182). Cases where the habitus is largely unimportant appear in other situations. For example, the habitus will not play much of a role in the formalized, rule-governed diplomacy that operates between modern states (Swartz 1997: 113). The habitus is most effective in situations where weak or nonexistent rules apply and where the learned dispositions can quietly govern action (Bourdieu 1990b: 145).

Structured structures and structuring structures. For Bourdieu, the process of socialization creates an understanding of what is possible and what is not possible for individuals within a specific social position. Inherent in the habitus is a "system of circular relations that unite *structures* and *practices*" (Bourdieu and Passeron 1977: 203; emphasis in original). The habitus "tends to reproduce those actions, perceptions and attitudes consistent with the conditions under which it was produced" (Swartz 1997: 103).

Bourdieu's conception of habitus as incorporating dispositions as both structured and structuring centralizes power, because not all courses of action are open to all people. As Bourdieu (1990b: 64) phrases it:

The relation to what is possible is a relation to power; and the sense of the probable future is constituted in the prolonged relationship with a world structured according to the categories of the possible (for us) and the impossible (for us), of what is appropriated in advance by and for others and what one can reasonably expect for oneself.

Power for Bourdieu is "power in relational terms" (Wolf 1999: 5), and a key focus of all of Bourdieu's research concerns the manner in which inequalities of power and social privilege are sustained through generations without conscious recognition or full-scale revolt (Swartz 1997: 190). Some of the power that Bourdieu mentions is more clearly defined as domination.

Bourdieu's notion of power helps to explain his interest in the formalized educational practices of modern France. While the educational system there, as in the United States, may be advertised as a structured method for reducing social inequality, in actuality the educational system has precisely the opposite role. Course content, testing procedures, the language employed and encouraged, and the pedagogic emphases all favor the socially dominant. The reproduction of the educational system reinforces and is reinforced by the attitudes and aspirations of the individuals within the various social positions in the educational field (Bourdieu 1977a; Bourdieu and Passeron 1977; also see Collins 1993).

Capital and Field

It is virtually impossible to understand fully the significance of the habitus without also grasping the importance of Bourdieu's linked concepts of capital and field. Archaeologists who have relied almost exclusively on Bourdieu's early work, most notably *Outline of a Theory of Practice*, have often underestimated or entirely ignored capital and field because Bourdieu tended to emphasize these two social elements more than habitus in his later works (Swartz 1997: 118). In *Distinction*, however, Bourdieu could not be clearer about the need to include capital and field in his analytical framework, even going so far as to provide a formula demonstrating this importance: "[(habitus) (capital)] + field = practice" (1984: 101).

Bourdieu's statements on capital demonstrate both his acceptance of, and at the same time his break with, Marx. While Bourdieu accepts the importance of economic capital in social life, he extends it to cover all forms of social power. Reminiscent of Marx (1954: 42–43), Bourdieu

(1986: 241) argues that capital is "accumulated labor (in its materialized form or its 'incorporated,' embodied form) which, when appropriated on a private, i.e., exclusive basis by agents or groups of agents, enables them to appropriate social energy in the form of reified or living labor." Bourdieu speaks of capital "accumulating," of individuals using capital to produce "profits," and of capital's ability to generate "interest." Human labor becomes embodied, largely in disguise, as economic capital (which can be converted into currency and objectified in property and property rights); cultural capital (which consists of many factors including educational training that may be converted into economic capital by obtaining a high-paying job based on one's education or class position), social capital (composed of network connections and also convertible into economic capital), and symbolic capital (legitimation). A key element for Bourdieu is how individuals and groups obtain and employ various forms of capital in diverse social situations. The distribution of the different kinds of capital is capable of conferring degrees of power and strength on various individuals within a sociohistoric formation (Skeggs 1997: 8). Given this formulation, it is no exaggeration to claim that Bourdieu's perspective represents an expanded labor theory of value (Beasley-Murray 2000; Swartz 1997: 74), a staple of Marxian analysis when examined from its economic side. Being a sociologist rather than an economist, however, Bourdieu's interests rest largely on the creation, manifestations, and practice of cultural, social, and symbolic capitals. His concern to broaden the concept of capital beyond economics—a concept that was not truly foreign to Marx (see Bloch 1985: 23; Godelier 1988: 50–51)—allows him to move the analysis of capital from strictly capitalist sociohistorical formations to cultures that are decidedly non-capitalist in orientation.

Bourdieu's (1986: 248–52) idea of social capital is fundamentally attached to concepts of social networks because it constitutes the actual or potential resources that can be marshaled in such a way as to be credentialed (also see Lin 2001). A socially important family name, a class affiliation, or membership in a prominent clan, lineage, or yacht club provides collective capital to all those individuals with that social credential. The volume of social capital that is possessed by a specific individual is founded on the size of the network connections that individual can effectuate and on the volume of the other capital the individual possesses. In this sense, social capital is never independent, because it has its constituent base within a socially defined group structure.

The network of relations that an individual or group maintains is, in Bourdieu's (1986: 249) terms, "the product of investment strategies, individual and collective, consciously or unconsciously aimed at establishing or reproducing social relationships that are directly usable in the short or long term." The accumulation of social capital is thus a form of labor that can be accomplished through an infinite number of practices, but which in the final analysis must include "an unceasing effort of sociability, a continuous series of exchanges in which recognition is endlessly affirmed and reaffirmed" (Bourdieu 1986: 250). The process of acquiring capital is how humans make history.

For Bourdieu (1986: 243), cultural capital exists in three states. It can be "embodied," meaning that it occurs as the sustained, durable dispositions of the habitus; it can be "objectified" or exist in the form of cultural goods like oil paintings, books, dictionaries, musical instruments, computers, and so forth; and it can be "institutionalized," as in the case of educational affiliations that are designed to bestow social prestige. Objectified and institutionalized cultural capital can be purchased, but embodied cultural capital cannot. In other words, individuals who have acquired wealth through their own unique striving or through the serendipitous coincidence of conscious strategy and uncontrollable outside factors (overnight dot-com millionaires and lottery winners, for instance) cannot simply acquire cultural capital through instantaneous purchase. They can inculcate cultural capital into habitus, but this process takes time and is thus historical. Recently made millionaires can seek to increase their store of cultural capital through objectified and institutionalized means. The building of large monuments in one's personal honor, the construction of skyscrapers bearing one's name, or an act of philanthropy with the caveat that the endowment or the hospital wing must bear one's name are all examples of objectified cultural capital. An important characteristic of objectified cultural capital with real implications for archaeologists is that this kind of capital has the potential to exist for centuries and to become recontextualized as new forms of objectified cultural capital. Cahokia, now a state historical park, perfectly illustrates the process of capital recontextualization. Modern-world archaeologists often encounter recontextualized cultural capital at historic homes or properties that have been purchased by historical or preservation societies and then renamed after the donor who provided the funds for the purchase. Institutionalized cultural capital can be purchased by enrolling oneself or one's children in prestigious day care centers, schools, academies, colleges, and universities. Bearers of certificates or diplomas from prestigious institutions have in effect attempted to maximize their capital and, at least in capitalist settings, labored to obtain a form of cultural capital to add to their eventual store of economic capital. Bourdieu has focused much of his research, both in educational facilities and elsewhere, on the acquisition, maintenance, and perpetuation of cultural capital in contemporary French society (Bourdieu 1984, 1993b; Bourdieu and Passeron 1977).

Symbolic capital represents for Bourdieu a situation of domination whereby the dominators have shifted their power from overt coercion and the threat of physical violence to symbolic manipulation (Swartz 1997: 82). For Bourdieu (Bourdieu and Passeron 1977: 4), any power is guilty of symbolic violence when it has the ability to impose meanings on things and at the same time to legitimate that power by concealing the relations that underlie it. Bourdieu (1990b: 126) illustrates symbolic violence by reference to gift giving. A wealthy donor who has the economic capital to endow the wing of a library exercises symbolic violence by the moral obligations and emotional attachments that accompany the gift. The endowment is "misrecognized" as altruistic philanthropy when it is in fact an exercise of power. The accumulation of economic capital in a modern, capitalist sociohistorical formation can be effectively transformed into symbolic capital by the act of sitting on numerous boards of directors. The very act of participation on that exalted social level produces symbolic power. Social organizations which employ widespread symbolic violence as an irreducible element of the habitus, such that all social members inculcate the need for power and position at the expense of others, have been termed "terrorist societies" (Lefebvre 1984: 147).

The biggest oversight of most archaeologists who have employed Bourdieu's concept of habitus is that they have often failed to include his idea of field. This omission is unfortunate because it is essentially impossible to understand Bourdieu's theory of practice without comprehending fields. Fields are the location of all social practice.

The concept of social fields has a long history in anthropology (see Barnes 1954; Lesser 1961; Radcliffe-Brown 1940), but its greatest refinement outside practice theory has occurred in the "field theory" of social psychology. Developed largely under the direction of Kurt Lewin (1951), the goal of field theory is "to describe the essential here-and-now situation (field) in which a person participates" (De Rivera 1976: 3). Social psychologists envision fields as the site of struggle and domination—"an interpersonal space of conflict and tension" (Mey 1972: 57)—and all practice is mediated through fields. Fields are therefore the loci of cultural production and history.

Fields also have tangible network characteristics, in terms of both theory (Lewin 1951: 248–51; Mey 1972: 105–18) and practical action (Gershenfeld 1986: 98–99), and Bourdieu repeatedly and concisely acknowledges his understanding that fields describe networks: "To think in terms of field is to *think relationally*" (emphasis in original), "In analytic terms, a field may be defined as a network, or a configuration, of objective relations between positions" (Bourdieu and Wacquant 1992: 96, 97), and finally, "To account for the infinite diversity of practices in a way that is both unitary and specific, one has to break with *linear thinking* . . .

and endeavor to reconstruct the networks of interrelated relationships" (Bourdieu 1984: 107; emphasis in original). Fields are thus "social networks of conflict in which players manoeuver to conserve or augment their address in relation to others in the same space" (Prior 2000: 143). As Bourdieu (1985: 724) phrases it: "The social field can be described as a multi-dimensional space of positions such that every actual position can be defined in terms of a multi-dimensional system of co-ordinates whose values correspond to the values of the different pertinent variables."

In his fruitful examination of Bourdieu's sociology, David Swartz (1997: 122–29) outlines the structural properties of fields as Bourdieu understands them:

1. *Fields are arenas of struggle for legitimation.* There are as many fields as there are forms of capital, and actors will struggle within each field to have the right to enact symbolic violence (amass symbolic capital).

2. *Fields are structured spaces of dominant and subordinate positions based on types and amounts of capital.* The dominant positions in a field struggle with the subordinate positions, employing three strategies: conservation (pursued by those in dominant positions with seniority in the field), succession (attempts by new entrants to gain a dominant position), and subversion (undertaken by those who can expect to gain little from the dominant position and who seek to challenge its very legitimacy). Bourdieu often compares a field to a game that does not incorporate codified rules that can be rigidly enforced (Bourdieu and Wacquant 1992: 98–100).

3. *Fields impose specific forms of struggle on the actors.* Both the dominated and the dominators within a field will accept on some level that the struggle is worth pursuing. Bourdieu refers to the deep structure of a field as its "doxa"—an investment in the game and its outcome, an interest in the game, and a commitment to the presuppositions of the game (Bourdieu 1990b: 66). Each doxa is field specific.

4. *Fields are structured by their own internal mechanisms and are thus somewhat but not entirely autonomous from the external environment.* Fields have differing amounts of relative autonomy, based on the degree to which their production is consumed by other producers within that field. Science constitutes the most autonomous field (because scientists consume the works of other scientists), academic realms and art maintain intermediate autonomy, and the political field is the least autonomous (Lash 1993: 198–99). Though external forces have the potential to impact the agents of a given field, the greater the autonomy of a field, the more likely it is to restructure the external into its own logic (Bourdieu and Wacquant 1992: 105–6).

An important element of Bourdieu's field analysis is the concept of field homology. This concept references the idea that different fields develop the same relative structures, so that individuals who are dominated in one field are also subordinate in others. Much of Bourdieu's research, particularly that focused on the French educational system, is intended to demonstrate field homology. He neatly summarizes this concept in the following terms:

> The different classes or sections of a class are organized around three major positions: the lower position, occupied by the agricultural professions, workers, and small tradespeople, which are, in fact, categories excluded from participation in "high" culture; the intermediate position, occupied on the one hand by the heads and employees of industry and business and, on the other hand, by the intermediate office staff (who are just about as removed from the two other categories as these categories are from the lower categories); and, lastly, the higher position, which is occupied by higher office staff and professionals.
>
> The same structure is to be seen each time an assessment is made of the cultural habits and, in particular, of those that demand a cultured disposition, such as reading, and theatre, concert, art-cinema, and museum attendance. (Bourdieu 1977a: 488)

But the homology of the fields is not the result of any meta-historical or supra-cultural properties that exist outside the parameters of human practice, because as Bourdieu (1977b: 83) explains, homology is an element of the habitus: "The unifying principle of practices in different domains [fields] . . . is nothing other than the habitus."

Mapping Fields

Bourdieu's research focuses on the field of power, with the most important forms of capital being economic and cultural. He concentrates on these forms of capital because modern-day, French capitalist society constitutes his research universe. In this context, economic capital—his "dominant principle of hierarchy"—is expressed as wealth, income, and property, while cultural capital—his second principle of hierarchy—consists of knowledge, socially constituted refinement, and educational credentials (Swartz 1997: 136–37). Much of Bourdieu's research represents his attempts to map the field of power in literary and artistic fields. He uses an illustrative heuristic device to indicate how this mapping process operates (Bourdieu 1984: 128–29, 262, 1993b: 38, 186, 1998b: 5). The generated social maps can be extremely intricate because they are intended to illustrate the "space" occupied by each position in a field.

Swartz (1997: 139) provides a useful diagram of Bourdieu's method (Figure 4.1). The largest rectangle represents the field of social classes or social space (Swartz 1997: 138). The total volume of capital is expressed by the vertical line running through the center of the box, while the relative amount of economic and cultural capital is expressed by the centrally placed horizontal line. Both lines are conceptualized as continua, such that the volume of capital is greater for positions located at the top of the box and lesser for those positions located at the bottom. Cultural capital decreases from left to right, while economic capital increases from left to right. The field of power—also differentiated in terms of economic and cultural capital—resides in the upper portion of the largest rectangle because that is the portion of the social space that has the greatest volume of capital. The artistic field, one of Bourdieu's major subjects of analysis, is situated inside the field of power in such a way that it rests closest to the pole having great cultural capital and little economic capital. The artistic field is thus dominated within the field of power, but dominant in terms of class position. The artistic field is also internally differentiated by the plus and minus signs, meaning that some artists have a greater total volume of capital than others. Overall, however, the total volume of the artist position, even on the plus side of the rectangle, is not exceptionally great when compared to other social positions.

Bourdieu puts this conceptual scheme into operation in several studies as a two-dimensional representation of relative social power vis-à-vis

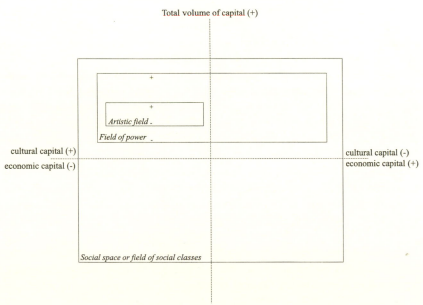

Figure 4.1. Diagram of Bourdieu's social space. Source: Swartz (1997: 139).

capital. For example, in *Distinction*, he locates a number of positions on the central vertical line, including—from top (high volume of total capital) to bottom (low volume of total capital): the professions, private-sector executives, engineers, public-sector engineers, social and medical service workers, art craftsmen and dealers, junior commercial executives/secretaries, technicians, office workers and commercial employees, supervisors, semi-skilled workers, skilled workers, and unskilled workers (Bourdieu 1984: 128–29). In contemporary France, therefore, the professions have the greatest volume of capital, while unskilled workers have the least. Moving from left (high cultural capital/low economic capital) to right (high economic capital/low cultural capital), the positions include artistic producers, higher-education teachers/secondary teachers/primary teachers, junior administrative executives, craft workers, small shopkeepers, industrialists, and commercial employers. Producers of art have high cultural capital and little economic capital, but they have a relatively high total volume of capital. Small shopkeepers may have great stores of economic capital but little cultural capital.

As a further aid to understanding this heuristic device, Bourdieu (Bourdieu and Wacquant 1992: 104–5) outlines the steps necessary for undertaking field analysis. The first step is to analyze the position of the field in terms of the field of power. For instance, the literary and artistic field as Bourdieu examines it is situated in the field of power in a dominated-dominant position. Artists, writers, and intellectuals are, in Bourdieu's terms, "the dominated fraction of the dominant class." They are members of the dominant class (they have a relatively high volume of total capital), but they are subordinate within it. The second step in the research process involves mapping the structure of the relations that obtain between the positions occupied by actors or institutions. These actors or institutions are the entities that compete for the legitimate form of authority (symbolic power) that exists within that field. The final step in the process concerns analyzing the agents' habitus, the different dispositions they have internalized as a feature of their specific social and economic conditions, and the likelihood, within the field, that they can actualize their opportunities (as a strategy).

Race Praxeology

The above brief outline suggests that Bourdieu's analytical field theory is well suited to provide a conceptual umbrella for an examination of past racialization, even though he never explores race to any extent in any of his analyses. He only occasionally references ethnicity. When he does mention social stratification vectors such as race, gender, and ethnicity, he typically subordinates them as "subsidiary characteristics" (Bourdieu

1984: 102) that compete with the "real underlying principles" (Bourdieu 1987: 7) of class formation. For Bourdieu, occupation has overwhelming importance in structuring class formation. He acknowledges that the "secondary" sources of social inequality can in fact create social divisions, but he tends to perceive these divisions as class internal rather than cross-cutting. At the same time, though, Bourdieu (1984: 102) does make it clear that "ethnic origin" and gender "may function, in the form of tacit requirements, as real principles of selection or exclusion without ever being formally stated." If we interpret "ethnic origin" to include a subjectively objectified racial characteristic, then it stands to reason that racial designation can serve as a "real principle of selection or exclusion."

Because Bourdieu's social space foregrounds the idea that classes are created only when they can "mobilize economic and cultural capital" (Swartz 1997: 155), his ideas cannot be used verbatim to understand the practice of race. Habitus, capital, and field instead must be interlinked in a manner that allows for the comprehension of the racial practices of particular sociohistoric formations. Failure to employ the complete triad of Bourdieu's analytical units would result in an impartial understanding of social complexity. As noted above, much archaeological application of practice theory has focused almost entirely on the habitus. Such exclusionary focus presents dispositions as one-dimensional features that have all the characteristics of essentialized whole-cultural traits. The inherent problems entailed by an incomplete use of Bourdieu's practice theory can be illustrated with reference to applications of practice theory to ethnicity. This exercise is pertinent because the same process of misrepresentation is potentially possible in the analysis of race.

Siân Jones (1997: 87–105; also see 1999: 225–27) has provided perhaps the most explicit application of Bourdieu's practice theory in her investigation of the archaeological dimensions of ethnicity. Jones's goal is to locate a theory of ethnicity that promotes an active view of social life, one in which ethnic identity is "a dynamic, contested, and multi-layered phenomenon" (Jones 1999: 221). She finds Bourdieu's concept of habitus to be useful and employs it as the basis of her theory of ethnic identity:

the concept of the habitus can be used to explain the way in which subjective ethnic classifications are grounded in the social conditions characterizing particular social domains. Ethnicity is not a passive reflection of similarities and differences in the cultural practices and structural conditions in which agents are socialized. Nor is ethnicity entirely constituted in the process of social interaction whereby epiphenomenal cultural characteristics are manipulated in the pursuit of economic and political interests. (Jones 1999: 226)

To stress the point that Bourdieu's theory of practice can be used to help archaeologists understand ethnicity in the past, Jones (1997) references

Carter Bentley's (1987) explicit effort to link habitus with ethnicity. She notes, however, that Bentley's application of habitus to ethnicity is somewhat problematic, because it is "not far removed from the traditional model of ethnicity as a passive reflection of the normative behaviour of a discrete group of people" (Jones 1997: 92). Faced with a similar criticism from another scholar (Yelvington 1991), Bentley (1991: 170) restates his perspective by arguing that the use of habitus allows the analyst to separate the overt, surface-level expressions of ethnicity from the deeply structured dispositions of the habitus. Bentley (1987: 29) states that the deep structure of the dispositions can produce an infinite number of surface expressions—or personal styles—that are recognizable "as being of a single type," even though the individuals acknowledging them can never concisely articulate their objective nature.

Jones (1997: 94) also accepts the critique that Bentley's analysis of ethnic formation occurs in isolation of "ethnic others" (Yelvington 1991: 162). Bentley envisions the creation of ethnic identity as a matter between the habitus and the surface-level cultural expressions, with no regard for the ethnic affiliations of proximate individuals who belonged to a differently defined group. Regarding "black and white Americans," for example, Bentley (1987: 33) observes that empirical studies indicate that blacks and whites reproduce cultural styles that differentiate their groups in ways that cannot be reduced to class alone. Because differences in the habitus of blacks and whites similarly can account for many of the conflicts between the groups, each group's habitus provides for the disparities within the racialized social space. Jones (1997: 93–94) disagrees with Bentley's conclusion here and stresses that "There are many examples where it seems highly implausible that the people brought together by the expression of a common ethnic identity share equally in a common habitus; ironically, for instance, Bentley's (1987) own example of black American ethnicity." The conceptual problem over black identity causes Jones to accept the *foundation* of Bentley's Bourdieuian analysis, but to propose in addition that the concept of habitus must be broadened to include "ethnic others" because "ethnic categories are almost always embedded in power relations of varying degrees of inequality" (Jones 1997: 96).

Jones's interpretation, though frequently insightful, suffers from two major problems. First, while she correctly identifies the most significant problem with Bentley's characterization of the relationship between cultural styles and black and white habitus, she fails to note its racial foundation. Her oversight causes her to underestimate the very power relations that she astutely notes are central to comprehending habitus fully. Failure to identify racial assignment as inherently and irreducibly related to power condemns her analytical framework to mere disparities between variant kinds of habitus. Second, in her concentration on habitus to the exclusion of field and capital, she dooms her study—just as Bentley (1987) had done earlier—to being incapable of actually creating a practice theory of ethnicity, her overt goal. She states that "Ethnicity is a multidimensional phenomenon constituted in different ways in different social domains" (Jones 1997: 100). By "domains" she clearly means "fields," but she does not exploit the important relationships between habitus, field, and capital that form the theoretical basis of Bourdieu's practice theory. She finds the habitus concept wanting and in need of reformation mostly because of her failure to complete it with capital and field. Her statement that the variability in ethnic expression—as an "objectification of cultural practices"—is "constituted by the intersection of the habitus with the prevailing social conditions in any given moment" (Jones 1997: 128) is precisely Bourdieu's point. Given the importance of the situational context, it is utterly predictable, for instance, that Miller's (1994: 207–8) empirical findings in Trinidad do not mirror Bourdieu's (1984) findings in France. No reason exists for the two sociohistorical formations to be identical, and any idea of compatibility is incongruous with practice theory and its archaeological variant, historical processualism. The intersection between the dispositions of the habitus and "any given moment" is precisely the point of practice theory.

Without question, the application of practice theory to studies of historical racialization using archaeology as a primary research tool is difficult. In order to begin to reach an intellectual accommodation with practice theory and racial analysis, we must be prepared to accept three important judgments. First, we must accept the idea that even though race is a social construct, it is a construct with meaning. Race is not simply a meta-narrative of modernity that exists in the abstract. Quite the contrary, the process of racialization creates meaningful categories and instills material inequalities (Smaje 1997). We can expect that the created categories will be instilled as dispositions within the habitus. Second, we must also be willing to distinguish between racist language and the construction of racial hierarchies (Bonilla-Silva 1997). Racialization results in more than the establishment of cognitive categories of identification and exclusion. Racialization actually excludes, and in so doing, it operates dialectically within the structure it establishes. Racial categorization thus has the ability (as situated within specific historical moments) to be both a structured structure and a structuring structure. And finally, we must be willing as social archaeologists to acknowledge that a racialized social structure mandates the unequal distribution of material benefits, work positions, educational opportunities, and a host of other social factors that have the potential to retain archaeological visibility. Racialization thus enacts symbolic violence through its "otherizing" process (Bonilla-Silva 1999: 903).

An acceptance of these three propositions entails a concomitant understanding that the social space and the material expressions that racialization embodies cannot be separated in an archaeological application of practice theory. Every archaeologist knows that understanding a past social structure—the epochal structures noted by Donham (1999)—is never entirely straightforward. The struggle to conceptualize the past does not disappear even in those cases where significant sociological analysis has already occurred. Consider, for example, the now-outdated sociological caste model of the Old South.

American sociologists formulated the caste model in the early twentieth century and employed the color line as a caste line, conceptualizing it as a barrier to inter-caste mobility (Davis 1942; Davis et al. 1941; Dollard 1937; Moore and Williams 1942; Warner 1936). Though some sociologists employed the terms "color-caste" and "quasi-caste" to distinguish the American system from that of traditional India (see, e.g., Abrahamson et al. 1976: 329), the applicability of the caste model to American social space was long ago refuted. For some sociologists, the model had the power to "obfuscate the most significant aspects of race relations" (Cox 1945: 368), but for others, the American caste system promised to offer "a solution of the race problem" (Park 1950: 185).

Sociologists designed the American caste model with the white caste situated above the black caste (Figure 4.2). Each caste contained an upper, middle, and lower class, and the color line (a–b) ran diagonally through the model at such an angle that a tiny black upper class was on a structural level with the lower tier of the white middle class. Though it appeared to represent social stasis, the sociologists who created the model did not envision the color line to be stationary. On the contrary, they recognized that it could in fact move as a result of "The gradual elaboration of the economic, educational, and general social activities of the Negro caste since slavery" (Davis et al. 1941: 11). This elaboration of opportunity—or what Bourdieu (1984: 372) terms "the choice of the necessary"—caused the color line to slide upward (to A–B) in such a manner that the size of the lower black class decreased as the black middle and upper classes expanded. The sociologists' hope was that the color line would eventually rotate on a central axis point (c), finally becoming vertical (d–e). The terminal position of the color line would create a "parallelism" that would produce Park's "solution to the race problem." The black caste would exist alongside the white caste, with each caste's classes mirroring one another.

Citizens of post-emancipation United States realize that the caste-focused sociologists' dream for the complete verticalization of the color line did not occur, even though this strategy was ostensibly the goal of the Jim Crow, separate-but-equal doctrine. The legislation that federal, state, and local politicians enacted under the aegis of this repressive doc-trine merely stigmatized (and further institutionalized) people of color with hierarchically enforced racial inferiority, and for a time the Jim Crow laws even worked to legitimate discrimination against certain European immigrants (Baker 1998: 88). If the color line had ever attained the posi-tion of complete verticality (d–e), then, given the history of American institutionalized racialization, the entire social system could be concep-tualized to have rotated 90° on its side in such a way that the white caste would have remained in the superordinate position.

The early twentieth-century caste model, though a provocative heuris-tic device, does not significantly assist our efforts to understand racial-ization. The class categories within the castes appear as objectively fixed through time. The caste-and-class structure offers little to promote real comprehension of how men, women, and children who were designated black and white struggled to create history. All we know from reading the histories and personal accounts of the Jim Crow era is that institu-tionalized, race-based discrimination, debasement, and violence were regularly perpetrated against people of color in the name of keeping the social order static.

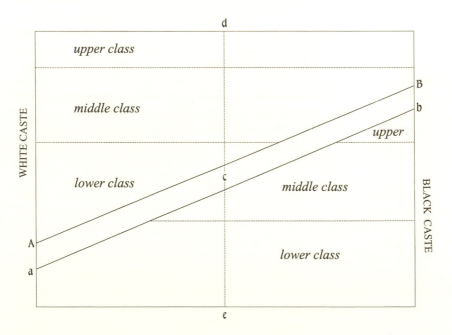

Figure 4.2. Early twentieth-century caste model of the American South. Source: Davis et al. (1941: 10).

What the caste model does provide, however, is a conceptual link to the economics of racial discrimination, particularly if we roughly equate the idealized vertical color line envisioned by some sociologists (see Figure 4.2, d–e) with Bourdieu's total volume of capital line (see Figure 4.1). In general, as one moves out of the black caste (or up the line of total volume of capital), one's distance from necessity decreases. The precise nature of the linkage between racial designation and poverty is understandably a complex and historically contingent issue that defies easy resolution and invariably fosters emotional response. It is true, nonetheless, that even though racial justice is not the same as economic justice, the two are clearly linked (Jackson 1997). An individual does not have to be a person of color to be poor, but it helps. As one social critic stated it:

The Negro is poor because he is black; that is obvious enough. But, perhaps more importantly, the Negro is black because he is poor. The laws against color can be removed, but that will leave the poverty that is the historic and institutionalized consequence of color. As long as this is the case, being born a Negro will continue to be the most profound disability that the United States imposes upon a citizen. (Harrington 1963: 73)

And, as Du Bois (1999: 14) succinctly stated it: "To be a poor man is hard, but to be a poor race in a land of dollars is the very bottom of hardships." The United States federal government was forced to confront the reality of the racialized social system it had created when the National Advisory Commission on Civil Disorders (the Kerner Commission) released its report on March 1, 1968. The authors of this official report unambiguously observed that "Our nation is moving toward two societies, one black, one white—separate and unequal" (quoted in Harris and Curtis 1998: 1). Studies conducted since 1968 reveal that blacks lag behind whites in income (with almost $16,000 difference in 1989), and that as a group blacks appear disproportionally below the poverty line (outnumbering whites 3:1 in 1989), occupy low-paying service jobs (23.5 percent versus the white figure of 12.2 percent in 1985) and experience greater unemployment (11.4 percent versus 4.5 percent in 1989) (Leiman 1993: 88–145). Social analysts thus find it impossible, when investigating some sociohistorical contexts, to separate race and class.

Once the realization is made that racial designation and class affiliation must be considered in tandem, the analyst wishing to employ the insights of practice theory discovers the urgency of rehabilitating the theory in such a way that assigned racial categorization is not relegated to a secondary level of stratification. The task of adjustment can be tremendously aided by reference to Leslie McCall's (1992) effort to realign practice theory with gender.

McCall argues that two readings of Bourdieu's conceptual framework are possible. The first reading, the one promoted by Bourdieu himself and the one noted above, accords primacy to occupational and educational capital as central determinants of social position. It is for this reason that Bourdieu's class positions are largely defined by the work people do as a reflection of their investment in cultural capital (e.g., educational credentials). In the second reading, however, McCall openly rejects occupational/educational primacy and concentrates on the interaction between gender and class distinction. Her frame of reference is Bourdieu's embodied cultural capital.

Focusing on the characteristics of the "secondary principles of societal division," McCall (1992: 841) posits that in Bourdieu's framework the secondary variables obtain their form and value in relation to capital. This means that Bourdieu's view maintains that gender is not a form of capital in and of itself. In this sense, Bourdieu's concept of gender is distinct from his view of ethnicity. He proposes that ethnic groups—which are reinforced, he says, "by principles of division relatively independent of economic or cultural practices" (Bourdieu 1985: 743)—can occupy positions in all social fields. Lower-ranked ethnic groups will tend to occupy fewer positions than those ethnicities that are ranked higher. Thus, the vertical classification of ethnic groups appears as an overlay on social space (McCall 1992: 842), having a conceptual appearance much like the classes in the old caste model. But McCall argues that under the terms of the second reading, gender can constitute embodied cultural capital because, as Bourdieu (1986: 243) says, embodied cultural capital appears "in the form of long-lasting dispositions of the mind and *body*" (emphasis added). A conceptual difficulty arises for Bourdieu because a person strives to accumulate cultural capital through the purposeful investment of time in self-improvement activities. People invest in historically and situationally defined cultural pursuits to improve their overall social position, with their activities rendering interest over time. For Bourdieu (1984: 153), as women seek the social construction of bodily appearance—and as they enter formerly exclusive androcentric professions—they create gendered forms of cultural capital and in effect redefine "the legitimate image of femininity." As McCall (1992: 844) astutely observes, however, even though Bourdieu argues that women with economic capital can best achieve society's ideal of beauty, the very physicality of this form of cultural capital, which Bourdieu misrecognizes as economic, becomes symbolic capital. McCall (1992: 847) argues that Bourdieu's view of habitus and capital fails to capture the significance of gender as embodied cultural capital because of his focus on the middle class as *the* site of contemporary struggle. In concentrating on the middle class, she argues that Bourdieu misses the perspective of the dominated classes, a group that includes women.

McCall's insightful exegesis of Bourdieu's understanding of social space can be applied to race as well, so that a racial designation can be considered to constitute embodied cultural capital. Like gender, race is an ambiguous form of capital because, while it is initially instilled from the outside, a social actor can strive for its accumulation specifically because of the initial identification. This means that even though blackness, for example, was initially designed as a racial identifier—intended to unequivocally separate "blacks" from "non-blacks," the "superior" from the "inferior"—it is also true that blackness has also become a site of conscious struggle ("black is beautiful"; the acceptance of the designation "black" in Brazil). Racial identity is a "long-term disposition" of the body. The same can also be said about whiteness or any other skin-color-based racial designation (see, e.g., Bonnett 1996).

By the same token, the idea of being racialized can be an element of the habitus. Bourdieu (1984: 471), though speaking of economically based social classes, employs the idea that the habitus defines what should be expected: "Objective limits become a sense of limits, a practical anticipation of objective limits acquired by experience of objective limits, a 'sense of place' which leads one to exclude oneself from the goods, persons, places and so forth from which one is excluded." But as McCall (1992: 849–50) illustrates, women who consciously venture into male-dominated professions find that they face several obstacles, including being labeled with derogatory terms. Such experiences represent a break with the established doxa—the fund of field-specific, commonsense knowledge—only to be replaced with a modified doxa that proposes that the struggle is worth the effort (also see Crossley 2002: 184). In this sense, the struggle noted by McCall appears structurally similar to the situation in which African Americans demonstrated that they did not "know their place" (that is, their externally defined positions in the dominated half of the field of power). The actions that appeared to violate the dominant understanding of what dispositions the black habitus should contain often resulted in acts of unspeakable terrorism perpetrated against African Americans (see, e.g., DeNevi and Holmes 1973).

Archaeologists wishing to pursue a historical processual paradigm must strive to model successfully the social space—habitus, fields, and capital—of the particular sociohistorical formation under study. Pauketat (2000, 2001), in his exemplary studies of the Mississippian polity at Cahokia, has arguably had the most success in applying practice theory to ancient history. It may be supposed, however, that a social archaeology using practice theory is even more conducive to situations for which abundant historical information exists. The reliability of this conclusion is of course open to debate, but at the very least it would appear that as a practical matter, the investigation of racialization requires the presence of some textual information that can be employed to conceptualize the basic structure of the sociohistorical formation under study.

A brief consideration of the experience of rural African Americans in the southern United States can illustrate the use of habitus, field, and capital as it pertains to racialization. The parameters of the pertinent social space can be envisioned to incorporate a field of power that existed much like Bourdieu's field of power in modern-day France, because both contexts were structured as capitalist social spaces.

Although the structure was by no means static, the classes of the agricultural segment of the antebellum American South included large planters, small planters and commercial farmers, non-slaveholding yeomen farmers, and poor whites (Figure 4.3) (Moore and Williams 1942: 344–45). The top class fraction, often designed "southern gentlemen," were idealized as "hospitable, gentlemanly, courteous, and more anxious to please than to be pleased" (Hundley 1860: 57). The bottom class fraction, with no economic capital in slaves or property, were conversely described in opposite terms: "there is no order of men in any part of the United States, with which I have any acquaintance, who are in a more debased and humiliated state of moral servitude, than are those white people who inhabit that part of the southern country, where the landed property is all, or nearly all, held by the great planters" (Ball 1837: 290). In conformity with the tenets of practice theory, we can presume that the members of the various class fractions vied for symbolic power through their acquisition of economic and cultural capital, with the majority of the capital being amassed by the large planters (with the highest total volume of capital). The positions of the various class fractions would be distributed according to their economic and cultural capital. An unlettered planter with 500 slaves would have high economic capital but low cultural capital, whereas a wealthy planter's capricious son who exhibited no interest in plantation management and only wished to employ his talents as an artist would have high cultural capital and low economic capital. The use of practice theory promotes the idea that specific actions by the planters—such as placing rows of stately live oaks on both sides of the main road into their estates—would be intended to increase the planter's store of cultural capital (as a mark of refinement) as actualized through his high amount of economic capital. The presence of the trees would enact symbolic violence on all those planters of lesser wealth who, while riding under them, would be urged to realize that they could not afford to purchase such grand amenities. Such ideas of cultural capital have even been immortalized in the romantic, fictional literature of the Old South, where whiteness is used as a metaphor for large planter symbolic power. For example, in *Gone with the Wind*, Margaret Mitchell describes Tara in unmistakable language:

Here under his [Gerald O'Hara's] feet would rise a house of whitewashed brick . . . and the red earth that rolled down the hillside to the rich river bottom land would gleam white as eiderdown in the sun—cotton, acres and acres of cotton . . . . From the avenue of cedars to the row of white cabins in the slave quarters, there was an air of solidness, of stability and permanence about Tara. (1936: 47–48)

This purposeful image of the white plantation mansion has become integral to the modern-day concept of the southern plantation, appearing

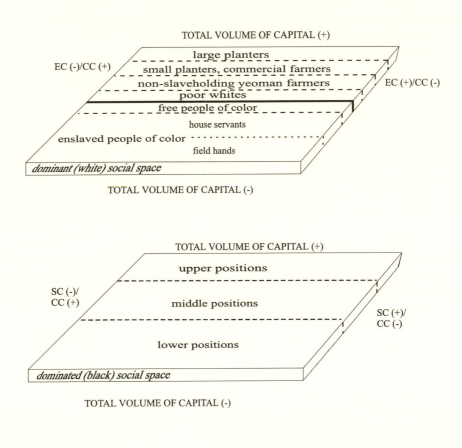

EC = economic capital
CC = cultural capital
SC = social capital

Figure 4.3. Social structure of the antebellum agricultural South.

regularly in fiction (see, e.g., McNeill 1975: 43), with the loss of whiteness serving as a metaphor for the decline of the planter's fortunes (see, e.g., Horner 1973: 12).

In her analysis of Oakley Plantation in Louisiana, Laurie Wilkie (2000: 226, 228) notes that the site of the habitus, at least early in life, is the household. It is in this initial environment that children learn the deep-structuring potentials, possibilities, and limitations of life that describe their social space. Education within the slave community, however, was diverse and multifaceted. In fact, the education of the bondsman or bondswoman had a unique double character, such that one set of habitus dispositions could actually be diametrically opposed to a second set of dispositions. The education of this bifurcated habitus was homologous with a similarly structured field of power. On the one hand, the large slave owner—a possessor of high economic capital (embodied in property, slaves, and realizable funds in the form of cash crops) and equally high cultural capital (legally white, educated, and well-connected) sought to instill a habitus on the slaves that inculcated two propositions: job training and a willingness to use job skills efficiently (Webber 1978: 26). As ancillary skills, many slaveowners also desired that their slaves be well-versed in obedience and, for house servants, in housekeeping skills as well.

Slaveowning plantation masters valued their slaves for their work abilities and classified them accordingly. Fanny Kemble, an astute observer of plantation social space, made these observations:

Our servants—those who have been selected to wait upon us in the house—consist of a man, who is quite a tolerable cook (I believe this is a natural gift with them, as with Frenchmen); a dairy-woman, who churns for us; a laundry-woman; her daughter, our housemaid, the aftersaid Mary; and two young lads of from fifteen to twenty, who wait upon us in the capacity of footmen. (1863: 22–23)

Rachel O'Connor, another plantation mistress, stated that "Patience cooks for me. Old Milly raises poultry, Old Leah spins wool, Old Dinah is nearly blind, but churns and feeds the cows and helps about all she can see to do. Charity is [the] washer and attends about the house" (Webb 1983: 252). A specific, readily identifiable individual performed each special task, but the primary point is that each task represents a position within the dominant social space. As a woman in a patriarchal social system, the plantation mistress was a dominated member of the dominant class, and the house servants (whatever their assigned duties) were dominated members of the dominated class. But at least as far as the planters were concerned, the social space occupied by the house servants carried more capital than those slaves who worked as field hands. We must remember, however, that the very presence of liveried house servants—waiting on a well-appointed, lavish dinner table and using the most refined manners in doing so—enacted a dualistic symbolic violence, both on the plantation's dinner guests and on the slaves being made to act as waiters.

The planters' pedagogic goal was to instill their own notion of a slave habitus (as a set of artificial dispositions) in their enslaved men, women, and children. Plantation journals written by slaveowners are replete with statements about the "proper" and "acceptable" conduct of their slaves. For example, writing October 1831, Rachel O'Connor observed that the slaves on a nearby plantation were "as peaceable as lambs" and that "They all behaved well" (Webb 1983: 63). The enactment of the "proper" slave behavior was so central to the practice of the slave plantation that many antebellum writers codified what they expected from their enslaved human chattel. Planter James J. Butler presented a fairly common vision of the correct slave attitude when he wrote:

The master should never establish any regulation among his slaves until he is fully convinced of its propriety and equity. Being thus convinced, and having issued his orders, implicit obedience should be required and rigidly enforced. Firmness of manner and promptness to enforce obedience, will save much trouble, and be the means of avoiding the necessity for much whipping. The negro should feel that his master is his law-giver and judge, and yet is his protector and friend, but so far above him, as never to be approached save in the most respectful manner. (1851: 328)

The comment that the master was "so far above" the slave is metaphorical at the same time that it figuratively expresses the ideological core of the racialized social structure. Another planter advised in 1861 that the plantation overseer should "Not allow Negroes to swear, do anything disrespectful, make noise in quarters, nor talk loudly while at work, nor allow quarreling or fighting" (Davis 1982: 118). These writers also stated, at least publicly, that it was incumbent on slaveowners to treat their slaves wisely. As one commentator phrased it, "No more beautiful picture of human society can be drawn than a well-organized plantation, this governed by the humane principles of reason" (Calhoun 1855: 716). Despite such views, it was also true that slaveowners could be "lords of the lash" (Helper 1860: 43) if they so wished. Using Nowak's (1983) terms, plantation owners exercised domination because they had the power to affect the social relations of the slaves. But, also as Nowak makes quite clear, the domination is never truly total.

The abundant slave uprisings and rebellions, which many plantation owners deathly feared on a daily basis and which are today legendary, suggests of course that many of the slaves' obsequious practices were feigned. The almost infinite variety of individual acts of defiance committed by slaves—from malingering to poisoning (Aptheker 1943: 140–49; Rosengarten 1986: 157–62)—indicates that the slaveowners' efforts to invent and instill a habitus of control were largely unsuccessful. We can designate the resistant actions of slaves "agency" if we wish, but this facile understanding would not offer any true sensitivity about how the slaves' actions were consciously and unconsciously situated within sociohistorically constructed fields.

The reason that planters were unable to control their slaves at all times would seem to be that some element of the African habitus was incompatible with bondage and submission. So modeled, this pan-cultural incompatibility would have whole-cultural characteristics. But, given that African slaves in the New World originated in diverse cultures throughout West and Central Africa, it is highly unlikely, as Jones (1997: 93–94) has noted, that men, women, and children held in bondage on a single plantation would share the same habitus. The deep theoretical deficiency with the whole-culture model is hereby glaringly exposed, because the central point is that, regardless of place of origin, the individuals held in bondage on the plantations of the New World were accorded positions in social space within a race-based, vertical structure that was historically contrived. Even in situations where slaves were purchased because they had some specific knowledge, such as on the techniques of rice cultivation, their value—as far as the planter was concerned—was as a holder of a social position. Once placed in that position (initially defined phenotypically and then redefined occupationally) enslaved men and women were expected to perform their tasks proficiently and wisely, based on an invented habitus that did not really exist. When Thomas Chaplin, a slaveowning planter in coastal South Carolina, wrote in late May 1851 that "My Negroes were hauling cotton today when their own sense should tell them they ought to be supplying" [laying in provisions] (Rosengarten 1986: 534), he was actually saying that he previously provided the necessary instruction to them and that they would have learned the proper actions if they had any sense. An underlying message might be that they did not follow the "proper" procedure because they were racially inferior and thus incapable of thinking like a white person.

A significant point, however, is that the pedagogic perspective that slaveowning planters brought to the plantation was not the only operative view. The slave community had its own dispositions to impart to its children (Webber 1978: 157–243). And, while the creation of slave identity was influenced by the institution of an artificial creolized culture, slave practice operated within a dualistic social space that is well-summarized by Du Bois (1999: 11) in his concept of "double consciousness":

It is a peculiar sensation, this double-consciousness, this sense of always looking at one's self through the eyes of others, of measuring one's soul by the tape of a world that looks on in amused contempt and pity. One ever feels his two-ness, — an American, a Negro; two souls, two thoughts, two unreconciled strivings; two warring ideas in one dark body, whose dogged strength alone keeps it from being torn asunder.

An important element of the contra-education slaves received in the quarters was the homologous invention of a social hierarchy that ran completely counter to that imposed from the dominant racial class. According to John Blassingame (1976: 150–51), an idealized social hierarchy within the slave community contained the following positions:

A. Upper class
    1. Conjurors
    2. Physicians and midwives
    3. Preachers
    4. Elders
    5. Teachers
    6. Creators and carriers of culture
    7. Entertainers
    8. Rebels
B. Middle class
    1. Creators of material culture
    2. Verbal artists
    3. Cool cats
    4. Self-employed slaves
    5. Bondsmen whose jobs frequently carried them away from the plantation
    6. Artisans who made the slaves' shoes, liquor, clothes, and houses
    7. Artisans who made the slaves' tools (blacksmiths, coopers)
    8. Unusually strong, handsome, pretty, or intelligent field hands
    9. Drivers who protected the slaves' interests
C. Lower class
    1. Temporary house servants and servants residing in the quarters
    2. Ordinary field hands
    3. Exploitative drivers
    4. Live-in house servants with long tenure
    5. Voluntary concubines
    6. Informants

Scholars may wish to quibble over Blassingame's use of the term "class," the labels employed, the precise ordering of the labor positions, and the general applicability of the model to all plantations throughout the New World, but the important point is structural: the slaves constructed and implemented a hierarchy that was distinct from that of slaveowning planters (see Figure 4.3). This system of stratification existed in the same physical space as the planters' hierarchical system, but the two were far from homologous in Bourdieu's sense.

Social capital was more important than economic capital in the slave community. While Blassingame's (1976) slave-quarter class system does indicate the significance of economic capital in his "middle class" positions, it is clear that social capital—as composed of network connections that embodied obligations and the administration of medical, religious, entertainment, and educational services—was much more important. And rebels, those men and women who would occupy the absolute bottom rung of the social ladder in the planters' structure (and who were in fact labeled criminals), were accorded a position in the upper class fraction of the slave's worldview. South Carolina planter Thomas Chaplin, in 1845, concisely summarized the variance in the dispositions in the dominant and dominated social spaces: "for in truth, the Negroes did not care as much about us as we did for them" (Rosengarten 1986: 348). For planters, slaves represented embodied economic capital (in the most literal sense of the term) and symbolic capital. For slaves, planters could never be conceputalized as any form of capital; in fact, the very idea is patently absurd. The social capital embodied in slaves was recognized at the time by one astute observer:

But slavery in the South is something more than a moral and political principle: it has become a fashionable taste, a social passion. The possession of a slave in the South carries with it the same sort of prestige as the possession of land in this country, as the possession of a horse among the Arabs: it brings the owner into connexion with the privileged class and forms a presumption that he has attained a certain social position. Slaves have thus in the South acquired a factitious value, and are coveted with an eagerness far beyond what the intrinsic utility of their services would explain. (Cairnes 1862: 90)

The structure of the antebellum slave plantation was not an aberrant phase of social interaction, within which individuals from the dominant social space exerted their power over individuals from the dominated social space. Systems of institutionalized racial oppression continued to thrive after 1865, as many of the same structural elements were drawn into systems of sharecropping and tenant farming (Orser 1988b: 48–81, 1991b).

It is paramount to understand that the racialized social structure did not die with slave emancipation. Southern planters with high volumes of total capital were so committed to their race-based, hierarchical system that they sought to import other peoples they had designated as non-whites into the South to continue to cultivate on their behalf. Their racially motivated goal was to hire immigrants rather than to rent farms to former slaves. Numerous planters faced with the labor implications of emancipation wrote to southern agricultural journals expressing their belief that former slaves refused to work, that they had a natural tendency to loaf, and that they would steal everything possible (see, e.g., G.A.N. 1867; Hassler 1871; T.A.W. 1869). For many plantation owners, the answer to their labor "problem" lay with the importation of "coolies," a general term they used for any people of color who were not of direct African descent (see, e. g., Anonymous 1866a, 1867a, 1869a; Bell 1867; Capron 1871: 572–76). But the attempted retention of the racialized power structure was not limited to people of color, because some planters—striving to maintain the consistency of their racialized belief system and wishing to use it to uphold the racialized social structure—argued that white workers should replace blacks. They could still dominate these "inferior" whites and at the same time not have to engage people of color, either free or newly freed. Germans, Irish, and "hardy" Swedes and Norwegians were all cited as possible substitute laborers (Anonymous 1866b, 1867b, 1869b; Schurz 1866: 40–42). Other planters argued for the racial advantages of peoples from warmer European climates (and not coincidently those considered outside the Aryan racial strain), expressing the belief that they would be better fitted to the demands of southern agriculture: "Although Germans, Irish, and Northerners can and will live and prosper in the Southern States, there is no doubt that emigrants from France, Spain, and Italy would be most readily and perfectly adapted to our climate" (Nott 1866: 173). As a result of such manipulation, the racialized field of southern agriculture was upheld within the larger racialized social structure. When enough "coolies" could not be enticed onto the South's plantations, southern plantation owners were forced to concede tenancy to former slaves. But in making this concession to the realities of their demand for labor, they continued to relegate peoples of color to the lowest social positions and created new forces of oppression that worked to suppress the acquisition of capital by those relegated to structural domination (see Litwack 1979; Magdol 1977; Rose 1978; Sutch and Ranson 1978; White and Leonard 1915).

The history of African American life in the agricultural South obviously contains myriad circumstances and many unique historical specificities, and the intent here is not to recount this history in any detail. The goal is simply to use southern agriculture as an illustration of how archaeologists might conceptualize one complex, multifaceted sociohistorical formation that incorporated racialization as a structuring structure. This admittedly brief account is designed to model the epochal structures of one element of this racialized history. The point is that such interpretation is required of archaeologists attempting practice theory because of the structural factors that engage human practice. The next task is to relate the field analytic perspectives of practice theory to artifacts and space, two indispensable variables of the archaeological field. This exegesis will further help to establish the important theoretical strengths of historical processualism.

Chapter 5
Materiality in the Practice of Race

The construction of past habitus, field, and capital for specific sociohistoric formations constitutes only half of the archaeological project. If social archaeologists cease their research with the modeling the social structure, no matter how complex the model may be, they are acting as historical sociologists and not archaeologists, even though the creation of the model is a necessary archaeological step. Archaeologists must be especially sensitive to and adept at developing insights that can be used to connect the actions that occurred within past social fields to the material symbolizations of those actions. Archaeologists are of course properly respected for employing a diverse array of source materials in their research, but even in the most transdisciplinary of efforts, a primary set of information must remain portable pieces of material culture and their large-scale partners, the immovable features impressed in or erected on the landscape. Even historical archaeologists—for whom textual materials of myriad kinds represent irreducibly significant sources of referential information—must ultimately position their investigations on a foundation of things and places. The requisite task for an archaeological practice theory, then, is to provide ways in which to conceptualize archaeologically relevant notions of things and places that interlink with the tenets of the theory. Our specific need here is to demonstrate the application of these ideas to race and racialization.

Artifacts as Commodities

Every practicing archaeologist is aware of the disciplinary transformation of the study of artifacts over the past several decades, and a full recounting of the intellectual maturation of thought about artifacts is unnecessary. Suffice to say that archaeological reasoning in relation to artifacts has been significantly modified from the beginning of the nineteenth century—when Jens Worsaae voiced the commonly held perception that artifacts were "mere curiosities" (Henry 1995: 20)—to the early twenty-first century—when Schiffer (1999) outlined his formalized communicative theory of material culture. Whether or not one chooses to accept the precepts of Schiffer's understanding of the archaeological project, most archaeologists at least may be prepared to accept one of his prime understandings: that archaeology is largely concerned with the interactions between humans and things (Reid 1995; Reid et al. 1975; Schiffer 1976: 4, 1999: 7; Walker et al. 1995: 2). The operative question, of course, is how social archaeologists should model and interpret the infinite variety of human-object interactions.

Given that archaeological theory is inextricably enmeshed with inquiries that conceptualize material culture, one of the most contested realms of archaeological thought quite understandably focuses on the precise nature of the human-designed transformations of artifacts and their meanings. Numerous scholars, including many archaeologists, have devised intricate chosecentric developmental schemata to describe the transmogrification of portable things, extending from stone-bronze-iron (Engelhardt 1866: 3) to tool-using cultures-technocracies-technopolies (Lefebvre 1984: 48–50; Postman 1993: 21–55).

Regardless of how one chooses to model the historical vectors of artifact philosophy, and despite the actual mechanisms of change accorded interpretative primacy, one of the most important understandings to emerge from the many ruminations on physical things is that "To be deprived of objects is to be deprived of social existence, of human relations with others and with oneself" (Lefebvre 1982: 84). Linked with the important association between social existence and physical objects is the indisputable fact of history that humans have increasing transformed ever-expanding numbers of artifacts into commodities—objects produced specifically for exchange. The historical trajectory of commodity presence has been so exponential over time that one observer has noted that between 1950 and 1990, the world's peoples had consumed as many commodities as all previous generations combined (Durning 1992: 38). The invention and spread of commodities is a topic with major significance for modern-world archaeologists.

Commodification refers to the act of assigning the characteristics of exchangeability to objects, attitudes, behaviors, and, in the case of slavery, people. When the rise of commodification is viewed as a metanarrative, various root causes can be assigned to it, including changes in political ideology, economic motivations, and modifications in religiosity, social structure, and human psychology (see, e.g., Brewer and Porter 1993; Douglas and Isherwood 1979; Greenblatt 1991; Jardine 1998). Analysts understandably disagree about the human benefits of increased commodification, and whether the individual consumer is "free to choose" (the position of those who put their faith in the regulatory power of the free-market system) or "free to lose" (the position of those who argue that the free-market system is inherently exploitative) remains a politically charged, and probably unresolvable, philosophical debate. In either case, increased commodity production, marketing, and acquisition do engender certain environmental costs (e.g., Durning 1992: 19–61; Goldsmith 1996: 81–91; Sale 1996: 216–19), and archaeologists have ably demonstrated the modern-day landscape effects of this ecosystemic stress (e.g., Rathje and Murphy 1992).

The temporal dimensions of the increased human interaction with commodities means that archaeologists of the modern world must redouble their efforts to understand commodities and the process of commodification. A conceptual shift that impels the addition of commodity awareness—as a base-level analytical category within modern-world archaeology—in addition to artifact-awareness, represents more than an overt acknowledgment of the postmodern concern for consumption over production (Slater 1997: 193–94). Rather, a conscious concern with commodities stresses the sociability of objects that resides at the core of human experience (Orser 1996a: 113). The goal of a totally social archaeology is thus to strive to envision objects as "not what they were made to be but what they have become" (N. Thomas 1991: 4), and to contemplate the objects' socially relevant contextualizations and recontextualizations over time and circumstance.

The exchange of objects and services is an ancient process in human history, and at least one student of the material aspects of human life has postulated that "without exchange, there is no society" (Braudel 1977: 15). While the transference and consumption of goods and services indeed has a venerable history across the globe, historians generally agree that the institution of a truly global, consumerist network is a creation of the modern world (Gottdiener 2000: 12; Stearns 2001: 1). The long-term antecedents of globalization are open to debate (see, e.g., Abu-Lughod 1989; Frank 1993a, 1998; Frank and Gills 1993), but by 1515, one observer of global commerce noted when thinking about the European trade connections with the African and Indian littorals, "trading in merchandise is so necessary that without it the world would not go on" (Jardine 1998: 327). Modern-world archaeologists must accept the challenge of conceptualizing many of their excavated artifacts as commodities to grasp the profound revolution wrought by the rise of consumerism in the West (Stearns 2001: 23). A significantly irreducible feature of modern consumerist practices involves the relationships that commodities embody.

Consumption and consumerism are impossible without commodities. In the most straightforward sense, commodities are merely objects that are expressly created for exchange. The immediate noesis when conceptualizing this view of commodities is that the definition may be restricted only to discrete objects. Careful reflection reveals, however, that humans have the power to convert services, narratives, recipes, landscapes, and even people into commodities if they wish. But individuals do not necessarily commoditize everything possible, because some entities can be excluded from the process for religious, mythical, or other sociohistorically defined reasons (Stone et al. 2000: 6). Commoditization is thus situational and historic.

Economists have analyzed and debated commoditization for many years, modeling the act of exchange in relatively straightforward terms, in which one commodity changes hands in return for a different commodity. The process of exchange thus appears relatively straightforward, while it is in truth laden with complexity. The exchanged objects need not be equal, nor must the exchange process be consummated immediately. The theory of exchange rests mainly in the bailiwick of the economist, but what interests social scientists about commodities is not that they can be exchanged, but that their exchange necessarily entails a social connection. To acquire exchange-meaning (that is, to enter a commodity state), a commodity must involve a minimum of two individuals: someone with the commodity who is willing to surrender it and someone without the commodity who would like to possess it and is thereby willing to enter into an exchange situation with the commodity holder (Orser 1996a: 113). The social transformation that accompanies exchange as a silent partner represents the commodity's substantive, albeit hidden, attributes:

A commodity appears, at first sight, a very trivial thing, and easily understood. Its analysis shows that it is, in reality, a very queer thing, abounding in metaphysical subtleties and theological niceties. So far as it is a value in use, there is nothing mysterious about it, whether we consider it from the point of view that by its properties it is capable of satisfying human wants, or from the point that those properties are the product of human labour. It is as clear as noon-day, that man, by his industry, changes the forms of the materials furnished by Nature, in such a way as to make them useful to him. The form of wood, for instance, is altered by making a table out of it. Yet, for all that, the table continues to be that common, every-day thing, wood. But, so soon as it steps forth as a commodity, it is changed into something transcendent. (Marx 1967: 71)

To become transcendent (that is, to embody the characteristic of exchange), two commodities must share a common feature in which both of them can be evaluated (Marx 1967: 37–38). In a famous illustration, Marx supposed that in a situation where one quarter measure of corn is exchanged for x cwt. of iron, the two, quite distinct commodities cannot be equal except in terms of a third entity. The third (and hidden) element for Marx was human labor, and his ruminations on the "labor theory of value" allowed him to create a theory of exploitation (Roemer 1988: 47).

The labor theory of value—in which labor is perceived as a surrogate measure for value—has understandably generated a huge literature that is outside the scope of this study (see, e.g., Cohen 1988: 209–38; Elster 1985: 127–41; Lichtenstein 1983: 152–63; Thompson 1983; Valtukh 1987: 71–77; Roemer 1988: 47–51; Whitaker 1968). For present purposes, the theoretical correctness and empirical veracity of the labor theory of value are less important than three insights that are encapsulated within it: (1) that commodities can have social meanings that are not immediately apparent to the individuals engaged in the transaction to obtain or to release them; (2) that the meanings of commodities are not static, but are free to change through time; and (3) that the process of commodification is inherently relational. The three significant implications embodied by the labor theory of value reveal the conceptual importance of value.

Judicious philosophical curiosity about value extends to Aristotle (Oates 1963) and appears in many scholarly traditions. Economists have long understood that commodities embody "use value"—meaning that they have the ability to satisfy a human want—and "exchange value"—that they can command a return of goods or services when their ownership is transferred from one individual to another. Members of modern capitalist societies typically envision exchange value in terms of price (thereby inexorably coupling exchange value and use value), but—given the mutable attributes of commodities—price and value are not synonymous concepts.

The lack of perfect conjunction between price and value is perhaps accorded its best expression by the concepts of "esteem" (Walsh 1901: 1), "aesthetic" (Simmel 1978: 73–74), or "sign" (Baudrillard 1998: 79) value. Esteem/aesthetic/sign values can embody both group- and individual-specific meanings and are therefore completely free to vary among all social positions and along all temporal and spatial vectors. Value of this sort can never be consistently constituted for all time.

The embodiment of exchange value is distinct from the embodiment of use value (Fine 1995: 143–44). In a non-market situation, exchange values may be envisioned to be bestowed through the productive process itself, such that the time consumed in production directly expresses the price sought by the seller. The producer's care and attention may be reflected in the physical demeanor of the object. A finely hand-crafted table would be assumed to have a different appearance from that of a quickly made, mass-produced table, even if they were both made of the same kind of wood. Use value is in one sense an objective attribute because it references a base-level human quality, need (Baudrillard 1998: 50). Esteem values on the other hand are purely social impositions.

Given the transitory, temporally specific nature of esteem value, a commodity's socially bequeathed properties cannot necessarily be read or inferred from the object itself. The three values of a commodity therefore operate as a tripartite dialectic (Gottdiener 2000: 25–28), such that no one kind of value need dominate in any particular sociohistoric formation or at any precise moment in history. One, two, or all three values can obtain expression, depending upon the situational context. This understanding has the practical purpose of dialectically linking production and consumption. Though Marx (1970: 196) is often credited with an almost single-minded obsession with production, he did explicitly state, "Production is thus at the same time consumption, and consumption is at the same time production. Each is simultaneously its opposite." "Consumption" is used here, then, to indicate "the processes by which consumer goods and services are created, bought [acquired], and used" (McCracken 1990: 139).

The consideration of a commodity's triadic values aptly demonstrates the complexity inherent in the substance of commoditized material objects. The linkage between value and physical appearance is minuscule, because the properties that humans bestow upon commodities are culturally defined, socially relevant, and historically situated. Commodities are, quite simply, "social things whose qualities are at the same time perceptible and imperceptible by the senses" (Marx 1967: 72). Ethnographers too numerous to cite have recognized the site-specific characteristics of commodities as elements of the social world and have irrefutably demonstrated the inherent sociality of things (see, e.g., Appadurai 1986; Haugerud et al. 2000; Howes 1996; Miller 1995). At the same time, it is important to understand that commoditization is a process, such that an object has the potential to move into and out of a commodity state throughout its "life history" (Kopytoff 1986). In one sense, objects do not remain in a commodity state throughout their existence, because they can be repeatedly recontextualized in ways that do not inherently involve exchange value. A person who purchases a hairbrush probably does not intend to reintroduce it to a second commodity state. We must also remember, however, that commodities need never lose the memory of their commodity state. Modern-day consumers are likely to imbue some former commodities with their original exchange values as they recall how much they had to surrender to obtain the object in the first place. Nonetheless, to be introduced into a use value setting, commodities must first be conceptualized as having exchange value. And, to enter the exchange value state, they must be presented as having use value. The late nineteenth-century growth of professional advertising and its current-day all-pervasive infusion into the quotidian world simultaneously indicate the paradoxicalness of the primacy of the artificial illusion of use value and the declining importance of use value in the impersonal, exchange value dominated marketplace (Durning 1992: 26–28; Wander 1984: xiii).

Modern-world archaeologists are exceptionally pressed to grapple with commodities because of the exponential growth of post-Columbian consumerism over time (Orser 1992a, 1994b). The institution of mass consumption commenced before the implementation of the capitalist enterprise (see, e.g., Braudel 1967; Jardine 1998; Mukerji 1983), but historians have unequivocally shown that a general growth in population, accompanied by an increase in economic capital attained by some European elite classes, provided the impetus for the growth of the so-called "consumer society" (e.g., Breen 1988). Defining a precise date for the institution of the consumer society is largely irrelevant to archaeological practice, and it is only pertinent to acknowledge that the transformation "is characterized less by dramatic events and famous individuals than by processes that take place over extended periods of time, begin and end at dates that are almost impossible to pinpoint, and involve the efforts of people who mostly remain anonymous" (Duplessis 1997: xi). Historians confirm that the institution of full-scale, society-wide, mass consumption grew substantially after 1400, and acknowledge with some assurance that "consumer culture is bound up with 'the whole of modernity'" (Slater 1997: 24). Modern-world archaeologists, concentrating as they do on the past 500 years or so, must surely engage commodification in some fashion or risk overlooking a major social force in modern history.

Some archaeologists of the modern world have acknowledged the historical reality of the intensified consumption of commodities in post-Columbian times and have accordingly sought to employ perspectives that promote the meanings behind the presence of mass-produced objects in archaeological deposits. Their views run the interpretive gamut from the simplicity of objective need to the subjectivity of ideational symbolism (for diverse perspectives, see Ferguson 1977; Little and Shackel 1992).

Using the household as a basic archaeological unit (e.g., Deetz 1982; Henry 1991; Klein 1991; Gibb 1996: 17–19; Wall 1994a)—also the standard unit for investigations of income poverty (Callan and Nolan 1998: 97)—some historical archaeologists have employed rigorous consumer behavior models in the effort to interpret the site-specific distribution of commodities. In an early statement of the objectives of archaeologically based consumer choice studies, Suzanne Spencer-Wood succinctly outlined the operative methodology:

Comparing the different data available from documentary and archaeological sources provides more information than can be gained from either source alone. The primary hypothesis [of the archaeological examination of consumer behavior] is that socioeconomic stratification significantly affects certain consumer behaviors, involving choices to acquire, and later archaeologically deposit, relatively expensive versus inexpensive goods. Such consumer choices are inferred primarily from quantitatively measured patterns in archaeological data. Through comparative site analyses, household variations in these patterns are explained through documented variations in socioeconomic status and/or other factors affecting consumer behavior. (1987b: xi)

From the beginning, then, the stated objective of consumer-choice archaeology was to employ textual sources of information to construct models of specific socioeconomic structures and then to use this information in conjunction with—and usually, comparatively against—the archaeological findings. The goal of such research was to examine "socioeconomic stratification as reflected in the distribution of material goods" (McBride and McBride 1987: 143).

Consumer-choice archaeologists always fully understood the impact of constraints on consumption that each household, as an essentialized historical unit, would have experienced in their quest for material objects. The frequently used term "socioeconomic status" in many of the early consumer choice studies amply expresses the interpretive primacy of purchasing power as the most significant factor influencing the presence of commodities in separate households. Capitalist-inspired common sense dictated that members of a household could purchase those objects they both desired and could afford. Within this often implicit model, those commodities that a household's members could obtain—within a fully capitalist setting—were thought to have crossed the "threshold of affordability" (Singer 1987: 85). These are the commodities that archaeologists unearth in their field investigations.

Consumer-choice archaeologists soon realized, however, that diverse factors beyond mere economics influenced the desire to purchase. The contributing elements existed both inside and outside the human body, and included place of residence, labor position, personality, perception, attitude, and ethnic and racial affiliation (see, e.g., Clark 1987: 384–86; Henry 1991: 4–10; Holt 1991: 55–56; Orser 1987: 124–26). Such readily apparent societal dispositions and personal characteristics form the basis of traditional consumer-choice analyses (see Magrabi et al. 1991: 12–15), and their adoption in the analysis of the past appeared relatively straightforward.

The application of consumer-choice models in historical archaeology is not without its legitimate critics (see, e.g., Gibb 1996: 237–38; Monks 1999) and, while consumption remains a topic of serious archaeological inquiry (see, e.g., Beaudry 1999: 119–20; Brown 1999; Courtney 1997: 15; Meadows 1999), explicit consumer-choice analyses per se are more difficult to locate after the early 1990s. Some of the hesitancy to apply consumer-choice models to past households may relate to the conceptual indeterminateness of precisely how consumer choice is "reflected" in archaeological deposits. Further confusion over measurement is perhaps suggested by the household economists' notion that the outcome of consumption is "household well-being," with "well-being" defined as "the state of health, comfort, or happiness that results from (among other things) the consumption of goods and services" (Magrabi et al. 1991: 14; also see Baudrillard 1998: 49–55). Such a vague and constantly fluid concept does not easily lend itself to archaeological assessment. Even in the presence of abundant historical documentation—even directly referencing the particular household under investigation—a firm archaeological understanding of "well-being" remains an interpretive difficulty if not an improbability.

The conceptual inability of modern-world archaeologists to grasp the most intangible elements of commodity consumption does not negate the significance of the analytical effort. Archaeologists have demonstrated the interpretive power inherent in the archaeological investigation of consumer choice. For example, in her gender-focused analysis of middle-class life in late eighteenth- and early nineteenth-century New York City, Diana Wall (1994a, 2000) provides an insightful examination of commodity usage in urban homes. Rather than to ground her analysis in the material dimensions of commodity acquisition, her stated goal is to examine the restructuring of gender roles and to decide the part that urban women may have played in creating domesticity and in reconstituting their spheres of activity. Wall envisions the family meal as a central feature of daily life, and one within which secular rituals were deeply embedded. In the words of one researcher, "personal rituals are variously used to transfer the meaning contained in goods to individual consumers" (McCracken 1986: 80). Wall argues that new activities are converted into traditions and old traditions are perpetuated through the enactment of such personal, daily rituals (Wall 1994a: 111). She further proposes that meals provide a unique perspective on the way in which women's roles—as expressed within the domestic sphere of activity—may have received expression. Her foundational idea is that the enactment of the social rituals that accompanied family meals, as well as those associated with the formalized institution of high tea, should be especially sensitive to reorganizations of the household's routine because changes in ritual—their presentation, enactment, and setting—would indicate broader, societal (in this case, gender-related) transformations. The inherent materiality of the social context is readily assured by the infrangible association between ceramics and the ways in which meals were enacted in the highly urbanized setting of the late eighteenth and early nineteenth centuries.

Wall focuses on archaeologically collected refined earthenware ceramics (manufactured for the most part in the Staffordshire factories of England) as indicators of the social changes that impacted dining habits. She divides her sample of eleven households into three temporal units: an early group, dating to the 1780s and occupationally related to a silversmith, a hatter, and two merchants; a middle group, dating to the 1800s and associated with a druggist, a grocer, a merchant, and a merchant or artisan; and a later group, dating to the 1820s and related to a physician, a druggist or boardinghouse keeper, and a merchant. Given her understanding of the social transformations that occurred during the 1780s-1820s period, Wall (1994a: 139) offers two suppositions about the ceramics: (1) because of the profound significance of meal rituals, the stylistic patterns exhibited on the ceramics should vary according to meal because the social meaning of each meal was distinct, an enactment of what McCracken (1986: 79) terms "possession rituals"; and (2) that the stylistic patterns of the ceramics should differ through time in accordance with the changing users' social contextualizations of the meals.

She separates the ceramic assemblages into five standard decorative categories—minimally decorated, shell-edged, Chinese landscape, floral, and other—to facilitate the identification of internal similarities and differences. These analytical categories allowed Wall (1994a: 140–42) to determine that the distribution of the decorative styles was indeed temporally sensitive. The early group contained almost 90 percent minimally decorated tablewares; the middle group had less than 30 percent minimally decorated tablewares and just over 60 percent shell-edged wares; and the later group had over 70 percent Chinese landscape styles and less than 10 percent minimally decorated and shell-edged styles. Wall also discerned that the exchange values of the ceramics rose over time. The price of teawares was consistently high throughout her period of interest, probably because they were objects of conscious display imbued with significantly high aesthetic/esteem/sign value. These objects appear to have been purchased despite their high cost because their use values were thus easily converted into sign values. During the same period, however, the households' members spent considerably less for their tablewares. The households' consumers actualized lower exchange values for their family-oriented commodities, while seeking to expend greatest financial resources on objects of display. By the 1820s, however, the cost of the tablewares was roughly equal to the cost of the teawares.

Wall (1994a: 162–63) ultimately uses the class-relevant and temporally sensitive ceramic variation to describe a social transformation that was rooted in the changing ideological relationship between men and women. Her interpretation is thus distanced from a conscious consumer choice model based on the consumers' internal and external needs, desires, and opportunities. She envisions the residents of the households as agents active within their own dominant spheres of activity. The woman's domain was the home and family, whereas the man's place was outside the home, within the economic and political spheres. Even within a conservative model of gender roles, the presence of different kinds of commodities in the various households is in the final analysis class-based (Wall 1994a: 173–76), with the relevant wealth measurement relying on real and personal property as referenced in the available tax records.

In another study, James Gibb (1996) investigates seventeenth-century Maryland by explicitly focusing on consumer behavior. He seeks to employ a robust consumer choice model that will significantly distance his interpretation from earlier conceptualizations of artifacts as mere reflectors of "socioeconomic status." To accomplish the required theoretical rigor, he relies upon the ideas of consumption theorists, most notably Grant McCracken (1990) and Daniel Miller (1987). Gibb adopts from these scholars the notion that consumption is a liberating, self-creative process that is inherently cultural.

Miller (1987: 33) embraces Hegel's concept of objectification as the foundation of his theory of culture, accordingly modeling consumption as a dynamic culture-creating process. He perceives an indivisibility of individuals and the things they possess, and argues that neither can be reduced to their constitutive parts as subject and object. Accordingly, material objects merely represent one form of culture, wherein the social relations embodied in mass consumption are predicated on culture and actually generate society (Miller 1987: 204). Thus, many of the cultural changes that have occurred in recent decades, including the rise of mass consumerism, have generally been positive and have provided increased opportunities for equality and social development. In tacit agreement with Wall's (1994a) general conceptual framework, Miller (1987: 212) envisions consumption as "concerned with the internalization of culture in everyday life."

McCracken (1990: 70) similarly perceives material objects to be in service to humans through the objects' abilities to perform "social and cultural work." He envisions consumer goods as objects embodying highly mutable meanings, with the consumer being actively engaged in a "cultural project" (McCracken 1990: 88). Self-actualization and identity creation is the eventual goal of this human endeavor, with the "consumer system" providing the cultural materials for self-completion. McCracken (1990: 20) notes that the linkage between consumption and a growing sense of individualism represents "one of the great cultural fusions of the modern world."

An important element of McCracken's (1990: 118–29) analysis is the Diderot Effect, a characteristic named for the eighteenth-century French philosopher Denis Diderot, who in his expansive and object-oriented encyclopedia espoused the idea of the complementariness of material objects. McCracken perceives the Diderot Effect to operate in two principal ways: it can constrain a consumer to stay within the limits of his or her general pattern of consumption, or it can force a consumer to modify his or her consumption pattern in such a manner that a wholly new pattern is created. The range of possible activity is culturally constrained, with the Diderot Unity being the sense of wholeness or harmony that results when all material objects in an assemblage appear to complement one another. In creating the Diderot Unity, the consumer must "take each product category and line it up with every other product category, so that their internal distinctions exist in parallel" (McCracken 1990: 120). Material culture lifestyles—as represented within the habitus—are thus Diderot Unities.

The Diderot Unity can have considerable conceptual utility in archaeological reasoning because it can help to explain the unequal distribution of artifact assemblages. According to McCracken (1990: 120), individuals appropriate material things based on a concept of cultural consistency, a cognitive uniformity that reflects "(1) the nature of the meaning that is contained in things, (2) the way in which this meaning enters into things, and (3) the manner in which the meaning of things is communicated by the 'object code'." As a result, material things take their meanings from their contextualizations. The objects in combination display an internal consistency that is enacted within and through the habitus and expressed within the social fields. Gibb adopts the insights provided by McCracken and Miller to argue that archaeologically collected artifacts were systemic objects employed in the constantly changing conceptualizations of self-image, and he proposes that archaeologists can employ archival and archaeological information to examine artifact assemblages to reveal the objects' "symbolic" contexts.

Gibb's central task is to investigate wealth in seventeenth-century Maryland, described as consisting of the totality of a person's possession of objects that were either already existing commodities or which had the potential to become commodities. His concentration, then, is on those things that "were deemed to have market value" and that were decidedly household-centered rather than invested in instruments of credit, mortgages, or other non-household-specific entities (Gibb 1996: 41). Gibb envisions the household as the locus for "articulating values, promoting strategies, and reconciling conflict within the basic residential group of a colonial society" (2). Consumer behavior is thus related to the acquisition of goods rather than to pure consumption per se (i.e., expenditure through use). He creates three propositions out of this framework that have clear cut implications for archaeological research: (1) all material culture is wealth or potential wealth until it is discarded; (2) wealth is situated in the household (also see Hayden 2001); and (3) households express their identities through their consumer choices, as a measure of their use of wealth (211). Most important, perhaps, he models wealth and consumer choice as pivotal in establishing and continuing inter-household relationships, with ethnicity, race, and class being merely extensions of consumer decisions rather than determinants (211). In other words, because his project is intended to rotate the analytical focus inward (within the household) rather than outward (to the social order), he minimizes the effects of race, class, and ethnicity; they are perceived as playing no role in the household political economy.

Gibb investigates his ideas on household consumption using two seventeenth-century sites in Maryland. He models the inhabitants of the sites as goal-directed individuals and argues that the relevant historical records indicate that they had six major concerns: (1) the perpetuation of the patrilineage; (2) the expression of personal power, honor, and social position of the male head of household and the virtue of the women in his care; (3) the assurance of the financial future of his children; (4) the maintenance of idealized family relations; (5) the achievement of self-sufficiency; and (6) an engagement with agriculture as a means of ensuring security, honor, and wealth (Gibb 1996: 212). These textually verifiable interfamilial interests unfortunately do not lend themselves to easy archaeological interpretation, except to associations that relate to architectural space, the siting of property, and the distribution of graves in cemeteries. Gibb (220–27) attempts to examine his conceptions about wealth in terms of the distribution of ceramic vessels, but finds the comparative samples to be inadequate.

That both Wall and Gibb acknowledge the limitations inherent in the quality and quantity of their data (Gibb 1996: 227; Wall 1994a: 206–7) merely indicates the nascent state of serious, commodity-focused, modern-world social archaeology. Even with inadequate information, however, we nonetheless rediscover from their in-depth investigations what the earliest consumer-choice archaeologists learned: that the association of consumerism with past social variables is exceedingly difficult. Wall (1994a: 157) focuses her investigation on social class, modeling urban social space along classic sociological grounds, where a middle class serves "as intermediaries between capitalists and labor." Her overt concentration on the class structure of urban New York causes her to minimize other social factors, even though she inherently understands their significance. She notes, for example, that middle-class male New Yorkers—

those individuals who moved within public economic and political spheres of activity—were not able to identify with the interests of the city's industrial workers because "a large proportion of [them] were foreign-born" (157). The obvious social gap between the American middle class and the foreign-born lower class raises the specter of how nativity, as operationalized as race, affected social interaction. We may well wonder what is inherently distinctive about being foreign-born that would incite inter-group difficulties between classes. Previously cited studies of American race and ethnicity suggest that the basis for misunderstanding originated within the historically developed habitus of the middle class. Within carefully controlled fields, members of the upwardly mobile middle class simply defined the foreign-born as Other and in so doing created an enforceable social chasm between themselves and these outsiders—men, women, and even children who were destined for low-paying, lowly regarded positions in the city's hierarchy of labor, a reality that Wall (1999: 103–4) later acknowledged. Gibb also does not envision racialization to have any significance within his interpretive framework for seventeenth-century Maryland because the household constitutes the locus of significant human practice. His vision that race, class, and ethnicity are secondary within the broader pursuit of household-centric wealth is meaningful because it allows him to negate all social variables beyond intra-household sex and age. Wealth has the practical function of creating and recreating the household's identity beyond the household (Gibb 1996: 43). His evaluation in this regard is profoundly important because the use of wealth for the establishment and reinforcement of visible social identity is at least partly based on the acquisition of commodities from outside the household. Gibb assents that "the world capitalist system constrained and directed household decision making" (44), but he minimizes the impact of this global market by asserting that the households based their consumerist decisions on their perceptions of the larger world rather than upon their perfect understanding of it. We can only conclude from his assessment that the households of English colonists within the sample all had equal access to the marketplace operating outside the households. This interpretation is difficult to sustain, however, because the pursuit of wealth is based on a household's ability to realize acquisition. It is extremely unlikely, even in a constantly developing colonialist environment, that all households were equally endowed with wealth-realizing potentialities. Thus, a dialectics of acquisition and meaning operates between the social relations enacted within the household and those that operate outside the household.

Economists know, however, that not all households have equal access to the marketplace or, once in the marketplace, an equivalency of opportunity. The sociohistorical circumstances of market-based class formation are of course infinitely complex and nuanced, and accordingly defy simple, uniform modeling. Economists have nonetheless demonstrated the clear linkage between initial endowments of capital and eventual class position (see Roemer 1988: 75–82) and numerous sociologists, including Bourdieu, have written extensively on the various possible connections between social position and economic capital, with race assignment often constituting a major determining attribute.

As noted previously, archaeologists in the past have generally been reluctant to engage the material effects of racialization. The precise reasons for this neglect remain somewhat unclear, but at least one archaeologist imagines that the archaeological conceptualization of racism as a totalizing structure has the power to limit individual action, thereby serving to make African American studies inconsistent with the current interest in agency (De Cunzo 1998: 43, 52). Paul Mullins has defied the trend of extracting racism from the conduct of human practice and has provided the most detailed and insightful studies involving the correlation of racial identity and consumption in modern-world archaeology (Mullins 1999a, b, 2001).

Mullins actively engages the importance of racialization and employs the writings of social commentators such as Du Bois (1999) as well as scholars who specifically investigated African American consumerism (e.g., Edwards 1932) to investigate the consumption profiles of three African American households in Annapolis, Maryland: the Maynard-Burgess House (occupied from 1850/58–1980s), the Courthouse Site (a neighborhood occupied from the mid-nineteenth century until the 1960s), and Gott's Court (an alley community inhabited from 1907–1952).

Though Mullins respects the significance of the household as a primary archaeological unit of analysis, unlike Gibb (and perhaps because of the different temporal focus) he does not minimize the impact of the outside world on the consumption habits of the houses' residents. Mullins argues quite the contrary, that the privilege of African American citizenship was imbued as much in consumption as in other rights. Instead of simply ascribing consumption to need, Mullins (1999a: 18) assigns it considerably more political-economic significance: "consumption was an African-American sociopolitical statement of civil aspirations, material desires, and resistance to monolithic racist caricatures." For African Americans, Mullins argues, consumption was a type of symbolic statement about basic human rights. The African American strategy of acquisition and ownership was requisite because American consumerist space was inherently racist, even to the point that the police could arrest African American window shoppers who, by their very presence, appeared to violate the rules of white consumption (Mullins 1999a: 41–77).

In a profound demonstration of the nuanced complexity of racialization, Mullins (1999a: 76) posits that racialization was more than a structure that had the power to limit African American practice. Racism has always been a potent force in American life, but Mullins shows how African American men and women could use it "as a launching pad for an utterly politicized African-American material symbolism" (77). The struggle was inherently material in scope and design.

Mullins (2001) employs the presence of bric-a-brac in the archaeological deposits of African-American homes to illustrate the subtleties of racialized consumption. The small ceramic statuettes—usually fashioned to resemble notable historical personages or bucolic figures—were more than the trivial objects of display most people imagine. Mullins proposes instead that the African American consumers of these objects contextualized them in flexible, symbolic ways. Bric-a-brac represented one way for African Americans to symbolize both their aspirations within, and the challenges they faced from, a racist society. As he insightfully observes, the producers of the apparently inconsequential curios did not imagine that they could be employed in such symbolically powerful ways, because the objects were simply insignificant to non-African Americans (Mullins 2001: 176). As African American consumers recontextualized the statuettes, however, they cemented their social place within the wider marketplace, but in such a manner that the dominant social space—and its carefully crafted, racist ideology—were not threatened. Bric-a-brac was thus a "daydreaming commodity" (164) in which the consumer's aspirations could be embodied, exclusive of the material realities in which the consumer was enmeshed. The sign value of bric-a-brac was immense when it was recontextualized within the African American home.

Mullin's research, perhaps more than any other currently existing body of work, demonstrates that the addition of racialization to archaeological consumption studies raises a profusion of seminal questions. These questions inherently involve practice.

The Practice of Consumption

In keeping with the ideas outlined in the previous chapter, a concept of consumption must be employed that is consistent with practice theory. Bourdieu's most explicit ideas on the societal use of material objects appears in *Distinction*, a book that is considered to have been responsible for the retheorization of consumption studies in much social science (Miles 2001: 67). *Distinction* has also received considerable archaeological citation since it first appeared in English. Even though most archaeologists are aware of the book, few appear to have recognized its applicability to archaeological thought. Part of the problem of archaeological adaptation may stem from Bourdieu's focus on the French middle class, a sociohistorical formation that many archaeologists may find difficult to equate with their research universe. The issue of correlation is not as significant a problem for modern-world archaeologists because many of the structural mechanics of exchange and production/consumption remain roughly homeostatic within the historical expression of the capitalist domain, with the obvious caveat of situationally sensitive transformations.

Bourdieu bases his analysis in an unambiguous class structure, in which his three primary dimensions of stratification—volume of capital, composition of capital, and social trajectory (complete with synchronic and diachronic dimensions) (Bourdieu 1984: 170)—provide the basis for analysis (see Swartz 1997: 162). Consumer behavior and lifestyle considerations are rooted in the habitus, the social space in which individuals are enculturated with their internal understandings and reasonable expectations, and then put into practice within the appropriate fields. Bourdieu rejects the inherent rationality of consumer-choice models— beginning with Adam Smith's "invisible hand" proposition that "I am rational, therefore I self-maximize" (McMurtry 1998: 127–32). He rejects the rational-actor model because the associations between economics and commodity selection are mediated by the habitus. Distinctions in habitus ensure that individuals with the same incomes do not necessarily obtain the same sets of material goods.

Thus seeking to abandon any sort of rational-choice perspective, Bourdieu (1984: 173) defines material preference as "taste": "the propensity and capacity to appropriate (materially or symbolically) a given class of classified, classifying objects or practices." For Bourdieu, "taste expresses the precise position of the individual in the networks of power relations" (Dant 1999: 21). The homology that occurs within the set of objects that an individual appropriates represents a Diderot Unity that exists in harmony with the habitus. Inherently understanding how their tastes are to be expressed, individuals enter different fields of practice. An individual's purchasing power therefore does not alone establish the parameters of consumer choice because the habitus constantly works to structure and to homologize the Diderot Unity. Any appearance that a direct linkage exists between income and consumption is only apparent because of the homology between taste and income. When economic analysts credit income as the only causal characteristic in commodity selection, they are actually measuring the homology between habitus and income (Bourdieu 1984: 375). While it is true that individuals purchase commodities "in order to take possession of a small concrete part of the style of life to which they aspire" (McCracken 1990: 111), this act of purchase does not occur outside the habitus.

Social archaeologists accepting practice theory must accordingly reject any simplistic "socioeconomic status"/commodities correlation. As Bourdieu (1984: 374) notes "Having a million does not in itself make one able to live like a millionaire." Individuals with the same relative incomes can surround themselves with quite distinct objects, in the course of "stylizing" their lives. The relation between the habitus and taste is thus truly dialectic. For archaeologists, habitus without taste—as represented by commodities—is as impossible as taste without habitus. In the context of class-based social structures, material culture lifestyles become reproduced and internalized as a classificatory system that exists within the social space and appears natural.

A significant element of Bourdieu's conceptual framework, and one that has particular relevance for modern-world archaeologists (and for any archaeologists investigating highly stratified sociohistorical formations), revolves around his idea that social spaces are sites of constant struggle. He proposes, for example, that a "basic opposition" exists between "tastes of luxury" and "tastes of necessity" that serves to create social distance between haves and have-nots (Bourdieu 1984: 183–84). Elite class members are able to realize greater expenditures of exchange values to satisfy the "taste for freedom" which their habitus incorporates and which is expressed in the Diderot Unity. In their search for material distinction, members of the dominant class are able to express their cultural capital through every facet of daily life, including the creation and practice of ceremonial rituals "governed by rules of etiquette and sociability" (Swartz 1997: 167). In Bourdieu's (1984: 55) terms, the elites' economic power distances them from want at the same time that it permits them to express their luxury and relative ease of living. Privileged elites thus maneuver in a world where they can operationalize "consumer sovereignty" (McMurtry 1998: 166).

The commodities obtained by the elites are not intended to be neutral. The presence of commodities, which may in fact serve to create a sense and even a reality of increased well-being, acts both as gift and curse. A whole array of inter-group conflicts occur as the market-based system positions individuals and groups into various social spaces. The individuals who feel the domination wrought by the marketplace experience insecurity and a host of social costs (Bourdieu 1998a: 29–44). As Marcuse observed:

The technical division of labor divides the human being itself into partial operations and functions, coordinated by the coordinators of the capitalist process. This technostructure of exploitation organizes a vast network of human instruments which produce and sustain a rich society. For unless he belongs to the *ruthlessly suppressed minorities*, the individual also benefits from this richness. (1972: 14; emphasis added)

Men and women who are not members of the elite social space, and who in fact are defined in contrast to the elites, are confronted with a dialectical taste of necessity that exists in opposition to the elite's taste of freedom. The sense-experience of those relegated to positions structurally beneath the elites, particularly those enmeshed in poverty (however defined), occurs against a backdrop of the elite's tastes for freedom (Charlesworth 2000: 56–57). Those individuals designated poor are frequently divided into "the undeserving poor" and the "deserving poor," with the former being stigmatized because they are responsible for their own condition (Bourdieu 1998a: 43; Gans 1995: 6–7). The habitus of the poor is circumscribed by their sense of helplessness and vulnerability, even though as individuals they may have great personal will to climb the social hierarchy. When all social relations are reduced to economistic value within a market-based sociohistorical formation, having little or no money is one of the individual's greatest social crimes. The socially designed stigma that attaches to economic poverty obtains because the individuals designated "poor" appear as dependents rather than as consumers. In other words, their access to the commodities of the marketplace is limited. In such situations, race-based discrimination can serve as one mechanism the elites—those men and women with complete freedom to consume and with the uppermost racial designation—can use to establish and recreate social differentiation (Gans 1995: 28–29; McMurtry 1998: 162; Roemer 1988: 118).

Bourdieu's (1984: 184) analysis of French class reveals the prominence of three "structures of consumption" distributed across three item-domains: food, culture (by which he means all those expressions regarded as "high culture"), and presentation (which includes clothing, the employment of servants, and beauty treatments). As must be expected given the existence of habitus and the unequal distribution of the many forms of capital across social space, the three item-domains are differentially apportioned. Individuals at the lower end of the social hierarchy realize less expenditure for high-cultural items (such as books and theater tickets) than those individuals within the elite. Tastes for food are homologous, such that the dominant class drink more milk and eat more chocolate than the working class, while members of the working class tend to prefer salty foods that are often gendered as masculine (Bourdieu 1984: 382–83).

Bourdieu repeatedly cautions against reading his interpretation as ultimately rooted in purchasing power rather than habitus, but it is nonetheless tempting to perceive his analysis as based in the final analysis on pure economic scaling. His dominant, elite class can be idealized as an example of Weber's (1968: 303) "property class." This reading of Bourdieu's framework, though alluring, is grossly incorrect. Even if we choose to ignore the importance of the habitus, a facile reading would be misguided because of the structural nature of the social hierarchy, such that the lifestyles of the non-elites "serve as a negative reference for the dominant class" (Swartz 1997: 169). Their lifestyles, rather than existing in a self-sustaining, exclusive reality, dialectically help to define the lifestyles of the elites.

Bourdieu's concentration on the dominant French classes of the late twentieth century means that he provides little discussion of an important dimension of taste with particular archaeological relevancy: the invention of taste through the introduction of new commodities. Bourdieu is able to take mass commoditization as a given reality in contemporary French society, but this is not a luxury afforded to most archaeologists, particularly those interested in the interaction between diverse cultures intent on cross-cultural exchange. Historians have often written about the "colonization of taste" that occurred in the colonial world, frequently positing that the acceptance of mass consumer goods "just happened" (Breen 1988: 84–85). Perspectives of this sort tend to promote the "global homogenization paradigm," in which analysts assume that the spread of foreign-made commodities into new cultural settings produces a worldwide, mass-produced culture that is growing increasing similar as all local manifestations of tradition are smothered into extinction (Howes 1996: 3–4). Thoughtful reflection reveals, however, that "globalization is not homogenization; on the contrary, it is the extension of the hold of a small number of dominant nations over the whole set of national financial markets" (Bourdieu 1998a: 38).

Studies by anthropologists have repeatedly demonstrated the fallacy of the idea that the introduction of previously unknown consumer goods is a natural process and one that necessarily works to create global homogeneity. Numerous studies have illustrated the "mutability of things in recontextualization" (N. Thomas 1991: 28), as individuals reinvent the meanings, usages, and even the perceptions of commodities. Research has also indicated that many of the individuals involved in an exchange situation do not necessarily conceive of the transferable commodities in the same way. For example, the Europeans who encountered the indigenous peoples of the New World typically referred to the objects they traded away as "trifles," and in the process imagined that they had received vastly greater value in return: "the more worthless and hollow the trifle, the more value is gained in the exchange" (Greenblatt 1991: 110). In this sense, they built exploitation into the exchange process, and justified it with their views about racial and cultural inferiority as they created the primitive Other, a construction that often contained some notion of poverty (McMurtry 1998: 162; Thomas 1991: 84–85). In many cases, the men and women Other who played an integral, productive role in the wider global economy, did not understand the non-local usage of the commodities they produced (Weiss 1996: 93).

Equally important as the social-structural nature of the social space, and especially significant here, is Bourdieu's (1984: 178) observation that the distance between the habitus incorporating the taste for freedom and the habitus with the taste for necessity can lead to "class racism." Class racism grafts notions of inferiority, stupidity, and general coarseness onto non-elites and in the process invents the "undeserving poor." The structural correlation between "class racism" and racialization should not be missed because the application of subjective social difference can include physiologic characteristics. In fact, it is the social-structural, definitional application of such characteristics of perceived physical appearance that leads to the creation of a racialized social structure in the first instance.

The accuracy of Bourdieu's assessment of class racism, or even appearance-based racism, is affirmed by patterns of urban African American consumption in the late 1920s and early 1930s (Edwards 1932). Advertisers attempted to entice African American consumers to purchase specific products by approaching them simply as economically conscious individuals. In imagining the African American consumer as "a simple-souled individual, little interested in or appreciating other appeals than price" (Edwards 1932: 199), advertisers disregarded any notion of African American taste. In anticipation of Bourdieu's analysis, Edwards's study demonstrated that different African American occupational classes (common and semi-skilled laborers, skilled laborers, and business and professional people) purchased different products (also see Mullins 1999b).

Bourdieu's comments about food preferences are especially interesting given the findings of Edwards's African American survey. Bourdieu (1984: 177) argues that as individuals rise in the social hierarchy, the proportion of income they will expend on inexpensive, fatty, heavy foods declines. This correlation may initially appear to be based solely on the amount of accessible economic capital, but Bourdieu notes that French foremen, who may actually earn more than clerical and commercial employees, generally have a more "popular" taste than do office workers, whose tastes more accurately mirror those of educated teachers. African Americans in the urban American South in the early decades of the twentieth century exhibited the same pattern: "Negro common and semi-skilled labor families in the urban South make their chief diet of heavy, energy-producing, muscle-building foods" (Edwards 1932: 56). Rather than representing some sort of homologous, universal habitus, however, the findings of the African American survey suggest the complex relationship that obtains between habitus, capital, and race. As

Mullins (1999a: 48–49, 2001: 158) notes, the dominant consumer culture in capitalism was irrepressibly white in design and implementation.

Material distinction is one of the primary implications of cultural and racial domination because non-elites (however they are defined) are compelled to substitute economically cheaper objects for those appropriated by the elites (Bourdieu 1984: 386–87). Working-class families thus surround themselves with reproductions rather than oil paintings, popular music rather than classical sonatas, and vinyl rather than leather furniture. The unequal distribution of material objects in this manner is a historical dimension of capitalism (Braudel 1985: 283–84). The social-structural character of the have/have-not dichotomy is designed to identify the material expressions of the elite as the "legitimate" (i.e., "authentic") culture, an expression that is accordingly misrecognized as objective and even natural (Bourdieu and Passeron 1977: 23–24). But the material appropriation of the elites only exists in opposition to the material cultural appropriation of the non-elites. The subjective illegitimacy of the non-elites' lifestyle is summarized as "popular culture" (Bourdieu 1990a: 150–55).

The elites often attempt to appear to upgrade the material culture of the dominated by reference to a "populi-culture," a thinly veiled, degraded version of the cultural goods of the dominant class fraction (Bourdieu and Wacquant 1992: 82–83). Bourdieu's position in this regard may at first appear to constitute an unflinching devotion to the dominant ideology thesis (e.g., Abercrombie et al. 1980), but the truth is quite the opposite. He instead argues for the conceptualization of an ongoing struggle among the dominant to maintain their primacy in the material culture hierarchy, while they allow some of their favored goods (or some approximation thereof) to fall into the hands of the dominated. Rather than robbing the dominated of their agency, Bourdieu's perspective merely illustrates the realities of the heart and soul of capitalism as an inherently unequalizing economic system. The modes of appropriation, both within the sociohistorical formation and cross-culturally, are understandably a complex and much-debated issue (see Howes 1996; Haugerud et al. 2000).

Spatial Practice

The social space within which the habitus is enacted in the fields and within which various forms of capital are amassed and dispensed does not exist in the abstract, but in actual, physical space. As is true of many theoretical sociologists, however, Bourdieu does not overtly concentrate on the geographic dimensions of social space. Topological space is nonetheless inherent in Bourdieu's notion of the field: "We may think of a field as a space within which an effect of field is exercised, so that what happens to any object that traverses this space cannot be explained solely by the intrinsic properties of the object in question. The limits of the field are situated at the point where the effects of the field cease" (Bourdieu and Wacquant 1992: 100). Bourdieu's conceptualization of a field is thus theoretic and social, but we may also simultaneously envision it literally as acreage, the boundaries of which terminate with the physical edges of the plot itself.

Bourdieu's notion of social space, though comprised of expressional and attitudinal positions assumed by social actors, necessarily involves places. To separate physical space from social space is to deny the reality of life because "The ordering of space in buildings [where some of the fields are enacted] is really about the ordering of relations between people" (Hillier and Hanson 1984: 2; also see Delle 1998: 37–40). This statement can easily be interpreted dualistically, so that the placement of rooms within a building helps structure and frame the interpersonal relations enacted within it (after Hall's [1963] proxemics), or we may imagine that the spaces actually interact with the individuals inside them to help create social relations. In either case, it is imperative that our understanding acknowledges that "social theory must be about the time-space constitution of social structure *right from the start*" (Thrift 2002: 114; emphasis in original). The homology between social space and physical space is of supreme importance to practice theory, because it is impossible to extract action from the locality of its enactment. Accordingly, the "socio-spatial dialectic" (Soja 1980)—characterized by the interaction between spatial structure and social structure—operates as an ongoing, constantly mutable process (Soja 1989: 57, 81).

The need to adopt the sociospatial dialectic at the outset is well represented by reconsidering commodities. As noted above, commodities incorporate both physical and social, real and imagined characteristics, and so it is impossible to identify the primary attributes that distinguish any particular commodity. But just as commodities are social and physical, they are also spatial. The very definition of "commodity"—as something intended for exchange—necessarily incorporates spatiality, because the object is designed to be transferred from person to person and from place to place. In economics, the inherent spatiality of commodities is aptly illustrated by the term "commodity chain" (see Jackson and Thrift 1995: 212–17). As the term implies, the commodity chain is the route that a specific commodity or group of commodities must travel before it reaches its final destination. The extent of commodity chains is typically minimal in pre- and non-capitalist settings. The seasonal exchange of horticultural goods produced by the sedentary Arikaras of the

North American northern plains for the bison hides processed by the nomadic Dakotas provides a ready example (for historic citations see Orser 1980: 146–52). In settings such as these, the direct producers of the commodities were also the individuals engaged in the trade, and so a two-element commodity chain operates. The commodity chain was only enlarged by a factor of 1 when the bison hides were re-exchanged to nomadic peoples living west of the Arikaras. The commodity chains were expanded during the earliest trading encounters between European explorers and indigenous peoples, so that the spatiality of the commodities would be structured as follows: factory → merchant → trader → native recipient. The spatial dimensions of the commodity chains are even broader today because of the addition of numerous suppliers and multi-level merchants. In the language of commodity flow analysis, today's commodity chains have great "depth" because they involve many commodity sites (Jackson and Thrift 1995: 215). A significant, albeit situationally sensitive, measure of time is also involved in any commodity chain, and it is equally impossible to remove the social elements of the commodity chains (see Collins 2000).

An analysis of the Kabyle house allowed Bourdieu (1990b: 271–83) the opportunity to explore spatial subjects, and many archaeologists are familiar with his examination. His fairly straightforward interpretation illustrated how the physical structure of the house design was dialectically structured with the practices that occurred within and around it. Given the specificity of Bourdieu's examination, it is perhaps conceptually easy to treat his analysis as merely ethnographic, with little or no nonspecific application. We must recognize at the same time, however, that all Bourdieu's social analyses incorporate spatiality, though not as overtly as the Kabyle house study. For example, his masterful investigation of the French academic field, while not directly addressing matters of physical space per se, nonetheless includes the concept that the "morphological transformations of the disciplines" incorporated necessary spatial transformations as well (Bourdieu 1988). As French intellectuals created the various academic disciplines and sought to distinguish them from one another (while concurrently seeking to imbue them with capital and power), they also sought spatial distance from disciplines with less capital and power. Hard scientists could therefore establish their intellectual capital and their scientific power and prestige through constructing high-tech laboratories, using grants provided by prestigious agencies, as well as by affiliating with important scientific institutes. Conversely, scholars in the humanities, who did not require sophisticated laboratories and who often labored in solitude without the assistance of numerous laboratory technicians, had a much more difficult time building academic capital. In keeping with the principal characteristics of the habitus, much of the search for intellectual capital is unconscious, seemingly relating strictly to the way in which the individual disciplines operate.

In a similar vein, the social distinctions of taste examined by Bourdieu (1984) in modern-day France also incorporate social spatiality. Men and women with high economic capital and low cultural capital tend to maintain spatial arrangements different from those of individuals with other amounts of capital. As a sociologist, Bourdieu is more concerned with the nature of social relations and does not provide much in the way of clues about the significance of space. Accordingly, he fails to present archaeologists with ways in which to use practice theory spatially.

Fortunately, Henri Lefebvre (1991), a contemporary of Bourdieu's, rectifies the spatial deficiencies in Bourdieu's practice theory and explicitly expounds upon the sociospatial dialectic in a manner wholly consistent with Bourdieu's outline. Lefebvre's writings are as dense and as difficult as Bourdieu's, but his views on the production of space are widely considered to represent "a touchstone of contemporary thinking" about spatiality (Dear and Flusty 2002: 131) and as such cannot be ignored by archaeologists pursuing practice theory.

The basis of Lefebvre's argument is that space is socially constituted, that it inherently incorporates social action, and that it is never innocent. These attributes clearly indicate that space is a social product and that it can be commoditized (Lefebvre 1979). Lefebvre argues that the already existing "science of space" is only adept at allowing for descriptive statements about what occurs in space. Proponents of the traditional "science of space" have generated a lengthy and complex discourse on space, but they have not been able to develop actual knowledge of space. What is required, says Lefebvre, is a "unitary theory" of space that can link together the three "fields" of spatial practice: the physical, the mental, and the social. In an archaeological example, Delle (1998: 38–39) refers to these three spaces as, respectively, material, cognitive, and social. The goal of Lefebvre's theory about "the space of social practice" is to illustrate how space is actually produced by individuals in action. He thus speaks of "social space" as the inseparable unity of the three spaces, and seeks to demonstrate that it "is constituted neither by a collection of things or an aggregate of (sensory) data, nor by a void packed like a parcel with various contents" (Lefebvre 1991: 27).

Lefebvre notes, however, that social space resists analysis because of its complexity and because it is often masked by illusions that bestow upon it a sense of naturalness and substance. Here we can identify the homology between illusions of space and illusions of race. Both conceptualizations, in the present and in their many historical expressions, seek to reify an imposed order. Both race and space exist as a reflection of their past, but both are constantly being expressed and enacted in the present through and because of their past (Lefebvre 1979: 286). In this sense, both race and space are transhistorical.

Lefebvre proposes that social space contains two kinds of relations, each of which is assigned a situationally appropriate location within a particular sociohistoric formation: the social relations of reproduction (biological and physiologic relations between males and females, age grades, and family members), and the relations of production (the division of labor and its organization in the form of hierarchically designed social functions). He employs a simple contrast between precapitalist and capitalist (or "modern neocapitalist") sociohistorical formations to illustrate the general way in which these relations operate in tandem to create social space. In precapitalist settings, the two relations are irreducibly locked together in order to reproduce the social order through time and despite internal strife, warfare, feuds, and inter-generational conflict. With the creation of capitalism, however, three interlocking levels were created: biological reproduction (the family), the reproduction of labor power (the working class per se), and the reproduction of social relations of production.

While we may wish to quibble with Lefebvre's broad-based, somewhat totalizing, cultural historical schema, two important ideas emerge from his conceptual framework: (1) that space embraces a vast array of social interconnections, each of which maintains a specific location, and (2) that a conceptual triad exists. The triad is perhaps the most significant element of Lefebvre's framework because it provides a way to conceptualize a spatially oriented practice theory. Lefebvre's triad consists of the following elements: spatial practice, representations of space, and representational spaces.

Spatial practice is the way in which a particular sociohistorical formation promotes and presupposes space as a dialectical process between the physical reality and the ways in which human action manipulates, uses, and recreates space. The spatial practice of a society—which is understandable as perceived space—is revealed through deciphering or decoding its space. The spatial practice of medieval Europe, for instance, incorporated the network of roads that connected monasteries, castles, and peasant communities, as well as all the other passageways and routes used by pilgrims and Crusaders. In a post-Columbian, capitalist polity, perceived space consists of the dialectics that operate between daily routine and all the properties of urbanity that comprise the city (e.g., road networks and high-rise buildings) and which inherently interconnect the work routine with leisure. Each society's social practice is cohesive but not necessarily coherent.

Representations of space are conceptualized spaces imagined by social planners, scientists, and urban designers. These spaces are usually designated by a system of consciously created verbal signs, and as such they constitute space conceived through subjective knowledge and ideology. Representations of space are always open to modification. Even though they may be abstract, representations of space have the ability to establish and reinforce relations between people and things and thus accordingly figure into social practice. In the European Middle Ages, representations of space were created from Christian concepts of the cosmos, Earth, heaven, and hell. In modern-day capitalist societies, the representations of space appear in advertising and other promotional media.

Representational spaces or spaces of representation are those that are directly lived through associated images, symbols, and mythic narratives. This space overlays physical space and is the space that individuals seek to change. Such spaces tend to be comprised of coherent systems of nonverbal symbols and signs. In medieval Europe, representational space determined the focal points of life in accordance with interpretations about important symbolic beliefs (churches, holy wells). In today's consumerist societies, shopping malls and department stores are spaces of representation.

Lefebvre (1991: 39–40) stresses that the three spaces operate as a perceived-conceived-lived triad which contributes to the production of space within a specific sociohistorical formation. The triad is internalized as part of the habitus. As men and women live spatially, they are mostly unaware of the importance of space because of the illusion that space is materially inherent. Space merely appears to pre-exist as a tableau upon which practice is enacted rather than as an active agent of social practice. In this sense, the dialectical relation between representations of space and spaces of representation can function as a trap, particularly in hierarchically ordered sociohistorical formations within which the spatial users are passive: "Only a small 'elite' see the trap and manage to sidestep it. The elitist character of some oppositional movements and social critiques should perhaps be viewed in this light. Meanwhile, however, the social control of space weighs heavy indeed upon all those consumers who fail to reject the familiarity of everyday life" (Lefebvre 1991: 233).

An important feature of Lefebvre's understanding of social space is the concept that spatial practice changes with the creation of new social practices. This understanding follows from Lefebvre's strong insistence that space is social. For practical purposes, Lefebvre's conceptualization in this regard serves to demonstrate one important sociohistoric characteristic of the modern world: the enactment of new social relations rooted in commodity exchange and the institution of new social relations of dependence. His view foregrounds the notion that the invention of mass commoditization, however it was received at the local scale, was as much a "Spatial Revolution" as anything else (Blaut 1993: 172). Wallerstein's (1979) "capitalist world-economy" comes nearest to Lefebvre's perspective, though it is not a perfect reflection of it.

Both Lefebvre and Bourdieu use a concept of "strategy" in their theoretic formulations. For Bourdieu, it constitutes a key concept in the theory of the field (Johnson 1993: 17–18). Rather than a strategy being comprised of a series of conscious, calculated maneuvers—as the term is commonly used—Bourdieu envisions it as a constituent element of the habitus that is manifested as a "feel for the game" (Bourdieu and Wacquant 1992: 128–29; also see Bourdieu 1977b: 214n2). Time is an important element of a strategy, because the actor involved may not anticipate the outcome of his or her action, and a final resolution of an action's effects may take some duration to be completed (Swartz 1997: 99–100). The accompanying uncertainty permits Bourdieu (1990a: 9–10) to eschew the use of social "rules," and to replace, for example, the "rules of kinship" with "matrimonial strategies."

Lefebvre (1991: 375) incorporates a compatible notion of spatial strategy in his theory of spatial production. As individuals produce space, the created space often functions in service to a dominant class, seeking to create and to reify spatial difference. Elites in a modern-day, capitalist setting imbue the "center" (where they live and conduct business) with more power, authority, and wealth than the "periphery" (the place they exploit), just as they differentiate "public" from "private" space with the construction of governmental and corporate office buildings. Even within such highly regulated spaces, however, social space is a field of action, wherein men and women are both "enabled and constrained," where they can both acquiesce and resist (Pred 1990: 9). The creation of social spaces within the habitus merely reflects overt and tacit potentialities and options; spatial understanding is thus "second nature" (Soja 1989: 129). The distribution of knowledge throughout the social structure—as incorporated within the habitus—is differential rather than uniform, with racialization being assigned as a determining attribute along with age, gender, and ethnicity (Thrift 1985: 369).

The intersection of class with the production of space necessarily and inescapably includes the creation and enactment of power relations, however they are historically designed and implemented (Pred 1985: 339). The struggle that operates as the relations of power incorporates more than simple conflict or competition between different social classes or class fractions, because exercised power has the ability to imprint space with its perspective (Darby 2000: 15–16). This imprint becomes an elite representation of space which, within the specifics of the sociohistorical circumstances, may or may not become a representational space.

The sociospatial dialectic that exists within Lefebvre's notion of social space is closely aligned with practice theory, because both inexorably include a notion of network relations. As noted in the previous chapter, Bourdieu was cognizant of network models even if he did not overtly develop them in his social analyses. Though Bourdieu tended to reject formal network theory because of its often rigid structure (Swartz 1997: 146), there is no question that his advice to "think relationally" must involve network modeling in some fashion (Bourdieu 1992: 228). Lefebvre's (1991: 53) perceived-conceived-lived triad is equally rooted in a conceptual base that incorporates the notion of a dense overlay of various networks of interaction. The active nature of the various networks is adequately expressed by conceptualizing "landscape" as both a noun and a verb (Darby 2000: 12).

Many scholars concerned with sociospatial matters have often eschewed formal network theory because of its propensity to be deterministic, formulaic, and particularistically empirical. Such criticisms are not entirely unwarranted, but a complete rejection of network theory is unfortunate, because network models—when used more than metaphorically—do have a contribution to make to practice theory. Interest in networks should be especially strong among archaeologists because of the inherently spatial nature of archaeological remains. Some understanding of networks is arguably the most pressing for modern-world archaeologists because of their need to conceptualize action and knowledge "at a distance" (Law and Hetherington 2002: 396), especially as it pertains to the operation of large-scale exchange networks of the sort that were created and maintained during and after the so-called Age of European Expansion.

One of the greatest deficiencies in social network analysis is that too many network analysts seek to remove their social actors from the physical spaces they occupy. The actors merely operate topologically in relation to one another, outside the parameters of any physical space. The greatest strength of social network analysis—that of "emphasizing relations that connect the social positions within a system" (Knoke and Kuklinski 1982: 10)—thus also constitutes its most profound weakness. Accepting the sociospatial dialectic means that the goal of the analysis should be to situate a social network within historic and spatial specificity, so that the individuals in a network enact their relationships as social practice.

Cultural anthropologist Donald Donham (1999) illustrates the interpretive value of operationalizing the sociospatial dialectic in his study of the Maale people of southern Ethiopia. Donham's investigation shows that Maale individuals envision political solidarity through a process

of "working together." Because Maale men and women enact many per-
mutations of working together, what may at first appear to be a fairly
straightforward social act is in fact complicated by a series of social relationships that involve dimensions of age and gender. The Maale also
express the complexity of "working" through the use of two verbs, *ma'-
dane* and *soofane*. Ma'dane refers to the process of doing something, such
as sweeping the floor or conducting a ritual. Soofane, on the other hand,
involves the conduct of work outside the home. An elder conducting a
ritual in his home would be described as ma'dane, but a man going to
the river to fetch water would be described as soofane. The activity must
require sustained physical exertion to be described as soofane. The
internal complexity of working together among the Maale is enhanced by
the conceptualization of soofane as male, public, and group oriented,
whereas ma'dane is envisioned as domestic, female, and individualizing.

To help illustrate the complex nature of the practice of working
together within Maale social space, Donham (1999: 146) provides two
explicit network models: a bloc model and a web model (Figure 5.1). The
nodes of the models are households and the lines connecting them are
their "working together" relations. The sociomatrices for the two kinds
of relationships appear distinct because in Donham's bloc model everyone works with everyone else, or in network jargon, all the nodes are
adjacent (Table 5.1). Within the confines of the networks, the Maale
employ three types of work arrangements: *helma* (a small bloc network),
mol'o (a large bloc network), and *dabo* (a web network). As explained by
Donham (1999: 146), "A helma is a small group of workers, usually three
or four, who work in a set cycle of rotation on each other's fields. Each
day that a helma assembles, the group works for about four hours, usually in the morning. Then workers go home and in the afternoon follow
their individual pursuits." The helma networks are constituted along age
and sex lines, such that male, female, and young people's helma exist.
The male helma are organized to perform the clearing, cultivating,
weeding, and harvesting of the large and small fields, the women's helma
performs weeding and harvesting, and the young people's helma weeds
large fields.

Donham's careful description of the Maale helma, as well as of the
other operative networks, indicates that the associations are created and
operated in terms of a sociospatial dialectic. We may well imagine a
helma to exist only in topologic social space, but this theoretical construct would be meaningless to the ethnography. The helma requires
both social connections and spatial associations to be enacted. Being
organized for the conduct of horticultural tasks, the bloc networks would
have no use without the presence of horticultural fields.

The dabo, the web network, is also inherently sociospatial. The dabo

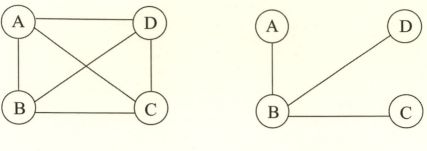

Figure 5.1. Donham's (1999) two network models.

web is created by sets of cooperating households which come together for the purpose of brewing beer. The social relations of the dabo are more complex and are potentially sustained for longer durations than either the helma or the mol'o, but the process of brewing beer itself incorporates the interaction of social and spatial connections:

First, finger millet had to be left in a damp pot to sprout and the resulting malt had to be ground. Other grain had to be stone ground, hour after hour of continuous work, and a large quantity of water brought from the stream about a mile away. Most women asked (and later gave) neighbors help with fetching water and sometimes with grinding, but these arrangements were not formalized and were not thought of as "working together." Finally, the malt and flour had to be mixed in a large pot of hot water and the brew poured into large gourds to ferment. (Donham 1999: 153, 155)

Examples of the sociospatial dialectic abound, with some instances being easier to recognize than others. The walled medieval European town provides a superb venue for providing further understanding of the

TABLE 5.1. Sociomatrices for Donham's Bloc and Web Models

	A	B	C	D
Bloc model				
A	—	1	1	1
B	1	—	1	1
C	1	1	—	1
D	1	1	1	—
Web model				
A	—	1	0	0
B	1	—	1	1
C	0	1	—	0
D	0	1	0	—

1 = connection; 0 = no connection.

sociospatial dialectic perceived in Lefebvre's terms. Of the many examples that exist, Rothenburg, Germany, is a useful heuristic device because of the perception that it represents the "Jewel of the Middle Ages" (Kootz 2000), and because its medieval walls are still extant (though somewhat reconstructed), giving the town a truly bounded appearance. To conceptualize Rothenburg, we must return to Lefebvre:

(Social) space is not a thing among other things, nor a product among other products: rather, it subsumes things produced, and encompasses their interrelationships in their coexistence and simultaneity—their (relative) order and/or (relative) disorder. It is the outcome of a sequence and set of operations, and thus cannot be reduced to the rank of a simple object. At the same time there is nothing imagined, unreal or "ideal" about it as compared, for example, with science, representations, ideas or dreams. Itself the outcome of past actions, social space is what permits fresh actions to occur, while suggesting others and prohibiting yet others. (1991: 73)

The castle at Rothenburg was constructed in the tenth century, and in 1274 the town became a free imperial city under King Rudolf of Habsburg. At this time, builders extended the town's walls to encompass a newly settled area of tradespeople. Encountering the narrow, winding lanes of Rothenburg today, tourists are immediately reminded of medieval spatial practice and at the same time, as a car roars past (outside the traffic-free zone), they are also forced to confront today's spatial practice. The juxtaposition of the practices of past and present is, however, nothing new because all peoples of all times have been forced to confront this temporal disjunction, even in landscapes that may appear "natural." Just as European explorers were forced to engage the "natural" landscape of the New World—or in Darby's (2000) view, "to landscape"—the seductive physical space of Rothenburg may encourage today's tourists to engage in self-deception that they may claim it as their own. The space, rather than being purely socialized by humanity, plays a socializing role as it is constantly constituted and reconstituted historically (Lefebvre 1991: 190–91). Rothenburg is thus at the same time perceived space (as a spatial entity composed of roads, buildings, and walls as well as the social relations that accompany them), conceived space (as representations created by the original builders, the reconstructors after the Allied bombing of the Second World War, and today's city managers), and as representational, lived, space (recreated as a symbolic medieval space replete with all the images the Middle Ages permit us to imagine).

Racial elements of social space are intertwined with the relations of power that are enacted and enforced within particular sociohistorical formations. Racially defined otherness can be commodified as well as anything else (Smith 1999: 88–92), and this commodification is usually spatially situated. Irrefutable testimony of the commodification of the Other is adequately demonstrated by the many exhibitions of indigenous people as oddities (such as the European display of Saartjie Baartman, the so-called "Hottentot Venus") in the powerful cities of Europe's commercial core (see, e.g., Altick 1978), and by the way in which Social Darwinism was given spatial expression in the physical design of the World's Columbian Exposition in 1893 (Baker 1998: 56–60).

In an especially enlightening and pertinent investigation, James Delle (1998) explicitly adopts Lefebvre's insights to examine social space in the coffee plantations of slaveholding Jamaica. Delle's analysis demonstrates that, beginning with the final decades of the eighteenth century—as capitalism entered a crisis phase (see Soja 1989: 27–28)—the power elites of Jamaica's plantation economy struggled to redefine the social space of the island. They accordingly altered the spatial dimensions of coffee production during the 1790–1865 period to keep pace with the dramatic social changes brought about by slave emancipation. During the transition in production from bound to wage labor, the spatialities of control and resistance were in almost constant conflict. During slave days, the overseers established sight lines of surveillance, and enslaved men and women frequently sought to enter places where the oversight was absent, such as the plantation hospital. After emancipation in 1834, plantation owners paid greater attention to the precise spatial extent of their coffee fields (and commissioned the drafting of intricate maps) so that they could invent a wage scale that could be quantifiably linked to the amount of land harvested by the wage laborers. In contradistinction to this action, wage earners, freed of a lifetime of enforced bondage, began to contest land ownership and use. All the actions were conducted within the sociospatial milieu of the coffee-growing estate.

Further insights into the racial features of the sociospatial dialectic can be observed by another cursory examination of a postbellum plantation situation, this one focused on the tenant farmers in the fifteen counties that comprise the piedmont region of South Carolina (Orser 1988b). Historians and social scientists generally have a priori divided the farmers of the region into three categories, based upon their social position relative to agricultural production and farm ownership. "Owners" owned their own land and farmed for their own benefit, "cash tenants" paid a fixed rent price to a landlord and raised a crop for their own use and disposition, and "share tenants" (sharecroppers and share renters) paid an unfixed rent based on the year's agricultural production and the amount of fertilizer the tenant and the landlord had each supplied to produce the year's crop. As an epochal structure, the three tenure groups only existed in relation to one another in a three-tiered hierarchy, which from top to bottom extended from owners to cash tenants to share tenants. Individuals racialized as both black and white appeared in each labor category, with the precise proportions of each group being historically determinate.

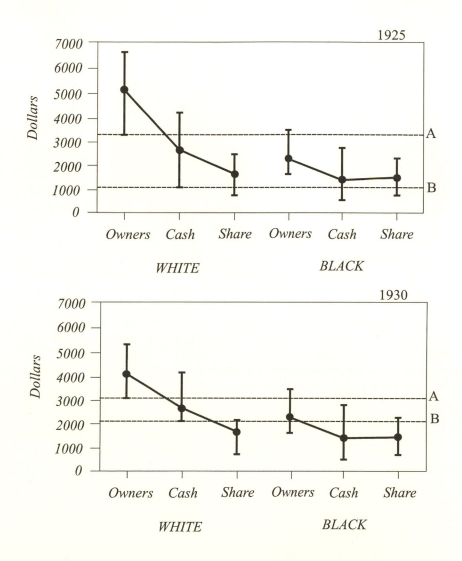

A = white owner threshold
B = white cash tenant threshold

Figure 5.2. Agricultural positions in the American South in 1925 and 1930. Source: Orser (1988b).

Official United States censuses for 1925 and 1930 suggest the degree of association between agricultural position and material acquisition, with a structural consistency, based on racial assignment, appearing in the assessed values of two spatial entities: land and buildings (Figure 5.2). White owners in 1925 controlled considerably more dollar-values of physical spatiality than did any other rural class, with white cash renters a distant second. About one-third of the white cash renters had moved upward beyond the white owner threshold (A), indicating that they had more economic capital than some owners, even though the white owners probably realized greater cultural capital. Most white share tenants and most black renters were situated above the white cash renter threshold (B), but significantly, the vast majority of black owners were beneath the white owner threshold. Racially based inequality is thus readily apparent in the distribution of valued rural space.

A temporal redistribution is evidenced in the 1930 values because the white owner threshold and the white cash renter threshold were closer together than they were only five years earlier. As expected of the epochal structure, and indicative of the unequal distribution of social space, white owners retained their elite position relative to the other racial agricultural classes, but their command of economic capital had decreased, even though a concomitant depletion of cultural capital was probably unlikely. About two-thirds of the white cash renters had moved above the white owner threshold (A), and the relative position of black owners changed little. The position of white share tenants dramatically worsened, as almost all of them were positioned beneath the white cash renter threshold. The same worsened condition obtained for black tenants, with the positions of the share tenants, both black and white, being practically equal.

The variable command of economic capital among the agricultural classes in 1930 is apparent (Table 5.2). Cash tenants commanded over 30 percent less economic capital than did owners, and share tenants commanded almost 28 percent less than cash tenants. The differentials between white and black class fractions, however, are even greater for black owners (against white owners) and black cash tenants (against white cash tenants). Only in the share tenant class was the differential less within the class than between the class and the next highest class (cash tenants).

In accordance with these statistics, historical records indicate that early twentieth-century African American tenant farmers living in the South Carolina piedmont occupied houses of lower quality, smaller size, and less substantial construction than did situationally comparable non-African Americans. The complexity of the social structure as racial regime is clearly revealed, however, in the lack of a clear linkage between the racial assignment of share tenants and their practically equal command of economic capital. At this point, we must recognize the important variance in racially defined cultural capital and the manner in which space was homologically apportioned based upon racial considerations. The ideological and physical terrorism experienced by African American tenant farmers during the early twentieth century was a violent response to the intersection of social practice and social space. The similar structural position between the poorest agriculturalists, regardless of racial assignment, may have been a contributing factor to the explosive growth of the Ku Klux Klan during the 1920s (Leiman 1993: 70).

As noted above, the race-based social structure was such that one group judged racially inferior could easily occupy the social space abandoned from or restricted to another perceived racially inferior group. This sentiment was neatly summarized by one promoter of Louisiana agriculture soon after the termination of the American Civil War:

Much has been said of chinese (sic) labor, but few seem to comprehend either the nature of the Asiatic, or our own peculiar condition. Some political writers seem to be afraid that the chinese will become a dangerous element of society; others that the mixing of the races would be unavoidable, and that we would soon be Mongolised. Is it possible that we could be so affected, influenced, and demoralized by these Celestials? *I have yet some faith in the superiority of our race,* and in the morality of our people. They will sooner become Americanized, than we Mongolised. The Chinese are peaceful, sober, law-abiding and intelligent, their climate is similar to ours, and they are familiar with the culture of sugar and

TABLE 5.2. Land and Building Value Means and Percent Differences for Class and Racial Class Fractions in the 15 South Carolina Piedmont Counties, 1930

	Mean ($)	*Difference (%)*
Class		
owners	3,009.24	–
cash tenants	2,086.99	–30.65
share tenants	1,503.90	–27.94
Racial class fractions		
owners		
white	4,109.02	–
black	1,909.45	–53.53
cash		
white	2,770.39	–
black	1,403.59	–49.34
share		
white	1,714.94	–
black	1,292.85	–24.74

Source: Orser (1988b: 109).

rice. We could not obtain more suitable laborers for the cultivation of our plantations. We must ever remember that the cultivation of the soil is our only source of prosperity. Laborers are needed, let them come from all parts of the world; they are welcome. (Bouchereau 1870: x; emphasis added)

The structural dimensions that permitted the substitution of peoples assigned to various racial groups into and out of the same relative slots of economic capital also operated in relation to physical space. Members of the dominant white class commonly conceived postbellum rural housing as transracial representations of space. For instance, Sir George Campbell (1879: 393), an English member of Parliament touring the southern United States in the late 1870s, observed that "Some of the smaller tenants live in places unfit for an Irishman, with no windows and showing much daylight between the logs." A similarity of racial domination translated into spatiality was also noted by former slave Charles Ball (1837: 139), when he said that the slave cabins he saw stood "in rows, much like the Indian villages which I have seen in the country of the Cherokees." Such sociospatial assessments express the tangled nature of nineteenth-century racialized social life in the United States. In addition, representational space was frequently intertwined with observable (and hence "objective") color, so that the dwellings of the elites were often described as white, while the houses of non-elites were described as "low" and even "black" (see, e.g., Dennett 1965: 178; Killion and Waller 1973: 34–35; Olmsted 1856: 416). In antebellum days, when slave cabins were frequently whitewashed, the treatment was often specifically designed to "keep them from spoiling the looks of the big house" (Social Science Institute 1945: 13).

This brief account of the postbellum American South allows insights into the composition of the epochal, sociospatial structure of the rural agricultural world in the late nineteenth and early twentieth centuries. At the same time, it permits us to perceive the relations between the social structure and racial identification, and the generally lower structural position of those individuals assigned to subordinate racial groups. The major problem with this cursory examination, however, is that its scale of analysis does not permit the presentation of a true practice perspective. In adopting the categories presented in the official census documents, we are forced into accepting artificial, reified social classifications that probably do not mirror the reality or complexity of the actual sociohistorical situations. As noted above, racial designation is highly subjective, and the same conclusion obtains for tenure class. Agricultural tenure was fluid and mutable, and it was not unusual that cash tenants one year were share tenants the next. It is entirely possible that the 1925 and the 1930 census figures represent the same farmers but categorized quite differently. In addition, between 1920 and 1930 over 444,000 African Americans migrated from the American South (Ransom and Sutch 1977: 196). This level of outmigration means that the two years' census figures may represent different populations. Such problems in these data cannot be overcome without an intensive, detailed investigation of postbellum plantation records and possibly the introduction of oral interviewing of former tenant farmers.

The presentation of the South Carolina census data does allow a limited glimpse of important elements of a racialized social structure, even though in this particular instance, we cannot examine practice as such. We can nonetheless perceive the relative distribution of people based upon the co-occurrence of their economic capital (as represented by agricultural situation) and their cultural capital (as demonstrated by assigned racial classification) within a racialized social structure. What is required, of course, is a more detailed analysis that has the ability to capture the many nuances of practice theory, while at the same time being able to present information about social space and the use of commodities in a racialized sociohistorical formation. This task can be accomplished in the next chapter by an intimate examination of the rural Irish during the early nineteenth century

Chapter 6
A Case Study of Archaeology and the Practice of Race from Early Nineteenth-Century Ireland

The previous chapters have outlined one perspective that may be employed in the archaeological analysis of historic racialization. The chapters are intended to present overviews of the history of the archaeological analysis of race and to provide a coherent framework for conducting an archaeological interpretation of race that is both theoretically rigorous and practically possible. I have specifically identified Bourdieu's practice theory, linked with Lefebvre's understanding of the production of social space, as one approach toward providing an archaeological analysis of race.

The preceding chapters make it clear that the focus of attention here is the modern world. As such, the methodology is one that can include the combination of information that is archaeological (excavated and personally observed) and textual (written outside the analyst's perception). The union of archaeological and textual sources also means that a multiscalar vision can be adopted, one that may include intra-site, extra-site, regional, national, and even international frames of reference. To present the kind of interpretation demanded by practice theory, it will be necessary to tack frequently, and perhaps not always linearly, between different geographic and temporal scales. This approach is required because history, though it appears from our vantage point to be completely linear, is in fact composed of constitutive tactics and strategies that occur every day (de Certeau 1988). It is the history of the everyday—the commonplace and the mundane practiced by millions of non-elites—that is often ignored, forgotten, or consciously misrepresented (see Parenti 1999; Trouillot 1995).

The focus in this chapter is on one group of individuals who lived in the townland of Ballykilcline in north County Roscommon, in the Republic of Ireland (Figure 6.1). The men and women who lived at Ballykilcline during the 1800–1848 period were simultaneously different from and yet similar to thousands of rural individuals who lived throughout Ireland at the time.

Ballykilcline provides an excellent arena for extended analysis because, in the early 1990s, historians forever linked the Irish with the process of becoming white (see, e.g., Allen 1994; Ignatiev 1995; Roediger 1991). The historical process in which the Irish were transmogrified from

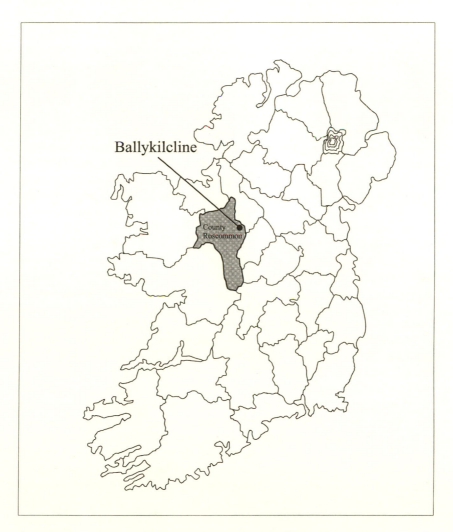

Figure 6.1. Location of Ballykilcline Townland in County Roscommon, Ireland

Other to Citizen has typically been perceived as constituting a socially significant element of the Irish diaspora. Historians believe this process began in the mid- to late nineteenth century, though Allen (1994) proposes that the process had much longer roots, in effect beginning in Ireland with the appearance of the colonialist English during the twelfth century. Ballykilcline is also useful because archaeologists under my direction have excavated two cabin sites there. These excavations have provided a unique body of information that can be used in conjunction with the rather abundant textual sources compiled about the townland.

To present an adequate account of the townland, however, we must often step outside its physical boundaries and explore the extra-townland social spaces within which the residents of Ballykilcline operated. The primary objective of this analysis is to examine the racial elements of life at Ballykilcline and to illustrate the residents' multilevel nexus of relationships and interactions inside the racialized social structure within which they found themselves. Conceptualized within Bourdieu's practice paradigm, the principal field of analysis will be the field of power organized around the parameters of a consciously created and studiously maintained racialization of the Irish men, women, and children who inhabited Ballykilcline and over 60,000 similar places throughout the island.

Before commencing the historical-archaeological investigation into the practice of daily life at Ballykilcline, we must return to Bonilla-Silva's (1997) outline of the structural nature of racialized social systems. Our first task must be to outline the epochal social space of rural Ireland as a backdrop to conceptualizing everyday life at Ballykilcline. The foundational understanding is that the early nineteenth-century residents of Ballykilcline did not operate within a social vacuum that was unique to their bounded settlement. Ballykilcline was a limited spatial representation to be sure, but it was also a lived, representational space as well. Tenants could have stepped over the boundaries of Ballykilcline and been conceptually aware that they had done so, but they did not become different men and women by performing this spatial act. Rather, in accordance with multiscalar, network-related practice theory, a primary understanding is that the daily lives of the Ballykilcline residents were interlinked with a series of complex, inter-generational and inter-geographic networks that were both structuring structures and structured structures.

Bonilla-Silva (1997: 474) presents a processual outline that illustrates the creation of a racialized social structure. His scheme is not a totalizing, universalized structure, but is rather merely a conceptual guide. All racialized social systems need not pass through the same steps in the process, and the various elements are not required to be sequentialized in every instance. Bonilla-Silva's framework simply provides a useful tool for examining racialization as a sociohistorical process. The general framework can be summarized in the following manner:

1. A racialized social structure is one that allocates various amounts and kinds of capital based upon socially constructed, racial lines; the racial distinctions can be based on any socially designated, totalizing attributes that serve to separate people into different essentialized categories.
2. The various "races" that are designed by the process of racialization are historically situated and constantly reflect back upon the system itself, such that the racial order structures social relations and is structured by them.
3. The development and maintenance of the racialized sociospatial structure gives rise to and at the same time is supported by a racial ideology, which can be termed "racism"; the racial ideology, however, is not merely superstructural, because it serves to structure social relations and in so structuring them becomes structured by them.
4. The rise of racialization often means that racialized social structures incorporate struggles and conflicts that have distinct racial characteristics.
5. The racialized social contestations will have the practicality of demonstrating the variant goals of the different, historically designed races, such that those individuals designated as of part of the "inferior race" seek to change the structure of the racial hierarchy, and those who deem themselves members of the "superior race" strive to maintain their elite position in the social order.

Bonilla-Silva's outline provides an excellent framework for determining whether a past social structure was in fact racialized. Thus we may initially ask: Did historic Ireland have a racialized social structure?

Epochal Structures

Archaeological research indicates that Ireland has been the site of numerous invasions and settlement schemes, beginning in the Mesolithic period, sometime around 7500 B.C. (Cooney 2000: 4). The rich history of cultural expression that exists throughout Ireland includes archaeological manifestations that are traditionally designated as falling within the Stone, Bronze, and Iron ages. The northern distribution of La Tène artifacts, most commonly associated with the arrival of the "Celts," has been the subject of considerable archaeological attention (see Cooney and Grogan 1994: 195–205; Duffy 2002: 34–38; Harbison 1988: 168–72; Waddell 1998: 288–90). The first major invasion by a powerful external people was that of the Vikings, which commenced in A.D. 795. They established settlements in Dublin, Wexford, Waterford, Cork, and Limerick (Duffy 1997: 24–25).

The Norse did not establish a settlement in County Roscommon, and in fact they raided only intermittently along the coast of Connacht, the westernmost province, within which Roscommon and Ballykilcline are situated. The only incursion of the Vikings into the interior of Roscommon was a raid in the parish of Baslick on the western side of the county (Duffy 1997: 25). At least two pertinent developments occurred as a result of the Viking presence in Ireland: they brought with them an international market (de Paor 1994: 102); and Irish chroniclers, in a precursor of modern racialist ideas, referred to the Vikings as "White Foreigners" (Norwegians, *Finn-gaill*) and "Black Foreigners" (Danes, *Dubh-gaill*) (Jones 1968: 76–77).

The Viking presence clearly impacted the Irish people, but the development of a proto-racialized social structure was not instituted until after the Anglo-Norman invasion. The initial English assaults on Ireland, which began in 1169, failed to institutionalize English cultural patterns, because the invaders were largely unable to unseat the powerfully entrenched Gaelic chieftains (see Duffy et al. 2001; Patterson 1994). When it became obvious that the small English force on the eastern coast of Ireland could not militarily subjugate the entire Irish population, the English settlers began to legislate to maintain their own cultural traditions. The Statute of Kilkenny, enacted in 1366, was an important tool in the English attempt to attain cultural domination by assuring that its own cultural members did not acculturate any Irish customs. The thirty-six clauses of this legal writ restated some of the measures introduced in the 1350s, but one important aspect of the legislation is that it marked an important shift in English-Irish relations (Brand 1998: 287). In one important and famous clause, the Statute maintained that

it is ordained and established, that every Englishman do use the English language, and be named by an English name, leaving off entirely the manner of naming used by the Irish; and that every Englishman use the English custom, fashion, mode of riding and apparel, according to his estate; and if any English, or Irish living among the English, use the Irish language amongst themselves, contrary to this ordinance, and thereof be attained, his lands and tenements, if he have any, shall be seized. (Crowley 2000: 15)

Edmund Spenser, an Englishman who passionately supported the utter subjugation of the Irish during Elizabethan colonialism, succinctly summarized the sentiment that rested behind the linguistic requirement:

"the speach being Irish, the heart must needes bee Irish: for out of the abundance of the heart, the tongue speaketh" (Spenser 1997: 71).

The Anglo-Normans also expressed their attempted dominance of the Irish religiously and spatially. Anglo-Norman priests granted absolution to murderers of the Irish because it was "no more sin to kill an Irishman than a dog or any other brute" (Allen 1994: 47), at the same time that their military engineers built castles and other fortifications. They situated these architectural landmarks within a network of nucleated rural settlements they constructed throughout their region of influence (see Barry 1987: 37–115; McNeill 1997).

Legislative statutes reinforced the idea that the situation in Ireland involved an inter-cultural conflict between an indigenous population and an invading force. The English settlers who lived in and around Dublin were thus encouraged to denigrate Irish culture and, by extension, those individuals who tenaciously clung to it. The statutes would not have been needed if so many English men and women had not been drawn to use Irish speech and customs of riding and dress. The Anglo-Normans, even in the face of their condescending perception of the Gaelic Irish, did not necessarily believe that they were incapable of accepting English civilization (Canny 1973: 580).

The situation in the vicinity of Ballykilcline during Anglo-Norman times and earlier is difficult to determine from textual sources. Being situated some distance from Dublin and other seats of Anglo-Norman power, the area was seldom explicitly mentioned. The presence of two ringforts within the nineteenth-century boundaries of the townland and two crannóga (semi-artificial islands intended for defensive habitation) in Lough Kilglass on the eastern boundary of the townland substantiate the long-term habitation of the area. Radiocarbon dates indicate that ringforts date from the fifth to the tenth centuries A.D. and that they served as habitation sites and cattle enclosures (Stout 1997: 22–34; Stout and Stout 1997: 44–49). Many crannóga in north Connacht continued to be used up to the seventeenth century (O'Conor 2001: 337).

The design and areal placement of ringforts were sociospatial. The current model of ringfort settlement holds that the space occupied by the early medieval, rural Irish túath, or petty kingdom (Patterson 1994: 9), was simultaneously social and spatial, with the settlement hierarchy producing and in turn being produced by the social hierarchy. Kings lived in the largest ringforts, while nobles lived in the next largest. Free land-owning kindred and free landless tenants lived in still smaller ringforts. Unfree tenant farmers and hereditary serfs are thought to have lived in dwellings outside the ringforts (Stout 1997: 95). Each polity was associated with an ecclesiastical center, and the entire network endured through the enactment of a complex, bidirectional nexus of clientship and tribute in cattle, feasting, and protection (both spiritual and martial) (see Patterson 1994: 150–78).

The English continued to hold a large territory around Dublin, which they called The Pale, and the monarchy attempted to reinforce its colonists along the east coast (Smith 1997: 46–47). (Accordingly, the phrase "beyond the pale" has come to mean anything that is uncouth, uncivilized, or out of the range of reasonable, polite society.) At the same time, traditional Irish chieftains fought for control of land and cattle throughout much of the rest of the island. The contests within the Kingdom of Connacht revolved mostly around the struggle of the O'Conors to maintain their power base (see Byrne 2000).

Beginning around 1530, the English "progressively redefined [Ireland] as a crucial and strategic springboard for colonisation and provisioning of, migration to and trade with the New World" (Smyth 2000: 158). The English redefinition of the Irish has pressed historians to ask how it was that "at the mid-sixteenth century, the Irish, a people with whom the English had always had some familiarity, came to be regarded as uncivilized, and what justifications were used for indiscriminate slaying and expropriation" (Canny 1973: 583).

Canny (1973: 583–95) focused his explanation for the development of a new English evaluation of the Irish on ideology. The English, he argued, were disgusted by the way in which the Irish had combined Christianity with their more ancient religious (pagan) traditions. Canny's understanding may be correct in part, but it cannot by itself offer the kind of structural comprehension required of racialization. According to Bonilla-Silva's (1997) perspective, the development of a racist *mentalité* can only develop after concerted efforts to institute a racialized social structure.

Historical sources indicate that with their greater intent to subjugate Ireland, late Tudor-era English colonialists sought to establish a ranked social hierarchy with a foundational base rooted in racial concepts. This structure was also interlinked with production. In their plantation schemes in Ulster, along the eastern boundary of Leinster, and in Munster (1580s-1620), the English power elite sought to replace recalcitrant Irish landholders with more pliable, loyal English subjects (Clarke 1994: 190; Hayes-McCoy 1994: 183). Beneath the layer of the upper class, the goal of replacing Irish (Catholic) farmers with English (Protestant) farmers, though partly ideological, is more pertinently analogous to the attempted replacement of African American farmers with non-African Americans after the American Civil War. The sought-after replacement of the Irish was based on the image of their paganism and barbarism, but it was also deeply rooted in the racialist idea that they were lazy and unproductive. To counter a common belief, one late seventeenth-century observer noted that "Ireland wants Skilful and Industrious Husband-men as much as any place. In the condition 'tis now you can't expect to see men Industrious. The Irish are reckon'd a lazy people; but this I don't attribute to the natural temper of the Men, and the abundance of Flegm in their Bodies as is generally suppos'd, but rather to the want of Employment, and Encouragement to work" (Anonymous 1697: 12). Over fifty years later, in 1749, Church of Ireland bishop and philosopher George Berkeley urged the Roman Catholic clergy to exhort their parishioners and "Make them sensible what a reproach it is that a nation which makes so great pretensions to antiquity, and is said to have flourished many ages ago in arts and learning, should in these our days, turn out a lazy, destitute, and degenerate race" (Fraser 1871: 441). The concept that Irish men and women would only work when they were encouraged (that is, taught a different work ethic) was a racialist theme that endured for over two hundred years: "The virtues of patience, of prudence, and industry seldom are included in the composition of an Irishman: he projects gigantic schemes, but wants perseverance to realize any work of magnitude: his conceptions are grand and vivid, but his execution is feeble and indolent" (Croker 1824: 12). The view of the Irish as racially inferior even made the diasporic journey to the United States (Knobel 1986: 50–55; Roediger 1991: 133).

Much of the ideological justification for the racialized social structure of post-Elizabethan Ireland occurred in the field of cultural production, specifically in what Bourdieu (1993b: 30) terms "the space of artistic position-taking." The position-takings expressed by artists seeking to represent the Irish—as undeniably distinct from the English—were irreducibly racialized. In a seminal study, Curtis (1971) has demonstrated how English visual artists untiringly portrayed the Irish as simian, uncouth, uncultured, and violent. Images of Irish men and women as subhuman and stubbornly resistant to "civilization" were mass-produced for wholesale English consumption as an indivisible element of the social structure. Their appearance in newspapers ensured that the images would be circulated to the widest possible number of non-Irish citizens. That such images continue to be used within the past three decades in the form of political cartoons, anti-Irish jokes, and mass-produced novelty items (see Curtis 1996: 82–97) merely demonstrates the tenacious capacity of a racialized social structure.

Visual and textual representations of the Irish before their full racialization stand in marked contrast to the images artists and other observers would make during the late eighteenth and early nineteenth centuries. During the Tudor period, for instance, drawings of the rural Irish show them as uncouth and uncultured, especially when they were presented in comparison to residents of the Pale. In such images, artists such as Albrecht Dürer in 1521 (Hayes-McCoy 1994: 179) and Lucas de Heere around 1575 (Canny 1989: 107) portrayed the Irish as unshaven, barefoot, with stringy hair, and wearing long, ragged mantles. At the same time, English governmental documents referred to the Irish as "savage, lazy, unwashed, ignorant, superstitious, and promiscuous" (Berleth 1994: 22). Even in these highly charged pictures and textual images, however, the artists and the chroniclers nonetheless depicted the Irish as humans devoid of simian characteristics (also see Canny 1989: 105; Duffy 2002: 92). The ape-like, cultural production of the Irish would only come later with their full racialization.

Hierarchical social structure was not new to the Irish. Using ancient Irish law tracts, Nerys Patterson (1994: 181–205) has forcefully demonstrated that the pre-Norman Irish maintained a complicated triadic ranking system that encompassed secular society, the Church, and poets. Two kinds of status existed within each social space, divided into sacred (lords, kings, clerics, poets, and the learned) and non-sacred, and within each status was a secondary segregation involving the individual's bound or free condition. Several legal barriers functioned to protect the structure's elites, and the system was in no way democratic or egalitarian. The habitus of each group allowed the hierarchy to produce and reproduce its structure, so that the children of the elites fully expected to be better fed, clothed, and cared for than the offspring of the non-elites. The social and spatial systems retained perfect homology, so that the men and women situated within the hierarchy did not expect to move out of their carefully structured social placement or their hierarchically designed settlement pattern. What was new to the Irish with the advent of English domination, however, was the institutionalized idea that because of their Irishness, all of them—regardless of their customary, familial-based positions in the traditional social space of pre-Norman Ireland—would be relegated to the same subordinate position within the racialized social order.

Located as it is in Connacht, County Roscommon was included in the huge tract of land in the west that was intended to be the resettlement area of the Irish during the devastating Cromwellian assaults (see Ellis 1988): "By Order of the Commissioners of the Parliament of England for the Affairs of Ireland, dated 14th October, 1653, all persons having right to favour and mercy were to remove and transplant themselves into the province of Connacht and county of Clare before the 1st May, 1654" (Simington 1949: xxxiii). The decree specifically mandated that Irish men, women, and children from Kildare, Meath, Queen's County (Laois), and Dublin would be resettled in the north Roscommon baronies of Roscommon, Ballintober, Ballymoe, and Boyle. Ballykilcline is located in the barony of Ballintober North. The English established their first power bases in County Roscommon in 1566, placing one garrison at Boyle Abbey about 32 kilometers (20 miles) north of Ballykilcline, and another at Roscommon Castle roughly 24 kilometers (15 miles) south of the townland (Cronin 1980: 109).

During the forced resettlement program, many of the land parcels in the area of Ballykilcline were placed under the direct control of Nicholas Mahon, the landlord whose seat of power was Strokestown Park House, located about 8 km from Ballykilcline. Mahon, an officer in Cromwell's command, had the assigned task of hunting down Irish Catholics who refused English domination (Hanley 1961: 228). The reward for his service was an extensive grant of land around Strokestown. Little is known about Ballykilcline for the next one hundred years, but in 1793, the townland was leased by the Crown to Charles Costelloe for a period of 41 years. Costelloe quickly turned the lease over to the Mahons, who would hold it until May 1, 1834 (House of Lords 1847: 4). When the Mahons were unable to negotiate the continuance of the lease, it and the direct oversight of Ballykilcline reverted to the Crown, as administered by the Commissioners of Her Majesty's Woods, Forests, Land Revenues, Works, and Buildings.

Mahon expressed his position of power within the Irish social space—as a former Cromwellian officer and a major landholder—through his house, begun in 1659, and demesne, both of which were consciously created to portray and promote "a new consciousness of space" (Lefebvre 1991: 125). As truly monumental (and still extant) architecture, the house and the demesne "embodies and imposes a clearly intelligible message. It says what it wishes to say—yet it hides a good deal more: being political, military, and ultimately fascist in character . . . it mask[s] the will to power and the arbitrariness of power beneath signs and surfaces which claim to express collective will and collective thought" (Lefebvre 1991: 143). The Mahons' statement of power was not merely metaphorical, however, because the house—which was formally called "The Bawn" (Weld 1832: 329–30)—was in fact the former fortified house, or bawn, complex of the local Gaelic chieftain, The O'Conor Roe. Samuel Lewis (1984, 1: 581) described the Mahons' house and demesne in his 1837 *Topographical Dictionary of Ireland*: "Bawn House, the noble mansion of Lord Hartland [Maurice Mahon, grandson of Nicholas] is situated to the east of the town, in a demesne of more than 100 acres: it consists of a centre with an Ionic portico, having a flat roof guarded by a balustrade, and heavy advancing wings, showing the original character of the whole edifice" (Figure 6.2) Arthur Young (1780: 184), when visiting the Mahon estate in the late 1770s, perfectly expressed the ideological aspects of the demesne:

Mr. Mahon's woods are all of his own planting . . . a vast number of hedge-rows well planted round many inclosures, which join those woods, *they all take the appearance of uniting into one great range of plantations*, spreading on each side [of] the house. It is one of the *strongest instances* of fine shade being speedily *formed in the midst of a bleak country* that I have any where met with, *being a perfect contrast to the neighborhood*. He began 35 years ago with ash, which trees are now 70 to 80 feet high. (emphasis added)

Documents indicate that the Mahons continued to "improve" their estate with plantings. For example, they obtained the following trees and bushes on October 23, 1841: "600 larch, 300 silver fir, 300 spruce, 200 Scotch, 300 oak, 300 ash, 20 varigated holly, 20 copper beech, 20 Portugal laurel, 20 arbutus, and 20 evergreen oak" (Pakenham-Mahon Papers, document 412.003). The Mahons, as landlords tended to do throughout the period of extreme "landlordism"—c. 1750–1850— "effected and controlled some of the most significant modifications in the cultural landscape" (Jones Hughes 1965: 79). Landlords like the Mahons, who were powerful within the Anglo-Irish colonialist structure of early nineteenth-century Ireland, thus attempted to effectuate a dominant "estate culture" (Foster 1993: 51).

Figure 6.2. Strokestown Park House as it looks today. Photo: C. E. Orser.

Conditions were not quite so grand for the region's Irish farmers (Figure 6.3). The 1749 Synge census completed for Ballykilcline on behalf of the diocese lists 30 male heads of household, 39 children under the age of fourteen, 27 children over the age of fourteen, and 3 female servants; wives are not mentioned (Coyle 1994). When Young (1780: 184) visited the area fifty years later, all he noticed about the tenants was that "they are better fed than 20 years ago, and better cloathed, but not more industrious, or better housed." Edward Wakefield (1812: 274), who traveled through the same area in June 1809, said that he found "a superabundant but miserable population. The picture which I here saw will not be easily effaced from my remembrance." In 1830, Isaac Weld observed that the Mahons had improved their tenants' housing:

Now although the appearance of want and wretchedness, both in houses and garments, are by no means obliterated entirely, yet the circumstances of the place have undergone decided amelioration, and many compact comfortable cottages, with well built firm walls of stone and mortar, and neatly slated roofs, had been lately built; whilst several of the old cabins had undergone repair. (1832: 317)

The census of 1851 reported that 473 males and females lived in 82 houses at Ballykilcline ten years earlier (Census of Ireland 1852: 186).

Figure 6.3. A "bogtrotter"'s cabin in County Roscommon in the 1840s. Originally appeared in the *Illustrated London News*.

Though we may not know many concrete details about the cultural history of Ballykilcline in the 1650–1750 period, language usage provides one avenue toward helping us to comprehend the changes confronted by the townland's residents. Numerous scholars have documented the role that language can play in the colonization process, with the adoption or rejection of the invaders' language being assigned a racial character. Individuals who accept the new language are given access to the elites' power structure and are often presented with greater opportunities for social advancement. African writer Ngũgĩ wa Thiong'o succinctly summarized the process:

We have already seen what any colonial system does: impose its tongue on the subject races, and then downgrade the vernacular tongues of the people. By so doing they make the acquisition of their tongue a status symbol; anyone who learns it begins to despise the peasant majority and their barbaric tongues. By acquiring the thought-processes and values of his adopted tongue, he becomes alienated from the values of his mother tongue, or from the language of the masses. (Ngũgĩ wa Thiong'o (1986: 72)

The process experienced by Ngũgĩ wa Thiong'o in twentieth-century Kenya mirrors the introduction of English in Ireland. At the beginning of the nineteenth century, Irish individuals spoke their native language throughout the majority of the island. English was dominant in much of Leinster (spreading westward from Dublin) and in southwest Ulster. Irish was probably already largely extinct in the counties of Antrim and Down in northeastern Ulster, the location of the earliest English plantations. Irish speakers constituted the majority in County Roscommon in 1800, but as early as 1814–19, it appears that only a minority could not understand English (Connolly 1982: 79). By 1851—after the mass evictions that included Ballykilcline—the number of Irish speakers dramatically declined (see Hindley 1990: 8,16). Today, Irish is spoken principally in tiny pockets along the western seaboard in the Gaeltacht, even though Irish remains the official language of the nation. Irish-language radio and television stations broadcast daily, and a resurgence in the use of Irish is underway.

The loss or retention of Irish as the principal quotidian language was political in the nineteenth century, just as it can be today (see, e.g., Boyle 2001). Not everyone who supported Irish social advancement favored the retention of Irish. For example, Daniel O'Connell, a prime promoter of Catholic emancipation—and a man about whom rural farmers created an extensive folk memory (Uí Ógáin 1996)—opined, when asked about the loss of Irish in 1833,

I am sufficiently utilitarian not to regret its gradual abandonment. A diversity of tongues is no benefit; it was first imposed on mankind as a curse, at the building of Babel. It would be of vast advantage to mankind if all the inhabitants spoke the same language. Therefore, although the Irish language is connected with many recollections that twine around the hearts of Irishmen, yet the superior utility of the English tongue, as the medium of modern communication, is so great, that I can witness without a sigh the gradual disuse of the Irish. (Crowley 2000: 153)

Some understanding of the transition from Irish to English in north County Roscommon can be gauged by textual sources. For example, in his 1830 survey of the county Weld (1832: 217, 699) made reference to

Figure 6.4. Brassington and Gale Plat of 1836.

the teaching of "Greek, Latin, and English" to Irish students and to formal instruction in "reading, writing, and arithmetic." John O'Donovan (1927: 57), the Irish scholar engaged by the Ordnance Survey who visited the Ballykilcline area in 1837, remarked with alarm how people's surnames were "being assimilated to those of their conquerors . . . Quilly to Cox! Mac Uiseoige to Lark! Mac Shane to Johnston, Breen to Brune! O'Braochain to Brougham!" Speaking specifically of Kilglass Parish, the location of Ballykilcline, the Reverend William Thompson discovered in 1816 that "English is the language spoken by the people in general; they all understand Irish, but it is not so much used among them as formerly" (Weld 1832: 490).

The detailed plat of Ballykilcline drawn by James Weale of the surveying firm of Brassington and Gale in 1836 for the Commissioners of Woods and Forests does not indicate the presence of any Irish names among the tenants (Figure 6.4). For instance, the residents of the two excavated house sites are recorded as "Mark Nary & Sons, Luke, James, and Edward." Current information does not indicate whether the use of these names represents the surveyors' gloss for English or whether the usage reflected actual townland practice. A perusal of all the other historical documentation relative to the townland implies, however, that the use of English names and the English language was fairly widespread in the area by the 1830s. Even Hugh O'Farrell, the tenants' attorney, used English names in his letters and other correspondence. Again, the use of English may simply represent the adoption of the "colonists' tongue" for legal matters. It is impossible to know whether the Ballykilcline tenants spoke Irish in their homes and whether they promoted the continuation of its usage. It is also possible that the retention of Irish was generationally relevant. When Douglas Hyde (1972: xi) collected Irish-language materials at the beginning of the twentieth century, he learned that many young people consciously chose not to speak Irish.

The adoption of English outside the Pale, to whatever extent, indicates that the colonizing English left a lasting cognitive mark upon rural Ireland. In terms of physical space, in addition to their structures—such as the monumental architecture of the Bawn—they also institutionalized the townland as the smallest administrative unit in Ireland (Cawley 1989: 221).

The concept for areal units like the townland has roots in Gaelic Ireland, where land divisions were associated with collective, lineage ownership (Patterson 1994: 170–71). Strong associations between families and townlands continue to the present, making the townland "the most intimate and enduring" physical unit in Ireland (Connell et al. 1998: 9). In County Roscommon, as throughout the Province of Connacht, the main land divisions as recorded in the early seventeenth century were, in decreasing size: baile, quarter, cartron, and gnive (1 baile = 4 quarters =

16 cartrons = 24 gnives) (McErlean 1983: 320). The presence of the word "Bally" (or *baile* in Irish) in "Ballykilcline" indicates that it was composed of four quarters. Two maps, dated 1836 and 1837 respectively, provide three (and possibly all four) of the ancient quarter names: Killtullyvary or Bungarrif, Aghamore, and Barravally. All these names encapsulate their Irish heritage: Killtullyvary = roughly, Church hill townland; Bungariff = rough bottom or end; Aghamore = great or large field; Barravally = high or hilly townland (Joyce 1996).

Approximately 62,000 townlands exist in Ireland today, ranging in size from .40 to 2,838 hectares (Garnham 1998: 547). In 1836, Brassington and Gale reported to the Commissioners of Woods and Forests that Ballykilcline measured just over 246 hectares (609 acres) in area. Thus, Ballykilcline was large for County Roscommon, where the average baile size was about 115 hectares (284 acres) (McErlean 1983: 324).

The manipulation of the physical landscape, the transition from Irish to English, and the general course of colonialist activity in Ireland as institutionalized in legislative action, indicate that many epochal structures were interwoven within Ireland. The years of our immediate archaeological interest are the 1800–1848 period (or, in other words, from the Act of Union to the mass evictions of the Great Hunger period). During this era, the most important epochal structure in rural Ireland centered on the agricultural arrangements procured by the individual families. Ballykilcline and the many townlands situated around it were inhabited by nuclear and extended families whose principal mode of production was agriculturally based, with the occupation of land taking the form of tenancy-at-will (that is, at the will of the landlord) (House of Lords 1847: 4).

The greatest social-structural division in the Irish countryside existed between landlords and tenants. Irish landlords were for the most part Anglo-Irish Protestants, whereas the tenants who rented from them were by and large Irish Roman Catholics. The guiding principle of the structure appears to be religious, but its basis was inherently racial. Just as the existence of African American slave owners appeared to violate the racial doctrine of the segregated United States (see, e.g., Johnson and Roark 1984), so too were some powerful landlords Irish Catholics (see Trench 1997). Regardless of the religious beliefs of those who received the rents, the tenancy system was invariable in creating lasting social distinctions:

England has subverted the conditions of Irish society. At first it confiscated the land, then it suppressed the industry by "Parliamentary enactments," and lastly, it broke the active energy by armed force. And thus England created those abominable 'conditions of society' which enable a small *caste* of rapacious lordlings to dictate to the Irish people the terms on which they shall be allowed to hold the land and to live upon it. (Marx and Engels 1971: 61; emphasis in original)

Tenant farming always has the potential to be contentious because of its inherent structural inequalities. There existed in Ireland an additional racialist element because of the English invention of the "Celtic subaltern" (Hingley 2000: 65–68). Even the Devon Commission, appointed by the British government in late 1843 specifically to investigate the nature of Irish agriculture, recognized the racialist element of Irish agriculture by their conclusion "that the principal cause of Irish misery was the bad relations between landlord and tenant. *Ireland was a conquered country, the Irish peasant a dispossessed man, his landlord an alien conqueror*" (Woodham-Smith 1991: 21; emphasis added).

The hierarchical structure of Irish farming, however, was not represented by the simple tenant:landlord dyad that characterized postbellum tenancy in the American South. The rural agricultural structure of Ireland was composed of a minimum of four social positions: cottier → subtenant → tenant → landlord. The historical specifics of this basic structure could be significantly blurred by reference to all farmers beneath the position of landlord as "peasants" or "the peasantry" (see, e.g., Doolan 1847; Foster 1846; MacDonnell 1823). The Commissioners of the Census for 1841 realized the inadequacy of the generalized term "peasants" because it ignored the significant social differentiation within the countryside. To create a heuristic measure that more adequately represented Irish complexity, they invented a four-part classification of housing that provided some of the exactitude they sought: "in the lowest, or fourth class, were comprised all mud cabins having only one room—in the third, a better description of cottage, still built of mud, but varying from 2 to 4 rooms and windows—in the second, a good farm house . . . having from 5 to 9 rooms and windows—and in the first, all houses of a better description than the preceding classes" (Commissioners of the Census 1843: xiv). The Commissioners' surrogate measure forever linked Irish farmers to their largest piece of material culture and at the same time clearly distinguished both the elite position of the landlords and the distinctions within the general tenant order (Table 6.1). The Commissioners contemplated combining the third- and fourth-class categories, but decided against it in order to emphasize the existence of the "mere hut" in Ireland (Commissioners of the Census 1843: xiv). They did hope, however, that the two categories could eventually be combined, because over three-quarters of Irish housing was classified as falling within the third or fourth class.

Without question, the social differentiation of early nineteenth-century rural Ireland was created by the intersection of economic and cultural capital. Important distinctions were also identified within the elite rank, with the Anglo-Irish gentry being differentiated in various ways.

One intriguing early nineteenth-century classification from Connacht includes three groups of "gentlemen":

1. "Half-mounted gentlemen," squireens with unpolished boots, hunting on good horses which jumped well but were never groomed, owning, and farming about 200 acres.

2. "Gentlemen every inch of them," but a bit short of cash, public-spirited and influential at elections.

3. "Gentlemen to the backbone," the oldest families, rather too grand for many but deeply respected by their tenantry, from whom they could at any time raise a formidable private army. (Trench 1997: 83)

Social and economic distinctions between tenants and landlords were generally worse in east Connacht than elsewhere—the location of Ballykilcline—with landlords often being grandly referred to as "lords of the soil" (Coleman 1999: 32).

The economic assets that an Irish tenant farming family could amass included: access to land, the labor of its members, and economic capital in the form of livestock, tools, furniture, and house (Harris 1999: 211). Such variance meant in practical terms that great distinctions occurred within the non-landowning masses, partly because various amounts of cultural capital could attach to kin groups irrespective of their access to land, labor, and livestock (see Clark 1979: 40–51). Any attempt to summarize the Irish agricultural structure necessarily leads to oversimplification and reification where none in fact existed (Connolly 1982: 16). Even the Commissioners of the 1841 census recognized that they "felt a difficulty in laying down any rule as to what really should be considered a farmer" (Commissioners of the Census 1843: xxiii). Rather than constituting a rigid system, wherein a tenant farmer could sequentially climb the rungs of an "agricultural ladder," Irish tenancy was similar to the structure experienced by tenant farmers in the American South (see Figure 5.2).

TABLE 6.1. Classes of Irish Houses in 1841

Housing class	Occupants	Number	Percentage
4	laborers	480,000	36.3
3	cottiers/small farmers	535,000	40.4
2	large farmers	265,000	20.0
1	landlords/gentry	43,000	3.3
Total		1,323,000	100.0

Source: Keating (1996: 11–12).

Irish tenure classes also tended to overlap and to blend into one another. The difference that did exist between the Irish and the American structures simply concerned the way in which the "races" were perceived. In the American case, race was used to separate racially superior tenants from those deemed racially inferior, whereas in Ireland, ostensibly all the tenants were, at least initially, in the subordinately defined racial group.

The variance that existed in the precise structure of Irish tenant farming means that several models of pre-1848 Irish tenancy are possible (Table 6.2). The principal difficulty in attempting to comprehend the hierarchical structure of pre-1848 Irish tenancy involves the often regional use of the descriptive terms themselves. Many historians have tended to distinguish between farmers and farm laborers, but the actual difference between these two agricultural labor classes is almost impossible to discern with any certainty (Beames 1983: 16).

The term "cottier" provides an excellent example of the problems inherent in the nomenclature of Irish tenancy. In much of southern Ireland the term "cottier" generally referenced a farmer on a small landholding, up to about 10 acres (4 hectares) in size. Elsewhere, including Connacht, a "cottier" was a farmer who paid all or part of his rent in labor to another farmer (Beames 1975: 352).

TABLE 6.2. Four Models of the Structure of Pre-1848 Irish Tenancy

Sigerson (1871)	Clark (1979)	Connolly (1982)	Beames (1983)
chief tenants (landlords)	large landed proprietors	landlords	landlords
upper tenants	large farmers	farmers, >50 acres farmers, 15–50 acres	middle rich peasantry, 15–30 acres
		farmers, <15 acres	middle rich peasantry, 5–15 acres
under tenants	small farmers	smallholders, <5 acres smallholders, 1–5 acres smallholders, >1 acres joint tenancies	poor peasantry, <5 acres
cottagers/ cottiers	laborer-landholders	cottiers and laborers	
	landless laborers	farm servants	laborers

Even the use of the term "landlord," as a static achieved status, is potentially problematic. Using Sigerson's (1871) scheme for illustration (see Table 6.2), the cottagers (cottiers) would pay rent in labor to an under tenant, and the under tenant would pay rent in cash to an upper tenant. This arrangement meant that the upper tenant was both a renter and a landlord. Thus, in pre-famine Ireland, under tenants, upper tenants, and landlords could all be conceivably and accurately termed "landlords."

A clear correlation obtained between quality of house and amount of land farmed, but the precise nature of this linkage is difficult to determine. Table 6.3 shows land holding statistics for Ireland as compiled during the 1841 census and amended by Bourke (1993: 78). An exact correlation between house class and landholding size—both measures assigned by census enumerators—is impossible to provide, but it is clear that most Irish farmers in the 1800–1848 period farmed less than 30 acres (12 hectares) and lived in third- and fourth-class housing.

Part of the Irish population, however, was not even placed on the social scale. These men, women, and children were members of that group typically defined as "landless laborers," or for administrative purposes, "destitute classes." In the early 1830s, His Majesty's Commissioners for Enquiring into the Condition of the Poorer Classes of Ireland conducted an island-wide survey in which they conducted interviews as part of their data-gathering process. Their report, published in 1835, enumerated the following "destitute classes": "Deserted and Orphan Children; Illegitimate Children and their Mothers; Widows having Families of young Children; The Impotent through Age or other permanent Infirmity; The Sick Poor, who in health are capable of earning their subsistence; The Able-bodied out of work, [and] Vagrancy" (Dublin et al. 1835: 3).

The structure provided by the 1841 census helps us to conceptualize the principal pattern of Irish farming, but the framework of the structure does not help us to comprehend the actual sociohistorical situation at Ballykilcline because of the great variation that was built into the

TABLE 6.3. Number of Individuals Holding Land in Ireland in 1841

Size of holding (acres)	Number of individuals	Percentage	Housing class
<2–10	310,436	44.9	4
10–30	252,799	36.6	3
30–60	79,338	11.5	2
> 60	48,623	7.0	1
Total	691,196	100.0	

Source: Bourke (1993: 78).

structure itself. Fortunately, however, the Brassington and Gale plat of 1836 permits a reconstruction of the landholding pattern at the townland.

The Brassington and Gale map was originally conceived as a spatial representation that the Commissioners of Woods and Forests could employ to understand the nature of agricultural production at Ballykilcline (see Andrews 1975). The Commissioners needed this map because the Ballykilcline tenants had commenced a rent strike as soon as the Crown had acquired the lease to the townland. The Commissioners thus had administrative reasons to know where each tenant family lived and farmed. The Brassington and Gale map acquired other meanings as well. Throughout the course of the rent strike, the Commissioners could use the plat to guide their strategy for assuming armed control of the townland. The roads into the townland—along with the locations of the "ringleaders'" houses—became focal points of interest in the Commissioners' attempts to force rent payment, to arrest those tenants they had identified as leaders, and to establish a police station within the townland. The Brassington and Gale map was thus even more of a surveillance tool than the Ordnance Survey plat because it included specific information about each landholder; the Ordnance Survey maps did not contain such precise information. Both government-sponsored maps still had significant geopolitical import because "Once mapped a place was ready to be owned, occupied, and 'civilized'" (Smith 2001: 94). The civilizing agent at Ballykilcline was to be enforced by the payment of rents, and the map was to be an important structuring element of that enforcement.

The surveyors who created the Brassington and Gale plat carefully indicated field boundaries, field areas (in acres, roods, and perches), the name of the head of each landholding family, the locations of their houses, and many other features (see Figure 6.4). The information presented on this plat can be analytically employed today, albeit with a firm understanding that it is inherently synchronic and possibly biased in its viewpoint (see Smith 1998, 2001). Even with these caveats in mind, however, the map can be an important historical source.

The size of each holding at Ballykilcline can be easily calculated (Table 6.4) and the basic hierarchical structure of the townland constructed from this information, both for individuals (Table 6.5) and for families (Table 6.6). This information suggests that the basic internal, hierarchical structure of Irish tenant farming was upheld at Ballykilcline. Well over half (62.0 percent) of the individual tenants farmed between 2 and 10 acres (.81–4.04 hectares), and only a minority (13.9 percent) farmed less than 2 acres. The statistics reveal, though that four families (McDermott, Donnellan, Nary, and Connor) held between 30 and 60 acres each (12.1–24.3 hectares). The important link between family affiliation and

TABLE 6.4. Individual Landholdings in 1836

Acreage	Holder	Acreage	Holder	Acreage	Holder
24.35	Hugh McDermott	7.89	Mary McDaniel	5.18	James Hanley
24.15	Patrick Donnellan	7.79	John Carnton	5.05	Thomas Mangan, Jr.
24.15	Edward Donnellan	7.71	Terence Reynolds	4.88	Patrick Stewart
16.37	Thomas McCormick	7.70	Patrick Reilly	4.78	Patrick Maguire
15.48	Patrick Collogan, Jr.	7.60	Honora Winter	4.72	Patrick McCormick
14.66	Owen Carolan	7.56	Edward Nary	4.33	Henry Stewart
13.65	Thomas Fallon	7.56	Luke Nary	4.33	William Stewart
13.52	William Brennan	7.56	James Nary	4.14	John Downey
13.33	James Mullera	7.56	Mark Nary	3.57	Daniel Coghlan
12.66	Patrick Connor	7.49	John Mangan	3.54	Terence Moran
12.26	Thomas Fitzmorris	7.28	James Kelly	3.26	Patrick Coyle
12.18	John McDermott	7.07	John Quin	3.26	James Foley
11.60	Patrick Reynolds	7.04	Patrick Collogan	2.90	James Stewart
11.54	Rev. Thomas Lloyd	7.04	Bridget Fallon	2.84	Eliza Reynolds
10.95	Patrick Finn	6.90	Patrick Nary	1.94	Ann Flower
10.75	Richard Padian	6.90	Bartolomew Nary	1.92	John Wynne
10.64	Thomas Costello	6.80	Patrick Kelly	1.63	Michael Coyle
10.64	John Costello	6.38	John Mullera	1.22	John Toolan
10.24	Byron O'Neill	6.38	Thomas Mullera	0.93	Mary Gallagher
9.83	Thomas Mangan, Sr	6.36	Terence Connor	0.77	John Clements
9.68	James Deafly	6.18	John Stewart	0.50	Thomas Moran
9.68	Patrick Deafly	6.13	John Moran	0.50	Edward Ginty
9.39	Michael Connor	5.86	Jane Mangan	0.50	Patrick Pellegan
8.47	Thomas McManus	5.84	James Connor	0.41	Bridget Mahon
8.19	Thomas Hanley	5.80	Martin Finn	0.37	John McCormick
7.95	Thomas McDermott	5.27	Michael McDermott		
7.92	Denis Connor	5.27	Thomas Reynolds		

size of holding can be observed by considering the number of family members on each holding (Table 6.7). The families at the bottom of the acreage scale tend to be represented by a single individual occupying a small plot of ground. The flexibility of the agricultural structure means, however, that the correlation between family size and size of holding is not absolute. For example, John Carnton held 25 fields and the Widow Honora Winter held 18, but in both cases their total holdings equaled less than 10 acres (4.04 hectares). Richard Padian, on the other hand, held only one field that was almost 11 acres (4.45 hectares) in size.

The connection between farm holdings and individuals or family members only offers the most basic, indirect information about economic capital. It is difficult from these statistics alone to discover much about the amassing and use of cultural capital. Some clues about cultural capital can be obtained, however, by considering the social networks that operated at Ballykilcline.

Networks of Social Interaction

The men and women of Ballykilcline, like the thousands of tenant farmers on the over 60,000 townlands of rural Ireland, were enmeshed in a complex, multiscalar nexus of interaction that involved countless people in disparate places. Ballykilcline was somewhat unique historically in the sense that it was the locus of a protracted rent strike, or what was then known as an "agrarian outrage."

TABLE 6.5. Breakdown of Individual Holdings, 1836

Acreage	Number of holders	Percentage
< 2	11	13.9
2–10	49	62.0
10–30	19	24.1
30–60	0	0.0
Total	79	100.0

TABLE 6.6. Breakdown of Family Holdings, 1836

Acreage	Number of holders	Percentage
< 2	8	19.0
2–10	11	26.2
10–30	19	45.2
30–60	4	9.5
Total	42	99.9

Table 6.7. Family Holdings, 1836

Family	Acreage	Number of fields	Number of holders
McDermott	49.75	7	4
Donnellan	48.30	4	2
Nary	44.04	6	6
Connor	42.17	17	5
Mangan	28.23	22	4
Reynolds	27.42	11	4
Mullera	26.09	6	3
Stewart	22.62	19	5
Collogan	22.52	4	2
McCormick	21.46	11	3
Costello	21.28	2	2
Fallon	20.69	4	2
Deafly	19.36	2	2
Finn	16.75	4	2
Carolan	14.66	2	1
Kelly	14.08	6	2
Brennan	13.52	3	1
Hanley	13.37	4	2
Fitzmorris	12.26	1	1
Lloyd	11.54	1	1
Padian	10.75	1	1
O'Neill	10.24	2	1
Moran	10.17	6	3
McManus	8.47	1	1
McDaniel	7.89	1	1
Carnton	7.79	25	1
Reilly	7.70	1	1
Winter	7.60	18	1
Quin	7.07	2	1
Coyle	4.89	2	2
Maguire	4.78	1	1
Downey	4.14	3	1
Coghlan	3.57	1	1
Foley	3.26	1	1
Flower	1.94	1	1
Wynne	1.92	1	1
Toolan	1.22	1	1
Gallagher	0.93	1	1
Clements	0.77	1	1
Pellegan	0.50	1	1
Ginty	0.50	1	1
Mahon	0.41	1	1

Mass protest has a long history in rural Ireland, with the first such action being recorded as occurring in Connacht in 1711 (Knott 1984: 96). In the early nineteenth century, rural men and women formed protest movements with names like Caravats, Shanavests, Ribbonmen, Defenders, Whiteboys, and Molly Maguires (see Beames 1982, 1983; Donnelly 1983; Kenny 1998; Knott 1984; Roberts 1983; Sigerson 1871: 278–333). These collective actions could have national, sectarian, and agrarian emphases with disparate goals (Clark 1979: 65–100). The avowedly nationalistic movements, such as the Ribbonmen, were devised as organized reactions to the construction of the racialized social order that situated the Irish, in toto, at the bottom of the English-designed social scale. According to one early nineteenth-century informer, the Ribbonmen's national aspirations sought nothing less than "to rebel, to separate themselves from the English government, and put down the Protestant religion" (Beames 1982: 136). The overt nationalistic movements largely failed to promote the kind of full-scale, systemic changes in agriculture many proponents desired, but they did accomplish, in some measure and in various ways, the creation of large-scale, extra-townland networks of interaction.

As might well be supposed, Anglo-Irish and British elites were concerned about the effects of the lower-echelon, collective, rural movements upon both the social character and the productive abilities of Irish agriculture, particularly if such movements could establish long-distance networks that would have at their core the rejection of the racialized social order. Many early nineteenth-century commentators recognized that the central cause of the agrarian disturbances revolved around issues of land tenure as a central deficiency in the structure of Irish agriculture. The system demanded, through its very structure, that Irish tenant farmers could expect little return on their labor beyond mere subsistence (see Foster 1846: 10–26; Marx and Engels 1971: 59–65). Other commentators, however, found it impossible to condemn the structure of agricultural production, and so they sought explanations that were more consistent with their general views about progress and capitalist development. For these observers, the problem with Irish agriculture was decidedly racial: because of religious affiliation and national temperament, the Irish were simply not able to perform as efficient tillers of the soil:

The people of Ireland have been accused of idleness and improvidence. These vices are attributed by many to the prevalent creed; and their supineness and want of industry are laid at the door of their religion. Others speak of them as the inherent characteristics of the Celtic race. . . . It has been asserted that even in America the Irish are to be known by their idleness, their want of cleanliness, and their improvident habits. (Pim 1848: 24, 26)

A clear linkage thus existed in early nineteenth-century Ireland between agrarian disturbance and the prevailing agriculture structure, largely because of the practice of conacre. Irish tenant farmers accepting conacre typically received around 0.5–1.0 acres (0.2 to 0.4 hectares) specifically for the production of potatoes, one of the principal foods of the rural Irish (Donnelly 1975: 19). Thousands of Irish tenants had accepted the potato as a food crop because of its hardy nature, its adaptability to the wet Irish climate, and its nutritional attributes (Salaman 1985: 243; Zuckerman 1998: 34–35). In productive years, Irish tenants could count on growing potatoes for food and other crops—oats, barley, wheat—for rent. Accepting conacre meant that even farmers with the smallest plots would potentially have food. But conacre also meant that they would be required to renegotiate their contracts every year. They would receive no long-term commitments within the conacre system. The practice of conacre was more prevalent in Connacht and Munster (southern Ireland) than in the other Irish provinces of Leinster and Ulster (O'Brien 1921: 11).

Agrarian unrest was common in County Roscommon in the early nineteenth century, with most of it arising because of the unequal distribution of land (Coleman 1999: 14). By the third decade of the nineteenth century, Kilglass Parish had developed a reputation for unruliness. O'Donovan observed in 1837 that Kilglass was "proverbial in this part of the county for its wickedness" (O'Donovan 1927: 57), and George Knox, the local Crown agent for Ballykilcline, noted that the townland's tenants "are the most lawless and violent set of people in the County of Roscommon" (Knox 1846: 136).

O'Donovan's opinion—and certainly Knox's—was undoubtedly occasioned by the Ballykilcline rent strike. The tenants' refusal to submit their rent monies to the Crown's representatives after 1834 provided a defining moment in the history of the townland. The Crown's detailed, bureaucratic account of the rent strike—which is undeniably representative of the colonialist understanding of their dominance in Ireland—provides unique information about the nature of the social networks that operated within the townland. To understand these networks, we must delve briefly into the history of the strike.

By 1836, two years after assuming direct administrative control of the townland, the Crown's agents realized that they would have difficulty collecting rents from the Ballykilcline tenants. As a result, they issued notices requiring the tenants to surrender possession of their holdings. Fifty-two of the 79 tenants (roughly 66 percent) agreed to the arrangement and were reinstated by the Crown as "care-takers" at an allowance of 6*d* per month. One condition of the arrangement was that the tenants—

who had undergone a significant structural transformation from tenants to caretakers—were required to surrender possession immediately upon the Crown's insistence. While most of the tenants initially agreed to the Crown's demands, the remaining third of them "absolutely refused to give up the Possession or to account with the Crown's Receivers for the Value of the Holdings in their Occupation" (House of Lords 1847: 4). When the Crown's agents appeared at the townland, several of the formerly agreeable tenants had changed their minds about becoming caretakers. Faced with escalating unrest, the Crown asked the police to intervene and to protect the men seeking to collect the rent arrears. The police, however, feared for their safety and refused to assist.

By 1842, the Crown decided to commence legal proceedings against the eight tenants whom they had identified as the rent strike's "ring leaders" (Thomas Fitzmorris, Thomas Mangan, John Quin, Patrick McCormick, John Wynne, Denis Connor, Patrick Nary, and Bartolomew Nary). But the true situation at Ballykilcline was much more fluid than the Crown's representatives had expected, because, for example, Thomas Fitzmorris (who had defaulted on his 1834–35 rent) had emigrated to America and Patrick Croghan had taken his land; Denis Connor (also an 1834–35 defaulter) had since died and his relatives had taken his land. In April 1842, then, the process server gave notice to four tenants: Thomas Magan (whom the Crown's agents described as in "good circumstances"), Patrick McCormick, John Wynne (both of whom the agents designated as having "very little property"), and Denis Connor. Only with the assistance of the emboldened police could the agents deliver the subpoenas to the remaining four tenants: Bartolomew Nary, his brother Patrick Nary (both of whom the agents observed were "very solvent"), John Quin ("very little property"), and Patrick Croghan. The landholding figures (see Table 6.4) indicate that, as individuals, the tenants identified as strike "ring leaders" were not among the group of tenants who held the most land. Thomas Mangan Sr. held 9.83 acres, John Quin 7.07 acres, Patrick McCormick 4.72 acres, John Wynne 1.92 acres, Denis Connor 7.92 acres, and Patrick and Bartolomew Nary, 6.90 acres each. When examined as members of families rather than as individuals, however, the situation appears quite different (see Table 6.7). The Mangans, McCormicks, Connors, and Narys all appear within the cohort holding over 20 acres, with the Narys and the Connors belonging to the over-40-acre group. Only Quin and Wynne, neither of whom had obvious family connections within the townland, appear near the bottom of the landholding list. (Patrick Croghan cannot be identified.)

One month after having served subpoenas on the tenants defined as the principal defaulters, the Clerk of Quit Rents communicated to the Ballykilcline tenants that they were required to pay their rent arrears on

May 31, 1842, in Strokestown, the locus of the Mahons' power. The tenants duly appeared as requested, but only one of them, Patrick Maguire (holding only 4.78 acres), paid the required amount. The other tenants refused to pay "saying they had not the Money, and that the Rent fixed upon their Lands was too much and more than they could pay" (House of Lords 1847: 18). In accordance with their refusal to pay the required rents, the tenants made a concerted plea to the Commissioners of Woods and Forests. Their petition explained the basis of their revolt and illustrated that their concerns revolved around issues of land tenure in accordance with other, island-wide agrarian rebellions. In the petition, they enumerated their situation:

1. that the "Right Honourable Maurice Lord Hartland [Maurice Mahon] subleased the lands to a Mr. Hogg" (who lived at the nearby Gilstown estate; Lewis 1984, 2: 98);
2. that both men charged their tenants a "Wreck Rent" (an unreasonably high rent);
3. that a Richard Brabazon, who subleased the land from either Lord Hartland or Charles Costello, of County Mayo, "called upon and collected from the congregated Assemblage of Tenants their former Receipts";
4. that in order to meet Brabazon's "high, enormous Rents," the tenants "did sacrifice Limb and Body" and they hoped that by becoming renters of the Crown they could release themselves from "the Cruelty of the grinding Landlords"; and
5. they requested that the Crown require the same rents as those assessed by Lord Hartland.

Perhaps to demonstrate that they believed they held a position of strength, the tenants added a bold conclusion to their petition: if the Commissioners did not agree to their demands, they would be forced to send a second petition to "Her most Gracious and Illustrious Majesty, tending to the Fraud and Imposition they are subjected to" (House of Lords 1847: 20).

The Commissioners elected not to accept the conditions of the tenants' petition and in fact stiffened their resolve to evict them. As a symbolic indication of the legality of their position as landlords, the Commissioners began to refer to the tenants as "Intruders on the Crown Lands of Ballykilcline." The tenants continued their intransigence, even with the increased threat of eviction, and escalated their resistance. In a letter dated April 8, 1843, John R. Malone, the Sub-Sheriff of County Roscommon, stated that when he arrested Bartolomew Nary in Strokestown, "the roads on every Side of me were surrounded, and the Prisoner would be certainly rescued from me had I not got him into One of the Police Stations along the Road." The tenants attacked the police depot and Malone could only get Nary to the jail in Roscommon town by traveling an indirect route. Malone then planned to arrest the other defendants, hoping to catch them at one of the local fairs. But, as he wrote in a letter to the townland's receivers, there was "no Fair or Market anywhere within Twenty Miles of their Places of Abode" that he and his men had not searched for them. In a final note of exasperation, Malone concluded, "I cannot devote myself from Market Day to Market Day looking after the Defendants" (House of Lords 1847: 30).

Malone's reluctance to send his men to every local market and fair in search of the Ballykilcline defendants becomes more understandable when we realize the frequency of such well-attended gatherings. Lewis' dictionary of Ireland, first published in 1837, provides the following dates for markets and fairs for the towns located within a twenty-mile radius of Ballykilcline: Cloone (County Leitrim) = fairs on February 12, April 5, May 26, June 13, July 10, August 26, September 29, November 2, December 20; Elphin = market every Wednesday, fairs on May 3, June 27, September 29, and December 10; Mohill (County Leitrim) = market every Thursday, fairs on the first Thursday of January, February 3, February 25, March 17, April 14, May 8, the first Thursday in June, July 31, August 1, August 18, the second Thursday in September, October 19, November 10, and the first Thursday in December; and Strokestown = weekly market and fairs on the first Tuesday in May, June, October, and November (Lewis 1984, 1: 379, 597, 2: 376, 581).

Little had changed at Ballykilcline by 1844. The tenants still refused to pay their rents, and the Crown's representatives continued to attempt to force payment. In May of that year, the Crown's bailiffs found the tenants more intractable than ever. According to Knox, when they attempted to serve notice "they were attacked by the Tenants, and not having the Protection of the Police were obliged to retreat, after only effecting the Service of Six or Seven of the Notices, and were it not that by chance they met a few Policemen on Duty they would certainly have been killed, as it was with the greatest Difficulty and fixed Bayonets that the Police could keep the Mob from them" (House of Lords 1847: 50). Knox further noted that the tenants had been "armed with Sticks, Stones, and Shovels" and that they had used "threatening language" when chasing the bailiffs from the townland. Knox sought permission to establish a police station directly within Ballykilcline ("One of the Houses held by the Narrys would, with some Repairs, make a Police Barrack") and offered that the Crown's forces should either evict the tenants and lock their houses or else "throw them down."

After the armed rebellion, the Crown's agents had to accept that the tenants of Ballykilcline were in overt opposition to the established system of tenure. The flow of rent monies from the townland had declined precipitously during the course of the strike, as increasing numbers of tenants joined the action (Table 6.8). The Commissioners thus decided that ejectment was the best solution for ending the rent strike. The tenants must also have begun to recognize that their options were evaporating, because on May 12, 1846, they sent a petition to the Commissioners of Woods and Forests, in which they described themselves as "459 Individuals of moral industrious Habits, exemplary, obedient, and implicit to their Landlady or Landlord." They argued that they were "penitent and regretful for any Misunderstanding which has occurred in the Event of the Case in question" (House of Lords 1847: 73). The petition was presented by The O'Conor Don, the traditional Gaelic chieftain of the region.

The government's men charged with overseeing Ballykilcline appeared disposed to accept the petition, probably hoping to see the troubles come to an end and undoubtedly wishing to see the tenants once again submitting their rents. Knox, the on-site agent, however, was not impressed by the tenants' profession of loyalty: "My firm Conviction therefore is that they never will become satisfactory Tenants to the Crown" (House of Lords 1847: 76). In February 1847, Richard Moore, Attorney General for Ireland, expressed his opinion that after several years of protest, the tenants of Ballykilcline must have become emboldened by the "Impression that the Crown either is unable or unwilling to turn them out." He concluded that they must be evicted, but decided that it would appear too cruel to do it in the middle of winter. But by 1847 the potato blight had reached County Roscommon, and it was virtually impossible for the tenants—like hundreds of thousands of others throughout the island—to pay their yearly rents, let alone their amassed arrears. With this reality made abundantly clear, the Crown decided to

TABLE 6.8. Defaulting Ballykilcline Tenants and Rent Collections, 1834–1841

Date	Defaulters	Rent			Decline(%)
		l.	*s.*	*d.*	
Before May 1834	—	412	0	2	—
May 1834–May 1835	8	376	13	5	8.6
May 1835–May 1836	21	287	0	5	23.8
May 1836–May 1837	40	100	4	7½	65.1
May 1837–May 1841	77	10	10	0	89.5

Source: House of Lords (1847).

evict the tenants. Between September 1847 and April 1848, four ship-loads of Ballykilcline tenants were transported first to Liverpool and then to New York (Scally 1995: 105–29). The Narys, upon whose land excavations occurred from 1998–2002, were among the evictees.

Historical documents do not reveal how Mark Nary and his family traveled to the United States, but we do know when Mark's nephews, Bartolomew ("Bartley") and Patrick, arrived. Bartolomew Nary, who had been arrested in Strokestown and held for trial, left Liverpool on the *Channing*, and arrived in New York on April 17, 1848. His younger brother, Patrick (also an original defendant and identified "ring leader"), had left on the *Roscius* six months earlier (Ellis 1977: 19) and had arrived in New York on October 22, 1847 (Glazier 1983: 136).

The official records of the rent strike compiled by the central actors of the British bureaucracy include a listing of the individuals with rent arrears from May 1, 1834, to January 7, 1842 (House of Lords 1847: 10–13). This list allows inferences to be made about the inter-family webs of interaction that were maintained at Ballykilcline, employing the assumption that individuals engaged in the rent strike may have conspired with the other non-paying tenants, as agent George Knox argued throughout the strike. It is also possible that some tenants joined the strike as it gained momentum when they noticed that their neighbors were withholding their rents with apparent impunity. Others may have been coerced into joining the strike or were physically assaulted for not participating (Scally 1995: 119). Those tenants who filed petitions claiming their innocence in the rent strike may simply have been adopting another strategy that would permit them to stay on their land, once the evictions became a reality.

The composition of the rent strike "ring leader" cohort changed throughout the course of the strike, or from 1835 to 1847 (Table 6.9). If we examine the composition of the ring leader group in 1835, just after the strike began, we note that the seven individuals who can be correlated with the 1836 Brassington and Gale plat held a total of 45.26 acres (mean = 6.47 acres). In 1846, however, the ten identified ring leaders held 94.27 acres (mean = 9.43). These figures suggest that larger tenants were attracted to the rent strike as it progressed. The same may be true of the largest landholding families, because three of the four largest were represented in 1846 (McDermott, Nary, and Connor). John Wynne, the smallest land holder in 1835, with only 1.92 acres, does not appear on the government's list of defaulters in 1841 (House of Lords 1847: 10–13), though he and his two children were evicted in September 1847 (Ellis 1977: 21).

The involvement of the largest landholders in the strike appears to have occurred at about the same time that the strikers were becoming increasingly determined and more overtly violent. The strategy that the largest holders employed may have involved waiting at the start of the action to see what would happen, and then joining once the rent strike took hold. It is possible that they enacted numerous authority vectors within the community to maintain the strike. For instance, the Crown's representatives thought that Richard Padian, a middling farmer in 1836, was an important leader of the strike. Peter Geraghty, the only priest at Ballykilcline, lodged with Padian's family (Scally 1995: 73–74). Geraghty would have had abundant cultural capital among the residents of the townland (but little economic capital), and this store of indirect capital may have helped Padian—who had no obvious relatives in the town-land—to hold a prominent position in maintaining the strike and in recruiting new participants. Individual priests could take either pro or anti positions in agrarian movements (see Connolly 1982: 219–63), and Geraghty's views are unknown. His residence with Padian's family, how-ever, suggests that he supported the strike (Scally 1995: 74–75).

The network of strikers was only one of the structures that existed in Ballykilcline during the rent strike. A second cohort was comprised of those tenants who openly disagreed with the strike action and who in some instances informed on the activities of their fellow tenants. The

TABLE 6.9. "Ring Leader" Cohort in 1835 and 1846 with Landholdings

		Holdings (acres), 1836	
"Defaulters," 1835	*"Defendants," 1846*	*Individual*	*Family*
Thomas Fitzmorris	Patrick Croghan	—	—
Thomas Mangan		9.83	28.23
John Quin		7.07	7.07
Patrick McCormick		4.72	21.46
John Wynne		1.92	1.92
Dennis Connor	John Connor[1]	6.36	42.17
Patrick Nary	Patrick Nary	6.90	44.04
Bartolomew Nary	Bartolomew Nary	6.90	44.04
	Richard Padian	10.75	10.75
	Patrick Collogan	15.48	22.52
	Michael Connor	9.39	42.17
	Terence Connor	6.36	42.17
	Patrick Stewart	4.88	22.62
	James Stewart	2.90	22.62
	James Reynolds	—	27.42
	Joseph Reynolds[2]	—	27.42
	Hugh McDermott	24.35	49.75
	Bernard McDermott[3]	—	49.75

[1] Brother of Denis Connor, who died around 1842.
[2] Younger brother of James Reynolds.
[3] Eldest son of Hugh McDermott.

documents suggest that at least three informants lived at Ballykilcline: Patrick Maguire, John Mullera, and Patrick Reilly. These men were relatively small landholders—4.78, 6.38, and 7.70 acres respectively—who together only held 18.86 acres. Their average holding was only 6.29 acres, even lower than that of the original defaulters (which includes Wynne's 1.92 plot). The anti-strike faction, however, had an important ally in the Rev. Thomas Lloyd, Rector of Kilglass, who lived in the Glebe House on the edge of Ballykilcline. Lines of tension between the tenants and Lloyd stemmed from two sources: (1) Lloyd's ardent support of the British Crown and its representatives in Ireland (House of Lords 1847: 14), and (2) the requirement that the Roman Catholic tenant farmers of Ballykilcline remit almost £760 in tithes to support the protestant Church of Ireland, of which Lloyd was the local representative (Lewis 1984, II: 98). Lloyd's household included his wife Eleanor and their seven children, but also five employed men and women from Ballykilcline: Barnard Regan (manservant), Anne Stewart (housekeeper and cook), Maria Gill (scullery girl), and Thomas Fox and Thomas Wynne (farmhands) (Scally 1995: 127–28). The extant information indicates that the service of these tenants to the Lloyds did not necessarily mean that they were exempt from eviction. Both Anne Stewart (aged 50) and Thomas Fox, a landless laborer, left Liverpool on the *Channing* on March 13, 1848, and arrived in New York City on April 18 (Ellis 1977: 15, 20; Glazier 1983: 316). Upon his arrival, Fox was classified as a shoemaker, perhaps a representation of the personal capital he had acquired while in Lloyd's employ.

The construction of the two factions at Ballykilcline, organized on the basis of their stance on the wisdom of the rent strike, could cross-cut family linkages. For example, Mary Maguire, the mother of informer Patrick Maguire, was also the mother-in-law of Terence Connor, one of the 1846 defendants. Such interconnections demonstrate the complexity of the networks that were produced and reproduced at Ballykilcline and show how the tenants could constantly refashion their social networks in relation to the circumstances they faced.

In addition to the presence of the two diametrically opposed factions at Ballykilcline during the height of the rent strike, it may be possible to reconstruct another cohort, based upon their collective presence at the bottom of the social hierarchy. Records indicate that a number of landless laborers lived at Ballykilcline. This group included Thomas Fox, his older brother and his wife and their two children; Thomas Geelan; Bernard Gill, possibly related to Maria Gill, the scullery girl; Michael Hoare, his wife, and their five children; James Kelly, his wife, and their eight children; Patrick Kelly, his wife Eliza Cline, and their five children; Michael McDonnell and his three children; John McGann; the widow Mary McGann and her six children; the widow Mary Madden and her two children; Catherine, Patrick, and Anne Mullera (relationship unknown); brothers James and Thomas Mullera; the widow Bridget Stewart and her three children; Anne Stewart, who worked for Lloyd; and Michael Wynne, his wife, and their three children. These 62 individuals are difficult to locate in the textual sources because they probably worked as landless laborers on conacre ground attached to one of the large landholders, who held the simultaneous labor positions of landlord and tenant. Historical rent accounts do not exist for subtenants who rented from other tenants. Anglo-Irish landlords generally would not know the names of these men and women, and often they would not even be aware that these subtenants lived on their estate, because they would have had no direct legal or social connection with them. The agricultural arrangements of subtenants were strictly intra-townland in scope.

Many of the social connections constructed at Ballykilcline were strong enough to be transferred to the United States as an element of the diaspora. For instance, St. Vincent's cemetery, in Waltham township, LaSalle County, Illinois, contains the graves of many Ballykilcline tenants, including John Stewart (evicted at age 21, arrived on the *Creole*), Patrick Mullera (evicted at age 29, arrived on the *Channing*), Thomas Hanley (evicted at age 60, arrived on the *Creole*), John Carrington (evicted at age 14 and traveled with the Hanley family), John Hoare, the son of a landless laborer (evicted at age 7, arrived on the *Channing*), and Edward Nary (evicted at age 42), whose house was excavated as part of the research from which this chapter derives.

The intra-townland social space was not merely a cognitive construct. On the contrary, it was undeniably rooted in the landscape. The distribution of the houses at Ballykilcline demonstrates that the tenants lived along the roads, in a "modern" pattern rather than in clachans, or nucleated settlements that existed as part of the rundale, or infield/outfield system of agriculture. The close association of the nucleated settlement form with the rundale system has lead to the general substitution of "rundale village" for clachan (Whelan 1994: 63). Historical geographers have debated the history of the clachan, and current thinking maintains that it was a sophisticated adaption to ecological and sociohistorical circumstances, including among them, the British intervention and creation of a racialist conceptualization of the Irish "peasantry" (see, e.g., Whelan 1992: 411–15, 1997: 81–82). The location of rundale villages in mountainous, hilly, and boggy areas indicates that this residence form developed during a period of resettlement in previously uninhabited areas. But settlement at Ballykilcline was along the roadways, with the fields generally stretching away from, or behind, the houses.

The roads into Ballykilcline, extending from the west, north, and east, provided entry points for the sheriff and the bailiffs seeking to serve notice on the tenants or even to evict them. It would have been difficult, within the confines of this spatial design, for the tenants to avoid the government's representatives while they were in their homes. In light of the spatial practice that the design structured and in turn was structured by, it is perhaps noteworthy that the 1846 defendants' network described a unilinear form that stretched along the main roadway through the center of the townland, extending from Richard Padian's home on the extreme eastern side of the townland to James Stewart's house on the extreme western side (Figure 6.5). This linear pattern of resistance may represent an attempt by the tenants to monitor the main points of entry into the townland and to retain control of the main route through their settlement. Agent George Knox clearly recognized the tactical impor-tance of the roadways, because he suggested to John Burke, the Clerk of Quit Rents, that "One of the Houses held by the Narrys would, with some Repairs, make a Police Barrack" (House of Lords 1847: 50). The cen-trality of the Bartolomew and Patrick Nary land may have been a factor in Knox's decision, but he later changed his mind about using one of the Nary houses, opting instead for the house of Richard Padian or Patrick Croghan because they were both "on the High Road leading from Strokestown to Ruskey" (House of Lords 1847: 71–72). This road is still the main route through the old townland of Ballykilcline.

The homes of the major informants against the strikers—John Mul-lera, Patrick Maguire, and the Rev. Thomas Lloyd—were all on the per-iphery. (The location of Reilly's home cannot be determined.) The most centralized location was Maguire's, being situated directly across the road from the homes of Bartolomew and Patrick Nary, two central figures in the strike. Maguire's labor position was such that he served as a personal carriage driver for both Thomas Lloyd and George Knox. This position would have given him some measure of cultural capital: "While he was hated and cursed by most of the townland, his position as Knox's driver still made him a man of importance among them, someone who *in ordinary times* should not be offended lightly" (Scally 1995: 69; emphasis added). The strategy for which Maguire opted was to agree with Lloyd and to support the Crown, even if it meant being hated, threatened, and even beaten by the striking tenants. Maguire undoubt-edly assumed this risky position to be justified and his analysis seems to have been correct. Knox informed the Crown's agents that only Maguire should have the right to stay in Ballykilcline after the mass evic-tions (Scally 1995: 105). Thus it would appear that Maguire transfigured his cultural capital—acquired in the townland through his unique posi-tion of driver—to align it with the dominant governmental forces. Mag-uire would have had no knowledge, of course, of how the strike would be resolved, but it is possible that he suspected the possibility of mass eviction. Lloyd may even have kept him informed of the government's plans. Evictions for non-payment of two years' rent were common in Ireland, with the first known example occurring in the English-occupied Pale in 1298 (Sigerson 1871: 16). Forced ejectment was one legal recourse

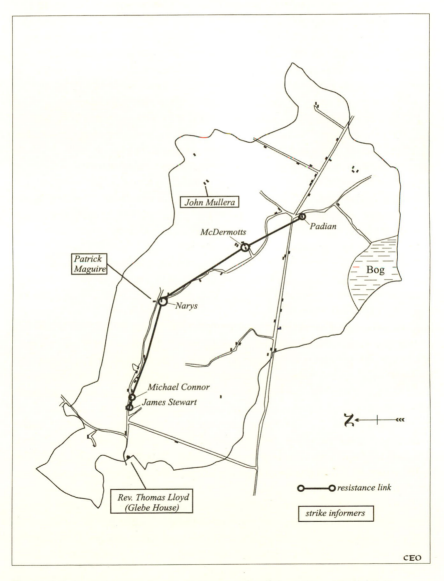

Figure 6.5. Spatial networks of resistance and collaboration at Ballykilcline.

available to early nineteenth-century landlords, along with the distraint of a tenant's property (Clark 1979: 29).

The tenants of Ballykilcline were also engaged in at least two important extra-townland networks. These networks of interaction would be completely unsuspected without the presence of archaeological information. Both networks involve the introduction of commodities into the townland and both specifically concern the movement of ceramics. The first network revolved around the production of Irish-made coarse earthenwares, and the second concerned the much more well-known manufacturing and marketing of English-made refined earthenwares.

The production of glazed coarse earthenwares has roots in medieval Europe, and in Ireland archaeologists have found examples at several medieval-period sites. Research suggests that the pre-modern coarse earthenware found in Ireland was both domestic- and foreign-made (Barry 1987: 100–3; Edwards 1999: 68; Mallory and McNeill 1991: 266). Archaeologists find coarse earthenware pieces in early modern deposits and usually designate them either "brownware," because of the color of their bodies, or "blackware," because of their extremely dark glazes (see Fanning and Hurst 1975; Sweetman 1979, 1980; White 1999). Coarse earthenware production in Ireland during the late eighteenth and early nineteenth centuries is poorly researched and so little concrete knowledge has been collected (McManus 1984).

One reason that the history and character of coarse earthenware production in Ireland is largely unknown is that it was generally a cottage industry, probably conducted by generations of family-affiliated potters who had both attained the necessary skills and acquired the required equipment. Most coarse earthenware potters may not have kept records of their activities, and those learned gentlemen who contemplated and wrote about Ireland's ceramic industry usually completely ignored the indigenous coarse earthenware industry. The late eighteenth-century comment of Thomas Wallace (1798: 243) is illustrative of the elite attitude about Irish-made coarse earthenwares: "If there exists any manufacture of this kind [of ceramics] beyond that of a few coarse tiles, and still coarser earthenware, it is so trivial as to deserve no notice." Elite English and Anglo-Irish capitalist "improvers" like Wallace perceived the Irish coarse earthenware to be insignificant to the Irish economy (also see Sheffield 1785: 243).

Comments by elite industrial promoters should not be assumed to be unimportant simply because an entire industry existed of which they knew nothing or cared little. Observations that denigrated Irish coarse earthenware usually incorporated a subtle subtextual assessment of the Irish themselves. In the mind of observers like Lord Sheffield (1785: 243), Irish coarse earthenware did not reflect "the ability and elegant taste of Mr. Wedgwood" because it was coarse, heavy, and earth-toned. Contemporary observers undoubtedly found it difficult to separate the manufactured material objects from the culture of their producers, and it is possible to observe, even in the few comments that were made about Irish-made coarse earthenware, a deeper conceptualization of the Irish people. Isaac Weld provided the most detailed account of the manufacture of coarse earthenwares in County Roscommon:

Amongst the articles manufactured in the immediate vicinity of Roscommon [town], may also be mentioned coarse pottery ware, consisting of pans, jugs, &c. These were mostly of a *reddish brown colour, or of brown mixed with yellow, in rude patterns,* or merely mottled, and considerable quantities were brought in to the markets. The clays of which these articles are made is not found on the spot, but brought in carts from the neighbourhood of the Shannon; neither is there any peculiar advantage from fuel. With the facility of carriage afforded by the canal, and with improved roads, it may be presumed that English earthenware will, in a few years more, completely supplant that of the country; and not only because it can be afforded on as reasonable or more reasonable terms, but *because it is likewise much better manufactured.* In fact, several of the small and *rude potteries* of the country, have, as I was informed, been already abandoned; but as long as there are any which afford a bare livelihood to the workmen, they will be continued, to the last, struggling for a precarious existence. (Weld 1832: 403–4; emphasis added)

Weld minimized the cultural significance of the earthenwares, and his use of descriptive terms, such as rude, should not be overlooked. Wakefield (1812, 1: 113–14) tended to have a better opinion of the local ceramic industry (at least around Belfast), but Weld's comments suggest that he perceived the English-made, fine white earthenware as modern, progressive, and forward-looking, whereas he viewed the Irish wares as traditional, old-fashioned, and retrogressive (for further comments, see Orser 2001b).

Weld indicated that coarse earthenwares were available as commodities at the local markets. William Makepeace Thackeray (1990: 119), writing in his Irish travel book of 1842, substantiated their presence and provided a useful account of the market in Killarney: "A sort of market is held here, and the place is swarming with blue cloaks, and groups of men talking; here and there is a stall with coarse linens, crockery, a cheese, and crowds of egg and milk-women are squatted on the pavement with their ragged customers or gossips."

Excavations at the two homes formerly inhabited by Mark Nary and his three sons revealed a minimum coarse earthenware vessel count of 8 in one cabin and 36 in the other (more extensively explored) cabin. The vessel forms—milk pans, bowls, jugs, and storage jars or crocks—suggest that the tenants employed the coarse earthenwares in their daily productive activities rather than as tablewares. It is likely that they generally employed the vessels in dairying and in food preparation and storage (Table 6.10).

No concrete information currently exists to explain the ways in which the men and women of Ballykilcline obtained their coarse earthenware vessels. A careful survey of Lewis' *A Topographical Dictionary of Ireland*, first published in 1837, indicates the presence of twenty-five "coarse" potteries throughout Ireland (Figure 6.6). Most of these potteries were clustered west of Belfast, but other important centers of production were located just south of Roscommon town (Weld 1832). Another locus of production was situated slightly northeast of Ballykilcline in the neighboring county of Leitrim.

The coarse earthenwares indicate that they were elements of a large-scale commodity network that stretched throughout Ireland, interconnecting traditional-style potters with the families of rural tenant farmers. The tenants themselves may have obtained the vessels at the local markets or from itinerant pedlars, who may have brought some vessels directly into the townland (see Ó Ciosáin 1997: 59–71). In either case, the practice of obtaining coarse earthenware vessels was inherently a constitutive element of a social process of interactive communication that brought Irish "peasants" into contact with people from far beyond the boundaries of their townlands. And, just as Edmund Spenser (1997: 78) observed in Elizabethan times, it is likely that the residents of rural townlands, including Ballykilcline, used the commodity-based interactions to obtain news of the larger world in which they lived. In this manner the coarse earthenwares may serve as metaphors for tenant social interaction and possibly even knowledge of the world beyond the townland.

The Irish-made coarse earthenwares provide only a partial glimpse of the commodity situation at Ballykilcline. Also included in the excavated samples are rather large numbers of English-made refined earthenwares, just the kind that Weld (1832) thought would quickly supplant the Irish wares (Table 6.11). The collections obtained from the two cabin sites

TABLE 6.10. Coarse Earthenware Minimum Vessel Counts and Forms from the Two Nary Cabins

Vessel form	Cabin 1	Cabin 2
milk pan	3	10
bowl	–	4
storage jar or crock	4	11
jug	1	10
unknown	–	1
Total	8	36

yield a minimum count of 130 vessels, 49 from one cabin and 81 from the other. (The differential vessel frequency in the two cabins is insignificant because of the concentration of excavation in Cabin 2.)

Two points about the two ceramic commodities are significant. First, the excavations revealed that after the evictions, the houses occupied by the tenants of Ballykilcline were destroyed and the largest stones

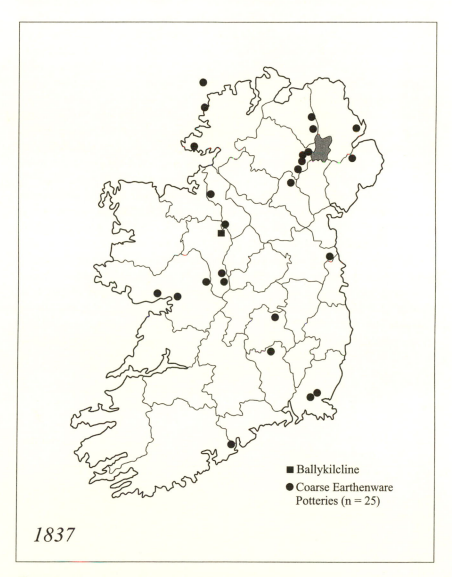

1837

■ Ballykilcline
● Coarse Earthenware
   Potteries (n = 25)

Figure 6.6. Locations of coarse earthenware potteries in 1837.

removed ("so as to prevent them being rebuilt"; House of Lords 1847: 88). No significant modification of the old Nary lands occurred between 1848 (the date of eviction) and 1998 (the date excavation commenced). As a result, the terminal use date for the artifacts is assured. Second, if it is indeed correct that the Narys only moved onto Ballykilcline in the 1820s, as one historian maintains (Scally 1995: 80), then the excavated commodities could have been introduced only within a maximum of 28 years (1820–1848). This short time span means, then, that significant commodity activity occurred within Ballykilcline throughout the period of the rent strike. It is intriguing to contemplate whether the tenants used the monies they withheld from the Crown to purchase their imported, refined earthenwares. If this scenario was in fact the case, then it suggests that the men and women of Ballykilcline resisted the British Crown's rent requirements at the same time that they bought into the British world market, ostensibly adopting what Weld (1832) surely would have considered refined dining habits. No evidence exists to indicate that traditional Irish potters made vessels that could be described as tablewares.

Ireland experienced a rapid and extensive introduction to the British world market during the 1740–1814 period (Cullen 1968; Whelan 1993). Several producers of tin-glazed earthenwares established potteries in Belfast and Dublin, but the Irish industries could not complete with the larger, better capitalized Staffordshire factories, and most of the Irish concerns were closed by the second decade of the nineteenth century (Dunlevy 1988: 21–22; Francis 2000, 2001; Westropp 1913, 1935). The dearth of Irish refined earthenware producers, however, did not mean

TABLE 6.11. Refined Earthenware Minimum Vessel Counts and Forms from the Two Nary Cabins

Vessel form	Cabin 1	Cabin 2
Teacup	14	23
Saucer	6	18
Plate	13	18
Platter	–	1
Soup bowl	2	4
Serving bowl	1	–
Small bowl	1	1
Pitcher	6	8
Teapot	1	–
Mug	4	3
Unknown	1	5
Total	49	81

that English-made ceramics did not reach Ireland. In fact, during the late eighteenth and early nineteenth centuries foresighted retailers began to establish ceramic outlets that would preclude the need to travel to local fairs and markets (Thomas 1971: 103–16). Wedgwood opened two outlets in Dublin, one in 1772 and another in 1808 (Dunlevy 1988: 22–23). A survey of three commercial directories for Ireland (Pigot 1823, 1824; Slater 1846) shows that the number of retail concerns selling English-made refined earthenware increased dramatically during the first half of the nineteenth century (Figure 6.7). By 1846, during the climax of the Ballykilcline rent strike, Strokestown, the nearest market town, had two "earthenware dealers": Edward Conroy and Nicholas Gilleran (Slater 1846: 141). The presence of the earthenware at Ballykilcline indicates that the tenants who lived there were participants in another network, this one with international dimensions. The precise mechanisms of this network are currently unknown.

The presence of English-made refined earthenware at Ballykilcline raises an important point about the complex correlation between racialization and material culture, and is directly pertinent for the application of a practice perspective to the townland. George Knox, the Crown's agent for the townland, offered two significant observations in 1846. His comments provide special insight into the practices of the Ballykilcline tenants as they operated within the epochal structures and social spaces of early nineteenth-century Ireland. On May 24, Knox notified the Clerk of Quit Rents that "There are not more than Fifty or Sixty Individuals residing on the Portion under Ejectment, and those are all *in a State of comparative Affluence towards the neighbouring Peasantry, most of them having Provisions to dispose of, and being worth from 20l. to 100l. each*" (House of Lords 1847: 76, emphasis added). On August 17, after the earliest effects of the potato blight had become clear, Knox wrote to the Commissioners of Woods and Forests and explained that

the Deprivation they have met with in the Loss of the Potato Crop this Second Season induces me to believe that very few of them could now pay it [the rent and the arrears]. At the same Time my private Opinion is, that those who could afford to do so are unwilling to come forward, *through Fear of the others* and my firm Belief also is, that NONE of them have the least Idea of becoming amenable to the Crown, or of taking out Leases, but that they are men endeavoring to put off the Proposals *until they reap the present Crop of Grain, and get possession of the Price of it*. . . . And I am quite certain that they will continue to keep the Possession in the same lawless Manner, until the Injunction be put into force against them. (House of Lords 1847: 80, emphasis added)

These two observations reveal that Knox, who was without question the government representative who came nearest to comprehending the true

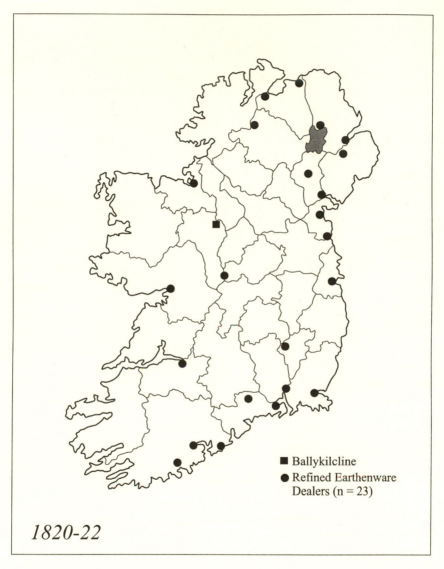

■ Ballykilcline
● Refined Earthenware
   Dealers (n = 23)

1820-22

Figure 6.7. Increase in retailers offering English-made refined earthenware, 1820–1846.

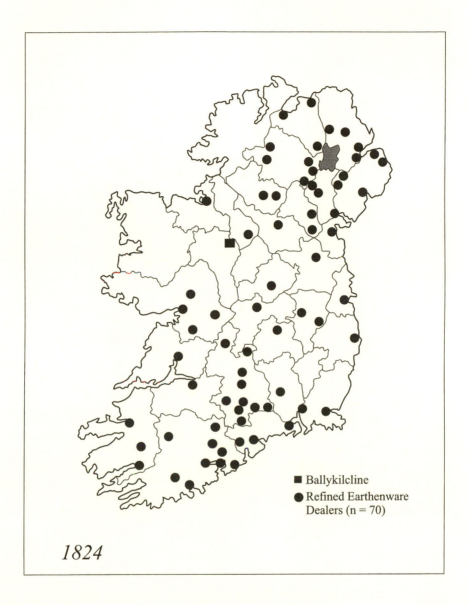

■ Ballykilcline

● Refined Earthenware
Dealers (n = 70)

1824

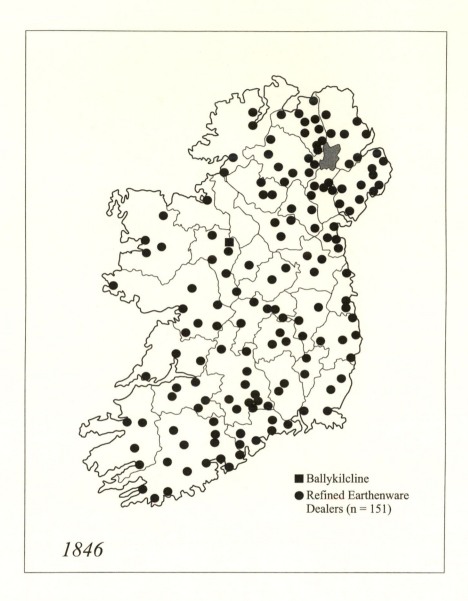

■ Ballykilcline
● Refined Earthenware
  Dealers (n = 151)

1846

condition and strategy of the Ballykilcline tenantry, believed that many of the tenants—including the "ring leaders"—possessed the necessary funds to pay their rents. In addition, Knox also believed that they were planning to retain their grain crops until such time as they could sell them for their own benefit. The Ballykilcline strikers were not looking to transfer their economic capital to the Crown.

Knox's assessments are intriguing in light of the artifactual evidence from the two Nary cabins. A breakdown of the coarse and refined earthenwares from the two cabins reveals that the overwhelming majority of vessels (74.7 percent) were refined earthenwares (Table 6.12). Overall, the fund of refined earthenware vessels outnumbered the coarse earthenwares by about a 3:1 ratio. This unequal distribution may suggest, even though the tenants still used their traditional, commercial network to obtain their utilitarian vessels, that they were beginning to rely heavily on imported, English-made wares. The unequal presence of refined to coarse earthenwares may indicate that Weld (1832) was correct in his assessment of the power of the English wares to supplant the Irish wares.

If we investigate the refined earthenware samples further, we discover that the collection contains 36.7 percent transfer-printed vessels (n = 18) from Cabin 1 and 38.3 percent (n = 31) from Cabin 2 (or 37.7 percent of all refined earthenware). If we accept Miller's (1980, 1991) argument that transfer-printed vessels were consistently the highest-priced English ceramics available during the early nineteenth century (during the height of Ballykilcline's habitation), then it appears that over one-third of the Nary family's imported ceramic collection was among the most expensive ceramics then available. Of course, this conclusion envisions the ceramics purely as economic commodities whose sign values are unknown. The presence of high-priced, English-made refined earthenwares, however, does indicate the oversimplification of innocently linking poverty with "the peasantry." Nonetheless, one must engage poverty as a subject matter to make this realization.

For their part, the British government's representatives gave the Ballykilcline tenants every opportunity to repent and to pay their rent arrears. In fact, in November 1846 the Attorney General of Ireland even

TABLE 6.12. Distribution of Coarse (Irish-made) and Refined (English-made) Ceramic Vessels at the Two Nary Cabins (frequency and percentage)

Ware type	Cabin 1	Cabin 2	Total
Coarse earthenware	8 (14.0)	36 (30.8)	44 (25.3)
Refined earthenware	49 (86.0)	81 (69.2)	130 (74.7)
Total	57(100.0)	117(100.0)	174(100.0)

invited the tenants to go to Dublin and to negotiate the rental terms for themselves. Five tenants accepted the Crown's offer, but then reneged and did not appear. Instead, they continued to defy the Crown and to practice life on their own terms. The tenants could not escape the racial identification that had been assigned to them in British society at large, but they could resist domination in their labor positions, if only for a time.

When the general recalcitrance of the Ballykilcline tenants is considered in conjunction with the archaeological findings, we can envision a sociohistorical scenario in which the tenants simply wished to retain their land and to be unmolested, even to the point of not paying rent for Irish land to the British Crown. As they made explicit in their petition of 1846 to the Commissioners of Woods and Forests, they believed that they had strong family connections with the places they occupied because they described themselves as: "your Petitioners and their Fathers before them, who occupied said Lands" (House of Lords 1847: 74). It thus appears that in refusing to pay their rents, the tenants simply sought to control their own daily lives by endeavoring to retain the monies they had collected from the sale of their crops and lesser produce. In maintaining control of their economic capital, it seems that the tenants sought to buy into the British marketplace at the same time that they defied the elites within the British Empire. It is possible that the acquisition of English ceramics could have raised the cultural capital of the tenants in the same way that Maguire's position as driver would have assisted him. The possession of objects like teacups within the cabins of the townland may have been a paradoxical reference to English refinement at the same time that their acquisition represented the tenants' ability to negotiate an avenue into the British marketplace.

To help us interpret the connection between race and identity in rural Ireland, it is useful to return to Mullins's research into African American consumerism during the late nineteenth century. Though the cultural histories and temporal associations of pre-famine Irish tenants and post-emancipation African Americans are utterly distinct, a certain similarity of practice does seem common to both populations. Mullins's (1999a, b, 2001) studies demonstrate that African Americans living in Annapolis, Maryland, struggled within the dominizing, racialized social structure that was constructed around them, and during the course of this struggle that they invented viable tactics that operated within the dominant consumerist space. The dialectical structure of black marginalization and white privilege was such that African American consumers "maneuvered between mass culture and class society, seeking the equity mass consumer culture promised and forging evidence that African America could reproduce dominant social and material symbolism" (Mullins

1999b: 35). African Americans embedded within Maryland's segregated social space tended to be relegated to service-related labor positions that white elites considered "appropriate for their race." Structural homology obtained in pre-famine, rural Ireland. Rural Irish men and women, designated the "inferior race," were largely relegated to tenant-at-will labor positions. Like African Americans in Annapolis, they were not expected to participate in the elite-dominated mass market along the same lines as their racial "betters." A major difference between the two groups, however, is that the African Americans received wages for their labor, albeit at grossly inadequate and unfair rates. The Ballykilcline tenants were expected to submit their surplus capital to the Crown as rent, rather than to have the freedom to use it to enter the British consumer market. A significant site of struggle for Irish tenant farmers, then, was to define their social location within a largely exclusionary world-system. For the tenants of Ballykilcline, the only possible way to effect this strategy was to withhold their rent monies; otherwise, the system was ostensibly closed to them.

The struggle of the Ballykilcline tenants to enter a consumerist space that was largely not intended for them obtained a significant symbolic dimension that accompanied the more facile economic motivations. The symbolic dimension was rooted in several spatial strategies. Some of the strategies have already been mentioned. The construction of Brassington and Gale's plat of the townland in 1836 and the Ordnance Survey map of 1837 are prime examples of the British attempt to define and to manipulate—and in the process also to control—the Irish landscape. The maps were intended to graft a British perspective of domination onto the land by ignoring Gaelic names, overlooking small pathways, and completely neglecting the housing locations of the sub-tenants. Other struggles were vastly more subtle. These contestations are again somewhat analogous to the social space of African American consumers in late nineteenth-century Annapolis. Subtleties of this nature can never be understood economically. As Lefebvre (1991: 80) noted: "Things and products that are measured, that is to say reduced to the common measure of money, do not speak the truth about themselves." Comprehension of the subtle contests require an examination of the mundane.

Mullins' (1999a: 162–70, 2001) explorations of the social significance of bric-a-brac usage among African Americans in Annapolis amply demonstrate the "complex symbolic terrain" within which African American consumption was practiced. The recontextualization of the seemingly unimportant statuettes allowed African Americans to find a space within the racialized structure in which they lived. Accordingly in Ireland, the formation of a pre-famine rural identity was a spatially situated process in which the struggle of the Ballykilcline tenants made abstract space visible. In foregrounding the townland's social practices, the tenants helped to create a representational space (Hetherington 1998: 67). This space, however, incorporated a double consciousness similar to that identified by Du Bois (1999: 11) in 1903, in which every African American "feels his two-ness." The same situation may well have obtained at Ballykilcline, such that all residents were legally British citizens at the same time that they were undeniably Irish. And, as was true for African Americans, the struggle of Irish tenant farmers was sociohistorical, material, and undeniably interlinked with relations of racialized power.

We may never know whether the men and women of Ballykilcline selected the fine earthenware ceramics they used or whether they simply purchased what was made available to them. This level of interpretation is currently unavailable. The archaeological research does demonstrate, however, that at least some of the residents used a number of vessels that had been differentially decorated. Several transfer-printed cups, saucers, plates, and one or two other vessel forms appear in the collection. Many of the transfer-printed designs exhibit peaceful, pastoral images, unlike the state of life at Ballykilcline after 1834. The Bridge at Lucano (Figure 6.8) was a typical image of this sort (Coysh and Henrywood 1982: 55–56). The quiet scene, with its resting cattle and unmolested birds gliding over the serene river, exudes peace and tranquility. But this pictorial quiescence may have embodied a representational space with a deeper meaning.

In two insightful studies of the possible meanings of early nineteenth-century transfer-printed English ceramics, Alasdair Brooks (1997, 1999) argues that the presentation of pastoral and other images worked in part to advance the ideology of a unified British identity. This identity-in-service-to-the-state was intended to be forged from the disparate English, Scottish, Welsh, and Irish local identities that existed within the physical boundaries of Great Britain. Many of the most prominent images of the early nineteenth century featured scenes of rural prosperity and calm, much like the Bridge at Lucano. That the bridge was actually in Italy, not in England or Ireland, probably did not matter as much as its idyllic calm.

Spatial representations such as the Bridge at Lucano must have created contradictory space (after Lefebvre 1991) in rural Irish homes. The daily presence of this space may have foregrounded the double consciousness experienced by Irish men and women who were officially designated "British" but culturally Irish (and inferior). Rather than serving to represent the straightforward acculturation of the rural Irish—in their imagined motivation to become British—the transfer-printed dishes they obtained symbolized the same struggle represented by the African American appropriation of seemingly insignificant bric-a-brac. The historical reality of the rent strike, promulgated against the British

Figure 6.8. Bridge at Lucano pattern found at Ballykilcline. Top: excavated sherds; bottom: reproduction plate. Reproduction is 26.5 cm in diameter. Courtesy Katherine Hull.

Crown itself, precludes the formulation of any simple archaeological interpretation. An interpretation that features any degree of acculturation on the part of the rural Irish would effectively eliminate the central significance of the invented racialized social structure that operated throughout Ireland and which was experienced as daily practice by the residents of Ballykilcline.

As ever-present, tangible representations of a space that could be conceived, the transfer prints at Ballykilcline may have empowered the tenants and even emboldened them in regard to the wisdom of their rent strike. Knox's letters clearly indicate that the Ballykilcline tenants enacted a carefully designed strategy of resistance within the epochal structures constructed around their rural lives. The historical reality of their mass eviction indicates that they did not have complete freedom of "agency," as some neoliberal archaeologists would like to pretend in such cases (see Orser 1996a: 177–82). Still, their enactment of a protracted rent strike indicates that they did have some level of negotiative power, if only temporarily.

One larger implication of the struggle represented by the residents of Ballykilcline may be that their efforts to "become White" (following Ignatiev 1995)—that is, to pull themselves collectively from the lowest racial category to the highest—may have been a process intermittently begun through the conduct of rent strikes and other rural "outrages." In other words, the Irish struggle against their wholesale racialization may have been waged as part of a diasporic process that required constant renegotiation within the specificities of each racialized sociohistorical space (Walter 2001: 22–24). Only future comparative research between archaeological collections excavated in Ireland and at diasporic sites throughout the world can even begin to address the intriguing elements of transcontinental, Irish racialization.

Chapter 7
Race, Practice, and Archaeology

The archaeological application of practice theory is only at the experimental stage. The novelty of this approach, especially as it pertains to the study of race—a topic that has yet to achieve prominence among archaeologists—mandates that this book must be viewed as an initial foray into a difficult and multifaceted realm of inquiry. Future archaeologists who opt to use practice theory to interpret past racialization—as well as other topics of concern to social archaeology—will undoubtedly deepen its application within the discipline. Archaeologists have the double-edged advantage of understanding the multivalent capacities of material culture in past sociohistorical settings while also openly adopting and adapting the substantive insights of cultural anthropologists, sociologists, and geographers, among others. Empirical archaeological analyses of recent history that employ an intellectually diverse conceptual toolkit will substantially enrich our intellectual treasury of understanding and in so doing help us to comprehend the historical antecedents of the world around us.

The many methodological advantages of modern-world archaeology, including perhaps most concretely the presence of often abundant textual resources, ensures that the recent past is an arena in which archaeologists can construct fully contextualized examinations. The relatively recent invention of modern-age theories of racialization makes perfect the match between the historical study of race and modern-world archaeology. The most recent centuries appear as a relatively short period when viewed from the perspective of the entirety of human history. Nonetheless, the myriad material and spatial dimensions of historical racialization during this age are infinitely complex and so their study is understandably far from exhausted.

The archaeological examination of racialization is perfectly suited to multiscalar analysis, because the application of racial theories was never merely site-specific. For example, the many applications of race prejudice and oppression that were given expression at thousands of slave-operated plantations throughout the New World were never simply "about" that single place. The foundational racial theory that upheld the operation of individual slave plantations pervaded the entire plantation regime. Its manifestations—though context-specific, extensively mutable, and even idiosyncratic—stretched through time and across space. Countless slaveowners resident on plantations reproduced the structural realities of slave-based production, even though each one of them was free to create and enact individual personal strategies. At the same time, innumerable men and women held in perpetual bondage struggled with the regime's epochal structures and sought their own strategies of survival and self-determination.

An important analytical strength of practice theory is that it recognizes the seminal significance of structures and actions, but it does not essentialize them. We cannot expect that the agriculturally rooted structure of early nineteenth-century rural America should be reproduced in early seventeenth-century America or even in early nineteenth-century Ireland, even though the basic structure of agriculturally based social inequality is roughly homologous through time and space. Owner/slave and landlord/tenant labor positions exist within the structures by definition, but the meanings of the positions and the ways in which individuals within the fields pursued and amassed diverse forms of capital are sociohistorically distinctive.

The considerable diversity in sociohistorical formations mandates that the archaeological analysis of a social variable as mutable as race can be approached in various ways. The topic is amenable both to in-depth, site-specific examination and to broader comparative study. Modern-world archaeologists intent on investigating past racialization can operationalize their research programs as site- and region-specific, and thus they may describe their research as "historic ethnography" if they wish (Schuyler 1988: 40–41). They can also undertake more overtly comparative projects of any scale, including the inter-site, race-based analyses suggested by Baker (1980: 35–36) or the internationally designed comparisons proposed by Deetz (1991: 8). The application of a highly contextualized practice theory will always ensure the practical difficulty of in-depth comparative analysis, but the insights gained will be profound and significant. The homologies between the structures of enforced African American agriculture and pre-famine Irish farm tenancy are particularly instructive in this regard. Irish landlords were not slaveowners, but numerous early nineteenth-century commentators perceived the two elite groups as occupying roughly equal structural positions within their respective social hierarchies.

Our purpose in examining early nineteenth-century rural Ireland is threefold: (1) to illustrate a way that practice theory can be applied to archaeological interpretation to examine historical racialization; (2) to indicate the epochal structures that were created and reproduced in early nineteenth-century Ireland; and (3) to offer specific information about the ways in which the epochal structures were negotiated and manipulated at Ballykilcline, only one of over 60,000 townlands in Ireland. We have sought to demonstrate the complexities of the constructed epochal structures as a way of properly contextualizing life at Ballykilcline, as seen through the perspective of the Nary house sites. We have sought to provide a useful interpretation of Ballykilcline, focusing on those elements of the sociohistorical formation that appear most relevant to racialization. But we must understand, given the insights of social network theory, that any contextualization of an actual past sociohistorical setting is infinitely complex and can be approached from several angles directed toward various scales.

One potentially fruitful topic that we have not engaged for the sake of brevity is "the theory and practice of improvement" (Bell and Watson 1986: 229–39; also see Bell 1987; Hull 1997). Even the briefest overview of improvement indicates its capacity for further illustrating the racialized realities of life in rural Ireland.

Agricultural improvement in Ireland was a topic of substantial concern to many early nineteenth-century commentators, and the relevant literature is huge (see, e.g., Griffith 1819; Desmond 1847; Robinson 1843, 1846). To summarize, these observers usually made two arguments about Irish agriculture: that the traditional methods of cultivation were "inefficient," and that the Irish did not dedicate enough land to production. Presenting their advice in various tracts and treatises, these improvers implored Irish landlords to fund drainage projects in bogs and low areas to make more land available for agriculture. They also urged Irish landlords to encourage their tenants to forsake their traditional tools for the latest scientific implements and to abandon their traditional system of cultivation. The many plans they advocated were ostensibly designed to increase the output of Irish agriculture, but the plans' implications were also directed toward a transformation of the Irish cultural habitus in a manner that would be more consistently English in outlook. The days of Gaelic herding and transhumance were forever banished as scientific improvers sought to cement the changes in both the social and the environmental landscapes.

Abundant evidence indicates the fitness of traditional Irish agricultural methods, but the most dramatic proof derives from the late 1840s, during the height of Irish mass starvation. During these years of profound destitution and disease, shippers exported tons of wheat, oats, cattle, sheep, pigs, bacon, eggs, butter, whiskey, ale, and other foodstuffs from Ireland to England (Kinealy 1997: 79–81). Countless men and women of Irish descent have not forgotten this transshipment of sorely needed food from Irish ports to English homes, and many individuals still argue that the English colonial overlords of Ireland conducted a protracted and deliberate assault on the Irish as members of "a different race from the rest of mankind" (Luckombe 1780: 41–42). Such deep-seated and historically reproduced understandings led the Irish radical John Mitchel to argue:

that a million and a half of men, women, and children were carefully, prudently, and peacefully *slain* by the English government. They died of hunger in the midst of abundance, which their own hands created; and it is quite immaterial to distinguish those who perished in the agonies of famine itself from those who died of typhus fever, which in Ireland is always caused by famine. (1860: 217; emphasis in original)

Such realities led Mitchel (1860: 219, 1868: 596) to coin the memorable phrase: "The Almighty, indeed, sent the potato blight, but the English created the famine."

Part of the controversy over agricultural methods arose because agricultural improvement was never simply about increasing the productive output of crops. Authors interested in scientific agriculture concomitantly advised the "improvement" of the "peasantry of Ireland" (see, e.g., Doolan 1847; Maberly 1847; MacDonnell 1823; Pim 1848). If asked, the authors of the social improvement literature would undoubtedly argue that their goal was merely an attempt to save the Irish from themselves and their traditions. They would fail to recognize the epochal structures they promoted with their practice.

The use of early nineteenth-century Irish tenant farming in the analysis provides an important site for the study of racialization, because it helps to throw into relief the important connections between race and class. Given the epochal structure of tenant farming, it would be relatively easy to propose that the Ballykilcline rent strike was simply a reaction to the inherent inequalities of farm tenancy. This interpretation would not be entirely incorrect, because many small farmers and tenants in early nineteenth-century Ireland saw themselves as "the victims of an institutionalized injustice" rooted in agriculture (Coleman 1999: 30). Historians have convincingly documented that the distribution of land in rural Ireland was a prominent variable in the cause of agrarian outrages (see, e.g., Clark and Donnelly 1983; Beames 1982: 111–39). This impressive body of evidence may encourage us to suppose that the tenants of Ballykilcline merely perceived a unique opportunity to redress the economic inequalities of tenancy when the Mahons lost their lease to the townland in 1834. Acting as rational economists, the tenants simply sought rent relief when the Crown obtained full control of the estate.

The class-conscious, rational-actor model is compelling, until we realize that non-elite Irish men and women had paid rents for many generations. Farmers in Gaelic society were expected to render rents of cattle, food, and even personal service to their kin and social betters in a complex network of clientship (Patterson 1994: 150–78). In the province of Connacht specifically, the English rulers instituted a more capitalist system of rent payments that was largely devoid of the strong social duties and responsibilities of the Gaelic system. The Composition of 1585 established the requirements for the payment of fixed rents throughout the province (Lennon 1994: 249–63). The payment of rents at Ballykilcline in the early nineteenth century was therefore not unusual or new.

What was new in Ireland in the early nineteenth century was the increasing effort of the English and others to accelerate the racialization of the Irish. The transformation of the pictorial representations of the Irish—from uncouth and uncivilized at the end of the sixteenth century to ape-like in the early nineteenth century—visually demonstrates the social transmogrification of Irish men, women, and children during the period. Information expressed in textual sources tends to mirror the visual images. A description of the Irish written in 1588 stresses their attitudes and comments on their way of life: "The people are of nature very glorious, frank, ireful, good horsemen, able to endure great pains, delighted in war, [of] great hospitality, of religion (for the most part) papists, great gluttons, and of a sensual and vicious life, deep dissemblers, secret in displeasure, of a cruel, revenging mind and irreconcilable" (Quinn 1966: 90). This is not a flattering image, but it is a far cry from Kingsley's highly racialized view of the Irish as "white chimpanzees" expressed almost three centuries later. George Lewis, in his examination of the "local disturbances" in Ireland, suggested a perspective that included racialization as early as 1836, even though the times in which he wrote did not facilitate this realization:

The treatment of the native Irish, *as an incurably barbarous race*, before the Reformation [pre-1536], and the various civil wars and confiscations which took place after the Reformation [post-1625], had, at the period of the Revolution, when King William's power was finally established in Ireland [1691], so completely broken up the framework of society, and so loosened men's notions as to the obligations of law and morality, that it would have been a difficult task for the wisest and most beneficent [sic] government to raise the mass of the Irish people to the general level of European civilization. (Lewis 1836: 46; emphasis added)

The question of Irish racialization, in addition to foregrounding the linkage between race and class, also helps to illustrate the need for modern-world archaeologists to wean themselves away from conceptualizing race as merely a social feature that has relevance to men, women, and children who can be described as having dark skin colors. Investigating the archaeology of racialization among peoples of color certainly must not be abandoned or lessened in importance, and historical archaeologists should continue to develop this line of inquiry in every sociohistorical setting in which such an analysis is pertinent. At the same time, however, archaeologists must also turn their considerable interpretive attention to sites associated with individuals who were not considered, either by others or by themselves, as being "of color." Chapter 2 unambiguously demonstrates how investigators employing archaeological information can use skin color and other physical attributes to manipulate our understanding of ancient peoples like the Native American mound builders and the European Celts. Pseudo-archaeologists have used the same conceptual approach to racialize the imaginary citizens of Atlantis. That the project of racialization can extend to the so-called lost kingdoms of antiquity demonstrates the pernicious nature of the racial application. Today's pseudo-archaeologists who assign a racialized sociohistorical structure to past life on Atlantis and other illusory places are probably not even aware of their acceptance of this unfortunate model.

The racialization of Atlantis foregrounds the extremely significant point that racial categorization has been so commonplace in the past few centuries that individuals who rely on such notions may not even acknowledge their debt to this body of thought. An important implication of this realization is that we cannot suppose a priori that the hidden dimensions of racialization were recognized and properly contextualized by the men and women who compiled the written records that historical archaeologists regularly use in their research. The possibility is strong that the elite commentators who left detailed accounts of their daily lives, and copious observations about the lives of others, accepted the racialized structures in which they lived. In fact, being educated elites, it is entirely possible that their intellectual ancestors created the human classifications in the first place. So ingrained were the racial elements of elite habitus in early nineteenth-century Ireland that Scottish-born, County Wicklow landlady Elizabeth Grant (1997: 35, 38) could not even see the irony in her journal comments of late 1840, when speaking of her Irish tenants: "a more improvident, idle set of human beings never were collected in a plentiful land. . . . it is heart-breaking to think of what will become of the creatures when we are away." Such comments provide substantial insights into the attitudes of real men and women, and they prove invaluable to archaeologists seeking to contextualize a past sociohistorical formation. The bias expressed in Grant's brief statement demonstrates the necessity for archaeological research. The practices that were strategized and enacted within past epochal structures may be entirely masked in the absence of archaeology.

As archaeologists of the recent past expand their research universe into realms never before investigated (see, e.g., Crass et al. 1998; Lawrence 2000; Mayne and Murray 2001), they will be confronted with increased opportunities to examine the racialized daily lives of nominally "white" European immigrants. The pressures such immigrants faced, and the ways in which the dynamics of racial designation were either transmogrified or made static with each diasporic wave of immigration, are vitally important archaeological topics. The archaeological investigation of Irish and Irish-American history provides only one opportunity to conduct this inquiry. Here we have concentrated only on the Irish side of the equation, but clearly much remains to be done.

Historians have demonstrated that Irish immigrants to the United States entered a social field in which the elite members were obsessed with the maintenance and policing of the color line (Ignatiev 1995; Roediger 1991). Each in-migrating group, being racially defined, was duly accorded its appointed place in the race hierarchy. Monumental mass immigration, however, significantly clouded the neat racial ideals of American society, and the racial categorization of the Irish was far from certain. Nativist Americans referred to Irish immigrants as "niggers turned inside out" and to African Americans as "smoked Irish" (Ignatiev 1995: 41). Kingsley's human chimpanzees and John Cobden's (1860) investigative polemic on the white Irish slaves of England unequivocally demonstrate that the racialization of the Irish was a transnational, socially relevant phenomenon that defied the vast distances of the diaspora.

The elite's placement of Irish immigrants on the "non-white" side of the American color line (see Roediger 1991: 133–56) helped to create and to reify a useful strategy in which an attitude of hatred was fostered between men and women of Irish and African heritage. Anecdotal evidence suggests that this perception is still occasionally promoted in the United States, and its possible maintenance lends credence to its tenacity within the habitus. The ability of many Irish men and women to accept the racial elements of an unfamilar elite-promoted, all-American habitus allowed many of them to transcend their initial ranking within the nation's race-based social hierarchy. It would be facile to contend that conflicts did not occur between Irish and African immigrants, but we must also recall that Frederick Douglass drew massive audiences to his anti-slavery speeches in Ireland during the early 1840s (Blassingame 1979).

The exuberant acceptance of Douglass by many residents of Ireland's largest cities should not be interpreted to mean that Irish men and women were color-blind or that the English power structure that controlled the island was necessarily well-disposed to a new racial order. The true sociohistorical situation was much more complicated, with most social variables being irrevocably intertwined with many others. At the same time, the racialization process is not simply historic. In Great

Britain, for example, the forced inclusion of Irish immigrants into the imagined homogeneity of the British Isles since the 1950s has been facilitated by their perceived whiteness, even though this categorization has not alleviated discrimination against them (Curtis 1996: 69–97; Hickman 1998).

Practice theory offers archaeologists a rigorous and interpretively robust perspective for investigating the many intertwined, interconnected social attributes of past historical life. The application of practice theory in a manner that consciously maximizes concepts of network interaction and the sociospatial dialectic expands the research universe of historical archaeology at the same time that it helps to refine the interpretation of specific sites. Regarding race specifically, a key element in its archaeological analysis lies in fully understanding the racialized structures of the particular sociohistorical formation under study. A thorough conceptualization of the epochal structures is central for a modern-world archaeology informed by practice theory, because these structures are the realms within which individuals practiced their daily lives. In addition, the operation of these structures included the conscious manipulation of material culture.

Modern-world archaeology, or any historical archaeology for that matter, offers satisfying advantages and unique challenges. The presence of text-based sources of information is unparalleled in significance because this material, even in its most biased state, offers insights into the epochal structures of everyday life. Historical archaeologists also face the daunting task of evaluating and controlling this material, while understanding, in the case of epochal structures, that it can never be assumed to offer all the information needed to contextualize and interpret the past. The addition of archaeological data allows the modern-world archaeologist to investigate the past in a uniquely fruitful manner, and though much remains to be done, we hope that this book provides a useful way forward.

References Cited

Abercrombie, N., S. Hill, and B. S. Turner. 1980. *The Dominant Ideology Thesis.* London: Allen and Unwin.

Abrahamson, M., E. II. Mizruchi, and C. A. Hornung. 1976. *Stratification and Mobility.* New York: Macmillan.

Abu-Lughod, J. L. 1989. *Before European Hegemony: The World System, A.D. 1250–1350.* New York: Oxford University Press.

Adair, J. 1968. *The History of the American Indians, Particularly Those Nations Adjoining to the Mississippi, East and West Florida, Georgia, South and North Carolina, and Virginia.* 1775. New York: Johnson Reprints.

Adams, R. N. 1975. *Energy and Structure: A Theory of Social Power.* Austin: University of Texas Press.

Adams, W. H., P. M. Bowers, and R. Mills. 2001. Commodity Flow and National Market Access: A Case Study from Interior Alaska. *Historical Archaeology* 35(2): 73–107.

Akin, M. K. 1992. The Noncurrency Functions of Chinese *Wen* in America. *Historical Archaeology* 26(2): 58–65.

Algaze, G. 1993. *The Uruk World System: The Dynamics of Expansion of Early Mesopotamian Civilization.* Chicago: University of Chicago Press.

Allen, J. M. 1998. *Atlantis: The Andes Solution.* Moreton-in-Marsh, England: Windrush Press,

Allen, T. W. 1994. *The Invention of the White Race.* Vol. 1, *Racial Oppression and Social Control.* London: Verso.

———. 2001. "Race" and "Ethnicity": History and the 2000 Census. *Cultural Logic.* Electronic journal at http://eserver.org/clogic/3–1%262/allen.html.

Allison, P. M. 1999. Introduction. In *The Archaeology of Household Activities,* ed. P. M. Allison, pp. 1–18. London: Routledge.

Altick, R. D. 1978. *The Shows of London.* Cambridge, Mass.: Belknap Press.

Amin, S. 1989. *Eurocentrism.* Trans. R. Moore. New York: Monthly Review Press.

Anderson, K. 1995. *Hitler and the Occult.* Amherst, N.Y.: Prometheus.

Andrews, J. H. 1975. *A Paper Landscape: The Ordnance Survey in Nineteenth-Century Ireland.* Oxford: Clarendon Press.

Anonymous. 1697. *The True Way to Render Ireland Happy and Secure or, A Discourse Wherein 'tis Shewn that 'tis the Interest both of England and Ireland to Encourage Foreign Protestants to Plant in Ireland.* Dublin: Andrew Crook.

————. 1866a. Miscellany—1. Coolies as a Substitute for Negroes. *DeBow's Review* 2: 215–17.

————. 1866b. Art. VI. The Vast Resources of Louisiana. *DeBow's Review* 2: 274–85.

————. 1867a. Department of Immigration and Labor—4. The Importation of Coolies. *DeBow's Review* 4: 362–64.

————. 1867b. Art. X. Department of Immigration and Labor—1. The Louisiana Bureau. *DeBow's Review* 4: 575–76.

————. 1869a. The Cooley-ite Controversy. *DeBow's Review* 6: 709–23.

————. 1869b. What German Emigrants Can Accomplish in Louisiana. *DeBow's Review* 6: 617–18.

Appadurai, A., ed. 1986. *The Social Life of Things: Commodities in Cultural Perspective.* Cambridge: Cambridge University Press.

Aptheker, H. 1943. *American Negro Slave Revolts.* New York: Columbia University Press.

Arnold, B. 1990. The Past as Propaganda: Totalitarian Archaeology in Nazi Germany. *Antiquity* 64: 464–78.

Arnold, J. E. 2000. Revisiting Power, Labor Rights, and Kinship: Archaeology and Social Theory. In *Social Theory in Archaeology*, ed. M. B. Schiffer, pp. 14–30. Salt Lake City: University of Utah Press.

Ascher, R. 1974. Tin Can Archaeology. *Historical Archaeology* 8: 7–16.

Atherton, J. H. 1983. Ethnoarchaeology in Africa. *African Archaeological Review* 1: 75–104.

Axtell, J. 1992. *Beyond 1492: Encounters in Colonial North America.* New York: Oxford University Press.

Babson, D. W. 1990. The Archaeology of Racism and Ethnicity on Southern Plantations. *Historical Archaeology* 24(4): 20–28.

Baker, L. D. 1998. *From Savage to Negro: Anthropology and the Construction of Race, 1896–1954.* Berkeley: University of California Press.

Baker, V. G. 1978. *Historical Archaeology at Black Lucy's Garden, Andover, Massachusetts: Ceramics from the Site of a Nineteenth Century Afro-American.* Andover, Mass.: Phillips Academy.

————. 1980. Archaeological Visibility of Afro-American Culture: An Example from Black Lucy's Garden, Andover, Massachusetts. In *Archaeological Perspectives on Ethnicity in America: Afro-American and Asian American Culture History*, ed. R. L. Schuyler, pp. 29–37. Farmingdale, N.Y.: Baywood.

Ball, C. 1837. *Slavery in the United States: A Narrative of the Life and Adventures of Charles Ball, a Black Man.* New York: John S. Taylor.

Barford, P., Z. Kobyliński, and D. Krasnodębski. 1991. Between the Slavs, Balts, and Germans: Ethnic Problems in the Archaeology and History of Podlasie. *Archaeologia Polona* 29: 123–60.

Barkey, K. and R. Van Rossem. 1997. Networks of Contention: Villages and Regional Structure in the Seventeenth-Century Ottoman Empire. *American Journal of Sociology* 102: 1345–82.

Barnes, J. A. 1954. Class and Community in a Norwegian Island Parish. *Human Relations* 7: 39–58.

————. 1972. *Social Networks.* Addison-Wesley Module in Anthropology 26. Reading, Mass.: Addison-Wesley.

Barry, T. B. 1987. *The Archaeology of Medieval Ireland.* London: Routledge.

Barth, F. 1969. Introduction. In *Ethnic Groups and Boundaries: The Social Organization of Cultural Difference*, ed. F. Barth, pp. 9–38. London: G. Allen and Unwin.

Bartlett, R. 1993. *The Making of Europe: Conquest, Colonization, and Cultural Change, 950–1350.* Princeton, N.J.: Princeton University Press.

Baudrillard, J. 1998. *The Consumer Society: Myths and Structures.* London: Sage.

Bauer, J. 2000. Genealogies of Race and Culture in Anthropology: The Marginalized Ethnographers. In *Race and Racism in Theory and Practice,* ed. B. Lang, pp. 123–37. Lanham, Md.: Rowman and Littlefield.

Baugher, S. 1982. Hoboken Hollow: A 19th Century Factory Worker's Housing Site. *Northeast Historical Archaeology* 11: 26–38.

Beals, H. K. 1980. Chinese Coins in Six Northwestern Aboriginal Sites. *Historical Archaeology* 14: 58–72.

Beames, M. 1975. Cottiers and Conacre in Pre-Famine Ireland. *Journal of Peasant Studies* 2: 352–54.

———. 1982. The Ribbon Societies: Lower-Class Nationalism in Pre-Famine Ireland. *Past and Present* 97: 128–43.

———. 1983. *Peasants and Power: The Whiteboy Movement and Their Control in Pre-Famine Ireland.* Sussex: Harvester Press.

Beasley-Murray, J. 2000. Value and Capital in Bourdieu and Marx. In *Pierre Bourdieu: Fieldwork in Culture,* ed. N. Brown and I. Szeman, pp. 100–119. Lanham, Md.: Rowman and Littlefield.

Beaudry, M. C. 1999. House and Household: The Archaeology of Domestic Life in Early America. In *Old and New Worlds,* ed. G. Egan and R. L. Michael, pp. 117–26. Oxford: Oxbow.

Becker, C. L. 1955. What are Historical Facts? *Western Political Quarterly* 7: 327–40.

Becker, M. J. 1995. Letter to the Editor. *Bulletin of the Society for American Archaeology* 13(2): 6.

Bell, D. A. 2000. *Race, Racism, and American Law.* 4th ed. Gaithersburg, Md.: Aspen Law and Business.

Bell, E. Q. 1867. Art. VII. In Lieu of Labor. *DeBow's Review* 4: 69–83.

Bell, J. 1987. The Improvement of Irish Farming Techniques Since 1750: Theory and Practice. In *Rural Ireland, 1600–1900: Modernisation and Change,* ed. P. O'Flanagan, P. Ferguson, and K. Whelan, pp. 24–41. Cork: Cork University Press.

Bell, J. and M. Watson. 1986. *Irish Farming: Implements and Techniques, 1750–1900.* Edinburgh: John Donald.

Benedict, R. 1934. *Patterns of Culture.* Boston: Houghton Mifflin.

———. 1942. *Race and Racism.* London: Routledge.

Bentley, G. C. 1987. Ethnicity and Practice. *Comparative Studies in Society and History* 29: 24–55.

———. 1991. Response to Yelvington. *Comparative Studies in Society and History* 33: 169–75.

Berleth, R. 1994. *The Twilight Lords: An Irish Chronicle.* New York: Barnes and Noble.

Beyerstein, D. 1996. Edgar Cayce: The "Prophet" Who "Slept" His Way to the Top. *Skeptical Inquirer* 20(1): 32–37.

Bieder, R. E. 1986. *Science Encounters the Indian, 1820–1880: The Early Years of American Ethnology.* Norman: University of Oklahoma Press.

Binford, L. R. 1962. Archaeology as Anthropology. *American Antiquity* 28: 217–25.

———. 1972. "Evolution and Horizon as Revealed in Ceramic Analysis in Historical Archaeology": A Step Toward the Development of Archaeological Science. *Conference on Historic Sites Archaeology Papers* 6: 117–26.

———. 1973. Interassemblage Variability: The Mousterian and the "Functional" Argument. In *The Explanation of Culture Change: Model in Prehistory,* ed. C. Renfrew, pp. 227–54. London: Duckworth.

———. 1977. Foreword. In S. South, *Method and Theory in Historical Archaeology,* pp. xi–xii. New York: Academic Press.

Binford, L. and S. Binford. 1966. A Preliminary Analysis of Functional Variability in the Mousterian of Lavallois Faces. *American Anthropologist* 68: 238–95.

Blackburn, D. G. 2000. Why Race Is Not a Biological Concept. In *Race and Racism in Theory and Practice*, ed. B. Lang, pp. 3–26. Lanham, Md.: Rowman and Littlefield.

Blakey, M. L. 1988. Racism Through the Looking Glass: An Afro-American Perspective. *World Archaeological Bulletin* 2: 46–50.

———. 1990. American Nationality and Ethnicity in the Depicted Past. In *The Politics of the Past*, ed. P. Gathercole and D. Lowenthal, pp. 38–48. London: Unwin Hyman.

Blanton, R. E. 1994. *Houses and Households: A Comparative Study*. New York: Plenum Press.

Blanton, R. E. and G. Feinman. 1984. The Mesoamerican World System. *American Anthropologist* 86: 673–82.

Blanton, R., S. Kowalewski, and G. Feinman. 1992. The Mesoamerican World-System. *Review* 15: 419–26.

Blassingame, J. W., 1976. Status and Social Structure in the Slave Community: Evidence from New Sources. In *Perspectives and Irony in American Slavery*, ed H. P. Owens, pp. 137–51. Jackson: University Press of Mississippi.

Blau, P. M. 1964. *Exchange and Power in Social Life*. New York: John Wiley and Sons.

Blaut, J. M. 1993. *The Colonizer's Model of the World: Geographical Diffusionism and Eurocentric History*. New York: Guilford Press.

Bloch, M. 1985. *Marxism and Anthropology: The History of a Relationship*. Oxford: Oxford University Press.

Boas, A. J. 1999. *Crusader Archaeology: The Material Culture of the Latin East*. London: Routledge.

Bonasera, M. C. and L. Raymer. 2001. Good for What Ails You: Medicinal Use at Five Points. *Historical Archaeology* 35(3): 49–64.

Bonilla-Silva, E. 1997. Rethinking Racism: Toward a Structural Interpretation. *American Sociological Review* 62: 465–80.

———. 1999. The Essential Social Fact of "Race." *American Sociological Review* 64: 899–906.

Bonnett, A. 1996. White Studies: The Problems and Projects of a New Research Agenda. *Theory, Culture, and Society* 13: 145–55.

Bonvillain, N. 2001. *Native Nations: Cultures and Histories of Native North America*. Upper Saddle River, N.J.: Prentice Hall.

Bordes, F. 1973. On the Chronology and Contemporaneity of Different Palaeolithic Cultures in France. In *The Explanation of Culture Change: Models in Prehistory*, ed. C. Renfew, pp. 217–26. London: Duckworth.

Bordes, F. and D. de Sonneville-Bordes. 1970. The Significance of Variability in Palaeolithic Assemblages. *World Archaeology* 2: 61–73.

Boswell, T. and W. J. Dixon. 1993. Marx's Theory of Rebellion: A Cross-National Analysis of Class Exploitation, Economic Development, and Violent Revolt. *American Sociological Review* 58: 681–702.

Bouchereau, L. 1870. *Statement of the Sugar and Rice Crops Made in Louisiana in 1869–70*. New Orleans: Young and Bright.

Boulding, K. 1989. *Three Faces of Power*. Newbury Park, Calif.: Sage.

Bourdieu, P. 1971. Intellectual Field and Creative Project. In *Knowledge and Control: New Directions for the Sociology of Education*, ed. M. F. D. Young, pp. 161–88. London: Collier-Macmillan.

————. 1977a. Cultural Reproduction and Social Reproduction. In *Power and Ideology in Education*, ed. J. Karabel and A. H. Halsey, pp. 487–511. New York: Oxford University Press.

————. 1977b. *Outline of a Theory of Practice*. Trans. R. Nice. Cambridge: Cambridge University Press.

————. 1984. *Distinction: A Social Critique of the Judgement of Taste*. Trans. R. Nice. Cambridge, Mass.: Harvard University Press.

————. 1985. The Social Space and the Genesis of Groups. *Theory and Society* 14: 723–44.

————. 1986. The Forms of Capital. In *Handbook of Theory and Research for the Sociology of Education*, ed. J. G. Richardson, pp. 241–58. New York: Greenwood Press.

————. 1987. What Makes a Social Class? On the Theoretical and Practical Existence of Groups. *Berkeley Journal of Sociology* 32: 1–18.

————. 1988. *Homo Academicus*. Trans. P. Collier. Stanford, Calif.: Stanford University Press.

————. 1990a. *In Other Words: Essays Towards a Reflexive Sociology*. Trans. M. Adamson. Stanford, Calif.: Stanford University Press.

————. 1990b. *The Logic of Practice*. Trans. R. Nice. Stanford, Calif.: Stanford University Press.

————. 1992. The Practice of Reflexive Sociology (The Paris Workshop). In P. Bourdieu and L. J. D. Wacquant, *An Invitation to Reflexive Sociology*, pp. 216–60. Chicago: University of Chicago Press.

————. 1993a. Concluding Remarks: For a Sociogenetic Understanding of Intellectual Works. In *Bourdieu: Critical Perspectives*, ed. C. Calhoun, E. LiPuma, and M. Postone, pp. 263–75. Chicago: University of Chicago Press.

————. 1993b. *The Field of Cultural Production: Essays on Art and Literature*. Ed. R. Johnson, New York: Columbia University Press.

————. 1998a. *Acts of Resistance: Against the Tyranny of the Market*. Trans. R. Nice. New York: New Press.

————. 1998b. *Practical Reason: On the Theory of Action*. Stanford, Calif.: Stanford University Press.

Bourdieu, P. and J.-C. Passeron. 1977. *Reproduction in Education, Society, and Culture*. Trans. R. Nice. London: Sage.

Bourdieu, P. and L. J. D. Wacquant. 1992. The Purpose of Reflexive Sociology (The Chicago Workshop). In P. Bourdieu and L. J. D. Wacquant, *An Invitation to Reflexive Sociology*, pp. 60–215. Chicago: University of Chicago Press.

Bourke, A. 1993. *"The Visitation of God"? The Potato and the Great Irish Famine*. Ed. J. Hill and C. Ó Gráda. Dublin: Lilliput Press.

Boyle, M. 2001. Edifying the Rebellious Gael: Uses of Memories of Ireland's Troubled Past Among the West of Scotland's Irish Catholic Diaspora. In *Celtic Geographies: Old Culture, New Times*, ed. D. C. Harvey, R. Jones, N. McInroy, and C. Milligan, pp. 173–91. London: Routledge.

Brace, C. L. 1982. The Roots of the Race Concept in American Physical Anthropology. In *A History of American Physical Anthropology, 1930–1980*, ed. F. Spencer, pp. 11–29. New York: Academic Press.

Braghine, A. 1997. *The Shadow of Atlantis*. 1940. Kempton, Ill.: Adventures Unlimited.

Brah, A. 1996. *Cartographies of Diaspora: Contesting Identities*. London: Routledge.

Brand, P. A. 1998. Statute of Kilkenny. In *The Oxford Companion to Irish History*, ed. S. J. Connolly, pp. 286–87. Oxford: Oxford University Press.

Braudel, F. 1967. *Capitalism and Material Life, 1400–1800*. Ed. M. Kochan, New York: Harper and Row.

————. 1977. *Afterthoughts on Material Civilization and Capitalism.* Trans. P. M. Ranum. Baltimore: Johns Hopkins University Press.

————. 1985. *The Structures of Everyday Life: The Limits of the Possible.* Trans. S. Reynolds. New York: Harper and Row.

Breen, T. H. 1988. "Baubles of Britain": The American and Consumer Revolutions of the Eighteenth Century. *Past and Present* 119: 73–104.

Brewer, J. and R. Porter, eds., 1993. *Consumption and the World of Goods.* London: Routledge.

Brinton, D. G. 1890. *Races and Peoples: Lectures on the Science of Ethnography.* New York: N. D. C. Hodges.

Bro, H. H. 1989. *A Seer out of Season: The Life of Edgar Cayce.* New York: New American Library.

Brooks, A. M. 1997. Beyond the Fringe: Transfer-Printed Ceramics and the Internationalization of Celtic Myth. *International Journal of Historical Archaeology* 1: 39–55.

————. 1999. Building Jerusalem: Transfer-printed Finewares and the Creation of British Identity. In *The Familiar Past? Archaeologies of Later Historical Britain,* ed. S. Tarlow and S. West, pp. 51–65. London: Routledge.

Brown, D. H. 1999. Class and Rubbish. In *Historical Archaeology: Back from the Edge,* ed. P. P. A. Funari, M. Hall, and S. Jones, pp. 151–63. London: Routledge.

Brubaker, R. 1993. Social Theory as Habitus. In *Bourdieu: Critical Perspectives,* ed. C. Calhoun, E. LiPuma, and M. Postone, pp. 212–34. Chicago: University of Chicago Press.

Brubaker, R. and F. Cooper. 2000. Beyond "Identity." *Theory and Society* 29: 1–47.

Bullen, R. P. 1970. Comments on Garry W. Stone's Paper: "Ceramics in Suffolk County, Mass., Inventories, 1680–1775." *Conference on Historic Site Archaeology Papers* 3: 127–28.

Bullen, A. K. and R. P. Bullen. 1945. Black Lucy's Garden. *Bulletin of the Massachusetts Archaeological Society* 6(2): 17–28.

Burt, R. S. and N. Lin. 1977. Network Time Series from Archival Records. In *Sociological Methodology 1977,* ed. D. R. Heise, pp. 224–54. San Francisco: Jossey-Bass.

Butler, J. J. 1851. Agricultural Department: 1.—Management of Negroes. *DeBow's Review* 10: 325–28.

Byrne, V. 2000. *A Thousand Years of the Hidden Annals of the Kingdom of Connaught, 366–1385 A.D.* Dublin: Scanway Graphics.

Cairnes, J. E. 1862. *The Slave Power: Its Character, Career, and Probable Designs, Being an Attempt to Explain the Real Issues Involved in the American Contest.* New York: Carleton.

Calhoun, C. 1993. Habitus, Field, and Capital: The Question of Historical Specificity. In *Bourdieu: Critical Perspectives,* ed. C. Calhoun, E. LiPuma, and M. Postone, pp. 61–88. Chicago: University of Chicago Press.

————. 1995. *Critical Social Theory: Culture, History, and the Challenge of Difference.* Oxford: Blackwell.

Calhoun, J. A. 1855. Management of Slaves. *DeBow's Review* 18: 713–19.

Callan, T. and B. Nolan. 1998. Ireland. In *Poverty: A Persistent Global Reality,* ed. J. Dixon and D. Macarov, pp. 93–115. London: Routledge.

Campbell, G. 1879. *White and Black: The Outcome of a Visit to the United States.* London: Chatto and Windus.

Canny, N. P. 1973. The Ideology of English Colonization: From Ireland to America. *William and Mary Quarterly* 30: 575–98.

————. 1976. *The Elizabethan Conquest of Ireland: A Pattern Established, 1565–76.* New York: Barnes and Noble.

————. 1989. Early Modern Ireland, c. 1500–1700. In *The Oxford Illustrated History of Ireland,* ed. R. F. Foster, pp. 104–60. Oxford: Oxford University Press.

Capron, H. 1871. *Report of the Commissioner of Agriculture for the Year 1870.* Washington, D.C.: U.S. Government Printing Office.

Carrithers, M. 1992. *Why Humans Have Cultures: Explaining Anthropology and Social Diversity.* Oxford: Oxford University Press.

Castleden, R. 2001. *Atlantis Destroyed.* London: Routledge.

Cawley, M. 1989. Rural People and Services. In *The Irish Countryside: Landscape, Wildlife, History, People.* ed. D. Gillmor, pp. 197–225. Dublin: Wolfhound Press.

Cayce, H. L., ed. 1968. *Edgar Cayce on Atlantis.* New York: Warner.

Census of Ireland. 1852. *The Census of Ireland for the Year 1851: Part I: Showing the Area, Population, and Number of Townlands and Electoral Divisions, County of Roscommon.* Dublin: Alexander Thom.

Champion, S. 1995. Jewellery and Adornment. In *The Celtic World,* ed. M. J. Green, pp. 411–19. London: Routledge.

Champion, T. ed. 1989. *Centre and Periphery: Comparative Studies in Archaeology.* London: Unwin Hyman.

————. 1996. La Tène. In *The Oxford Companion to Archaeology,* ed. B. M. Fagan, p. 379. New York: Oxford University Press.

Charlesworth, S. 2000. Bourdieu, Social Suffering, and Working-Class Life. In *Reading Bourdieu on Society and Culture,* ed. B. Fowler, pp. 49–64. Oxford: Blackwell.

Chase-Dunn, C. 1992. Theoretical Approaches to World-System Analysis. In *Perspectives and Issues in International Political Economy,* ed. C. Polychroniou, pp. 3–20. Westport, Conn.: Praeger.

————. 1993. Comment on "Bronze Age World System Cycles" by A. G. Frank. *Current Anthropology* 34: 407–8.

————. 1996. World-Systems: Similarities and Differences. In *The Underdevelopment of Development: Essays in Honor of Andre Gunder Frank,* ed. S. C. Chew and R. A. Denemark, pp. 246–58. Thousand Oaks, Calif.: Sage.

Chase-Dunn, C. and T. D. Hall, eds. 1991. *Core-Periphery Relations in Precapitalist Worlds.* Boulder, Colo.: Westview Press.

Cheek, C. D. 1997. Setting an English Table: Black Carib Archaeology on the Caribbean Coast of Honduras. In *Approaches to the Historical Archaeology of Mexico, Central and South America,* ed. J. Gasco, G. C. Smith, and P. Fournier-Garcia, pp. 101–9. Los Angeles: Institute of Archaeology, University of California.

Childe, V. G. 1926. *The Aryans: A Study of Indo-European Origins.* New York: Knopf.

Childress, D. H. 1986. *Lost Cities and Ancient Mysteries of South America.* Stelle, Ill.: Adventures Unlimited Press.

————. 1992. *Lost Cities of North and Central America.* Stelle, Ill.: Adventures Unlimited Press.

Citro, C. F. and R. T. Michael, eds. 1995. *Measuring Poverty: A New Approach.* Washington, D.C.: National Academy Press.

Clark, L. 1987. Gravestones: Reflectors of Ethnicity or Class? In *Consumer Choice in Historical Archaeology,* ed. S. M. Spencer-Wood, pp. 383–95. New York: Plenum Press.

Clark, G. and S. Piggott. 1966. *Prehistoric Societies.* New York: Knopf.

Clark, S. 1979. *Social Origins of the Irish Land War.* Princeton, N. J.: Princeton University Press.

Clark, S. and J. S. Donnelly, Jr., eds. 1983. *Irish Peasants: Violence and Political Unrest, 1780–1914.* Madison: University of Wisconsin Press.

Clarke, A. 1994. The Colonisation of Ulster and the Rebellion of 1641 (1603–60). In *The Course of Irish History*, ed. T. W. Moody and F. X. Martin, pp. 189–203. Niwot, Colo.: Roberts Rinehart.

Clarke, D. L. 1968. *Analytical Archaeology.* London: Methuen.

Cleland, C. E. 2001. Historical Archaeology Adrift? *Historical Archaeology* 35(2): 1–8.

Cleland, C. E. and J. E. Fitting. 1968. The Crisis of Identity: Theory in Historical Archaeology. *Conference on Historic Site Archaeology Papers* 2(2): 124–38.

Cobden, J. C. 1860. *The White Slaves of England.* New York: C. M. Saxton, Barker.

Coe, M. D. 1993. *Breaking the Maya Code.* London: Thames and Hudson.

Cohen, G. A. 1988. *History, Labour, and Freedom: Themes from Marx.* Oxford: Clarendon Press.

Cole, J. R. 1980. Cult Archaeology and Unscientific Method and Theory. In *Advances in Archaeological Method and Theory*, vol. 3, ed. M. B. Schiffer, pp. 1–33. New York: Academic Press.

Coleman, A. 1999. *Riotous Roscommon: Social Unrest in the 1840s.* Dublin: Irish Academic Press.

Collins, J. 1993. Determination and Contradiction: An Appreciation and Critique of the Work of Pierre Bourdieu on Language and Education. In *Bourdieu: Critical Perspectives*, ed. C. Calhoun, E. LiPuma, and M. Postone, pp. 116–38. Chicago: University of Chicago Press.

Collins, J. K. 2000. Tracing Social Relations in Commodity Chains: The Case of Grapes in Brazil. In *Commodities and Globalization: Anthropological Perspectives*, ed. A. Haugerud, M. P. Stone, and P. D. Little, pp. 97–109. Lanham, Md.: Rowman and Littlefield.

Collins, K. 1990. *The Cultural Conquest of Ireland.* Cork: Mercier Press.

Collis, J. 1996. Celts and Politics. In *Cultural Identity and Archaeology: The Construction of European Communities*, ed. P. Graves-Brown, S. Jones, and C. Gamble, pp. 167–78. London: Routledge.

Commissioners of the Census. 1843. *Report of the Commissioners Appointed to Take the Census of Ireland, for the Year 1841.* Dublin: Alexander Thom.

Connell, P., D. A. Cronin, and B. Ó Dálaigh. 1998. Introduction. In *Irish Townlands: Studies in Local History*, ed. P. Connell, D. A. Cronin, and B. Ó Dálaigh, pp. 9–13. Dublin: Four Courts Press.

Connolly, S. J. 1982. *Priests and People in Pre-Famine Ireland, 1780–1845.* Dublin: Gill and Macmillan.

Coon, C. S. 1939. *The Races of Europe.* New York: Macmillan.

Cooney, G. 2000. Reading a Landscape Manuscript: A Review of Progress in Prehistoric Settlement Studies in Ireland. In *A History of Settlement in Ireland*, ed. T. Berry, pp. 1–49. London: Routledge.

Cooney, G. and E. Grogan. 1994. *Irish Prehistory: A Social Perspective.* Dublin: Wordwell.

Cotz, J. A. 1975. A Study of Ten Houses in Paterson's Dublin Area. *Northeast Historical Archaeology* 4: 44–52.

Courtney, P. 1997. The Tyranny of Constructs: Some Thoughts on Periodisation and Culture Change. In *The Age of Transition: The Archaeology of English Culture, 1400–1600*, ed. D. Gaimster and P. Stamper, pp. 9–23. Oxford: Oxbow.

Cowgill, G. L. 2000. "Rationality" and Contexts in Agency Theory. In *Agency in Archaeology*, ed. M-A Dobres and J. Robb, pp. 51–60. London: Routledge.

Cox, O. C. 1945. Race and Caste: A Distinction. *American Journal of Sociology* 50: 360–68.

———. 1970. *Caste, Class, and Race: A Study in Social Dynamics.* 1948. New York: Monthly Review Press.

Coyle, L. 1994. *A Parish History of Kilglass, Slatta, and Rooskey.* Boyle: Kilglass Gaels G.A.A. Club.

Coysh, A. W. and R. K. Henrywood. 1982. *The Dictionary of Blue and White Printed Pottery, 1780–1880.* Vol. 1. Woodbridge, Suffolk: Antique Collectors' Club.

Crass, D. C., S. D. Smith, M. A. Zierden, and R. D. Brooks, eds. 1998. *The Southern Colonial Backcountry: Interdisciplinary Perspectives on Frontier Communities.* Knoxville: University of Tennessee Press.

Cremo, M. A. and R. L. Thompson. 1993. *Forbidden Archaeology: The Hidden History of the Human Race.* San Diego: Bhaktivedanta Institute.

Croker, T. C. 1824. *Researches in the South of Ireland, Illustrative of the Scenery, Architectural Remains, and the Manners and Superstitions of the Peasantry with an Appendix, Containing a Private Narrative of the Rebellion of 1798.* London: John Murray.

Cronin, T. 1980. The Elizabethan Colony in Co. Roscommon. In *Irish Midland Studies: Essays in Commemoration of N. W. English,* ed. H. Murtagh, pp.107–20. Athlone: Old Athlone Society.

Crossley, N. 2002. *Making Sense of Social Movements.* Buckingham: Open University Press.

Crowell, A. L. 1997. *Archaeology and the Capitalist World System: A Study from Russian America.* New York: Plenum Press.

Crowley, T. 2000. *The Politics of Language in Ireland, 1366–1922: A Sourcebook.* London: Routledge.

Crumley, C. L. 1974. *Celtic Social Structure: The Generation of Archaeologically Testable Hypotheses from Literary Evidence.* Museum of Anthropology Anthropological Paper 54. Ann Arbor: University of Michigan.

Cullen, L. M. 1968. *Anglo-Irish Trade, 1660–1800.* Manchester: Manchester University Press.

Curtin, P. D. 1990. *The Rise and Fall of the Plantation Complex: Essays in Atlantic History.* Cambridge: Cambridge University Press.

Curtis, L. 1996. *Nothing but the Same Old Story: The Roots of Anti-Irish Racism.* Belfast: Sásta.

Curtis, L. P., Jr. 1971. *Apes and Angels: The Irishman in Victorian Caricature.* Washington, D.C.: Smithsonian Institution Press.

Custer, J. F. 2001. Working Together: Who Cares? *SAA Archaeological Record* 1(4): 21–22.

D'Altroy, T. N. and C. A. Hastorf, eds. 2001. *Empire and Domestic Economy.* New York: Kluwer Academic/Plenum Press.

Dames, M. 1992. *Mythic Ireland.* London: Thames and Hudson.

Dant, T. 1999. *Material Culture in the Social World: Values, Activities, Lifestyles.* Buckingham: Open University Press.

Darby, W. J. 2000. *Landscape and Identity: Geographies of Nation and Class in England.* Oxford: Berg.

Davin, A. 1996. *Growing Up Poor: Home, School, and Street in London, 1870–1914.* London: Rivers Oram Press.

Davis, A. 1942. *The Relation Between Color Caste and Economic Stratification in Two "Black" Plantation Counties.* Chicago: University of Chicago Libraries.

Davis, A, B. B. Gardner, and M. R. Gardner. 1941. *Deep South: A Social Anthropological Study of Caste and Class.* Chicago: University of Chicago Press.

Davis, R. L. F. 1982. *Good and Faithful Labor: From Slavery to Sharecropping in the Natchez District, 1860–1890.* Westport, Conn.: Greenwood Press.

Dawdy, S. L. 2000a. Preface. *Historical Archaeology* 34(3): 1–4.

———. 2000b. Understanding Cultural Change Through the Vernacular: Creolization in Louisiana. *Historical Archaeology* 34(3): 107–23.

Deagan, K. 1978. The Material Assemblage of 16th Century Spanish Florida. *Historical Archaeology* 12: 25–50.

———. 1982. Avenues of Inquiry in Historical Archaeology. In *Advances in Archaeological Method and Theory*, vol., 5, ed. M. B. Schiffer, pp. 151–77. New York: Academic Press.

———. 1983. *Spanish St. Augustine: The Archaeology of a Colonial Creole Community.* New York: Academic Press.

———. 1985. Spanish-Indian Interaction in Sixteenth-Century Florida and Hispaniola. In *Cultures in Contact: The European Impact on Native Cultural Institutions in Eastern North America, A.D. 1000–1800*, ed. W. W. Fitzhugh, pp. 281–318. Washington, D.C.: Smithsonian Institution Press.

———. 1987. *Artifacts of the Spanish Colonies in Florida and the Caribbean, 1500–1800.* Vol. 1, *Ceramics, Glassware, and Beads.* Washington, D.C.: Smithsonian Institution Press.

———. 1988. Neither History nor Prehistory: The Questions that Count in Historical Archaeology. *Historical Archaeology* 22(1): 7–12.

———. 1991. Historical Archaeology's Contributions to Our Understanding of Early America. In *Historical Archaeology in Global Perspective*, ed. L. Falk, pp. 97–112. Washington, D.C.: Smithsonian Institution Press.

———. 1995. After Columbus: The Sixteenth-Century Spanish-Caribbean Frontier. In *Puerto Real: The Archaeology of a Sixteenth-Century Spanish Town in Hispaniola*, ed. K. Deagan, pp. 419–56. Gainesville: University Press of Florida.

———. 2002. *Artifacts of the Spanish Colonies in Florida and the Caribbean, 1500–1800.* Vol. 2, *Portable Personal Possessions.* Washington, D.C.: Smithsonian Institution Press.

Deagan, K. and J. M. Cruxent. 2002a. *Archaeology at La Isabela: America's First European Town.* New Haven, Conn.: Yale University Press.

———. 2002b. *Columbus' Outpost Among the Taínos: Spain and America at La Isabela, 1493–1498.* New Haven, Conn.: Yale University Press.

Dear, M. J. and S. Flusty. 2002. Editors' Introduction to "The Production of Space" by Henri Lefebvre. In *The Spaces of Postmodernity: Readings in Human Geography*, ed. M. J. Dear and S. Flusty, p. 131. Oxford: Blackwell.

de Beaumont, G. 1839. *Ireland: Social, Political, and Religious*, ed. W. C. Taylor, London: R. Bentley.

de Camp, L. S. 1970. *Lost Continents: The Atlantis Theme in History, Science, and Literature.* New York: Dover.

de Certeau, M. 1988. *The Practice of Everyday Life.* Trans. S. Rendall. Berkeley: University of California Press.

DeCorse, C. R. 1989. Material Aspects of Limba, Yalunka, and Kuranko Ethnicity: Archaeological Research in Northeastern Sierra Leone. In *Archaeological Approaches to Cultural Identity*, ed. S. J. Shennan, pp. 125–40. London: Unwin Hyman.

De Cunzo, L. A. 1983. Economics and Ethnicity: An Archaeological Perspective on Nineteenth Century Paterson, New Jersey. Doctoral dissertation, University of Pennsylvania.

———. 1998. A Future After Freedom. *Historical Archaeology* 32(1): 42–54.

Deetz, J. 1967. *Invitation to Archaeology.* Garden City, N.Y.: Natural History Press.

———. 1968. Late Man in North America: Archaeology of European Americans. In *Archaeological Archaeology in the Americas*, ed. B. J. Meggers, pp. 121–30. Washington, D.C.: Anthropological Society of Washington.

————. 1977. *In Small Things Forgotten: The Archaeology of Early American Life.* Garden City, N.Y.: Anchor/Doubleday.

————. 1982. Households: A Structural Key to Archaeological Explanation. *American Behavioral Scientist* 25: 717–24.

————. 1983. Scientific Humanism and Humanistic Science: A Plea for Paradigmatic Pluralism in Historical Archaeology. *Geoscience and Man* 23: 27–34.

————. 1991. Introduction: Archaeological Evidence and Sixteenth- and Seventeenth-Century Encounters. In *Historical Archaeology in Global Perspective,* ed. L. Falk, pp. 1–9. Washington, D.C.: Smithsonian Institution Press.

————. 1996. *In Small Things Forgotten: An Archaeology of Early American Life.* Rev. ed. New York: Anchor Press/Doubleday.

Delle, J. A. 1998. *An Archaeology of Social Space: Analyzing Coffee Plantations in Jamaica's Blue Mountains.* New York: Plenum Press.

Deloria, V. Jr. 1995. *Red Earth, White Lies: Native Americans and the Myth of Scientific Fact.* New York: Scribner.

DeNevi, D. P. and D. A. Holmes, eds. 1973. *Racism at the Turn of the Century: Documentary Perspectives, 1870–1910.* San Rafael, Calif.: Leswing Press.

Dennett, J. R. 1965. *The South as It Is, 1865–1866.* ed. H. M. Christman, London: Sidgwick and Jackson.

de Paor, L. 1994. The Age of the Viking Wars (9th and 10th Centuries). In *The Course of Irish History,* rev. ed., T. W. Moody and F. X. Martin, pp. 91–106. Niwot, Colo.: Roberts Rinehart.

De Rivera, J. 1976. Introduction. In *Field Theory as Human-Science: Contributions of Lewin's Berlin Group,* ed. J. De Rivera, pp. 1–36. New York: Gardner Press.

Desmond, D. 1847. *Project for the Reclamation of One Million Acres of Waste Lands in Ireland.* Dublin: George Folds.

Diehl, M., J. A. Waters, and J. H. Thiel. 1998. Acculturation and the Composition of the Diet of Tucson's Overseas Chinese Gardeners at the Turn of the Century. *Historical Archaeology* 32(4): 19–33.

Dietz, T. 2001. The Agenda. In *Negotiating Poverty: New Directions, Renewed Debate,* ed. N. Middleton, P. O'Keefe, and R. Visser, pp. 19–25. London: Pluto Press.

DiMaggio, P. 1979. Review Essay: On Pierre Bourdieu. *American Journal of Sociology* 84: 1460–74.

Dixon, J. K. 1972. *The Vanishing Race: The Last Great Indian Council.* 1913. New York: Popular Library.

Doan, J. E. 1999. How the Irish and the Scots Became Indians: Colonial Traders and Agents and the Southeastern Tribes. *New Hibernia Review* 3: 9–19.

Dobres, M. A. and J. Robb, eds. 2000a. *Agency in Archaeology.* London: Routledge.

————. 2000b. Agency in Archaeology: Paradigm or Platitude? In *Agency in Archaeology,* ed. M-A Dobres and J. Robb, pp. 3–17. London: Routledge.

Dollard, J. 1937. *Caste and Class in a Southern Town.* New York: Harper.

Domínguez, V. R. 1986. *White by Definition: Social Classification in Creole Louisiana.* New Brunswick, N.J.: Rutgers University Press.

Dongoske, K. E., M. Yeatts, R. Anyon, and T. J. Ferguson. 1997. Archaeological Cultures and Cultural Affiliation: Hopi and Zuni Perspectives in the American Southwest. *American Antiquity* 62: 600–8.

Donham, D. L. 1999. *History, Power, and Ideology: Central Issues in Marxism and Anthropology.* Berkeley: University of California Press.

Donnelly, C. and N. Brannon. 1998. Trowelling Through History: Historical Archaeology and the Study of Early Modern Ireland. *History Ireland* 6(3): 22–25.

Donnelly, C. J. and A. J. Horning. 2002. Post-Medieval and Industrial Archaeology in Ireland: An Overview. *Antiquity* 76: 557–61.

Donnelly, J. S., Jr. 1975. *The Land and the People of Nineteenth-Century Cork: The Rural Economy and the Land Question.* London: Routledge.

———. 1983. Pastorini and Captain Rock: Millenarianism and Sectarianism in the Rockite Movement of 1821–4. In *Irish Peasants: Violence and Political Unrest, 1780–1914,* ed. S. Clark and J. S. Donnelly, Jr., pp. 102–39. Madison: University of Wisconsin Press.

Donnelly, I. 1976. *Atlantis: The Antediluvian World.* 1882. New York: Dover.

Doolan, T. 1847. *Practical Suggestions on the Improvement of the Present Condition of the Peasantry of Ireland.* London: George Barclay.

Dooley, B. 1998. *Black and Green: The Fight for Civil Rights in Northern Ireland and Black America.* London: Pluto Press.

Douglas, M. and B. Isherwood. 1979. *The World of Goods.* New York: Basic Books.

Douglass, Frederick. 1979. *The Frederick Douglass Papers, Series One: Speeches, Debates, and Interviews.* Vol. 1, *1841–46,* ed. J. W. Blassingame. New Haven, Conn.: Yale University Press.

Dowd, G. E. 1992. *A Spirited Resistance: The North American Indian Struggle for Unity, 1745–1815.* Baltimore: Johns Hopkins University Press.

Doyle, R. 1995. *The Barrytown Trilogy: The Commitments, The Snapper, The Van.* New York: Penguin.

Drucker, L. M. 1981. Socioeconomic Patterning of an Undocumented Late 18th Century Lowcountry Site: Spiers Landing, South Carolina. *Historical Archaeology* 15(2): 58–68.

D'Souza, D. 1995. *The End of Racism: Principles for a Multiracial Society.* New York: Free Press.

Dublin, R., D. Murray, C. Vignoles, R. M. O'Ferrall, J. Carlile, F. Hort, J. Corrie, J. L. W. Naper, and W. B. Wrightson. 1835. *Selection of Parochial Examinations Relative to the Destitute Classes in Ireland.* Dublin: Milliken and Son.

Du Bois, W. E. B. 1999. *The Souls of Black Folk.* 1903. Ed. H. L. Gates, Jr. and T. H. Oliver, New York: W.W. Norton.

Duffy, P. J., D. Edwards, and E. FitzPatrick, eds. 2001. *Gaelic Ireland, c. 1250–c.1650: Land, Lordship, and Settlement.* Dublin: Four Courts Press.

Duffy, S. 1997. Origins. In *Atlas of Irish History,* ed. S. Duffy, pp. 10–31. New York: Macmillan.

———. 2002. *The Illustrated History of Ireland.* Chicago: Contemporary Books.

Dunlevy, M. 1988. *Ceramics in Ireland.* Dublin: National Museum of Ireland.

Duplessis, R. S. 1997. *Transitions to Capitalism in Early Modern Europe.* Cambridge: Cambridge University Press.

Durkheim, E. 1915. *The Elementary Forms of the Religious Life: A Study in Religious Sociology.* Trans. J. W. Swain, London: Allen and Unwin.

Durning, A. T. 1992. *How Much is Enough? The Consumer Society and the Future of the Earth.* New York: W.W. Norton.

Eagan, C. M. 2001. "White," If "Not Quite": Irish Whiteness in the Nineteenth-Century Irish-American Novel. *Éire-Ireland* 36: 66–81.

Earle, T. K. 2001. Institutionalization of Chiefdoms: Why Landscapes Are Built. In *From Leaders to Rulers,* ed. J. Haas, pp.105–24. New York: Kluwer Academic/Plenum Press.

Edens, C. 1992. Dynamics of Trade in the Ancient Mesopotamian "World System." *American Anthropologist* 94: 118–39.

Edwards, N. 1999. *The Archaeology of Early Medieval Ireland.* London: Routledge.

Edwards, P. K. 1932. *The Southern Urban Negro as a Consumer.* Englewood Cliffs, N.J.: Prentice-Hall.

Ekholm, K. and J. Friedman. 1982. "Capital Imperialism" and Exploitation in the Ancient World-System. *Review* 6: 87–110.

Elias, P. D. 1993. Anthropology and Aboriginal Claims Research. In *Anthropology, Public Policy, and Native Peoples in Canada,* ed. N. Dyck and J. B. Waldram, pp. 233–70. Montreal: McGill-Queen's University Press.

Ellis, E. 1977. *Emigrants from Ireland, 1847–1852: State-Aided Emigration Schemes from Crown Estates in Ireland.* Baltimore: Genealogical Publishers.

Ellis, P. B. 1988. *Hell or Connaught: The Cromwellian Colonization of Ireland, 1652–1660.* Belfast: Blackstaff Press.

———. 1991. *A Dictionary of Irish Mythology.* Oxford: Oxford University Press.

Ellis, R. 1999. *Imagining Atlantis.* New York: Vintage.

Elster, J. 1985. *Making Sense of Marx.* Cambridge: Cambridge University Press.

Emerson, M. C. 1994. Decorated Clay Tobacco Pipes from the Chesapeake: An African Connection. In *Historical Archaeology of the Chesapeake,* ed. P. A. Shackel and B. J. Little, pp. 35–49. Washington, D.C.: Smithsonian Institution Press.

———. 1999. African Inspirations in a New World Art and Artifact: Decorated Tobacco Pipes from the Chesapeake. In *"I, Too, Am America": Archaeological Studies of African-American Life,* ed. T. A. Singleton, pp. 47–81. Charlottesville: University Press of Virginia.

Engelhardt, C. 1866. *Denmark in the Early Iron Age, Illustrated by Recent Discoveries in the Peat Mosses of Slesvig.* London: Williams and Norgate.

Engels, F. 1974. Selection from "Karl Marx." In *K. Marx, F. Engels, V. Lenin on Historical Materialism: A Collection.* 1878. Comp. T. Borodulina, New York: International Publishers.

Entine, J. 2000. *Taboo: Why Black Athletes Dominate Sports and Why We Are Afraid to Talk About It.* New York: Public Affairs Press.

Epperson, T. W. 1990a. "To Fix a Perpetual Brand": The Social Construction of Race in Virginia, 1675–1750. Doctoral dissertation, Temple University.

———. 1990b. Race and the Disciplines of the Plantation. *Historical Archaeology* 24(4): 29–36.

———. 1996. The Politics of "Race" and Cultural Identity at the African Burial Ground Excavations, New York City. *World Archaeological Bulletin* 7: 108–17.

———. 1997. Whiteness in Early Virginia. *Race Traitor* 7: 9–20.

———. 1999. Constructing Difference: The Social and Spatial Order of the Chesapeake Plantation. In *"I, Too, Am America": Archaeological Studies of African-American Life,* ed. T. A. Singleton, pp. 159–72. Charlottesville: University Press of Virginia.

———. 2001. "A Separate House for the Christian Slaves, One for the Negro Slaves": The Archaeology of Race and Identity in Late Seventeenth-Century Virginia. In *Race and the Archaeology of Identity,* ed. C. E. Orser, Jr., pp. 54–70. Salt Lake City: University of Utah Press.

Etter, P. A. 1980. The West Coast Chinese and Opium Smoking. In *Archaeological Perspectives on Ethnicity in America: Afro-American and Asian American Culture History,* ed. R. L. Schuyler, pp. 97–101. Farmingdale, N.Y.: Baywood.

Evans, D. E. 1995. The Early Celts: The Evidence of Language. In *The Celtic World,* ed. M. J. Green, pp. 8–20. London: Routledge.

Ewen, C. R. 1991. *From Spaniard to Creole: The Archaeology of Cultural Formation at Puerto Real, Haiti.* Tuscaloosa: University of Alabama Press.

Fagan, B. M. 1984. *Clash of Cultures.* New York: W.H. Freeman.

Fairbanks, C. H. 1983. Historical Archaeological Implications of Recent Investigations. *Geoscience and Man* 23: 17–26.

———. 1984. The Plantation Archaeology of the Southeastern Coast. *Historical Archaeology* 18(1): 1–14.

Fanning, T. and J. G. Hurst. 1975. A Mid-Seventeeth-Century Pottery Group and Other Objects from Ballyhack Castle, Co. Wexford. *Proceedings of the Royal Irish Academy* 75 (C): 103–18.

Fanon, F. 1968. *The Wretched of the Earth*. Trans. C. Farrington, New York: Grove Press.

Farnsworth, P. 1992. Missions, Indians, and Cultural Continuity. *Historical Archaeology* 26(1): 22–36.

Farris, G. J. 1979. "Cash" as Currency: Coins and Tokens from Yreka Chinatown. *Historical Archaeology* 13: 48–52.

Feder, K. L. 1984. Irrationality and Popular Archaeology. *American Antiquity* 49: 525–41.

———. 1994. *A Village of Outcasts: Historical Archaeology and Documentary Research at the Lighthouse Site*. Mountain View, Calif.: Mayfield.

———. 2002. *Frauds, Myths, and Mysteries: Science and Pseudoscience in Archaeology*. 4th ed. Boston: McGraw-Hill.

Fee, J. M. 1993. Idaho's Chinese Mountain Gardens. In *Hidden Heritage: Historical Archaeology of the Overseas Chinese*, ed. P. Wegars, pp. 65–96. Amityville, N.Y.: Baywood.

Feinman, G. M. 1996. Conclusions. In *Pre-Columbian World Systems*, ed. P. N. Peregrine and G. M. Feinman, pp. 115–21. Madison, Wis.: Prehistory Press.

Fell, B. 1976. *America B.C.: Ancient Settlers in the New World*. New York: Pocket Books.

Ferguson, L., ed. 1977. *Historical Archaeology and the Importance of Material Things*. Special Publication 2. Tucson, Ariz.: Society for Historical Archaeology.

———. 1992. *Uncommon Ground: Archaeology and Early African America, 1650–1800*. Washington, D.C.: Smithsonian Institution Press.

———. 1999. "The Cross Is a Magic Sign": Marks on Eighteenth-Century Bowls from South Carolina. In *"I, Too, Am America": Archaeological Studies of African-American Life*, ed. T. A. Singleton, pp. 116–31. Charlottesville: University Press of Virginia.

Fine, B. 1995. From Political Economy to Consumption. In *Acknowledging Consumption: A Review of New Studies*, ed. D. Miller, pp. 127–63. London: Routledge.

Fitzpatrick, A. P. 1996. "Celtic" Iron Age Europe: The Theoretical Basis. In *Cultural Identity and Archaeology: The Construction of European Communities*, ed. P. Graves-Brown, S. Jones, and C. Gamble, pp. 238–55. London: Routledge.

Flagg, B. J. 1998. *Was Blind, But Now I See: White Race Consciousness and the Law*. New York: New York University Press.

Flanagan, L. 1992. *A Dictionary of Irish Archaeology*. Dublin: Gill and Macmillan.

Flem-Ath, R. and R. Flem-Ath. 1995. *When the Sky Fell: In Search of Atlantis*. New York: St. Martin's Press.

Fontana, B. L. 1965. On the Meaning of Historic Sites Archaeology. *American Antiquity* 31: 61–65.

———. 1968. Bottles, Buckets, and Horseshoes: The Unrespectable in American Archaeology. *Keystone Folklore Quarterly* 13: 171–84.

Forty, A. 1986. *Objects of Desire: Design and Society, 1750–1980*. London: Thames and Hudson.

Foster, J. W. 1873. *Pre-historic Races of the United States of America.* Chicago: S.C. Griggs.

Foster, R. F. 1993. *Paddy and Mr. Punch: Connections in Irish and English History.* London: Penguin.

Foster, T. C. 1846. *Letters on the Condition of the People of Ireland.* London: Chapman and Hall.

Fournier-García, P. and F. A. Miranda-Flores. 1992. Historic Sites Archaeology in Mexico. *Historical Archaeology* 26(1): 75–83.

Francis, P. 2000. *Irish Delftware: An Illustrated History.* London: Jonathan Horne.

———. 2001. *A Pottery by the Lagan: Irish Creamware from the Downshire China Manufactory, Belfast, 1787–c. 1806.* Belfast: Institute of Irish Studies, Queen's University.

Frank, A. G. 1966. The Development of Underdevelopment. *Monthly Review* 18: 17–31.

———. 1993a. Bronze Age World System Cycle. *Current Anthropology* 34: 383–429.

———. 1993b. Transitional Ideological Modes: Feudalism, Capitalism, Socialism. In *The World-System: Five Hundred Years or Five Thousand?,* ed. A. G. Frank and B. K. Gills, pp. 200–220. London: Routledge.

———. 1998. *Re-Orient: Global Economy in the Asian Age.* Berkeley: University of California Press.

———. 1999. Abuses and Uses of World Systems Theory in Archaeology. In *World-Systems Theory in Practice: Leadership, Production, and Exchange,* ed. P. N. Kardulias, pp. 275–95. Lanham, Md.: Rowman and Littlefield.

Frank, A. G. and B. K. Gills, eds. 1993. *The World-System: Five Hundred Years or Five Thousand?* London: Routledge.

Franklin, M. 2001. A Black Feminist-Inspired Archaeology? *Journal of Social Archaeology* 1: 108–25.

Fraser, A. C., ed. 1871. *The Works of George Berkeley, D.D.* Oxford: Clarendon Press.

Frazer, B., ed. 1999. Archaeologies of Resistance in Britain and Ireland. *International Journal of Historical Archaeology* 3: 1–129.

Frazier, E. F. 1964. *The Negro Church in America.* New York: Schocken.

Freeman, P. 2001. *Ireland and the Classical World.* Austin: University of Texas Press.

Friedman, J. 1994. *Cultural Identity and Global Process.* London: Sage.

Gallup, G. H., Jr. and F. Newport. 1991. Belief in Paranormal Phenomena Among Adult Americans. *Skeptical Inquirer* 15(2): 137–46.

Gans, H. J. 1995. *The War Against the Poor: The Underclass and Antipoverty Policy.* New York: Basic Books.

Garnham, N. 1998. Townland. In *The Oxford Companion to Irish History,* ed. S. J. Connolly, p. 547. Oxford: Oxford University Press.

Gasco, J., G. C. Smith, and P. Fournier-García, eds. 1997. *Approaches to the Historical Archaeology of Mexico, Central and South America.* Los Angeles: Institute of Archaeology, University of California.

G. A. N. 1867. Laborers Wanted. *Southern Cultivator* 25: 69.

GAP (Group for the Advancement of Psychiatry). 1987. *Us and Them: The Psychology of Ethnonationalism.* New York: Brunner/Mazel.

Gaughwin, D. 1992. Trade, Capital, and the Development of the Extractive Industries of Northeast Tasmania. *Australasian Historical Archaeology* 10: 55–64.

Geremek, B. 1997. *Poverty: A History.* Trans. A. Kolakowska. Oxford: Blackwell.

Gero, J. M. 2000. Troubled Travels in Agency and Feminism. In *Agency in Archaeology,* ed. M. A. Dobres and J. Robb, pp. 34–39. London: Routledge.

Gershenfeld, M. K. 1986. Kurt Lewin: Intergroup Relations and Applications in

Current Action Research. In *The Lewin Legacy: Field Theory in Current Practice*, ed. E. Stivers and S. Wheelan, pp. 95–100. Berlin: Springer-Verlag.

Getches, D. H., D. M. Rosenfelt, and C. F. Wilkinson. 1979. *Cases and Materials on Federal Indian Law*. St. Paul, Minn.: West.

Gibb, J. G. 1996. *The Archaeology of Wealth: Consumer Behavior in English America*. New York: Plenum Press.

Gibbon, G. 1989. *Explanation in Archaeology*. Oxford: Blackwell.

Gibbons, L. 1991. Race Against Time: Racial Discourse and Irish History. *Oxford Literary Review* 13: 95–113.

Gildersleeve, C. R. 1978. The International Border City: Urban Spatial Organization in a Context of Two Cultures Along the United States-Mexico Boundary. Doctoral dissertation, University of Nebraska.

Gills, B. K. and A. G. Frank. 1992. World System Cycles, Crises, and Hegemonial Shifts, 1700 B.C. to 1700 A.D. *Review* 15: 621–87.

Gilroy, P. 1993. *The Black Atlantic: Modernity and Double Consciousness*. Cambridge, Mass.: Harvard University Press.

Glassie, H. 1968. *Pattern in the Material Culture of the Eastern United States*. Philadelphia: University of Pennsylvania Press.

——. 1975. *Folk Housing in Middle Virginia: A Structural Analysis of Historic Artifacts*. Knoxville: University of Tennessee Press.

Glazier, I. A., ed. 1983. *The Famine Immigrants: Lists of Irish Immigrants Arriving at the Port of New York, 1846–1851*. Vol. 2, *July 1846–June 1848*. Baltimore: Genealogical Publishing.

Glørstad, H. 2000. Freedom of Speech Is Always Freedom from the Speech of Others, or Rather Control of Their Silence: On Pierre Bourdieu and Archaeology. In *Philosophy and Archaeological Practice: Perspectives for the 21st Century*, ed. C. Holtorf and H. Karlsson, pp. 185–202. Göteborg, Sweden: Bricoleur Press.

Gmelch, S. B. 1976. The Emergence of an Ethnic Group: The Irish Tinkers. *Anthropological Quarterly* 49: 225–38.

Godelier, M. 1988. *The Mental and the Material: Thought, Economy, and Society*. Trans. M. Thom. London: Verso.

Godwyn, J. 1996. *Arktos: The Polar Myth in Science, Symbolism, and Nazi Survival*. Kempton, Ill.: Adventures Unlimited Press.

Goggin, J. M. 1960. *The Spanish Olive Jar: An Introductory Study*. Yale University Publications in Anthropology 62. New Haven, Conn.: Yale University Press.

——. 1968. *Spanish Majolica in the New World: Types of the Sixteenth to Eighteenth Centuries*. Yale University Publications in Anthropology 72. New Haven, Conn.: Yale University Press.

Goldberg, D. T. 1993. *Racist Culture: Philosophy and the Politics of Meaning*. Oxford: Blackwell.

Goldberg, M. Y. 1999. Spatial and Behavioural Negotiation in Classical Athenian City Houses. In *The Archaeology of Household Activities*, ed. P. M. Allison, pp. 142–61. London: Routledge.

Goldsmith, E. 1996. Global Trade and the Environment. In *The Case Against the Global Economy: And for a Turn Toward the Local*, ed. J. Mander and E. Goldsmith, pp.78–91. San Francisco: Sierra Club Books.

Gonzáles, N. L. 1988. *Sojourners of the Caribbean: Ethnogenesis and Ethnohistory of the Garifuna*. Urbana: University of Illinois Press.

Goodrick-Clarke, N. 1998. *Hitler's Priestess: Savitri Devi, the Hindu-Aryan Myth, and Neo-Nazism*. New York: New York University Press.

Gordon, M. 1964. *Assimilation in American Life: The Role of Race, Religion, and National Origins.* New York: Oxford University Press.

Gossett, T. F. 1963. *Race: The History of an Idea in America.* Dallas, Tex.: Southern Methodist University Press.

Gottdiener, M. 2000. Approaches to Consumption: Classical and Contemporary Perspectives. In *New Forms of Consumption: Consumers, Culture, and Commodification,* ed. M. Gottdiener, pp. 3–31. Lanham, Md.: Rowman and Littlefield.

Gould, R. V. 1996. Patron-Client Ties, State Centralization, and the Whiskey Rebellion. *American Journal of Sociology* 102: 400–429.

Gould, S. J. 1981. *The Mismeasure of Man.* New York: W.W. Norton.

Gramsci, A. 1971. *Selections from the Prison Notebooks of Antonio Gramsci.* Ed. Q. Hoare and G. N. Smith. New York: International Publishers.

Grant, E. 1997. *The Highland Lady in Ireland: Journals, 1840–50.* Ed. P. Pelly and A. Tod. Edinburgh: Canongate.

Green, M. J., ed. 1995. *The Celtic World.* London: Routledge.

Green, M. K. 1995. Cultural Identities: Challenges for the Twenty-First Century. In *Issues in Native American Cultural Identity,* ed. M. K. Green, pp. 1–38. New York: Peter Lang.

Greenblatt, S. 1991. *Marvelous Possessions: The Wonder of the New World.* Chicago: University of Chicago Press.

Greenwood, R. S. 1980. The Chinese on Main Street. In *Archaeological Perspectives on Ethnicity in America: Afro-American and Asian American Culture History,* ed. R. L. Schuyler, pp. 113–23. Farmingdale, N.Y.: Baywood.

————. 1993. Old Approaches and New Directions: Implications for Future Research. In *Hidden Heritage: Historical Archaeology of the Overseas Chinese,* ed. P. Wegars, pp. 375–403. Amityville, N.Y.: Baywood.

————. 1996. *Down by the Station: Los Angeles Chinatown, 1880–1933.* Monumenta Archaeologica 18. Los Angeles: Institute of Archaeology, University of California.

Griffith, R. 1819. *Practical Domestic Politics: Being a Comparative and Prospective Sketch of the Agriculture and Population of Great Britain and Ireland.* London: Sherwood, Neely, and Jones.

Griggs, H. J. 1999. Go gCuire Dia Rath Agus Blath Ort (God Grant that You Prosper and Flourish): Social and Economic Mobility Among the Irish in Nineteenth-Century New York. *Historical Archaeology* 33(1): 87–101.

Gundaker, G. 2000. Discussion: Creolization, Complexity, and Time. *Historical Archaeology* 34(3): 124–33.

Günther, H. F. K. 1970. *The Racial Elements of European History.* 1927. Trans. G. C. Wheeler, Port Washington, N.Y.: Kennikat Press.

Gust, S. M. 1993. Animal Bones from Historic Urban Chinese Sites: A Comparison of Sacramento, Woodland, Tucson, Ventura, and Lovelock. In *Hidden Heritage: Historical Archaeology of the Overseas Chinese,* ed. P. Wegars, pp. 177–212. Amityville, N.Y.: Baywood.

————. 2001. Appendix C: Analysis of Animal Bones. In *Block Technical Report: Historical Archaeology I-880 Cypress Replacement Project, Block 1,* ed. M. Praetzellis, pp. C-1–C-18. Oakland: California Department of Transportation.

Hackbarth, M. 1995. Letter to the Editor. *Bulletin of the Society for American Archaeology* 13(2): 6–7.

Hagood, M. J. 1939. *Mothers of the South: Portraiture of the White Tenant Farm Woman.* Chapel Hill: University of North Carolina Press.

Hall, E. T. 1963. Proxemics: The Study of Man's Spatial Relations. In *Man's Image in Medicine and Anthropology*, ed. I. Galdston, pp. 422–45. New York: International Universities Press.

Hall, G. M. 1992. The Formation of Afro-Creole Culture. In *Creole New Orleans: Race and Americanization*, ed. A. R. Hirsch and J. Logsdon, pp. 58–87. Baton Rouge: Louisiana State University Press.

Hall, M. 2000. *Archaeology and the Modern World: Colonial Transcripts in South Africa and the Chesapeake.* London: Routledge.

Hall, T. D. 1999. World-Systems and Evolution: An Appraisal. In *World-Systems Theory in Practice: Leadership, Production, and Exchange*, ed. P. N. Kardulias, pp. 1–23. Lanham, Md.: Rowman and Littlefield.

Hall, T. D. and C. Chase-Dunn. 1993. The World-Systems Perspective and Archaeology: Forward into the Past. *Journal of Archaeological Research* 1: 121–43.

———. 1996. Comparing World Systems: Concepts and Hypotheses. In *Pre-Columbian World Systems*, ed. P. N. Peregrine and G. M. Feinman, pp. 11–25. Madison, Wis.: Prehistory Press.

Hamilton, H. C., trans. 1887. *The Geography of Strabo.* Vol. 1. London: George Bell.

Hammond, C., trans. 1996. *Julius Caesar: Seven Commentaries on the Gallic War, with an Eighth Commentary by Aulus Hirtus.* Oxford: Oxford University Press.

Hancock, G. 1995. *Fingerprints of the Gods.* New York: Three Rivers Press.

———. 2002. *Underworld: The Mysterious Origins of Civilization.* New York: Crown.

Hancock, G. and R. Bauval. 1996. *The Message of the Sphinx: A Quest for the Hidden Legacy of Mankind.* New York: Three Rivers Press.

Hancock, G. and S. Faiia. 1998. *Heaven's Mirror: Quest for the Lost Civilization.* New York: Three Rivers Press.

Haney-López, I. F. 1996. *White by Law: The Legal Construction of Race.* New York: New York University Press.

Handler, J. S. 1997. An African-Type Healer/Diviner and His Grave Goods: A Burial from a Plantation Slave Cemetery in Barbados, West Indies. *International Journal of Historical Archaeology* 1: 91–130.

Handler, J. S., R. S. Corruccini, and R. J. Mutaw. 1982. Tooth Mutilation in the Caribbean: Evidence from a Slave Burial Population in Barbados. *Journal of Human Evolution* 11: 297–313.

Hanley, G. 1961. Nicholas Mahon and 17th Century Roscommon. *Irish Genealogist* 3: 228–35.

Hannaford, I. 1996. *Race: The History of an Idea in the West.* Baltimore: Johns Hopkins University Press.

Harbison, P. 1988. *Pre-Christian Ireland: From the First Settlers to the Early Celts.* London: Thames and Hudson.

Hardesty, D. L. and B. J. Little. 2000. *Assessing Site Significance: A Guide for Archaeologists and Historians.* Walnut Creek, Calif.: Altamira Press.

Hardin, M. A. 1979. The Cognitive Basis of Productivity in a Decorative Art Style: Implications of an Ethnographic Study for Archaeologists' Taxonomies. In *Ethnoarchaeology: Implications of Ethnography for Archaeologists*, ed. C. Kramer, pp. 75–101. New York: Columbia University Press.

Harding, J. and A. Barclay. 1999. An Introduction to the Cursus Monuments of Neolithic Britain and Ireland. In *Pathways and Ceremonies: The Cursus Monuments of Britain and Ireland*, ed. A. Barclay and J. Harding, pp. 1–8. Oxford: Oxbow.

Harrington, J. C. 1952. Historic Site Archaeology in the United States. In *Archaeology of Eastern United States*, ed. J. B. Griffin, pp. 335–44. Chicago: University of Chicago Press.

Harrington, M. 1963. *The Other America: Poverty in the United States.* Baltimore: Penguin.

Harris, F. R. and L. A. Curtis, eds. 1998. *Locked in the Poorhouse: Cities, Race, and Poverty in the United States.* Lanham, Md.: Rowman and Littlefield.

Harris, M. 1968. *The Rise of Anthropological Theory: A History of Theories of Culture.* New York: Thomas Y. Crowell.

Harris, R-A. M. 1999. Negotiating Patriarchy: Irish Women and the Landlord. In *Reclaiming Gender: Transgressive Identities in Modern Ireland,* ed. M. Cohen and N. J. Curtin, pp. 207–25. New York: St. Martin's Press.

Harrison, F. V. 1995. The Persistent Power of "Race" in the Cultural and Political Economy of Racism. *Annual Review of Anthropology* 24: 47–74.

Harrold, F. B. and R. A. Eve, eds. 1995. *Cult Archaeology and Creationism: Understanding Pseudoscientific Beliefs About the Past.* Iowa City: University of Iowa Press.

Hassler. 1871. Labor, Small Grain, etc. *Southern Cultivator* 29: 90.

Haugerud, A., M. P. Stone, and P. D. Little, eds. 2000. *Commodities and Globalization: Anthropological Perspectives.* Lanham, Md.: Rowman and Littlefield.

Hayden, B. 2001. The Dynamics of Wealth and Poverty in the Transegalitarian Societies of Southeast Asia. *Antiquity* 75: 571–81.

Hayes-McCoy, G. A. 1994. The Tudor Conquest (1534–1603). In *The Course of Irish History,* ed. T. W. Moody and F. X. Martin, pp. 174–88. Niwot, Colo.: Roberts Rinehart.

Hedstrom, P. and S. Ringen. 1990. Age and Income in Contemporary Society. In *Poverty, Inequality, and Income Distribution in Comparative Perspective: The Luxembourg Income Study,* ed. T. M. Smeeding, M. O'Higgins, and L. Rainwater, pp. 57–76. Washington, D.C.: Urban Institute.

Helper, H. R. 1860. *The Impending Crisis of the South: How to Meet It.* New York: A.B. Burdick.

Henry, D., ed. 1995. *Viking Ireland: Jens Worsaae's Accounts of His Visit to Ireland, 1846–47.* Balgavies, Scotland: Pinkfoot Press.

Henry, S. L. 1987. Factors Influencing Consumer Behavior in Turn-of-the-Century Phoenix, Arizona. In *Consumer Choice in Historical Archaeology,* ed. S. M. Spencer-Wood, pp. 359–81. New York: Plenum Press.

———. 1991. Consumers, Commodities, and Choices: A General Model of Consumer Behavior. *Historical Archaeology* 25(2): 3–14.

Herity, M. and G. Eogan. 1977. *Ireland in Prehistory.* London: Routledge.

Herm, G. 1976. *The Celts: The People Who Came out of the Darkness.* London: Weidenfeld and Nicolson.

Herskovits, M. J. 1958. *The Myth of the Negro Past.* Boston: Beacon Press.

Hertz, N. 2002. *The Silent Takeover: Global Capitalism and the Death of Democracy.* London: Arrow.

Herzog, D. 1998. *Poisoning the Minds of the Lower Orders.* Princeton, N.J.: Princeton University Press.

Hetherington, K. 1998. *Expressions of Identity: Space, Performance, Politics.* London: Sage.

Hewson, P. 1988. Bono: The White Nigger. In *Across the Frontiers: Ireland in the 1990s, Cultural—Political—Economic,* ed. R. Kearney, pp. 188–91. Dublin: Wolfhound Press.

Hickman, M. J. 1998. Reconstructing Deconstructing "Race": British Political Discourses about the Irish in Britain. *Ethnic and Racial Studies* 21: 288–307.

Higman, B. W. 1998. *Montpelier, Jamaica: A Plantation Community in Slavery and Freedom, 1739–1912.* Kingston, Jamaica: University Press of the West Indies.

Hillier, B. and J. Hanson. 1984. *The Social Logic of Space.* Cambridge: Cambridge University Press.

Hindley, R. 1990. *The Death of the Irish Language: A Qualified Obituary*. London: Routledge.

Hingley, R. 2000. *Roman Officers and English Gentlemen: The Imperial Origins of Roman Archaeology*. London: Routeldge.

Hinsley, C. M. 1989. Revising and Revisioning the History of Archaeology: Reflections on Region and Context. In *Tracing Archaeology's Past: The Historiography of Archaeology*, ed. A. L. Christenson, pp. 79–96. Carbondale: Southern Illinois University Press.

Hoberman, J. 2000. Totem and Taboo: The Myth of Race in Sports. *Skeptic* 8(1): 35–38.

Hodder, I. 1979. Economic and Social Stress and Material Culture Patterning. *American Antiquity* 44: 446–54.

———. 1982. *Symbols in Action: Ethnoarchaeological Studies of Material Culture*. Cambridge: Cambridge University Press.

———. 1986. *Reading the Past: Current Approaches to Interpretation in Archaeology*. Cambridge: Cambridge University Press.

Hodgen, M. T. 1971. *Early Anthropology in the Sixteenth and Seventeenth Centuries*. Philadelphia: University of Pennsylvania Press.

Holmes, T. R. 1899. *Caesar's Conquest of Gaul*. London: Macmillan.

Holt, C. A. 1991. Plants, Humans, and Culture: An Edible Model of Consuming Behavior. *Historical Archaeology* 25(2): 46–61.

Hope, M. 1991. *Atlantis: Myth or Reality?* London: Arkana.

Hopkins, T. K. 1982. The Study of the Capitalist World-Economy: Some Introductory Considerations. In *World-Systems Analysis: Theory and Methodology*, ed. T. K. Hopkins and I. Wallerstein, pp. 9–38. Beverly Hills, Calif.: Sage.

Horner, L. 1973. *Mistress of Falconhurst*. Greenwich, Conn.: Fawcett.

Horning, A. J. 2001. "Dwelling Houses in the Old Irish Barbarous Manner': Archaeological Evidence for Gaelic Architecture in an Ulster Plantation Village. In *Gaelic Ireland: Land, Lordship, and Settlement, c. 1250–c.1650*, ed. P. J. Duffy, D. Edwards, and E. FitzPatrick, pp. 375–96. Dublin: Four Courts Press.

Horvath, S. M, Jr. 1983. Ethnic Groups as Subjects of Archaeological Inquiry. In *Forgotten Places and Things: Archaeological Perspectives on American History*, ed. A. E. Ward, pp. 23–25. Albuquerque, N.M.: Center for Anthropological Studies.

House of Lords. 1847. *Lands of Ballykilcline, County Roscommon. Returns to Orders of the House of Lords, Dated 16th and 19th February 1847*. London: Her Majesty's Stationery Office.

Howes, D. 1996. Introduction: Commodities and Cultural Borders. In *Cross-Cultural Consumption Global Markets, Local Realities*, ed. D. Howes, pp. 1–16. London: Routledge.

Hubert, H. 1966. *The Rise of the Celts*. 1934. New York: Biblo and Tannen.

Huelsbeck, D. R. 1991. Faunal Remains and Consumer Behavior: What *Is* Being Measured? *Historical Archaeology* 25(2): 62–76.

Hull, K. L. 1997. An Analysis of Land Drainage at Gorttoose, County Roscommon, Ireland. Master's thesis, University of Missouri, Columbia.

Hundley, D. R. 1860. *Social Relations in Our Southern States*. New York: Henry B. Price.

Hyde, D. 1972. *The Religious Songs of Connacht*. 1906. Shannon: Irish Academic Press.

Ignatiev, N. 1995. *How the Irish Became White*. New York: Routledge.

Ignatiev, N. and J. Garvey, eds. 1996. *Race Traitor*. New York: Routledge.

Jackson, J. L., Jr. 1997. Why Race Dialogue Stutters. *The Nation* 264(12): 22–24.

Jackson, P. and N. Thrift. 1995. Geographies of Consumption. In *Acknowledging Consumption: A Review of New Studies*, ed. D. Miller, pp. 204–37. London: Routledge.

James, S. 1993. *The World of the Celts*. London: Thames and Hudson.

James, S. R., Jr. 1988. A Reassessment of the Chronological and Typological Framework of the Spanish Olive Jar. *Historical Archaeology* 22(1): 43–66.

Jardine, L. 1998. *Worldly Goods: A New History of the Renaissance*. New York: W.W. Norton.

Jeans, D. N. 1988. World Systems Theory: A Theoretical Context for Australian Historical Archaeology. In *Archaeology and Colonisation: Australia in the World Context*, ed. J. Birmingham, D. Baristow, and A. Wilson, pp. 57–63. Sydney: Australian Society for Historical Archaeology.

Jelks, E. B. 1968. Observations on the Scope of Historical Archaeology. *Historical Archaeology* 2: 1–3.

Johnson, J. C. 1994. Anthropological Contributions to the Study of Social Networks: A Review. In *Advances in Social Network Analysis: Research in the Social and Behavioral Sciences*, ed. S. Wasserman and J. Galaskiewicz, pp. 113–51. Thousand Oaks, Calif.: Sage.

Johnson, M. P. and J. L. Roark. 1984. *Black Masters: A Free Family of Color in the Old South*. New York: W.W. Norton.

Johnson, R. 1993. Pierre Bourdieu on Art, Literature, and Culture. In P. Bourdieu, *The Field of Cultural Production*, ed. R. Johnson, pp. 1–25. New York: Columbia University Press.

Jones, G. 1968. *A History of the Vikings*. London: Oxford University Press.

Jones, S. 1997. *The Archaeology of Ethnicity: Constructing Identities in the Past and Present*. London: Routledge.

———. 1999. Historical Categories and the Praxis of Identity: The Interpretation of Ethnicity in Historical Archaeology. In *Historical Archaeology: Back from the Edge*, ed. P. P. A. Funari, M. Hall, and S. Jones, pp. 219–32. London: Routledge.

Jones Hughes, T. 1965. Society and Settlement in Nineteenth-Century Ireland. *Irish Geography* 5(2): 79–96.

Jordan, P. 2001. *The Atlantis Syndrome*. Trupp, Gloucestershire: Sutton Publishing.

Josephy, A. M., Jr. 1994. *500 Nations: An Illustrated History of North American Indians*. New York: Knopf.

Joyce, A. A. 2000. The Founding of Monte Albán: Sacred Propositions and Social Practices. In *Agency in Archaeology*, ed. M.-A. Dobres and J. Robb, pp. 71–91. London: Routledge.

Joyce, P. W. 1996. *Irish Local Names Explained*. 1923. Dublin: Roberts Books.

Joyner, C. 1984. *Down by the Riverside: A South Carolina Slave Community*. Urbana: University of Illinois Press.

Kardulias, P. N., ed. 1999. *World-Systems Theory in Practice: Leadership, Production, and Exchange*. Lanham, Md.: Rowman and Littlefield.

Keating, J. 1996. *Irish Famine Facts*. Dublin: Teagasc.

Kelly, M. C. S. and R. E. Kelly. 1980. Approaches to Ethnic Identification in Historical Archaeology. In *Archaeological Perspectives on Ethnicity in America: Afro-American and Asian American Culture History*, ed. R. L. Schuyler, pp. 133–43. Farmingdale, N.Y.: Baywood.

Kemble, F. A. 1863. *Journal of a Residence on a Georgia Plantation in 1838–1839*. New York: Harper.

Kennedy, R. G. 1994. *Hidden Cities: The Discovery and Loss of Ancient North American Civilization*. New York: Penguin.

Kenny, K. 1998. *Making Sense of the Molly Maguires*. New York: Oxford University Press.

Kertzer, D. I. and D. Arel, eds. 2002. *Census and Identity: The Politics of Race, Ethnicity, and Language in National Censuses.* Cambridge: Cambridge University Press.

Killion, R. and C. Waller, eds. 1973. *Slavery Time When I Was Chillun Down on Marster's Plantation: Interviews with Georgia Slaves.* Savannah, Ga: Beehive Press.

Kinealy, C. 1997. *A Death-Dealing Famine: The Great Hunger in Ireland.* London: Pluto Press.

King, T. F. 2000. *Federal Planning and Historic Places: The Section 106 Process.* Walnut Creek, Calif.: Altamira Press.

King, A. and J. A. Freer. 1995. The Mississippian Southeast: A World-Systems Perspective. In *Native American Interactions: Multiscalar Analyses and Interpretations in the Eastern Woodlands,* ed. M. S. Nassaney and K. E. Sassaman, pp. 266–88. Knoxville: University of Tennessee Press.

Klein, T. H. 1991. Nineteenth-Century Ceramics and Models of Consumer Behavior. *Historical Archaeology* 25(2): 77–91.

Kniffen, F. B. and S. B. Hilliard. 1988. *Louisiana: Its Land and People.* Rev. ed. Baton Rouge: Louisiana State University Press.

Knobel, D. T. 1986. *Paddy and the Republic: Ethnicity and Nationality in Antebellum America.* Middletown, Conn.: Wesleyan University Press.

Knoke, D. and J. H. Kuklinski. 1982. *Network Analysis.* Newbury Park, Calif.: Sage.

Knott, J. W. 1984. Land, Kinship, and Identity: The Cultural Roots of Agrarian Agitation in Eighteenth- and Nineteenth-Century Ireland. *Journal of Peasant Studies* 12: 93–108.

Knox, G. 1846. Letter to John Burke. Quit Rent Office Papers, C2, Cases and Opinions, (2B.38.120). Dublin: National Archives of Ireland.

Kohl, P. L. 1987. The Use and Abuse of World Systems Theory: The Case of the Pristine West Asian State. In *Advances in Archaeological Method and Theory,* vol. 11, ed. M. B. Schiffer, pp. 1–35. San Diego: Academic Press.

Kootz, W. 2000. *Rothenburg on the Tauber.* Heidelberg: Kunstverlag Edm. von König.

Kopytoff, I. 1986. The Cultural Biography of Things: Commodization as Process. In *The Social Life of Things: Commodities in Cultural Perspective,* ed. A. Appadurai, pp. 64–91. Cambridge: Cambridge University Press.

Kroeber, A. L. 1919. On the Principle of Order in Civilization as Exemplified by Changes in Fashion. *American Anthropologist* 21: 235–63.

———. 1936. So-Called Social Science. *Journal of Social Philosophy* 1: 317–40.

———. 1944. *Configurations of Culture Growth.* Berkeley: University of California Press.

———. 1948. *Anthropology.* New York: Harcourt, Brace.

———. 1966. *An Anthropologist Looks at History.* ed. T. Kroeber, Berkeley: University of California Press.

Kroeber, A. L. and J. Richardson. 1940. Three Centuries of Women's Dress Fashions: A Quantitative Analysis. *University of California Anthropological Records* 5: 111–53.

Kurien, P. 1994. Colonialism and Ethnogenesis: A Study of Kerala, India. *Theory and Society* 23: 385–417.

LaDuke, W. 1992. Indigenous Environmental Perspectives: A North American Primer. *Native Americas Journal* 9(2): 52–71.

Landberg, L. C. W. 1967. Problems of Post-1800 Urban Sites Archaeology at Old Sacramento, California. *Historical Archaeology* 1: 71–78.

Lane, J. F. 2000. *Pierre Bourdieu: A Critical Introduction.* London: Pluto Press.

Larsen, C. S. 1993. On the Frontier of Contact: Mission Bioarchaeology in La

Florida. In *The Spanish Missions of La Florida*, ed. B. G. McEwan, pp. 322–56. Gainesville: University Press of Florida.

Lash, S. 1993. Pierre Bourdieu: Cultural Economy and Social Change. In *Bourdieu: Critical Perspectives*, ed. C. Calhoun, E. LiPuma, and M. Postone, pp. 193–211. Chicago: University of Chicago Press.

Lasswell, H. and A. Kaplan. 1950. *Power and Society*. New Haven, Conn.: Yale University Press.

Law, J. and K. Hetherington. 2002. Materialities, Spatialities, Globalities. In *The Spaces of Postmodernity: Readings in Human Geography*, ed. M. J. Dear and S. Flusty, pp. 390–401. Oxford: Blackwell.

Lawler, E. J. and J. Yoon. 1996. Commitment in Exchange Relations: Test of a Theory of Relational Cohesion. *American Sociological Review* 61: 89–108.

Lawrence, S. 1999. Towards a Feminist Archaeology of Households: Gender and Household Structure on the Australian Goldfields. In *The Archaeology of Household Activities*, ed. P. M. Allison, pp. 121–41. London: Routledge.

———. 2000. *Dolly's Creek: An Archaeology of a Victorian Goldfields Community*. Melbourne: Melbourne University Press.

Laxton, E. 1996. *The Famine Ships: The Irish Exodus to America*. New York: Henry Holt.

Leacock, E. B., ed. 1971. *The Culture of Poverty: A Critique*. New York: Simon and Schuster.

Lee, D., trans. 1977. *Plato: Timaeus and Critias*. London: Penguin.

Lefebvre, H. 1979. Space: Social Product and Use Value. In *Critical Sociology: European Perspectives*, ed. J. W. Freiberg, pp. 285–95. New York: Irvington.

———. 1982. *The Sociology of Marx*. Trans. N. Guterman. New York: Columbia University Press.

———. 1984. *Everyday Life in the Modern World*. Trans. S. Rabinovitch. New Brunswick, N.J.: Transaction Books.

———. 1991. *The Production of Space*. Trans. D. Nicholson-Smith. Oxford: Blackwell.

Le Hir, M-P. 2000. Cultural Studies Bourdieu's Way: Women, Leadership, and Feminist Theory. In *Pierre Bourdieu: Fieldwork in Culture*, ed. N. Brown and I. Szeman, pp. 123–44. Lanham, Md.: Rowman and Littlefield.

Leiman, M. M. 1993. *Political Economy of Racism*. London: Pluto Press.

Lennon, C. 1994. *Sixteenth-Century Ireland: The Incomplete Conquest*. Dublin: Gill and Macmillan.

Lenski, G. 1966. *Power and Privilege*. New York: McGraw-Hill.

Leonard, R. D. 1993. The Persistence of an Explanatory Dilemma in Contact Period Studies. In *Ethnohistory and Archaeology: Approaches to Postcontact Change in the Americas*, ed. J. D. Rogers and S. M. Wilson, pp. 31–43. New York: Plenum Press.

Leone, M. P. 1995a. A Historical Archaeology of Capitalism. *American Anthropologist* 97: 251–68.

———. 1995b. Letter to the Editor. *Bulletin of the Society for American Archaeology* 13(5): 3.

Leone, M. P. and C. A. Crosby. 1987. Epilogue: Middle Range Theory in Historical Archaeology. In *Consumer Choice in Historical Archaeology*, ed. S. M. Spencer-Wood, pp. 397–410. New York: Plenum Press.

Leone, M. P. and P. B. Potter, Jr. 1988. Introduction: Issues in Historical Archaeology. In *The Recovery of Meaning: Historical Archaeology in the Eastern United States*, ed. M. P. Leone and P. B. Potter, Jr., pp. 1–22. Washington, D.C.: Smithsonian Institution Press.

———. 1994. Historical Archaeology of Capitalism. *Bulletin of the Society for American Archaeology* 12(4): 14–15.

————, eds. 1999. *Historical Archaeologies of Capitalism.* New York: Kluwer Academic/ Plenum Press.

Leone, M. P., P. B. Potter, Jr., and P. A. Shackel. 1987. Toward a Critical Archaeology. *Current Anthropology* 28: 283–302.

Lesser, A. 1961. Social Fields and the Evolution of Society. *Southwestern Journal of Anthropology* 17: 40–48.

Levathes, L. 1996. *When China Ruled the Seas: The Treasure Fleet of the Dragon Throne, 1405–1433.* New York: Oxford University Press.

Lewin, K. 1951. *Field Theory in Social Science: Selected Theoretical Papers.* ed. D. Cartwright, New York: Harper.

Lewis, G. C. 1836. *On Local Disturbances in Ireland and on the Irish Church Question.* London: B. Fellowes.

Lewis, O. 1959. *Five Families: Mexican Case Studies in the Culture of Poverty.* New York: Basic Books.

————. 1966. *La Vida: A Puerto Rican Family in the Culture of Poverty—San Juan and New York.* New York: Random House.

Lewis, S. 1984. *A Topographical Dictionary of Ireland.* 1837. Baltimore: Genealogical Publishing.

Lichtenstein, P. M. 1983. *An Introduction to Post-Keynesian and Marxian Theories of Value and Price.* Armonk, N.Y.: M. E. Sharpe.

Lightfoot, K. G. 1995. Culture Contact Studies: Redefining the Relationship Between Prehistoric and Historical Archaeology. *American Antiquity* 60: 199–217.

Lin, N. 2001. *Social Capital: A Theory of Social Structure and Action.* Cambridge: Cambridge University Press.

Lipman-Blumen, J. 1994. The Existential Bases of Power Relationships: The Gender Role Case. In *Power/Gender: Social Relations in Theory and Practice,* ed. H. L. Radtke and H. J. Stam, pp. 108–35. London: Sage.

Lister, F. C. and R. H. Lister. 1976. *A Descriptive Dictionary for 500 Years of Spanish-Tradition Ceramics: 13th Through 18th Centuries.* Special Publication 1. Tucson, Ariz.: Society for Historical Archaeology.

————. 1978. The First Mexican Maiolicas: Imported and Locally Produced. *Historical Archaeology* 12: 1–24.

Little, B. J. 1994. People with History: An Update on Historical Archaeology in the United States. *Journal of Archaeological Method and Theory* 1: 5–40.

Little, B. J. and P. A. Shackel, eds. 1992. *Meanings and Uses of Material Culture.* Historical Archaeology 26, 3. Tucson, Ariz: Society for Historical Archeaology.

Littlefield, D. C. 1981. *Rice and Slaves: Ethnicity and the Slave Trade in Colonial South Carolina.* Urbana: University of Illinois Press.

Litwack, L. F. 1979. *Been in the Storm So Long: The Aftermath of Slavery.* New York: Knopf.

Lloyd-Morgan, G. 1995. Appearance, Life, and Leisure. In *The Celtic World,* ed. M. J. Green, pp. 95–120. London: Routledge.

Longacre, W. A. 1970. *Archaeology as Anthropology: A Case Study.* Anthropological Papers of the University of Arizona 17. Tucson: University of Arizona Press.

Lovell, T. 2000. Thinking Feminism With and Against Bourdieu. In *Reading Bourdieu on Society and Culture,* ed. B. Fowler, pp. 27–48. Oxford: Blackwell.

Loveman, M. 1999. Is "Race" Essential? *American Sociological Review* 64: 891–98.

Lucie-Smith, E. 1994. *Race, Sex, and Gender in Contemporary Art.* New York: H. N. Abrams.

Luckombe, P. 1780. *A Tour Through Ireland.* Dublin: J. and R. Bryn.

Lukes, S. 1974. *Power: A Radical View.* London: Macmillan.

Maberly, [Mrs.]. 1847. *The Present State of Ireland and Its Remedy.* London: James Ridgway.

MacDonnell, E. [Hibernicus] 1823. *Practical Views and Suggestions on the Present Condition and Permanent Improvement of Ireland.* Dublin: J. Carrick and Son.

MacPherson, S. and R. Silburn. 1998. The Meaning and Measurement of Poverty. In *Poverty: A Persistent Global Reality,* ed. J. Dixon and D. Macarov, pp. 1–19. London: Routledge.

McAnany, P. A. 2001. Cosmology and the Institutionalization of Hierarchy in the Maya Region. In *From Leaders to Rulers,* ed. J. Haas, pp. 125–48. New York: Kluwer Academic/Plenum Press.

McBride, W. S. and K. A. McBride. 1987. Socioeconomic Variation in a Late Antebellum Southern Town: The View from Archaeological and Documentary Sources. In *Consumer Choice in Historical Archaeology,* ed. S. M. Spencer-Wood, pp. 143–61. New York: Plenum Press.

McCall, L. 1992. Does Gender Fit? Bourdieu, Feminism, and Conceptions of Social Order. *Theory and Society* 21: 837–67.

McCann, W. J. 1988. The National Socialist Perversion of Archaeology. *World Archaeological Bulletin* 2: 51–54.

———. 1990. "Volk und Germanentum": The Presentation of the Past in Nazi Germany. In *The Politics of the Past,* ed. P. Gathercole and D. Lowenthal, pp. 74–88. London: Unwin Hyman.

McCracken, G. 1986. Culture and Consumption: A Theoretical Account of the Structure and Movement of the Cultural Meaning of Consumer Goods. *Journal of Consumer Research* 13: 71–84.

———. 1990. *Culture and Consumption: New Approaches to the Symbolic Character of Consumer Goods and Activities.* Bloomington: Indiana University Press.

McErlean, T. 1983. The Irish Townland System of Landscape Organisation. In *Landscape Archaeology in Ireland,* ed. T. Reeves-Smyth and F. Hamond, pp. 315–39. Oxford: British Archaeological Report.

McEwan, B. G. 1992. The Role of Ceramics in Spain and Spanish America During the 16th Century. *Historical Archaeology* 26(1): 92–108.

———. ed. 1993. *The Spanish Missions of La Florida.* Gainesville: University Press of Florida.

———. 1995. Spanish Precedents and Domestic Life at Puerto Real: The Archaeology of Two Spanish Homesites. In *Puerto Real: The Archaeology of a Sixteenth-Century Spanish Town in Hispaniola,* ed. K. Deagan, pp. 197–229. Gainesville: University Press of Florida.

McGuire, R. H. 1982. The Study of Ethnicity in Historical Archaeology. *Journal of Anthropological Archaeology* 1: 159–78.

———. 1983. Ethnic Group, Status, and Material Culture at the Rancho Punta de Agua. In *Forgotten Places and Things: Archaeological Perspectives on American History,* ed. A. E. Ward, pp. 193–203. Albuquerque, N.M.: Center for Anthropological Studies.

———. 1986. Economics and Modes of Production in the Prehistoric Southwestern Periphery. In *Ripples in the Chichimec Sea: New Considerations of Southwestern-Mesoamerican Interactions,* ed. F. J. Mathien and R. H. McGuire, pp. 243–69. Carbondale: Southern Illinois University Press.

———. 1996. The Limits of World-Systems Theory for the Study of Prehistory. In *Pre-Columbian World Systems,* ed. P. N. Peregrine and G. M. Feinman, pp. 51–64. Madison, Wis.: Prehistory Press.

McIlroy, J. and M. Praetzellis, eds. 1997. *Vanished Community: 19th-Century San*

Francisco Neighborhoods From Fourth Street to Mission Creek and Beyond. Rohnert Park, Calif.: Anthropological Studies Center, Sonoma State University.

McKay, J. 1975. A Theoretical Approach to Historical Archaeology. *Conference on Historic Site Archaeology Papers* 9(2): 129–40.

McManus, M. 1984. Coarse Ware. In *Ireland's Traditional Crafts.* ed. D. Shaw-Smith, pp. 186–90. London: Thames and Hudson.

McMurtry, J. 1998. *Unequal Freedoms: The Global Market as an Ethical System.* Toronto: Garamond Press.

McNeill, G. 1975. *The Plantation.* New York: Bantam.

McNeill, T. 1997. *Castles in Ireland: Feudal Power in a Gaelic World.* London: Routledge.

Magdol, E. 1977. *A Right to the Land: Essays on the Freedmen's Community.* Westport, Conn.: Greenwood Press.

Magrabi, F. M., Y. S. Chung, S. S. Cha, and S-J Yang. 1991. *The Economics of Household Consumption.* New York: Praeger.

Malefijt, A. de W. 1974. *Images of Man: A History of Anthropological Thought.* New York: Knopf.

Mallory, J. P. and T. E. McNeill. 1991. *The Archaeology of Ulster: From Colonization to Plantation.* Belfast: Institute of Irish Studies, Queen's University.

Marcuse, H. 1972. *Counterrevolution and Revolt.* Boston: Beacon Press.

Marquardt, W. H. 1992. Dialectical Archaeology. In *Archaeological Method and Theory,* vol. 4, ed. M. B. Schiffer, pp. 101–4. Tucson, Ariz.: University of Arizona Press.

Martin, P. S. 1971. The Revolution in Archaeology. *American Antiquity* 36: 1–8.

Marx, K. 1954. *The Communist Manifesto.* 1848. Trans. S. Moore. Chicago: Henry Regnery.

————. 1967. *Capital: A Critique of Political Economy.* 1887. New York: International Publishers.

————. 1970. *A Contribution to the Critique of Political Economy.* 1859. Ed. M. Dobb. New York: International Publishers.

————. 1983. *The Portable Marx.* Comp. E. Kamenka. New York: Penguin.

Marx, K. and F. Engels. 1970. *The German Ideology.* 1846–47. Ed. C. J. Arthur. New York: International Publishers.

————. 1971. *Ireland and the Irish Question.* Moscow: Progress Publishers.

Matthews, C. 1996. *The Elements of the Celtic Tradition.* Shaftesbury, Dorset: Element.

Maybury-Lewis, D. 1997. *Indigenous Peoples, Ethnic Groups, and the State.* Boston: Allyn and Bacon.

Mayne, A. and T. Murray. 2001. *The Archaeology of Urban Landscapes: Explorations in Slumland.* Cambridge: Cambridge University Press.

Meadows, K. 1999. The Appetites of Households in Early Roman Britain. In *The Archaeology of Household Activities,* ed. P. M. Allison, pp. 101–20. London: Routledge.

Megaw, R. and V. Megaw. 1995. The Nature and Function of Celtic Art. In *The Celtic World,* ed. M. J. Green, pp. 345–75. London: Routledge.

Meltzer, D. J. 1998. Introduction: Ephraim Squier, Edwin Davis, and the Making of an American Archaeological Classic. In *Ancient Monuments of the Mississippi Valley by Ephraim G. Squier and Edwin H. Davis,* ed. D. J. Meltzer, pp. 1–95. Washington, D.C.: Smithsonian Institution Press.

Merrill, A. P. 1869. Southern Labor. *DeBow's Review* 6: 586–92.

Mey, H. 1972. *Field-Theory: A Study of Its Application in the Social Sciences.* Trans. D. Scott. New York: St. Martin's Press.

Meyer, M. D. and S. B. Stewart, eds. 2000. *Block Technical Report: Historical Archaeology I-880 Cypress Replacement Project, Block 3*. Oakland: California Department of Transportation.

Miles, R. 1989. *Racism*. London: Routledge.

Miles, S. 2001. *Social Theory in the Real World*. London: Routledge.

Milisauskas, S. 1978. *European Prehistory*. New York: Academic Press.

Miller, D. 1987. *Material Culture and Mass Consumption*. Oxford: Blackwell.

———. 1994. *Modernity, An Ethnographic Approach: Dualism and Mass Consumption in Trinidad*. Oxford: Berg.

———. 1995. Consumption Studies as the Transformation of Anthropology. In *Acknowledging Consumption: A Review of New Studies*, ed. D. Miller, pp. 264–95. London: Routledge.

Miller, D. and C. Tilley. 1984. Ideology, Power, and Prehistory: An Introduction. In *Ideology, Power, and Prehistory*, ed. D. Miller and C. Tilley, pp. 1–15. Cambridge: Cambridge University Press.

Miller, G. L. 1980. Classification and Economic Scaling of 19th Century Ceramics. *Historical Archaeology* 14: 1–40.

———. 1991. A Revised Set of CC Index Values for Classification and Economic Scaling of English Ceramics from 1787 to 1880. *Historical Archaeology* 25(1): 1–25.

Miller, J. C. 1988. *Way of Death: Merchant Capitalism and the Angola Slave Trade, 1730–1830*. Madison: University of Wisconsin Press.

Mills, C. W. 1959. *The Sociological Imagination*. New York: Oxford University Press.

Milne, C. and P. Crabtree. 2000. Revealing Meals: Ethnicity, Economic Status, and Diet at Five Points, 1800–1860. In *Tales of Five Points: Working-Class Life in Nineteenth-Century New York*, vol. 2, ed. R. Yamin, pp. 130–96. West Chester, Pa.: John Milner Associates.

Min, P. G. and R. Kim. 2000. Formation of Ethnic and Racial Identities: Narratives by Young Asian-American Professionals. *Ethnic and Racial Studies* 23: 735–60.

Mintz, S. W. and R. Price. 1976. *An Anthropological Approach to the Afro-American Past: A Caribbean Perspective*. Philadelphia: Institute for the Study of Human Issues.

Mitchel, J. 1860. *The Last Conquest of Ireland (Perhaps)*. Glasgow: Cameron and Ferguson.

———. 1868. *The History of Ireland from the Treaty of Limerick to the Present Time*. New York: D. and J. Sadlier.

Mitchell, J. C. 1974. Social Networks. *Annual Review of Anthropology* 3: 279–99.

Mitchell, M. 1936. *Gone With the Wind*. New York: Macmillan.

Mitchell, T. 1990. Everyday Metaphors of Power. *Theory and Society* 19: 545–77.

Monks, G. G. 1999. On Rejecting the Concept of Socio-Economic Status in Historical Archaeology. In *Historical Archaeology: Back from the Edge*, ed. P. P. A. Funari, M. Hall, and S. Jones, pp. 204–16. London: Routledge.

Moore, L. E. 1995a. Letter to the Editor. *Bulletin of the Society for American Archaeology* 13(1): 3.

———. 1995b. Letter to the Editor. *Bulletin of the Society for American Archaeology* 13(4): 3–4.

Moore, R. 2001. Educational Malpractice: Why Do So Many Biology Teachers Endorse Creationism? *Skeptical Inquirer* 25(6): 38–43.

Moore, S. M. 1981. *An Antebellum Barrier Island Plantation: In Search of an Archaeological Pattern*. Doctoral dissertation, University of Florida. University Microfilms, Ann Arbor.

————. 1985. Social and Economic Status on the Coastal Plantation: An Archaeological Perspective. In *The Archaeology of Slavery and Plantation Life*, ed. T. A. Singleton, pp. 141–60. Orlando: Academic Press.

Moore, T. 1857. *The Poetical Works of Thomas Moore.* New York: Leavitt and Allen.

Moore, W. E. and R. M. Williams. 1942. Stratification in the Ante-Bellum South. *American Sociological Review* 7: 343–51.

Moreland, J. 2001. *Archaeology and Text.* London: Duckworth.

Mouer, L. D. 1993. Chesapeake Creoles: The Creation of Folk Cultures in Colonial Virginia. In *The Archaeology of 17th-Century Virginia*, ed. T. R. Reinhart and D. J. Pogue, pp. 105–66. Courtland: The Archaeological Society of Virginia.

Mouer, L. D., M. E. N. Hodges, S. R. Potter, S. L. H. Renaud, I. Noël Hume, D. J. Pogue, M. W. McCartney, and T. E. Davidson. 1999. Colonware Pottery, Chesapeake Pipes, and "Uncritical Assumptions." In *"I, Too, Am America": Archaeological Studies of African-American Life*, ed. T. A. Singleton, pp. 75–115. Charlottesville: University Press of Virginia.

Mukerji, C. 1983. *From Graven Images: Patterns of Modern Materialism.* New York: Columbia University Press.

Muldoon, J. 2000. Race or Culture: Medieval Notions of Difference. In *Race and Racism in Theory and Practice*, ed. B. Lang, pp. 79–97. Lanham, Md.: Rowman and Littlefield.

Mullins, P. R. 1996. The Contradiction of Consumption: An Archaeology of African America and Consumer Culture, 1850–1930. Doctoral dissertation, University of Massachusetts, Amherst.

————. 1999a. *Race and Affluence: An Archaeology of African America and Consumer Culture.* New York: Kluwer Academic/Plenum Press.

————. 1999b. Race and the Genteel Consumer: Class and African-American Consumption, 1850–1930. *Historical Archaeology* 33(1): 22–38.

————. 2001. Racializing the Parlor: Race and Victorian Bric-a-Brac Consumption. In *Race and the Archaeology of Identity*, ed. C. E. Orser, Jr, pp. 158–76. Salt Lake City: University of Utah Press.

Mullins, P. R. and R. Paynter. 2000. Representing Colonizers: An Archaeology of Creolization, Ethnogenesis, and Indigenous Material Culture Among the Haida. *Historical Archaeology* 34(3): 73–84.

Nash, D. 1976. Reconstructing Poseidonios' Celtic Ethnography: Some Considerations. *Britannia* 7: 111–26.

Ngũgĩ wa Thiong'o. 1986. *Decolonising the Mind: The Politics of Language in African Literature.* Oxford: James Currey.

Nicholson, A. 1847. *Ireland's Welcome to the Stranger: or, Excursions through Ireland in 1844 and 1845, for the Purpose of Personally Investigating the Condition of the Poor.* London: Charles Galpin.

————. 1998. *Annals of the Famine in Ireland 1851.* Ed. M. Murphy. Dublin: Lilliput Press.

Noël Hume, I. 1964. Archaeology: Handmaiden to History. *North Carolina Historical Review* 41: 215–25.

————. 1969. *A Guide to Artifacts of Colonial America.* New York: Knopf.

————. 1972. *Historical Archaeology.* New York: Knopf.

Norton-Taylor, D. 1974. *The Celts.* New York: Time-Life.

Nostrand, R. L. 1970. The Hispanic-American Borderland: Delimitation of an American Culture Region. *Annals of the Association of American Geographers* 60: 638–61.

Nott, J. C. 1866. Art. IV. Climates of the South in Their Relations to White Labor. *DeBow's Review* 1: 166–73.

Nowak, L. 1983. *Property and Power: Towards a Non-Marxian Historical Materialism.* Dordrecht: Reidel.

Oates, J. C. 1987. *On Boxing.* Garden City, N.Y.: Dolphin/Doubleday.

Oates, W. J. 1963. *Aristotle and the Problem of Value.* Princeton, N.J.: Princeton University Press.

O'Brien, G. 1921. *The Economic History of Ireland, From the Union to the Famine.* London: Longmans, Green.

Ó Ciosáin, N. 1997. *Print and Popular Culture in Ireland, 1750–1850.* New York: St. Martin's Press.

O'Connell, J. 2002. Travellers in Ireland: An Examination of Discrimination and Racism. In *Racism and Anti-Racism in Ireland,* ed. R. Lentin and R. McVeigh, pp. 49–62. Belfast: Beyond the Pale.

O'Conor, K. D. 2001. The Morphology of Gaelic Lordly Sites in North Connacht. In *Gaelic Ireland, c. 1250 - c. 1650: Land, Lordship, and Settlement,* ed. P. J. Duffy, D. Edwards, and E. FitzPatrick, pp. 329–45. Dublin: Four Courts Press.

O'Dovonan, J. 1927. *Letters Containing Information Relative to the Antiquities of the County of Roscommon, Collected During the Progress of the Ordnance Survey in 1837,* vol. 2, ed. M. O'Flanagan, Bray, typescript.

Olmsted, F. L. 1856. *A Journey in the Seaboard Slave States with Remarks on Their Economy.* New York: Dix and Edwards.

Olsen, B. and Z. Kobylínski. 1991. Ethnicity in Anthropological and Archaeological Research: A Norwegian-Polish Perspective. *Archaeologia Polona* 29: 5–27.

Olsen, J. W. 1983. An Analysis of East Asian Coins Excavated in Tucson, Arizona. *Historical Archaeology* 17(2): 41–55.

Omi, M. and H. Winant. 1983. By the Rivers of Babylon: Race in the United States. *Socialist Review* 13: 31–65.

Orser, C. E. Jr. 1980. An Archaeological and Historical Socioeconomic Analysis of Arikara Mortuary Practice. Doctoral dissertation, Southern Illinois University, Carbondale.

———. 1987. Plantation Status and Consumer Choice: A Materialist Framework for Historical Archaeology. In *Consumer Choice in Historical Archaeology,* ed. S. M. Spencer-Wood, pp. 121–37. New York: Plenum Press.

———. 1988a. The Archaeological Analysis of Plantation Society: Replacing Status and Caste with Economics and Power. *American Antiquity* 53: 735–51.

———. 1988b. *The Material Basis of the Postbellum Tenant Plantation: Historical Archaeology in the South Carolina Piedmont.* Athens: University of Georgia Press.

———. 1989. On Plantations and Patterns. *Historical Archaeology* 23(2): 28–40.

———. 1990. Archaeological Approaches to New World Plantation Slavery. In *Archaeological Method and Theory,* vol. 2, ed. M. B. Schiffer, pp. 111–54. Tucson: University of Arizona Press.

———. 1991a. The Archaeological Search for Ethnicity in the Historic United States. *Archaeologia Polona* 29: 109–21.

———. 1991b. The Continued Pattern of Dominance: Landlord and Tenant on the Postbellum Cotton Plantation. In *The Archaeology of Inequality,* ed. R. H. McGuire and R. Paynter, pp. 40–54. Oxford: Blackwell.

———. 1992a. Beneath the Material Surface of Things: Commodities, Artifacts, and Slave Plantations. *Historical Archaeology* 26(3): 95–104.

———. 1992b. The Illinois and Michigan Canal: Historical Archaeology and the Irish Experience in America. *Éire-Ireland* 27: 122–34.

————. 1994a. The Archaeology of African-American Slave Religion in the Antebellum South. *Cambridge Archaeological Journal* 4: 33–45.

————. 1994b. Consumption, Consumerism, and Things from the Earth. *Historical Methods* 27: 61–70.

————. 1996a. *A Historical Archaeology of the Modern World.* New York: Plenum Press.

————. 1996b. Can There Be an Archaeology of the Great Famine? In *"Fearful Realities": New Perspectives on the Famine,* ed. C. Morash and R. Hayes, pp. 77–89. Dublin: Irish Academic Press.

————. 1997a. Archaeology and Modern Irish History. *Irish Studies Review* 18: 2–7.

————. 1997b. Of Dishes and Drains: An Archaeological Perspective on Irish Rural Life in the Great Famine Era. *New Hibernia Review* 1: 120–35.

————. 1998a. Archaeology of the African Diaspora. *Annual Review of Anthropology* 27: 63–82.

————. 1998b. The Challenge of Race to American Historical Archaeology. *American Anthropologist* 100: 661–68.

————. 2000a. The Father of Atlantis: Ignatius Donnelly Created the Modern Myth and Modeled Pseudo-Archaeology. *Scientific American Discovering Archaeology* 2(5): 24–25.

————. 2000b. Why Is There No Archaeology in Irish Studies? *Irish Studies Review* 8: 157–65.

————. 2001a. The Anthropology in American Historical Archaeology. *American Anthropologist* 103: 621–32.

————. 2001b. Vessels of Honor and Dishonor: The Symbolic Character of Irish Earthenware. *New Hibernia Review* 5: 83–100.

————. ed. 2001c. *Race and the Archaeology of Identity.* Salt Lake City: University of Utah Press.

————. 2001d. Race and the Archaeology of Identity in the Modern World. In *Race and the Archaeology of Identity,* ed. C. E. Orser, Jr., pp. 1–13. Salt Lake City: University of Utah Press.

Orser, C. E., Jr. and B. M. Fagan. 1995. *Historical Archaeology.* New York: HarperCollins.

Ortner, S. B. 1984. Theory in Anthropology Since the Sixties. *Comparative Studies in Society and History* 26: 126–66.

Osborne, S. D. 1995. "The Voice of the Law": John Marshall and Indian Land Rights. In *Issues in Native American Cultural Identity,* ed. M. K. Green, pp. 57–80. New York: Peter Lang.

Otto, J. S. 1977. Artifacts and Status Differences: A Comparison of Ceramics from Planter, Overseer, and Slave Sites on an Antebellum Plantation. In *Research Strategies in Historical Archaeology,* ed. S. South, pp. 91–118. New York: Academic Press.

————. 1980. Race and Class on Antebellum Plantations. In *Archaeological Perspectives on Ethnicity in America: Afro-American and Asian American Culture History,* ed. R. L. Schuyler, pp. 3–13. Farmingdale, N.Y.: Baywood.

————. 1984. *Cannon's Point Plantation, 1794–1860: Living Conditions and Status Patterns in the Old South.* New York: Academic Press.

Packenham-Mahon Papers. Manuscript Division, National Library of Ireland, Dublin.

Padgett, J. F. and C. K. Ansell. 1993. Robust Action and the Rise of the Medici, 1400–1434. *American Journal of Sociology* 98: 1259–1319.

Pailes, R. A. and J. W. Whitecotton. 1979. The Greater Southwest and the

Mesoamerican "World" System: An Explanatory Model of Frontier Relationships. In *The Frontier*, vol. 2, *Comparative Studies*, ed. W. W. Savage, Jr. and S. I. Thompson, pp. 105–21. Norman: University of Oklahoma Press.

Parenti, M. 1999. *History as Mystery*. San Francisco: City Lights Books.

Park, R. E. 1928. The Bases of Race Prejudice. *Annals of the American Academy of Political and Social Science* 140: 11–20.

————. 1950. *Race and Culture*. Glencoe, Ill.: Free Press.

Patterson, N. T. 1994. *Cattle-Lords and Clansmen: The Social Structure of Early Ireland*. 2nd ed. Notre Dame, Ind.: University of Notre Dame Press.

Patterson, T. C. 1995. *Toward a Social History of Archaeology in the United States*. Fort Worth: Harcourt Brace.

————. 2001. *A Social History of Anthropology in the United States*. Oxford: Berg.

Pauketat, T. R. 2000. The Tragedy of the Commoners. In *Agency in Archaeology*, ed. M.-A. Dobres and J. Robb, pp. 113–29. London: Routledge.

————. 2001. Practice and History in Archaeology. *Anthropological Theory* 1: 73–98.

Paynter, R. 1982. *Models of Spatial Inequality Settlement Patterns in Historical Archaeology*. New York: Academic Press.

————. 1990. Afro-Americans in the Massachusetts Historical Landscape. In *The Politics of the Past*, ed. P. Gathercole and D. Lowenthal, pp. 49–62. London: Unwin Hyman.

————. 2000a. Historical and Anthropological Archaeology: Forging Alliances. *Journal of Archaeological Research* 8: 1–37.

————. 2000b. Historical Archaeology and the Post-Columbian World of North America. *Journal of Archaeological Research* 8: 169–217.

Paynter, R. and R. H. McGuire. 1991. The Archaeology of Inequality: Material Culture, Domination, and Resistance. In *The Archaeology of Inequality*, ed. R. H. McGuire and R. Paynter, pp. 1–27. Oxford: Blackwell.

Paynter, R., S. Hautaniemi, and N. Muller. 1994. The Landscapes of the W. E. B. Du Bois Boyhood Homesite: An Agenda for an Archaeology of the Color Line. In *Race*, ed. S. Gregory and R. Sanjek, pp. 285–318. New Brunswick, N.J.: Rutgers University Press.

Pellegrino, C. 1991. *Unearthing Atlantis: An Archaeological Odyssey*. New York: Random House.

Pennick, N. 1996. *Celtic Sacred Landscapes*. London: Thames and Hudson.

Peregrine, P. N. 1995. Networks of Power: The Mississippian World-System. In *Native American Interactions: Multiscalar Analyses and Interpretations in the Eastern Woodlands*, ed. M. S. Nassaney and K. E. Sassaman, pp. 245–65. Knoxville: University of Tennessee Press.

————. 1996. Introduction: World-Systems Theory and Archaeology. In *Pre-Columbian World Systems*, ed. P. N. Peregrine and G. M. Feinman, pp. 1–10. Madison, Wis.: Prehistory Press.

Peregrine, P. N. and G. M. Feinman, eds. 1996. *Pre-Columbian World Systems*. Madison, Wis.: Prehistory Press.

Perry, W. and R. Paynter. 1999. Artifacts, Ethnicity, and the Archaeology of African Americans. In *"I, Too, Am America": Archaeological Studies of African-American Life*, ed. T. A. Singleton, pp. 299–310. Charlottesville: University Press of Virginia.

Pettula, T. K. 1993. Kee-Oh-Na-Wah'-Wah: The Effects of European Contact on the Caddoan Indians of Texas, Louisiana, Arkansas, and Oklahoma. In *Ethnohistory and Archaeology: Approaches to Postcontact Change in the Americas*, ed. J. D. Rogers and S. M. Wilson, pp. 89–109. New York: Plenum Press.

Phillips, P. 1980. *The Prehistory of Europe.* London: Allen Lane.

Piggott, S. 1965. *Ancient Europe from the Beginnings of Agriculture to Classical Antiquity.* Chicago: Aldine.

Pigot. 1823. *The Commercial Directory for Ireland, Scotland, &c, 1820, 1821, 1822.* London: Pigot and Company.

————1824. *Pigot and Co.'s City of Dublin and Hibernia Provincial Directory.* London: Pigot and Company.

Pim, J. 1848. *The Condition and Prospects of Ireland, and the Evils Arising from the Present Distribution of Landed Property: With Suggestions for a Remedy.* Dublin: Hodges and Smith.

Postman, N. 1993. *Technopoly: The Surrender of Culture to Technology.* New York: Vintage.

Postone, M., E. LiPuma, and C. Calhoun. 1993. Introduction: Bourdieu and Social Theory. In *Bourdieu: Critical Perspectives*, ed. C. Calhoun, E. LiPuma, and M. Postone, pp. 1–13. Chicago: University of Chicago Press.

Powell, T. G. E. 1958. *The Celts.* New York: Praeger.

Praetzellis, A. C. 1991. The Archaeology of a Victorian City: Sacramento, California. Doctoral dissertation, University of California, Berkeley.

————. 1999. The Archaeology of Ethnicity: An Example from Sacramento, California's Early Chinese District. In *Old and New Worlds*, ed. G. Egan and R. L. Michael, pp. 127–35. Oxford: Oxbow Books.

Praetzellis, A., M. Praetzellis, and M. Brown III. 1987. Artifacts as Symbols of Identity: An Example from Sacramento's Gold Rush Era Chinese Community. In *Living in Cities: Current Research in Urban Archaeology*, ed. E. Staski, pp. 38–47. Special Publication 5. Tucson, Ariz.: Society for Historical Archaeology.

Praetzellis, M., ed. 2001a. *Block Technical Report: Historical Archaeology I-880 Cypress Replacement Project, Block 1.* Oakland: California Department of Transportation.

————. 2001b. *Block Technical Report: Historical Archaeology I-880 Cypress Replacement Project, Blocks 19, 20, 21, and 37.* Oakland: California Department of Transportation.

————. 2001c. *Block Technical Report: Historical Archaeology I-880 Cypress Replacement Project, Blocks 27, 28, and 31.* Oakland: California Department of Transportation.

Praetzellis, M. and A. Praetzellis. 1990. *The Mary Collins Assemblage: Mass Marketing and the Archaeology of a Sacramento Family.* Rohnert Park, Calif.: Anthropological Studies Center, Sonoma State University.

————. 1997. *Historical Archaeology of an Overseas Chinese Community in Sacramento, California.* Rohnert Park, Calif.: Anthropological Studies Center, Sonoma State University.

Praetzellis, M. and S. B. Stewart, eds., 2001. *Block Technical Report: Historical Archaeology I-880 Cypress Replacement Project, Blocks 4, 5, 6, and 9.* Oakland: California Department of Transportation.

Pred, A. 1985. The Social Becomes the Spatial, the Spatial Becomes the Social: Enclosures, Social Change, and the Becoming of Places in Skåne. In *Social Relations and Spatial Structures*, ed. D. Gregory and J. Urry, pp. 337–65. New York: St. Martin's Press.

————. 1990. *Making Histories and Constructing Human Geographies: The Local Transformation of Practice, Power Relations, and Consciousness.* Boulder, Colo.: Westview Press.

Prior, N. 2000. A Different Field of Vision: Gentlemen and Players in Edinburgh, 1826–1851. In *Reading Bourdieu on Society and Culture*, ed. B. Fowler, pp. 142–63. Oxford: Blackwell.

Quimby, G. I. 1939. European Trade Articles as Chronological Indicators for the Archaeology of the Historic Period in Michigan. *Papers of the Michigan Academy of Science, Arts, and Letters* 24: 25–31.

———. 1966. *Indian Culture and European Trade Goods: The Archaeology of the Historic Period in the Western Great Lakes Region.* Madison: University of Wisconsin Press.

Quimby, G. I. and A. Spoehr. 1951. Acculturation and Material Culture: I. *Fieldiana: Anthropology* 36: 107–47.

Quinn, D. B. 1966. *The Elizabethans and the Irish.* Ithaca, N.Y.: Cornell University Press.

Radcliffe-Brown, A. R. 1940. On Social Structure. *Journal of the Royal Anthropological Society of Great Britain and Ireland* 70: 1–12.

———. 1952. *Structure and Function in Primitive Society: Essays and Addresses.* New York: Free Press.

Raftery, B. 1996. Iron Age Studies in Ireland: Some Recent Developments. In *The Iron Age in Britain and Ireland: Recent Trends*, ed. T. C. Champion and J. R. Collis, pp. 155–61. Sheffield: J. R. Collis Publications, Department of Archaeology and Prehistory, University of Sheffield.

Rankin, H. D. 1987. *Celts and the Classical World.* London: Croom Helm.

Ransom, R. L. and R. Sutch. 1977. *One Kind of Freedom: The Economic Consequences of Emancipation.* Cambridge: Cambridge University Press.

Raper, A. F. 1936. *Preface to Peasantry: A Tale of Two Black Belt Counties.* Chapel Hill: University of North Carolina Press.

Rathje, W. and C. Murphy. 1992. *Rubbish! The Archaeology of Garbage.* New York: HarperCollins.

Reckner, P. E. and S. A. Brighton. 1999. "Free from All Vicious Habits": Archaeological Perspectives on Class Conflict and the Rhetoric of Temperance. *Historical Archaeology* 33(1): 63–86.

Redor, D. 1992. *Wage Inequalities in East and West.* Trans. R. Bourgault. Cambridge: Cambridge University Press.

Reid, J. J. 1995. Four Strategies After Twenty Years: A Return to Basics. In *Expanding Archaeology*, ed. J. M. Skibo, W. H. Walker, and A. E. Nielsen, pp. 15–21. Salt Lake City: University of Utah Press.

Reid, J. J., M. B. Schiffer, and W. L. Rathje. 1975. Behavioral Archaeology: Four Strategies. *American Anthropologist* 77: 836–48.

Reitz, E. J. 1987. Vertebrate Fauna and Socioeconomic Status. In *Consumer Choice in Historical Archaeology*, ed. S. M. Spencer-Wood, pp. 101–19. New York: Plenum Press.

———. 1992. The Spanish Colonial Experience and Domestic Animals. *Historical Archaeology* 26(1): 84–91.

———. 1993. Evidence for Animal Use at the Missions of Spanish Florida. In *The Spanish Missions of La Florida*, ed. B. G. McEwan, pp. 376–98. Gainesville: University Press of Florida.

Reitz, E. J. and C. M. Scarry. 1985. *Reconstructing Historic Subsistence with an Example from Sixteenth-Century Spanish Florida.* Special Publication 3. Tucson, Ariz.: Society for Historical Archaeology.

Renfrew, C. 1996. Prehistory and the Identity of Europe or, Don't Let's be Beastly to the Hungarians. In *Cultural Identity and Archaeology: The Construction of European Communities*, ed. P. Graves-Brown, S. Jones, and C. Gamble, pp. 125–37. London: Routledge.

Renfrew, C. and P. Bahn. 1991. *Archaeology: Theories, Methods, and Practice.* New York: Thames and Hudson.

Reno, R. L. 1996. Fuel for the Frontier: Industrial Archaeology of Charcoal

Production in the Eureka Mining District, Nevada, 1869–1891. Doctoral dissertation, University of Nevada, Reno.

Riis, J. A. 1971. *How the Other Half Lives: Studies Among the Tenements of New York.* 1890. New York: Dover.

Riley, C. L. 1967. American Historical Anthropology: An Appraisal. In *American Historical Anthropology: Essays in Honor of Leslie Spier,* ed. C. L. Riley and W. W. Taylor, pp. 3–21. Carbondale: Southern Illinois University Press.

Ripley, W. Z. 1899. *The Races of Europe: A Sociological Study.* New York: D. Appleton.

Roberts, P. E. W., 1983. Caravats and Shanavests: Whiteboyism and Faction Fighting in East Munster, 1802–11. In *Irish Peasants: Violence and Political Unrest, 1780–1914,* ed. S. Clark and J. S. Donnelly, Jr., pp. 64–101. Madison: University of Wisconsin Press.

Robinson, D. 1843. *Report of the System Pursued in the Management of the Irish Waste Land: Improvement Society's Estates in Ireland during the Year 1842.* London: S. and J. Bentley, Wilson, and Fley.

———. 1846. *Practical Suggestions for the Reclamation of Waste Lands, and the Improvement in the Condition of the Agricultural Population of Ireland.* London: Darling and Son.

Robinson, L. 1976. *Edgar Cayce's Story of the Origin and Destiny of Man.* New York: Berkley Books.

Roediger, D. R. 1991. *The Wages of Whiteness: Race and the Making of the American Working Class.* London: Verso.

Roemer, J. E. 1988. *Free to Lose: An Introduction to Marxist Economic Philosophy.* Cambridge, Mass.: Harvard University Press.

Rolston, B. and M. Shannon. 2002. *Encounters: How Racism Came to Ireland.* Belfast: Beyond the Pale Press.

Rose, P. I. 1974. *They and We: Racial and Ethnic Relations in the United States.* New York: Random House.

Rose, W. L. 1978. Jubilee and Beyond: What Was Freedom? In *What Was Freedom's Price?* ed. D. G. Sansing, pp. 3–20. Jackson: University Press of Mississippi.

Rosengarten, T. 1986. *Tombee: Portrait of a Cotton Planter.* New York: William Morrow.

Ross, A. 1974. *Pagan Celtic Britain.* London: Cardinal.

Roth, R. 1961. *Tea-Drinking in 18th-Century America: Its Etiquette and Equipage.* United States National Museum Bulletin 225. Washington, D.C.: Smithsonian Institution Press.

Rowlands, M., M. Larsen, and K. Kristiansen, eds. 1987. *Centre and Periphery in the Ancient World.* Cambridge: Cambridge University Press.

Russell, B. 1938. *Power: A New Social Analysis.* New York: W.W. Norton.

Sacks, K. B. 1989. Toward a Unified Theory of Class, Race, and Gender. *American Ethnologist* 16: 534–50.

Salaman, R. 1985. *The History and Social Influence of the Potato.* 1949. Rev. ed. Cambridge: Cambridge University Press.

Sale, K. 1996. *Rebels Against the Future: The Luddites and Their War on the Industrial Revolution, Lessons for the Computer Age.* Reading, Mass.: Addison-Wesley.

Samford, P. 1996. The Archaeology of African-American Slavery and Material Culture. *William and Mary Quarterly* 3rd ser., 53: 87–114.

Sanderson, S. K., ed. 1995. *Civilizations and World-Systems: Two Approaches to the Study of World-Historical Change.* Walnut Creek, Calif.: Altamira Press.

Sanjek, R. 1994. The Enduring Inequalities of Race. In *Race,* ed. S. Gregory and R. Sanjek, pp. 1–17. New Brunswick, N.J.: Rutgers University Press.

Savage, K. 1997. *Standing Soldiers, Kneeling Slaves: Race, War, and Monument in Nineteenth-Century America.* Princeton, N.J.: Princeton University Press.

Scally, R. J. 1995. *The End of Hidden Ireland: Rebellion, Famine, and Emigration.* New York: Oxford University Press.

Scarry, C. M. 1993. Plant Production and Procurement in Apalachee Province. In *The Spanish Missions of La Florida,* ed. B. G. McEwan, pp. 357–75. Gainesville: University Press of Florida.

Scott, J. C. 1990. *Domination and the Arts of Resistance: Hidden Transcripts.* New Haven, Conn.: Yale University Press.

Schiffer, M. B. 1976. *Behavioral Archaeology.* New York: Academic Press.

Schiffer, M. B. with A. R. Miller. 1999. *The Material Life of Human Beings: Artifacts, Behavior, and Communication.* London: Routledge.

Schortman, E. and P. Urban. 1987. Modeling Interregional Interaction in Prehistory. In *Advances in Archaeological Method and Theory,* vol. 11, ed. M. B. Schiffer, pp. 37–95. San Diego: Academic Press.

———. eds. 1992. *Resources, Power, and Interregional Interaction.* New York: Plenum Press.

———. 1994. Living on the Edge: Core/Periphery Relations in Ancient Southeastern Mesoamerica. *Current Anthropology* 35: 401–30.

Schrader, O. 1890. *Prehistoric Antiquities of the Aryan Peoples: A Manual of Comparative Philology and the Earliest Culture.* Trans. F. B. Jevons. London: Charles Griffin.

Schurz, C. 1866. *Report of Carl Schurz on the States of South Carolina, Georgia, Alabama, Mississippi, and Louisiana.* Senate Executive Document 2, 39th Congress, 1st Sess. Washington, D.C.: U. S. Government Printing Office.

Schutz, H. 1983. *The Prehistory of Germanic Europe.* New Haven, Conn.: Yale University Press.

Schuyler, R. L. 1970. Historical Archaeology and Historic Sites Archaeology as Anthropology: Basic Definitions and Relationships. *Historical Archaeology* 4: 83–89.

———. 1980a. Archaeology of Asian American Culture: An Annotated Bibliography. In *Archaeological Perspectives on Ethnicity in America: Afro-American and Asian American Culture History,* ed. R. L. Schuyler, pp. 124–30. Farmingdale, N.Y.: Baywood.

———. 1980b. Preface. In *Archaeological Perspectives on Ethnicity in America: Afro-American and Asian American Culture History,* ed. R. L. Schuyler, pp. vii–viii. Farmingdale, N.Y.: Baywood.

———. 1988. Archaeological Remains, Documents, and Anthropology: A Call for a New Culture History. *Historical Archaeology* 22(1): 36–42.

Schweizer, T. 1997. Embeddedness of Ethnographic Cases: A Social Networks Perspective. *Current Anthropology* 38: 739–60.

Scott, J. 1991. *Social Network Analysis: A Handbook.* London: Sage.

Scott, J. C. 1990. *Domination and the Arts of Resistence: Hidden Transcripts.* New Haven, Conn.: Yale University Press.

Scrope, G. P. 1847. *Extracts of Evidence Taken by the Late Commission of Inquiry into the Occupation of Land in Ireland, on the Subject of Waste Land Reclamation.* London: James Ridgway.

Sen, A. 1982. *Poverty and Famines: An Essay on Entitlement and Deprivation.* Oxford: Clarendon Press.

Shanks, M. and C. Tilley. 1987. *Re-Constructing Archaeology: Theory and Practice.* Cambridge: Cambridge University Press.

———. 1988. *Social Theory and Archaeology.* Albuquerque: University of New Mexico Press.

Sheffield, J. 1785. *Observations on the Manufactures, Trade, and Present State of Ireland.* Dublin: R. Moncrieffe, L. White, and P. Byrne.

Shennan, S. J. 1989. Introduction: Archaeological Approaches to Cultural Identity. In *Archaeological Approaches to Cultural Identity*, ed. S. J. Shennan, pp. 1–32. London: Unwin Hyman.

———. 1991. Some Current Issues in the Archaeological Identification of Past Peoples. *Archaeologia Polona* 29: 29–37.

Shephard, S. J. 1987. Status Variation in Antebellum Alexandria: An Archaeological Study of Ceramic Tableware. In *Consumer Choice in Historical Archaeology*, ed. S. M. Spencer-Wood, pp. 163–98. New York: Plenum Press.

Shermer, M. 1997. *Why People Believe Weird Things: Psuedoscience, Superstition, and Other Confusions of Our Time*. New York: W.H. Freeman.

Shoemaker, N. 1997. How Indians Got to be Red. *American Historical Review* 102: 624–44.

Shropshire, K. L. 1996. *In Black and White: Race and Sports in America*. New York: New York University Press.

Sigerson, G. 1871. *History of the Land Tenures and Land Classes of Ireland, with an Account of the Various Secret Agrarian Confederacies*. London: Longmans, Green, Reader, and Dyer.

Silverberg, R. 1986. *The Mound Builders*. Athens: Ohio University Press.

Silverman, M. 2001. *An Irish Working Class: Explorations in Political Economy and Hegemony, 1800–1950*. Toronto: University of Toronto Press.

Simeoni, D. 2000. Anglicizing Bourdieu. In *Pierre Bourdieu: Fieldwork in Culture*, ed. N. Brown and I. Szeman, pp. 65–86. Lanham, Md.: Rowman and Littlefield.

Simington, R. C. 1949. *Books of Survey and Distribution, Being Abstracts of Various Surveys and Instruments of Title, 1636–1703*. Vol. 1, *County of Roscommon*. Dublin: Stationery Office.

Simmel, G. 1955. *The Web of Group-Affiliations*. Trans. R. Bendix, Glencoe, Ill.: Free Press.

———. 1978. *The Philosophy of Money*. Trans. T. Bottomore and D. Frisby, London: Routledge and Kegan Paul.

Singer, D. A. 1987. Threshold of Affordability: Assessing Fish Remains for Socio-economics. In *Consumer Choice in Historical Archaeology*, ed. S. M. Spencer-Wood, pp. 85–99. New York: Plenum Press.

Singleton, T. A. 1980. The Archaeology of Afro-American Slavery in Coastal Georgia: A Regional Perception of Slave Household and Community Patterns. Doctoral dissertation, University of Florida.

———. 1999. An Introduction to African-American Archaeology. In *"I, Too, Am America": Archaeological Studies of African-American Life*, ed. T. A. Singleton, pp. 1–17. Charlottesville: University Press of Virginia.

Skeggs, B. 1997. *Formation of Class and Gender: Becoming Respectable*. London: Sage.

Slater, D. 1997. *Consumer Culture and Modernity*. Cambridge: Polity Press.

Slater, I. 1846. *I. Slater's National Commercial Directory of Ireland*. Manchester: I. Slater.

Smaje, C. 1997. Not Just a Social Construct: Theorising Race and Ethnicity. *Sociology* 31: 307–27.

Smedley, A. 1993. *Race in North America: Origin and Evolution of a Worldview*. Boulder, Colo.: Westview Press.

———. 1998. "Race" and the Construction of Human Identity. *American Anthropologist* 100: 690–702.

Smith, A. 1993. *An Inquiry into the Nature and Causes of the Wealth of Nations: A Selected Edition*. 1776. ed. K. Sutherland, Oxford: Oxford University Press.

Smith, A. P. 1998. Landscapes of Power in Nineteenth Century Ireland: Archaeology and Ordnance Survey Maps. *Archaeological Dialogues* 5: 69–84.

———. 2001. Mapping Cultural and Archaeological Meanings: Representing Landscapes and Pasts in 19th-Century Ireland. Doctoral dissertation, University of Massachusetts, Amherst.

Smith, B. 1997. The English Conquest. In *Atlas of Irish History*, ed. S. Duffy, pp. 32–49. New York: Macmillan.

Smith, L. T. 1999. *Decolonizing Methodologies: Research and Indigenous Peoples*. London: Zed Books.

Smyth, W. J. 2000. Ireland a Colony: Settlement Implications of the Revolution in Military-Administrative, Urban and Ecclesiastical Structures, c. 1550 to c. 1730. In *A History of Settlement in Ireland*, ed. T. Barry, pp. 158–86. London: Routledge.

Snowden, F. M. 1991. *Before Color Prejudice: The Ancient View of Blacks*. Cambridge, Mass.: Harvard University Press.

Social Science Institute. 1945. *Unwritten History of Slavery: Autobiographical Account of Negro Ex-Slaves*. Social Science Source Document 1. Nashville, Tenn.: Fisk University.

Soja, E. W. 1980. The Socio-Spatial Dialectic. *Annals of the Association of American Geographers* 70: 207–25.

———. 1989. *Postmodern Geographies: The Reassertion of Space in Critical Social Theory*. London: Verso.

Sopko, J. 2000. Farmstead Archaeology and the Impact of Agrarian Change at Three Sites in Eastern New York State. In *Nineteenth- and Early Twentieth-Century Domestic Site Archaeology in New York State*, ed. J. P. Hart and C. L. Fisher, pp. 149–75. Albany: New York State Education Department.

South, S. 1955. Evolutionary Theory in Archaeology. *Southern Indian Studies* 7: 10–32.

———. 1977. *Method and Theory in Historical Archaeology*. New York: Academic Press.

———. 1978. Pattern Recognition in Historical Archaeology. *American Antiquity* 43: 223–30.

———. 1988a. Santa Elena: Threshold of Conquest. In *The Recovery of Meaning: Historical Archaeology in the Eastern United States*, ed. M. P. Leone and P. B. Potter, Jr., pp. 27–71. Washington, D.C.: Smithsonian Institution Press.

———. 1988b. Whither Pattern? *Historical Archaeology* 22(1): 25–28.

———. ed. 1994. *Pioneers in Historical Archaeology: Breaking New Ground*. New York: Plenum Press.

Sowell, T. 1994. *Race and Culture: A World View*. New York: Basic Books.

———. 1998. *Conquests and Cultures: An International History*. New York: Basic Books.

Spence, L. 1995. *History of Atlantis*. 1926. London: Senate.

Spencer-Wood, S. M. 1987a. Introduction. In *Consumer Choice in Historical Archaeology*, ed. S. M. Spencer-Wood, pp. 1–24. New York: Plenum Press.

———. 1987b. Preface. In *Consumer Choice in Historical Archaeology*, ed. S. M. Spencer-Wood, xi–xii. New York: Plenum Press.

Spenser, E. 1997. *A View of the State of Ireland*. 1633. ed. A. Hadfield and W. Maley, Oxford: Blackwell.

Squier, E. G. and E. H. Davis. 1998. *Ancient Monuments of the Mississippi Valley*. 1848. Ed. D. J. Meltzer, Washington, D.C.: Smithsonian Institution Press.

Stapp, D. C. 1993. The Documentary Record of an Overseas Chinese Mining Camp. In *Hidden Heritage: Historical Archaeology of the Overseas Chinese*, Ed. P. Wegars, pp. 3–31. Amityville, N.Y.: Baywood.

Stanislawski, M. B. 1978. If Pots Were Mortal. In *Explorations in Ethnohistory*, ed. R. A. Gould, pp. 201–27. Albuquerque: University of New Mexico.

Staski, E. 1987. Border City, Border Culture: Assimilation and Change in Late 19th Century El Paso. In *Living in Cities: Current Research in Urban Archaeology*, ed. E. Staski, pp. 48–55. Special Publication 5. Tucson, Ariz.: Society for Historical Archaeology.

———. 1993. The Overseas Chinese in El Paso: Changing Goals, Changing Realities. In *Hidden Heritage: Historical Archaeology of the Overseas Chinese*, ed. P. Wegars, pp. 125–49. Amityville, N.Y.: Baywood.

Stearn, J. 1967. *Edgar Cayce: The Sleeping Prophet*. Garden City, N.Y.: Doubleday.

Stearns, P. N. 2001. *Consumerism in World History: The Global Transformation of Desire*. London: Routledge.

Steward, J. H. 1955. *Theory of Culture Change: The Methodology of Multilinear Evolution*. Urbana: University of Illinois Press.

Stewart, S. B. and M. Praetzellis, eds. 2001. *Block Technical Report: Historical Archaeology I-880 Cypress Replacement Project, Blocks 22, 24, and 29*. Oakland: California Department of Transportation.

Stiebing, W. H., Jr. 1984. *Ancient Astronauts, Cosmic Collisions and Other Popular Theories About Man's Past*. Buffalo, N.Y.: Prometheus.

Stone, M. P., A. Haugerud, and P. D. Little. 2000. Commodities and Globalization: Anthropological Perspectives. In *Commodities and Globalization: Anthropological Perspectives*, ed. A. Haugerud, M. P. Stone, and P. D. Little, pp. 1–29. Lanham, Md.: Rowman and Littlefield.

Stout, G. and M. Stout. 1997. Early Landscapes: From Prehistory to Plantation. In *Atlas of the Irish Rural Landscape*, ed. F. H. A. Aalen, K. Whelan, and M. Stout, pp. 31–63. Cork: Cork University Press.

Stout, M. 1997. *The Irish Ringfort*. Dublin: Four Courts Press.

———. 2000. Early Christian Ireland: Settlement and Environment. In *A History of Settlement in Ireland*. ed. T. Barry, pp. 81–109. London: Routledge.

Strathern, M. 1991. *Partial Connections*. Savage, Md.: Rowman and Littlefield.

Sutch, R. and R. Ransom. 1978. Sharecropping: Market Response or Mechanism of Race Control? In *What Was Freedom's Price?* ed. D. G. Sansing, pp. 51–69. Jackson: University Press of Mississippi.

Swartz, D. 1997. *Culture and Power: The Sociology of Pierre Bourdieu*. Chicago: University of Chicago Press.

Sweely, T. L., ed. 1999. *Manifesting Power: Gender and the Interpretation of Power in Archaeology*. London: Routledge.

Sweetman, D. 1979. Archaeological Excavations at Ferns Castle, Co. Wexford. *Proceedings of the Royal Irish Academy* 79(C): 217–45.

———. 1980. Archaeological Excavations at King John's Castle, Limerick. *Proceedings of the Royal Irish Academy* 79(C): 207–29.

Tabone, C. 1998. Malta. In *Poverty: A Persistent Global Reality*, ed. J. Dixon and D. Macarov, pp. 116–35. London: Routledge.

T. A. W. 1869. The Labor Question. *Southern Cultivator* 27: 57.

Thackeray, W. M. 1990. *The Irish Sketchbook, 1842*. 1843. Dublin: Gill and Macmillan.

Thomas, C. 1894. *Report on the Mound Explorations of the Bureau of Ethnology*. Twelfth Annual Report of the Bureau of Ethnology to the Secretary of the Smithsonian Institution, 1890–91. Washington, D.C.: U.S. Government Printing Office.

Thomas, D. H. 1988. Saints and Soldiers at Santa Catalina: Hispanic Designs for Colonial America. In *The Recovery of Meaning: Historical Archaeology in the Eastern United States*, ed. M. P. Leone and P. B. Potter, Jr., pp. 73–140. Washington, D.C.: Smithsonian Institution Press.

————. ed. 1989. *Columbian Consequences.* Vol. 1, *Archaeological and Historical Perspectives on the Spanish Borderlands West.* Washington, D.C.: Smithsonian Institution Press.

————. ed. 1990. *Columbian Consequences.* Vol. 2, *Archaeological and Historical Perspectives on the Spanish Borderlands East.* Washington, D.C.: Smithsonian Institution Press.

————. ed. 1991. *Columbian Consequences.* Vol. 3, *The Spanish Borderlands in Pan-American Perspective.* Washington, D.C.: Smithsonian Institution Press.

————. 1993. The Archaeology of Mission Santa Catalina de Guale: Our First 15 Years. In *The Spanish Missions of La Florida*, ed. B. G. McEwan, pp. 1–34. Gainesville: University Press of Florida.

Thomas, John 1971. *The Rise of the Staffordshire Potteries.* New York: Augustus M. Kelley.

Thomas, Julian 1996. *Time, Culture and Identity: An Interpretive Archaeology.* London: Routledge.

————. 1999. *Understanding the Neolithic.* 2nd ed. London: Routledge.

Thomas, J. E. 1993. An Examination of Early 19th Century Settlement in the Ohio Valley as Reflected in the Kelley Historic Site. Master's thesis, Kent State University.

Thomas, N. 1991. *Entangled Objects: Exchange, Material Culture, and Colonialism in the Pacific.* Cambridge, Mass.: Harvard University Press.

Thompson, E. P. 1993. *Customs in Common.* New York: New Press.

Thompson, R. H. 1983. The Ox, the Slave, and the Worker: A Pedagogic Exercise in Marx's Labor Theory of Value. *Dialectical Anthropology* 8: 237–40.

Thornton, J. 1992. *Africa and Africans in the Making of the Atlantic World, 1400–1680.* Cambridge: Cambridge University Press.

Thrift, N. J. 1985. Flies and Germs: A Geography of Knowledge. In *Social Relations and Spatial Structures*, ed. D. Gregory and J. Urry, pp. 366–403. New York: St. Martin's Press.

————. 2002. On the Determination of Social Action in Space and Time. In *The Spaces of Postmodernity: Readings in Human Geography*, ed. M. J. Dear and S. Flusty, pp. 106–19. Oxford: Blackwell.

Tregle, J. G., Jr. 1992. Creoles and Americans. In *Creole New Orleans: Race and Americanization*, ed. A. R. Hirsch and J. Logsdon, pp. 131–85. Baton Rouge: Louisiana State University Press.

Trench, C. C. 1997. *Grace's Card: Irish Catholic Landlords, 1690–1800.* Cork: Mercier Press.

Trigger, B. G. 1980. *Gordon Childe: Revolution in Archaeology.* New York: Columbia University Press.

————. 1989. *A History of Archaeological Thought.* Cambridge: Cambridge University Press.

Trombold, C. D. 1991. *Ancient Road Networks and Settlement Hierarchies in the New World.* Cambridge: Cambridge University Press.

Trouillot, M-R. 1995. *Silencing the Past: Power and the Production of History.* Boston: Beacon Press.

Uí Ógáin, R. 1996. *Immortal Dan: Daniel O'Connell in Irish Folk Tradition.* Dublin: Geography Publications.

United States Department of Commerce. 1993. *1990 Census of Population: Social and Economic Characteristics, United States.* Washington, D.C.: Government Printing Office.

Upham, S. 1982. *Politics and Power: An Economic and Political History of the Western Pueblo.* New York: Academic Press.

————. 1986. Imperialists, Isolationists, World Systems, and Political Realities:

Perspectives on Mesoamerican-Southwestern Interaction. In *Ripples in the Chichimec Sea: New Considerations of Southwestern-Mesoamerican Interactions*, ed. F. J. Mathien and R. H. McGuire, pp. 205–19. Carbondale: Southern Illinois University Press.

Valtukh, K. K. 1987. *Marx's Theory of Commodity and Surplus-Value*. Trans. B. Kutyrev. Moscow: Progress Publishers.

Vance, R. B. 1929. *Human Factors in Cotton Culture: A Study of the Social Geography of the American South*. Chapel Hill: University of North Carolina Press.

———. 1935. *Human Geography of the South: A Study in Regional Resource and Human Adequacy*. Chapel Hill: University of North Carolina Press.

———. 1936. *How the Other Half is Housed: A Pictorial Record of Sub-Minimum Farm Housing in the South*. Chapel Hill: University of North Carolina Press.

Voget, F. W. 1975. *A History of Ethnology*. New York: Holt, Rinehart, and Winston.

Von Däniken, E. 1970. *Chariots of the Gods? Unsolved Mysteries of the Past*. Trans. M. Heron. New York: Bantam.

von der Porten, E. P. 1972. Drake and Cermeno in California: Sixteenth-Century Chinese Ceramics. *Historical Archaeology* 6: 1–22.

Wacquant, L. J. D. 1992. Toward a Social Praxeology: The Structure and Logic of Bourdieu's Sociology. In P. Bourdieu and L. J. D. Wacquant, *An Invitation to Reflexive Sociology* pp. 1–59. Chicago: University of Chicago Press.

Waddell, J. 1998. *The Prehistoric Archaeology of Ireland*. Galway: Galway University Press.

Wade, M. L. 2000. From Eighteenth- to Nineteenth-Century Racial Science: Continuity and Change. In *Race and Racism in Theory and Practice*, ed. B. Lang, pp. 27–43. Lanham, Md.: Rowman and Littlefield.

Wakefield, E. 1812. *An Account of Ireland, Statistical and Political*. Vol. 2. London: Longman, Hurst, Rees, Orme, and Brown.

Walker, W. H., J. M. Skibo, and A. E. Nielsen. 1995. Introduction: Expanding Archaeology. In *Expanding Archaeology*, ed. J. M. Skibo, W. H. Walker, and A. E. Nielsen, pp. 1–12. Salt Lake City: University of Utah Press.

Wall, D. diZ. 1994a. *The Archaeology of Gender: Separating the Spheres in Urban America*. New York: Plenum.

———. 1994b. Family Dinners and Social Teas: Ceramics and Domestic Rituals. In *Everyday Life in the Early Republic*, ed. C. E. Hutchins, pp. 249–84. Winterthur, Del.: Henry Francis du Pont Winterthur Museum.

———. 1999. Examining Gender, Class, and Ethnicity in Nineteenth-Century New York City. *Historical Archaeology* 33(1): 102–17.

———. 2000. Family Meals and Evening Parties: Constructing Domesticity in Nineteenth-Century Middle-Class New York. In *Lines that Divide: Historical Archaeologies of Race, Class, and Gender*, ed. J. A. Delle, S. A. Mrozowski, and R. Paynter, pp. 109–41. Knoxville: University of Tennessee Press.

Wallace, T. 1798. *An Essay on the Manufactures of Ireland*. Dublin: Campbell and Shea.

Wallerstein, I. 1974. *The Modern World-System: Capitalist Agriculture and the Origins of the European World-Economy in the Sixteenth Century*. New York: Academic Press.

———. 1979. *The Capitalist World-Economy*. Cambridge: Cambridge University Press.

———. 1980. *The Modern World-System II: Mercantilism and the Consolidation of the European World-Economy, 1600–1750*. New York: Academic Press.

Wallerström, T. 1997. On Ethnicity as a Methodological Problem in Historical Archaeology: A Northern Fennoscandian Perspective. In *Visions of the Past:*

Trends and Traditions in Swedish Medieval Archaeology, ed. H. Andersson, P. Carelli, and L. Ersgård, pp. 299–352. Stockholm: Almquist and Wiksell.

Walsh, C. M. 1901. *The Measurement of General Exchange-Value.* New York: Macmillan.

Walter, B. 2001. *Outsiders Inside: Whiteness, Place, and Irish Women.* London: Routledge.

Wander, P. 1984. Introduction to the Transaction Edition. In H. Lefebvre, *Everday Life in the Modern World* pp. vii–xxiii. New Brunswick, N.J.: Transaction Books.

Wasserman, S. and K. Faust. 1994. *Social Network Analysis: Methods and Applications.* Cambridge: Cambridge University Press.

Warner, W. L. 1936. American Caste and Class. *American Journal of Sociology* 42: 234–37.

Wauchope, R. 1962. *Lost Tribes and Sunken Continents: Myth and Method in the Study of American Indians.* Chicago: University of Chicago Press.

Webb, A. B. W. 1983. *Mistress of Evergreen Plantation: Rachel O'Connor's Legacy of Letters, 1823–1845.* Albany: State University of New York Press.

Webber, T. L. 1978. *Deep like the Rivers: Education in the Slave Quarter Community, 1831–1865.* New York: W.W. Norton.

Weber, M. 1963. *Basic Concepts in Sociology.* Trans. H. P. Secher, New York: Citadel Press.

———. 1968. *Economy and Society: An Outline of Interpretive Sociology,* ed. G. Roth and C. Wittich, New York: Bedminster Press.

Weisman, B. R. 1993. Archaeology of Fig Springs Mission, Ichetucknee Springs State Park. In *The Spanish Missions of La Florida,* ed. B. G. McEwan, pp. 165–92. Gainesville: University Press of Florida.

Weiss, B. 1996. Coffee Breaks and Coffee Connections: The Lived Experience of a Commodity in Tanzanian and European Worlds. In *Cross-Cultural Consumption: Global Markets, Local Realities,* ed. D. Howes, pp. 93–105. London: Routledge.

Weld, I. 1832. *Statistical Survey of the County of Roscommon, Drawn up Under the Direction of the Royal Dublin Society.* Dublin: R. Graisberry.

Wells, P. S. 1980. *Culture Contact and Culture Change: Early Iron Age Central Europe and the Mediterranean World.* Cambridge: Cambridge University Press.

———. 2001. *Beyond Celts, Germans, and Scythians.* London: Duckworth.

Wesler, K. W. 1996. Letter to the Editor. *Bulletin of the Society for American Archaeology* 14(1): 3–4.

Wesolowski, W. 1979. *Classes, Strata, and Power.* Trans. G. Kolanliewicz, London: Routledge.

West, J. A. 1993. *Serpent in the Sky: The High Wisdom of Ancient Egypt.* Wheaton, Ill.: Quest Books.

Westropp, M. S. D. 1913. Notes on the Pottery Manufacture in Ireland. *Proceedings of the Royal Irish Academy* 32(C): 1–27.

———. 1935. *Irish Pottery and Porcelain.* Dublin: Stationery Office.

Westropp, T. J. 1912. Brasil and the Legendary Islands of the North Atlantic: Their History and Fable. A Contribution to the "Atlantis" Problem. *Proceedings of the Royal Irish Academy* 30(C): 223–63.

Wheaton, T. R. and P. H. Garrow. 1985. Acculturation and the Archaeological Record in the Carolina Lowcountry. In *The Archaeology of Slavery and Plantation Life,* ed. T. A. Singleton, pp. 239–59. Orlando, Fla.: Academic Press.

Wheaton, T. R., A. Friedlander, and P. H. Garrow. 1983. *Yaughan and Curriboo Plantations: Studies in Afro-American Archaeology.* Atlanta: Archaeological Services Branch, National Park Service.

Wheeler, M. 1956. *Archaeology from the Earth.* Baltimore: Penguin.

Whelan, K. 1992. Beyond a Paper Landscape: John Andrews and Irish Historical Geography. In *Dublin, City and Country: From Prehistory to Present, Studies in*

Honour of J. H. Andrews, ed. F. H. A. Aalen and K. Whelan, pp. 379–424. Dublin: Geography Publications.

————. 1993. Ireland in the World-System, 1600–1800. In *The Early-Modern World-System in Geographical Perspective*, ed. H-J. Nitz, pp. 204–18. Stuttgart: Franz Steiner Verlag.

————. 1994. Settlement Patterns in the West of Ireland in the Pre-Famine Period. In *Decoding the Landscape*, ed. T. Collins, pp. 60–78. Galway: Centre for Landscape Studies, Social Sciences Research Centre.

————. 1997. The Modern Landscape: From Plantation to Present. In *Atlas of the Irish Rural Landscape*, ed. F. H. A. Aalen, K. Whelan, and M. Stout, pp. 67–103. Cork: Cork University Press.

Whitaker, A. C. 1968. *History and Criticism of the Labor Theory of Value in English Political Economy.* 1904. New York: A. M. Kelley.

White, E. V. and W. E. Leonard. 1915. *Studies in Farm Tenancy in Texas.* Bulletin 21. Austin: University of Texas Press.

White, F. 1999. An Assemblage of Post-Medieval Local Wares from Merchants Road, Galway. Unpublished master's thesis, National University of Ireland, Galway.

White, J. R. 1975. Historic Contact Sites as Laboratories for the Study of Culture Change. *Conference on Historic Site Archaeology Papers* 9(2): 153–63.

Wilkie, L. A. 2000. *Creating Freedom: Material Culture and African American Identity at Oakley Plantation, Louisiana, 1840–1950.* Baton Rouge: Louisiana State University Press.

Wilkinson, D. 1987. Central Civilization. *Comparative Civilizations Review* 17: 31–59.

Willey, G. R. and P. Phillips. 1958. *Method and Theory in American Archaeology.* Chicago: University of Chicago Press.

Willey, G. R. and J. A. Sabloff. 1993. *A History of American Archaeology.* 3rd ed. New York: W.H. Freeman.

Williams, R. 1990. *Hierarchical Structures and Social Value: The Creation of Black and Irish Identities in the United States.* Cambridge: Cambridge University Press.

Williams, S. 1991. *Fantastic Archaeology: The Wild Side of North American Prehistory.* Philadelphia: University of Pennsylvania Press.

Wilson, C. 1999. *From Atlantis to the Sphinx.* New York: Fromm.

Wilson, C. and R. Flem-Ath. 2001. *The Atlantis Blueprint: Unlocking the Ancient Mysteries of a Long-Lost Civilization.* New York: Delacorte Press.

Winter, J. A., ed. 1971. *The Poor: A Culture of Poverty, or a Poverty of Culture?* Grand Rapids, Mich.: Eerdmans.

Wissler, C. 1923. *Man and Culture.* New York: Thomas Y. Crowell.

————. 1927. The Culture-Area Concept in Social Anthropology. *American Journal of Sociology* 32: 881–91.

Wittry, W. L. 1963. The Bell Site, Wn9, An Early Historic Fox Village. *Wisconsin Archaeologist* 44: 1–57.

Wolf, E. R. 1982. *Europe and the People Without History.* Berkeley: University of California Press.

————. 1984. Culture: Panacea or Problem? *American Antiquity* 49: 393–400.

————. 1990. Facing Power: Old Insights, New Questions. *American Anthropologist* 92: 586–96.

————. 1994. Perilous Ideas: Race, Culture, and People. *Current Anthropology* 35: 1–12.

————. 1999. *Envisioning Power: Ideologies of Dominance and Resistance.* Berkeley: University of California Press.

————. 2001. *Pathways to Power: Building an Anthropology of the Modern World.* Berkeley: University of California Press.

Woodham-Smith, C. 1991. *The Great Hunger: Ireland, 1845–1849.* 1962. London: Penguin.

Woodward, A. 1978. The Study of Historic Archaeology in America. In *Historical Archaeology: A Guide to Substantive and Theoretical Contributions,* 1937. ed. R. L. Schuyler, pp. 16–17. Farmingdale, N.Y.: Baywood.

Woofter, T. J., Jr. G. Blackwell, H. Hoffsommer, J. G. Maddox, J. M. Massell, B. O. Williams, and W. Wynne, Jr. 1936. *Landlord and Tenant on the Cotton Plantation.* Washington, D.C.: U.S. Government Printing Office.

Wrong, D. H. 1980. *Power: Its Forms, Bases, and Uses.* New York: Harper and Row.

Wylie, J. and R. E. Fike. 1993. Chinese Opium Smoking Techniques and Paraphernalia. In *Hidden Heritage: Historical Archaeology of the Overseas Chinese,* ed. P. Wegars, pp. 255–303. Amityville, N.Y.: Baywood.

Wyman, M. 1993. *Round-Trip America: The Immigrants Return to Europe, 1880–1930.* Ithaca, N.Y.: Cornell University Press.

Yamin, R. 1997. New York's Mythic Slum: Digging Lower Manhattan's Infamous Five Points. *Archaeology* 50(2): 44–53.

———, ed. 2000. *Tales of Five Points: Working-Class Life in Nineteenth-Century New York.* 6 vols. West Chester, Pa.: John Milner Associates.

———, ed. 2001. Becoming New York: The Five Points Neighborhood. *Historical Archaeology* 35(3): 1–135.

Yelvington, K. A. 1991. Ethnicity as Practice? A Comment on Bentley. *Comparative Studies in Society and History* 33: 158–68.

Young, A. 1780. *A Tour of Ireland with General Observations on the Present State of that Kingdom made in the Years 1776, 1777, and 1778.* London: T. Cadell and J. Dodsley.

Young, A. L. 1996. Archaeological Evidence of African-Style Ritual and Healing Practices in the Upland South. *Tennessee Anthropologist* 21: 139–55.

Young, R. J. C. 1995. *Colonial Desire: Hybridity in Theory, Culture, and Race.* London: Routledge.

Zangger, E. 1992. *The Flood from Heaven: Deciphering the Atlantis Legend.* New York: William Morrow.

Ziesing, G. H. and M. Praetzellis, eds., 2001. *Block Technical Report: Historical Archaeology I-880 Cypress Replacement Project, Block 2.* Oakland: California Department of Transportation.

Zimmerman, L. J. 1989. Made Radical by My Own: An Archaeologist Learns to Understand Reburial. In *Conflict in the Archaeology of Living Traditions,* ed. R. Layton, pp. 60–67. London: Unwin Hyman.

Zuckerman, L. 1998. *The Potato: How the Humble Spud Rescued the Western World.* New York: North Point Press.

Index